Hitler's Japanese Confidant

Hitler's Japanese Confidant

General Ōshima Hiroshi and MAGIC Intelligence, 1941-1945

Carl Boyd

Foreword by Peter Paret

 University Press of Kansas

Published by the University Press of Kansas (Lawrence, Kansas 66049), which
was organized by the Kansas Board of Regents and is operated and funded by
Emporia State University, Fort Hays State University, Kansas State University,
Pittsburg State University, the University of Kansas, and Wichita State
University

Library of Congress Cataloging-in-Publication Data

Boyd, Carl.
    Hitler's Japanese confidant : General Ōshima Hiroshi and MAGIC
intelligence, 1941–1945 / Carl Boyd ; foreword by Peter Paret.
        p.   cm. — (Modern war studies)
    Includes bibliographical references and index
    ISBN 0-7006-0569-X
    1. World War, 1939–1945—Cryptography.   2. Ōshima, Hiroshi, 1886–1975.
3. Diplomats—Japan—Biography.   4. Japan—Foreign relations—
Germany.   5. Germany—Foreign relations—Japan.   I. Title.
II. Series.
D810.C88B69   1993
940.54′85—dc20   92-28142

British Library Cataloguing in Publication Data is available.

Printed in the United States of America
10 9 8 7 6 5 4 3 2 1

The paper used in this publication meets the minimum requirements of the
American National Standard for Permanence of Paper for Printed Library
Materials Z39.48-1984.

To the memory of my father
Earl S. Boyd (1905–1984)

and

my friend and colleague
Heinz K. Meier (1929–1989)
Dean, College of Arts and Letters,
Old Dominion University, 1975–1985

Contents

Illustrations, Tables, and Maps

Tables

Maps

Foreword

American and British efforts during World War II to understand the intentions and grand strategy of the Third Reich fall into two main periods. The first, from the time of Munich, or at the latest from the German occupation of Prague in March 1939, to the invasion of Russia in June 1941, was a period of uncertainty, of guesswork, and sometimes of miscalculations in predicting major German decisions. The invasion of Russia clarified everything. Germany retained a capacity of strategic surprise, but the broad lines of policy were now fixed and remained so—against all reason—until the unconditional surrender of the Dönitz government in May 1945. Intelligence on political attitudes and on grand strategic decisions is notoriously difficult to evaluate, but as long as Germany was unable to win the war in Russia or unwilling to bring it to an end by negotiation, its options were severely limited. Not that high-level information became less important in this second phase, but once acquired such information was easier to interpret within the tight constraints under which Germany now fought.

One of Washington's most important sources on the thinking of Hitler and of his senior assistants was the Japanese ambassador to Germany, Ōshima Hiroshi. He had been in Germany since 1934, first as military attaché and from 1938 on as ambassador. He was recalled in the fall of 1939 but reappointed in December of the following year, after which he remained in Berlin until the last days of the war. A few months before the start of his second tour of duty, the U.S. Signal Intelligence Service broke the Japanese diplomatic code, and from then on Ōshima's frequent messages and reports to Tokyo were deciphered and their translated texts sent to President Roosevelt, General Marshall, and the senior intelligence staff. Ōshima's intercepts throw new light on Germany's conduct of the war and on German-Japanese relations; Washington's reaction to their contents also tells us something about the way in which this country fought the war. Carl Boyd has carefully analyzed the messages and placed them in their political and military context, and his study should prove as enlightening to historians today as the original texts were to the president and his chief of staff in the early 1940s.

Ōshima was an intelligent, experienced observer, but his lack of objectivity made him less useful to his country than he should have been. He held decidedly expansionist views, and until it became clear that the battle of Stalingrad was turning into a major German disaster, he repeatedly urged his government to attack the Soviet Union. He saw the war too exclusively from the perspectives of German and Japanese interests, overestimated German strength, and found it difficult to think globally—at least until Anglo-American naval and air power showed him that the Allies could coordinate their measures, which Germany and Japan never managed to do. His suggestions to Hitler and Ribbentrop during the second half of the war that Germany should seek a negotiated peace with Russia reflected a new realism, and belatedly he may have come to understand that Hitler's racial and ideological fantasies and the policy of mass murder in Russia and Eastern Europe made it impossible for Germany to seek this way out. It often seems that Germany and Japan had a more realistic understanding of each other's position than of their own. But Ōshima's partisan observations and conclusions were themselves enlightening. They offered Washington a direct insight into the outlook and methods of an enemy who persisted in fighting a modern war with primitive political concepts and equally primitive strategies. Carl Boyd's resurrection of Ōshima's messages has resulted in an interesting, unusual contribution to the history of World War II, and also a challenging case study of the ambiguities of high-level intelligence.

Peter Paret
Institute for Advanced Study
Princeton

Preface

This study relies heavily on the messages of Ōshima Hiroshi, the Japanese ambassador in Germany between February 1941 and May 1945, and on the messages from several wartime Japanese foreign ministers.[1] Ambassador Ōshima arrived in Berlin when Hitler was near the peak of his power, and Ōshima's intercepted and deciphered messages from Berlin document the pulse of the Third Reich from the eve of the fateful invasion of the Soviet Union to the end of the war in Europe. A staggering store of German documents fell into Allied hands because of the swift collapse of the Third Reich in the spring of 1945. Thousands of tons of records were captured, and the history of National Socialist Germany is probably better documented than any other modern society in existence for little more than twelve years. Nevertheless, several decades after the surrender of Berlin, the declassification of the Japanese MAGIC messages between Germany and Japan makes available a new perspective. Ōshima's messages greatly enrich our knowledge of conditions in the vanquished Nazi state, and they also show the role that this unique Japanese connection played in the Anglo-American strategic conduct of war in Europe.

The precise rendering of Ōshima's words in this book has an importance for historians and other readers interested in World War II. Ōshima's original enciphered secret messages and their deciphered versions in Japanese are no longer available; only the English translations from the latter exist. Available in the National Archives and Records Administration, Record Group 457, this collection is extremely voluminous and sometimes cumbersome for researchers to use. The individual translations of Japanese diplomatic messages alone number more than 115,000 sheets. What a wealth of documents this collection represents. Where else can one find such an array of writing by of major Japanese diplomats during World War II? Many Japanese of the era did not publish memoirs—Ōshima, for example—and those who did sometimes glossed over murky issues, lacked specific knowledge of certain matters, or found that their memories failed as they reflected on complex and sometimes embarrassing situations.

I have culled over 2000 messages from Ōshima out of the impressive and complex collection of Japanese communications from the embassy in Berlin to Tokyo. Moreover, I have relied on Ōshima's original messages in most instances and not on the more easily used but incomplete MAGIC summaries often cited by other authors.[2] For the most part this material has only recently been declassified. Thus, there are a number of reasons why the reader may well like to have full access to English translations of Ōshima's contemporary reports and the replies from his superiors in Tokyo.

Although chapters 1–5 and 8 are an outgrowth of articles I published in British and American journals in 1987–1989, they incorporate new material, analysis, and revision in the context of a booklength study of Ōshima, cipher intelligence, and Hitler. These articles, which appeared in *Intelligence and National Security* and *Cryptologia*, are listed in the bibliography.

Every author of a study that is long in preparation welcomes the opportunity to acknowledge publicly debts of gratitude. I became interested in German-Japanese relations long before the MAGIC messages were declassified, more than twenty-five years ago when I was a graduate student at the University of California, Davis, and I am indebted to my adviser there, Peter Paret, who introduced me to the study of war in a broad historical context and who since has stood ready to help at every turn as my professional career has developed. Other former professors have also remained particularly supportive over the years, among them Joseph O. Baylen, Robert H. Ferrell, and Maurice Matloff.

I am grateful for financial support for research from the College of Arts and Letters, Old Dominion University and from the American Philosophical Society. Moreover, the freedom provided by a two-year visiting professorship at the U.S. Army Center of Military History in Washington, D.C., enabled me to do a lot of research and writing for this study. I owe a special thanks for the army appointment to William A. Stofft, the former chief of military history, now commandant, U.S. Army War College. Through his good offices this study has benefited from my contacts with an array of helpful professionals: William H. Cunliffe and John Taylor at the National Archives; David Keough, Rod Paschall, John Slonaker, Richard J. Sommers, and Dennis Vetock at the U.S. Army Military History Institute; Henry F. Schorreck and Donald Gish at the National Security Agency, who painstakingly read and offered suggestions to improve an earlier version of this manuscript; Glenn S. Cook and John N. Jacob at the George C. Marshall

Research Library; Billy A. Arthur, Alexander S. Cochran, Jr., Graham A. Cosmas, Albert E. Crowdrey, Edward J. Drea, Arnold G. Fisch, Jr., Mary C. Gillett, Kim B. Holien, Patrick J. Holland, Ray Skates, and Hannah Zeidlik at the U.S. Army Center of Military History; Elizabeth Denier, Robert Parks, and Raymond Teichman at the Franklin D. Roosevelt Library; and William K. Beatty, Kevin Leonard, and Patrick M. Quinn at Northwestern University Archives.

A number of other people have given helpful advice, including many World War II veterans of intelligence operations and an equal number of generous scholars. Akagi Kanji, Wallace A. Bacon, Harold C. Deutsch, Henry F. Graff, David Kahn, Malcolm Muir, Jr., William W. Quinn, Willis L. M. Reese, Frank B. Rowlett, Suzuki Kenji, Gerhard L. Weinberg, and Wallace R. Winkler.

Finally, many people at Old Dominion University have played no small role. My students have often been responsive in discussions about codes, ciphers, and international relations from 1919 to 1945, and I am particularly indebted to graduate students Pamela W. Wheary for her careful cartographic work and Sheryl L. Mednik and Chiyoko T. Quasius for their intelligent editorial assistance. Furthermore, it is a pleasure to thank publicly my colleagues in the Department of History—Craig M. Cameron, Patrick J. Rollins, and Christopher W. A. Szpilman—who through their scholarly example, friendly encouragement, and intellectual collegiality have contributed more than they know.

I am also indebted to the editors of the University Press of Kansas, particularly Michael Briggs, acquisitions editor, and Megan Schoeck, production editor, whose imaginative suggestions have helped immeasurably to make my work much easier.

Abbreviations

AC of S	Assistant Chief of Staff
CMH	Center of Military History
COMINCH	Commander in Chief
COMINT	Communications Intelligence
COS	Chiefs of Staff Committee or Chiefs of Staff
DMI	Director of Military Intelligence
ETO	European Theater of Operations
ETOUSA	European Theater of Operations, U.S. Army
FDRL	Franklin D. Roosevelt Library
FUSAG	First U.S. Army Group
GC&CS	Government Code and Cipher School
GCMRL	George C. Marshall Research Library
GPU	Gosudarstvennoye Politicheskoye Upravleniye (State Political Directorate)
GSC	General Staff Corps
IMTFE	International Military Tribunal for the Far East
IPS	International Prosecution Section
JDZB	Japanisch-Deutsches Zentrum Berlin
JIC	Joint Intelligence Sub-Commmittee
MID	Military Intelligence Division
MIS	Military Intelligence Service
NKVD	Narodnyy Komissariat Vnutrennikh Del (People's Commissariat of Internal Affairs)
NSA	National Security Agency
OKW	Oberkommando der Wehrmacht (Armed Forces High Command)
ONI	Office of Naval Intelligence

OSS	Office of Strategic Services
PSIS	Pacific Strategic Intelligence Section
SHAEF	Supreme Headquarters, Allied Expeditionary Force
SIGINT	Signal Intelligence
SIS	Signal Intelligence Service
SLU	Special Liaison Unit
SRDJ	Individual Translations, Japanese Diplomatic Messages
SRH	Special Research History
SRMA	Discrete Records of Historical Cryptologic Import, U.S. Army
SRMN	Discrete Records of Historical Cryptologic Import, U.S. Navy
SRS	Summaries
SSA	Signal Security Agency
SSO	Special Security Officer
TICOM	Target Investigation Committee
WD	War Department
WDGS	War Department General Staff
WT	War Trials

Hitler's Japanese Confidant

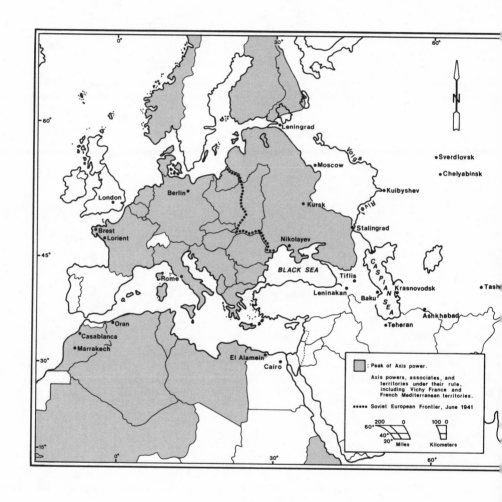

Peaks of Axis power in Europe, Africa, and Asia, 1939–1945

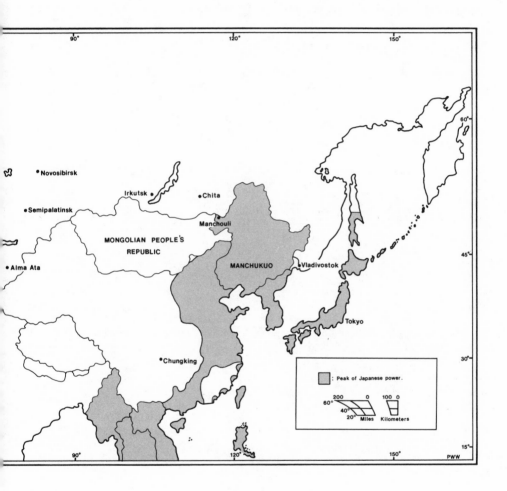

Introduction

George C. Marshall, chief of staff of the army, identified one of the most important intelligence sources in World War II when he wrote in September 1944 that the Japanese ambassador to Berlin was the United States' "main basis of information regarding Hitler's intentions in Europe." The U.S. Army's Signal Intelligence Service (SIS) deciphered Ambassador Ōshima Hiroshi's messages "from Berlin reporting his interviews with Hitler and other officials to the Japanese Government," Marshall explained.[1]

Ōshima's messages were enciphered in Japan's most sophisticated cipher system, but the Japanese system was solved in late 1940 to the point that intercepted Japanese messages could be read with at least moderate ease and accuracy. Nevertheless, the Japanese issued key replacements that always presented American cryptanalysts with the renewed problem of working to break the system analytically until fragmentary parts of a possible solution began to build up. Eventually the new key would be found and then used for decipherment.

The top cipher system used by the Japanese Foreign Ministry was solved after more than a year of extremely difficult work. SIS head William F. Friedman and especially Frank B. Rowlett, one of the earliest members of the SIS who worked primarily on the Japanese diplomatic intercepts, were largely responsible for the solution. In the 1930s Friedman often referred to his dedicated staff of cryptanalysts as "magicians," and it was probably this appellation that gave rise to the term MAGIC. MAGIC was the initial cover name used by the Americans for all intelligence produced by the solution of foreign codes and ciphers, which included the messages enciphered by the PURPLE machine system as well as all other systems used by the Japanese.[2]

Ōshima's detailed cipher reports to Tokyo were an invaluable source of information for the Americans and the British. The Japanese ambassador had a thorough knowledge of important German wartime secrets, and he reported everything to his superiors in Tokyo. En route, Ōshima's messages were intercepted, deciphered, and translated as a result of American code-breaking activities, which filled a significant gap in Allied intelligence in Europe left by ULTRA, the name the British gave to the intelligence obtained from breaking the German high-grade wireless traffic enciphered on the ENIGMA machine. As a participant in the ULTRA venture has written, the British were unable to read the secret traffic of the topmost German chiefs, but "the Americans, by reading the reports sent to Tokyo by the Japanese ambassador in Berlin, gleaned information about Hitler's plans and his state of mind. The Japanese ambassador and his staff knew the right people and got around."[3]

On the American side, MAGIC specialist Rowlett has written that "the information provided by Ōshima was of incalculable importance in leading the Allies to victory in World War II. . . . I consider that our timely access to his messages is one of the greatest intelligence achievements of all time."[4] One of Marshall's closest wartime associates involved with MAGIC held similar views about the importance of Ōshima's messages. A colonel during the war, Carter W. Clarke was chief of the Military Intelligence Service of the War Department General Staff from July 1941 to June 1944 and then became deputy chief of the Military Intelligence Service (MIS). A retired brigadier general who worked in intelligence for much of his distinguished thirty-nine-year army career, Clarke stated in 1983 that he knew "of nothing in the field of intelligence in all military history that equals in importance and value of the Ōshima messages. I have neither the words nor the capability adequate to assess and describe such priceless information."[5] And with reference to one message concerning the production of munitions in Germany that Ōshima sent to Tokyo in August 1944, other MIS officers said it was "worth all the expenses of maintaining the SSA [Signal Security Agency]."[6]

Each of two quite different developments in the 1930s—was dramatic and essential to this most successful intelligence operation during the war. One concerns the profundity of Ōshima's relations with the hierarchy of Hitler's Germany; the other, the remarkable accomplishments of cryptanalysts. Regarding the first, the astonishing flow of information from Berlin was greatly enriched by Ōshima's personal qualities and by the unique position he occupied in National Socialist Germany. A peculiar trust and a oneness of interests had built up among Hitler, Ōshima, and Joachim von Ribbentrop during Ōshima's first six-year tour of duty in Berlin.

Ōshima, born in Gifu Prefecture in 1886, came from a family that was prominent in the modernization of Japan. His father, Ōshima Ken'ichi, was war minister (30 March 1916–29 September 1918) in the Ōkuma and Te-

Ambassador Ōshima at his desk in the Japanese embassy, Berlin, in 1939 soon after the Japanese Foreign Ministry stopped using RED *and had adopted a new cryptographic system. Thus, Americans were unable "to read his mail" because* PURPLE *had not yet been solved. (From the author's collection)*

rauchi cabinets, and after graduation from the military academy in 1905, the younger Ōshima enjoyed a successful military career while following his family's tradition of loyal service to the emerging Japanese nation. In 1934 Ōshima arrived in Germany as the newly appointed Japanese military attaché. An army colonel who spoke nearly flawless German, within a year Ōshima had gained direct access to Ribbentrop, then Hitler's personal ambassador at large, and by the autumn of 1935 he had met privately with Hitler.[7] Through a great deal of intrigue and backstairs maneuvering in Berlin and with the support of the Japanese Army General Staff and certain pro-Axis elements in Tokyo, Ōshima moved from the rank of colonel and position of attaché in 1934 to lieutenant general and ambassador in 1938.[8]

Ōshima had long advocated military schemes to ally Japan with the European Axis powers, but Hitler's haste to conquer in September 1939 weakened and temporarily discredited Ōshima's plans. When the ambassador was recalled from Berlin not long after the German invasion of Poland in 1939,

Ribbentrop, Germany's foreign minister, tried to persuade the Japanese government to keep Ōshima at his Berlin post. Explaining his wishes to the German ambassador in Tokyo, with instructions to relay his views to the appropriate parties in that capital, Ribbentrop said that Ōshima had always understood "the aims of our policy" and that the Japanese general continued to enjoy "the complete confidence of the Führer and the German army." Ribbentrop argued, therefore, that Ōshima would be "better in the position to represent Japanese interests in Berlin than a new ambassador."[9]

Ribbentrop failed to have his way, however, and in late 1939 Ōshima returned to Japan via the United States. From Tokyo in mid-December Ōshima predicted a German victory and claimed that Hitler's armed forces had "superior, entirely new weapons that we have not thought of."[10] Ribbentrop knew that Ōshima had long been proponent of rightist interests, and it was now clear that his confidence in the former ambassador was not misplaced. Indeed, Ribbentrop instructed the German ambassador in Tokyo, Eugen Ott, to assist Ōshima in any way possible in the promotion of closer German-Japanese relations. Ōshima was given permission to use secret German codes to communicate directly with Ribbentrop in Berlin, but although he visited the German embassy several times in 1940, Ōshima claimed that he had no need to contact the German foreign minister.[11]

Ōshima's year in Japan before his reassignment to Berlin was spent promoting right-wing, pro-Axis groups. He advocated a pro-German policy in various discussions with Karakawa Yasuo (chief of the Europe-America Section), Yamagata Arimitsu (chief of the German Section), and Usui Shigeki (chief of the Subversion and Propaganda Section) of the Army General Staff. They were enthusiastic about Ōshima's ideas, and so were members of the House of Representatives of the Imperial Diet when Ōshima spoke to that group. He also met with Hata Shunroku (war minister, 30 August 1939–22 July 1940) who, in Ōshima's words, "was a very quiet person . . . waiting to see what would happen." Similarly, Ōshima met with Prime Minister Konoe Fumimaro twice in 1940. "I talked about Germany and expressed my opinion," Ōshima said, "However, since Prince Konoe was a smart person, he just listened to me and never expressed his opinion." In sharp contrast, Ōshima received a very warm reception in several meetings with Matsuoka Yōsuke, foreign minister in the second Konoe cabinet. "He wanted to listen to my story," Ōshima said proudly, but then continued in a more reserved tone: "Mr. Matsuoka was particularly interested in the problem of the Soviet Union and he set aside for himself an allotted time twice a week to reflect on the Soviet problem."[12]

Ōshima found that many Japanese admired Hitler's boldness. Ōshima and Shiratori Toshio, former Japanese ambassador to Italy, were leading members of the anti-British, pro-German groups. Shiratori, who returned to Japan shortly before Ōshima, energetically toured the country to make a series of pro-German addresses, and in 1940 the two former Axis ambassadors lectured widely before Japanese political audiences.[13] Ōshima said: "I always maintained close contact with Mr. Shiratori. We went here and there during our campaign. We also wrote articles in *Bungei Shunjū*." Soon after returning to Tokyo, Ōshima published at least two pro-German pieces in an attempt to sway Japanese public opinion.[14] Ōshima also said that while in Japan in 1940 he "was making decisions based on the assumption that Germany would win the war."[15]

The success of the German armed forces was impressive. A deceptive lull followed the conquest of Poland, but in April Denmark and Norway fell victim, and during the next two months the Netherlands, Belgium, Luxembourg, and France were overrun by Hitler's forces. These sweeping victories strengthened the political position of pro-Axis forces in Japan. Conditions in Europe appeared to offer the Japanese new opportunities for expansion southward, particularly into French Indo-China and the Dutch East Indies. Japan did not want to be left behind, and public opinion was summed up in a new popular slogan in the summer of 1940: "Don't miss the bus!" Between appointments as ambassador to Germany, Ōshima often used the phrase in pro-Axis public lectures when explaining that Japan should be a part of the unique redistribution of European colonies.[16]

The new government, the second Konoe cabinet (22 July 1940–18 July 1941), reflected the change in public attitude. The new foreign minister, Matsuoka, set forth a policy of strengthening political ties with Germany and Italy, and after Japan concluded the military tripartite agreement with these countries in late September 1940, Matsuoka gave Ōshima the opportunity to return to Berlin. The appointment was announced on 20 December 1940, three months after the Japanese diplomatic cipher system was solved.

Ōshima's reappointment was extremely popular. At a lavish farewell party on 15 January 1941, Foreign Minister Matsuoka, noting that "General Ōshima has studied modern Germany for a couple of decades," declared in a speech that "his thorough knowledge of German affairs far exceeds one's imagination. And he has developed the highest personal trust among the leading members of the German government, thus he can have heart-to-heart talks with them."[17]

Long before Ōshima returned to Berlin, indeed throughout the late 1930s, American cryptanalysts and Japanese-language translators recognized the importance of the connections Ōshima enjoyed in the upper echelons of Hitler's government. They regarded him as an invaluable source of information, especially concerning Axis strategic plans and military operations in

Europe.[18] Ōshima's pivotal position was also recognized by other signal intelligence specialists after he returned to Berlin in February 1941. As another U.S. Army cryptanalyst and Japanese-language translator recalled,

> Of the thousands of intercepts I translated during my wartime service, the ones from Ōshima were always the most alluring to me. I used to look for them to read, even though we translators were supposed to work on the messages in the order of receipt, regardless of whom or where they came from. Ōshima's messages, transmitted from Berlin, of course, and often reflecting his conversations with Hitler or Albert Speer . . . , seemed to come from the very heart of the evil enemy we were fighting. . . . As a fledgling historian I felt in reading the words of Ōshima that I was standing at the center of the universe.[19]

Obviously, then, the Ōshima connection, fully manifested on the eve of the war, paid extremely handsome dividends during the war. Because of the incredibly sophisticated and difficult work of a handful of Americans who made up the cryptologic intelligence community[20] in the 1930s, the war in the 1940s was shortened, the loss of life was reduced, and the Americans and their allies were assured of an eventual victory.

According to a U.S. Navy report declassified in 1984, early work to solve Japanese cryptographic systems revealed by 1930 the "Japanese intention of the conquest and annexation of Manchuria, China, and the East Indies."[21] In spite of the alarming implications of this early revelation, the peacetime depression economy severely hampered the clandestine operations of U.S. Navy and Army cryptologic services. These two services were equally important in the field of communications intelligence (COMINT) in the interwar period, but the work of Army COMINT is particularly important to this study.

After World War I the U.S. Army's Cipher Bureau, MI-8, the eighth section of the Military Intelligence Division (MID), the so-called Black Chamber, sought to obtain information of present, immediate value. It operated in New York City under the cover name "Code Compilation Company, Inc."[22] Major Herbert O. Yardley, director of the bureau, and a small staff made several breakthroughs in the 1920s, including solving the Japanese diplomatic, military attaché and naval attaché codes used for communications during the Washington Disarmament Conference, 12 November 1921–6 February 1922. Therefore, U.S. representatives were privy to secret instructions that Japan's negotiators received daily, and the Americans forced the Japanese to accept a smaller naval ratio vis-à-vis the United States and Great Britain, knowing that Japan would eventually assent to such an

American proposal.[23] Always operating under severe budget restrictions, MI-8 survived until the new secretary of state, Henry L. Stimson, withdrew crucial State Department funds and in effect closed it down in 1929. Stimson claimed that mutual trust worked best in international affairs, and his now-famous dictum—"Gentlemen do not read each other's mail"—was his reaction upon reading some deciphered Japanese messages supplied by MI-8.[24] This attitude seemed unrealistic in view of the threats to peace that MI-8 had already discovered in decoded Japanese diplomatic messages. Thus, the U.S. Army Signal Corps secretly assumed responsibility for cryptanalytic work in 1930, when the operation was set up in the Munitions Building in Washington, D.C.

SIS was thus founded in 1930 for the purpose of establishing in peacetime a small section of code and cipher specialists who were in constant training.[25] SIS inherited the working files of the Black Chamber, and William F. Friedman, his assistants—Frank B. Rowlett, Abraham Sinkov, and Solomon Kullback—and Japanese linguist John B. Hurt formed a unique team in the American COMINT community. These five SIS cryptanalysts had a special sense of mission well beyond the simple training aspect in their charter from the secretary of war, although they knew that what they were doing was in some way illegal if the spirit of the Stimson edict and federal communications law were followed.[26]

The primary COMINT objective of both the army and the navy was to develop the capability to read efficiently the signal communications of the armed services of major foreign powers in time of war. Thus, the small U.S. cryptographic forces gave Japan the highest priority, followed by Germany.

The U.S. Navy initially directed the main thrust of its COMINT effort against Japanese naval communications, and with no small degree of success. In 1921 naval intelligence obtained a photostat copy of the Red Book, cover name for the Imperial Japanese Navy Secret Operations Code, 1918. In 1926 a revised and updated edition of the Red Book was obtained, not to be confused with the later "RED machine" system. The Red Book was completely translated and fully available in 1930. It provided detailed information on the Imperial Japanese Navy's Orange 1930 Grand Maneuvers, including simulated air raids on Tokyo from the American carriers *Lexington* and *Saratoga*. A 1943 naval intelligence report concluded that "the most astonishing discovery was that the Japanese had a very good idea of American War Plans, as annually rehearsed at the Army and Navy War Colleges, and had taken suitable measures to take a devastating toll of attrition during our steam-roller advance to the relief of the Philippines."[27] Not surprisingly, U.S. war plans were modified in light of Japan's intentions. The U.S. Navy

Signal Intelligence Service, ca. 1935. Seated, Mrs. Louise Newkirk Nelson; standing, left to right, Herrick F. Bearce; Solomon Kullback; Captain H. G. Miller, USA; William F. Friedman; Abraham Sinkov; Lieutenant L. T. Jones, USCG; Frank B. Rowlett. John B. Hurt was ill when the picture was taken. (Courtesy of Wallace R. Winkler)

also gained at this time a healthy respect for the Japanese ability to launch night torpedo attacks.

The interwar period saw great change in the field of communications intelligence. On 1 December 1930, the Red Book was superseded by the Blue Book (named after the color of its binder). This new edition of the Imperial Japanese Navy secret code remained effective until 31 October 1938, but unlike the Red code, this one was acquired by the U.S. Navy the "hard way"—that is, by cryptographic analysis and reconstruction.

One of the more important pieces of information gained through the Blue Book concerned the Japanese battleship *Nagato's* postmodernization trials in 1936. The navy's codebreaking agency called Op-20-G (then named Communications Security Group, Washington, D.C.) learned that the *Nagato's* new top speed was 26 + knots. By inference, this was the prospective speed of the modernized battleship *Mutsu* and the new Japanese battleships which were about to be built. American naval planners had believed that the

Frank B. Rowlett at his desk in Arlington Hall Station, Arlington, Virginia, 1948. (Courtesy of Wallace R. Winkler)

Nagato class of battleship (including the *Mutsu*) was good for only 23 1/2 knots, therefore, the U.S. Navy's new battleships (then in blueprint stage) were designed to have a top speed of 24 knots, a narrow but sufficient margin of superiority over their Japanese counterparts. But with this new piece of intelligence, the design of American battleships was modified. Thus, the *North Carolina* (keel laid 27 October 1937), the *Washington* (keel laid 14 June 1938), and ten additional U.S. battleships were built with a maximum speed of 27 knots, a superiority of 1 knot rather than a deficiency of 2 knots compared with Japanese battleships.[28]

In June 1939 the Japanese Navy introduced yet another code, called JN25 by American cryptanalysts. Op-20-G had limited progress in attacking this main Japanese operations code when a second, enlarged edition, JN25b, was introduced on 1 December 1940. David Kahn has written that "by December 1941 only about 10 percent of the text of an average JN25b message could be read. This was due less to Japanese cryptographic superiority than to the navy's insufficiency of cryptanalysts, in part because it was helping the army decipher" Japanese diplomatic messages.[29]

Frequently throughout the decade before the attack on Pearl Harbor, the U.S. Army's codebreaking efforts required naval assistance. The Army emphasized code production work during the first two years after SIS was established, but by 1933 more importance was attached to work on Japanese diplomatic intercepts because it was thought that the old Black Chamber files would provide SIS with a valuable head start. There was also a new sense of urgency because Japanese aggression in Manchuria provided evidence that earlier intercepts were correct in forecasting Japanese intentions.

Increase in Japanese diplomatic traffic and greater efforts applied by SIS in 1935 to solve Japanese intercepts led to the solution in 1936 of a cipher system introduced in the early 1930s, the Japanese Cipher Machine, Type A, or, as American cryptographers named it, the "RED machine."[30] This was a major cryptanalytic breakthrough. Also during the mid-1930s the content of the increasingly voluminous Japanese diplomatic traffic aroused American interest and suspicion. Partially decoded Tokyo Foreign Ministry communications with Japanese embassies suggested that Japan was interested in negotiating a tripartite treaty with Germany and Italy. The aggressive tone of preliminary negotiations reflected in these messages prompted U.S. Army G-2 to have SIS give highest priority to the exploitation of Japanese diplomatic traffic between Tokyo and the two European Axis capitals. Because of the considerable capacity of the RED machine and the increased volume of Tokyo-Berlin-Rome communications dealing with tripartite negotiations, SIS found itself overwhelmed by early 1937. Its limited resources, particularly Japanese linguists, enabled SIS to translate only a small fraction of hundreds of deciphered Japanese messages made available by the efficient RED machine.[31]

To alleviate this situation, the Navy participated in the exploitation of the RED machine intercepts. Under the terms of an army-navy agreement, the Op-20-G became responsible for deciphering and translating Japanese diplomatic messages originating on odd calendar days, and SIS handled messages originating on even calendar days. This arrangement evenly distributed the workload and permitted fuller consideration of foreign secret communications by various U.S. government intelligence agencies.

This "odd-even" arrangement also helped to reduce SIS's workload in the

In Berlin on 20 April 1939, Ōshima introduces Hitler to Shiratori Toshio, Japanese ambassador to Italy. (Source: National Archives)

translation of tedious code manual systems used in all Japanese diplomatic communications. However, the army and navy retained autonomy in other aspects of this COMINT operation. The arrangement did not apply, for example, to the cryptanalytic recovery of the codes and transposition keys employed in Japanese cipher systems, nor did it apply to the respective intercept missions of the two services.

The volume of enciphered Japanese messages continued to increase in the late 1930s, and SIS continued to give Japanese diplomatic intercepts its highest priority. Although efforts were also increased to intercept and exploit the relatively low-powered transmissions of the Japanese Army, espe-

Ōshima and Hitler with Ribbentrop in the center, Berlin, 22 February 1939.
(Source: National Archives)

cially after the onset of the Sino-Japanese War in July 1937, SIS had greater success in handling Japanese diplomatic messages. Op-20-G, on the other hand, was particularly successful in its work to handle some of the Japanese naval radio circuits. Thus, the navy's workload was divided between the requirements for processing Op-20-G's share of the Japanese diplomatic intercepts and its work on the Japanese naval systems. The increasingly aggressive and rapidly expanding Japanese Navy understandably commanded growing concern and attention in U.S. naval COMINT operations.

With threats of another global war came an enormous increase in the workload of the small cryptographic units of the two U.S. armed services. In 1938, as the tension caused by militant forces in Europe became more evident, SIS was finally authorized to increase its staff from seven to eleven, and not long after the Munich crisis in late 1938, three additional people joined SIS.[32] Most significantly, in late 1938 the Japanese Foreign Ministry started to distribute a new cipher machine to its diplomatic missions that had RED machines. The new system, intended to be employed for the most secret of Japanese diplomatic communications, was largely in place in the spring of 1939, and soon traffic in the RED machine system almost completely disappeared. Because of the significant loss of Japanese intelligence, it is not surprising that both the army and navy were alarmed and thus placed great emphasis on the recovery of the new Japanese cipher system.

Op-20-G had not been altogether successful in solving Japanese naval systems, particularly JN25, and with the mounting Japanese naval threat and the failure of all efforts to solve the new Japanese cipher system used for diplomatic communications, the navy decided by the end of 1939 to shift some of its cryptanalytic effort from the new diplomatic system to the Japanese naval systems. SIS, however, continued to concentrate on the diplomatic intercepts, and finally, in the fall of 1940, the solution was discovered to the new Cipher Machine, Type B, called the "PURPLE machine" by American cryptographers.

The bulk of SIS's magical work during the eighteen months required to break PURPLE concentrated on analytical efforts and the construction of a PURPLE machine analog. The Japanese translation workload in both SIS and Op-20-G operations had been greatly reduced. Therefore, with the availability of the new PURPLE machine analog in late 1940, not unlike the situation that occurred in the 1930s when the RED machine system was solved, the sudden demand for Japanese linguists became too great for SIS to handle alone. Furthermore, there was an enormous flow of diplomatic traffic among the three Axis capitals, for the tripartite military pact had been concluded on 27 September 1940. It was not only important to process PURPLE intercepts on a current basis after September, but in order to restore intelli-

Hitler and Ōshima talking in Berlin, 2 March 1939. (Source: National Archives)

gence continuity during the eighteen-month PURPLE blackout it was essential to translate selected messages from the vast backlog of enciphered intercepts.

Again the army and navy implemented the odd-even day formula inaugurated initially for the RED machine system, and this time, the arrangement continued in force until early 1942. Like the previous arrangement, the odd-even day formula dealing with PURPLE did not apply to intercept activities of the two armed services. It is worth noting, particularly on the eve of the attack on Pearl Harbor, that practically all Japanese diplomatic traffic was carried by the transoceanic commercial radio circuits, and coverage of those circuits was shared by the army and navy in a coordinated effort. There was also a daily exchange of translations between the two services and a special exchange when anything of particular importance came up.[33]

The system of SIS or SSA production of information evolved throughout the war, and developments are discussed in context later in this book. However, certain steps by which an enemy message passed from its originator to MIS were fundamental, and six basic steps are illustrated in a drawing prepared under the direction of the U.S. Army assistant chief of staff, G-2, in 1946 (see the photograph on p. 15).[34]

1. The interception of traffic in large volume was performed mostly by

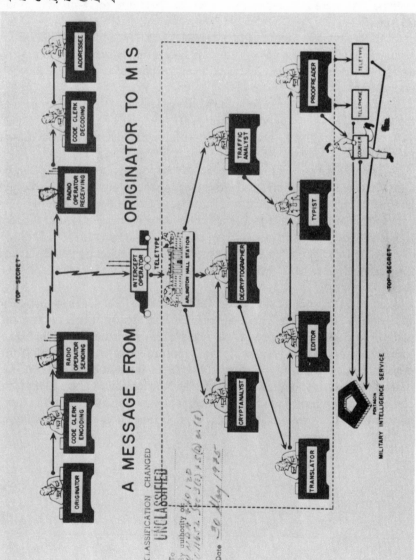

Diagram showing the "route" of an enemy message from interception to the Pentagon. (Source: National Security Agency)

fixed installations, not by mobile units in trucks, as suggested by the illustrator. The monthly volume of messages handled by Arlington Hall Station increased tremendously during the war, from 46,865 messages in February 1943 to 381,590 messages in July 1945. Transmission from the intercept stations to Arlington Hall was chiefly by special teletype lines, which increasingly took precedence over other means such as cable and air mail. Four teletype lines were in operation in December 1941 and forty-six were in use by August 1945.

2. Traffic analysis of intercepted messages was one of several functions of Arlington Hall Station that was not strictly cryptanalytic in character. Similar activities included secret ink solution and exploitation of telephone communications.

3. The solution of foreign cryptographic systems was the chief concern of the cryptanalysts who founded SIS in 1930.

4. Decryptographers worked closely with cryptanalysts on messages sent in solved or partially solved systems.

5. The translation desk was particularly important in the case of Japanese messages. (John Hurt, as the original Japanese linguist at SIS, did not hesitate to apply his broad cultural knowledge and understanding of Japanese society in an effort to render accurate, sensitive translations in modern English.)

6. After translation, editors, typists, and proofreaders prepared the text for transmission to MIS in the War Department, assistant chief of staff, G-2.

The complex work of Arlington Hall specialists, particularly that done years before the Japanese strike at Pearl Harbor, greatly influenced the war, and the specialists developed an extremely efficient means of producing information. Ōshima was also an intrinsic part of the great drama of World War II, particularly in the European theater of operations (ETO). He was uniquely suited to play the role of confidant to German military leaders, including Hitler, but the labor of American cryptanalysts turned Ōshima into an inadvertent informer of incalculable importance in leading the Allies to victory.

1

Ōshima and the Magic Road to Pearl Harbor

Ōshima's revelations through MAGIC helped to form a circuitous route to Pearl Harbor, a massing of circumstantial evidence that tended to suggest the outbreak of hostilities, yet the pieces of the puzzle did not come together soon enough to stay the calamity in Hawaii on 7 December 1941. Nevertheless, Ōshima's well-known rapport with Hitler and Ribbentrop placed the Japanese ambassador in the center of the Axis coalition. Although this situation was generally appreciated by MAGIC analysts before the attack, several opportunities were missed to form a clearer picture of impending disaster. Part of the problem was that Ōshima's reports were usually viewed in terms of what was already known or suspected, in the context of the German-Soviet war, for example, or in terms of Hitler's hopes that Japan would attack the Soviet Union. In 1941 Ōshima was often looked to by American cryptanalysts for evidence to back their suspicions or to confirm reports from other intelligence sources. With the surprise of Pearl Harbor came a massive reassessment of earlier MAGIC reports, and Ōshima's role was at last viewed with renewed appreciation. After the attack Ōshima continued at his post in Berlin where his embassy served as the hub for the vast majority of important Eurasian Axis communications.

Ōshima was the linchpin in German-Japanese communications. Although Ribbentrop had failed to convince the Japanese government that Ōshima should remain at his post in Berlin in 1939, when Ōshima was reappointed the different circumstances in wartime Europe late in 1940 and the fact that the MAGIC operation was in place made Ōshima pivotal to Anglo-American strategic planning. The Tripartite Pact was signed in late September, and on the day of the announcement of Ōshima's reappointment, 20 December 1940, the interim Japanese ambassador, Kurusu Saburō met with Ribbentrop in Berlin. He was told by the German foreign minister, "I am

Soon after his second appointment as ambassador to Germany, Ōshima is greeted by Ribbentrop at the latter's estate at Fuschl, near Salzburg, Austria, 23 February 1941. (From the author's collection)

sorry to see you go, but I am glad that Tokyo has appointed Ambassador Ōshima to succeed you here."[1] Clearly, the National Socialists were delighted with the news, and Ōshima, with a great deal of fanfare, was warmly greeted as a friend of the Third Reich upon his return to Berlin.[2] Not long afterward, Hitler's propaganda minister, Paul Joseph Goebbels, wrote in his diary: "Ōshima is really one of the most successful champions of Axis policies. A monument ought later to be erected in his honor in Germany."[3]

Ōshima soon reestablished direct contact with Hitler and Ribbentrop, providing American cryptanalysts with an invaluable source of raw intercept data that continued until V-E Day. Referred to in the Nationalist Socialist press as "Germany's old friend," Ōshima, six days after his return, conferred with Ribbentrop at Fuschl, the foreign minister's Austrian estate outside Salzburg. On 27 February Ōshima, dressed in military uniform, presented his diplomatic credentials to Hitler at the Berghof near Berchtesgaden.[4]

The chief piece of MAGIC intelligence obtained from Ōshima in the spring of 1941 concerned the German attack on the Soviet Union. Precise, detailed information quickly reached American cryptanalysts, and their ringside seat

Ambassador Ōshima arriving at Obersalzberg, accompanied by Ribbentrop, to present his credentials to Hitler, 27 February 1941. (Source: National Archives)

gave them a unique perspective of German and Japanese policies toward the Soviet Union.

Ōshima was in the center of German-Japanese discussions when Japanese Foreign Minister Matsuoka visited Germany in late March. (Washington had learned from MAGIC messages of the forthcoming visit five weeks earlier.[5]) Two days before he met Matsuoka, who had figured prominently in Ōshima's reassignment to Berlin, Hitler promised Ōshima that he would seek an "intimate exchange of opinions inasmuch as Foreign Minister Matsuoka has deliberately made a long trip to Germany in connection with future Japanese-German cooperation."[6] On 27 March Matsuoka had the first of several meetings with Hitler. Ōshima and his German counterpart from Tokyo, Ambassador Ott, were also present at the initial meeting. Hitler hinted that a German-Soviet war might break out. Matsuoka suggested that although "it would be practically impossible to foretell what . . . attitude the government of Japan would take at the time of such an eventuality . . . , [as a personal opinion he] *could not visualize Japan not striking* at the Soviet Union from the (Manchukuo?) area if war was declared between Germany and the Soviet Union."[7] However, the web of diplomacy with Germany's Axis partner was made more intricate during Matsuoka's return trip across the Soviet Union, for in Moscow on 13 April the Soviet-Japanese Neutrality Pact was concluded.

Hitler receives Ambassador Ōshima's credentials in the Berghof while Ribbentrop looks on, 27 February 1941. (Source: National Archives)

Discussion of major issues during Matsuoka's trip caused such an enormous increase of message traffic between Tokyo and Berlin that a special keying system called HIKAL was introduced. It was solved by cryptanalysts at the Munitions Building in Washington on the night of 16 April 1941, and soon afterward Ōshima wired news to Matsuoka in Japan of Hitler's intention to attack the Soviet Union. The SIS translator of the multipart message wrote that he worked late into the night on the first parts of Ōshima's message.

> Goering was outlining to Ōshima Germany's plan to attack Russia . . . , giving the number of planes and numbers and types of divisions to be used for this drive and that. I was too excited for sleep that night. It was the liveliest news for many a day. . . . We and the British informed the Russians about . . . [Hitler's plan], but they were too dumbfounded to believe it at first.[8]

On several occasions before the invasion was launched on 22 June 1941, Ōshima confirmed for MAGIC listeners the coming of the war, and he offered strategic assessments that had long-range implications. He met with Hitler and Ribbentrop on 3 June and again with Ribbentrop the next day. Ōshima reported to Tokyo that "both men tell me that in every probability war with Russia cannot be avoided."[9] A few days later Ōshima cryptically advised his superiors in Tokyo that "for the time being I think it would be a good idea for you, in some inconspicuous manner, to postpone the departure of Japanese citizens for Europe via Siberia. You will understand why."[10]

As the war in Europe was about to assume new dimensions by engulfing the Soviet Union, Tokyo became eager for estimates of the impact on the United States. The new concern of the Japanese Foreign Ministry and Ōshima's responses served to heighten awareness in Washington of the deterioration of U.S. relations with Japan. Tokyo wired Ōshima bluntly: "During your conversation[s] with Hitler and Ribbentrop the other day, what impression did you get as to the German government's opinion regarding the probable date of the United States' entry into the war? Please reply at once."[11] About ten days later Ōshima replied that he did not know how German authorities viewed the matter, but he was, quite typically, willing to offer his own opinion. Ōshima was convinced that the coming German-Soviet war was going to end in a short time and there would be no time for Great Britain and the United States to give the Soviet Union any concrete aid; nor would there be enough time to conclude a political agreement. As for the United States, Ōshima estimated that

Japanese Foreign Minister Matsuoka Yōsuke talking with Ōshima in the Japanese embassy, Berlin, 29 March 1941. (Source: National Archives)

she will at first wait to see what would happen, and if in the mean-time it becomes evident that Soviet Russia is being defeated, she will not give Russia any aid. The question then would be the increase of aid to Britain along with the intensification of anti-German public opinion. However, with the defeat of Soviet Russia, this would prob-ably pass as a mere temporary phenomenon, and this would lead her to forego her plans of joining the war.[12]

His assessment came on the eve of the important 2 July 1941 Imperial Conference, when the Japanese government decided that the southern ad-vance policy was to be implemented, even if the action ultimately led to war with the United States.[13]

No doubt Ōshima, whose staff members always read the foreign press and reported significant developments to their ambassador, was aware of President Franklin D. Roosevelt's lend-lease proposal to Congress made soon after the president's reelection. Yet Ōshima erred, not unlike other top-ranking Japanese government officials, in his estimate of American reaction to Axis aggression. There is no evidence that Ōshima's assessment in mid-June had any influence on the United States, although Ōshima's message was translated and available in Washington five days before President Roosevelt, at a press conference on 24 June, promised U.S. aid to the Soviet Union. Nor is there any evidence concerning Ōshima's reaction to U.S. con-gressional approval to grant lend-lease credit of $1 billion to the Soviet Un-ion.

If Tokyo was anxious to learn of Hitler's intentions from Ōshima, Ōshima seemed to want information about his own government's intentions. But Tokyo would tell the ambassador only of the broad outline of Japanese policy.[14] Five weeks after the Germans invaded the Soviet Union, Ōshima warned his government that the United States would eventually join the war. "The problem is not whether or not America will go to war on the basis of international law, but just to what extent America has the power and facili-ties to extend aid to Britain. I would like to know concretely just what your prognostications in regard to this are."[15] However, throughout the summer Ōshima, like all of Japan's ambassadors, was kept in the dark about his gov-ernment's plans to go to war with the western powers, unfortunately so from an American point of view. Surely such a revealing message to Ōshima con-cerning the forthcoming Pearl Harbor attack would have fallen victim to MAGIC, as did the messages concerning the forthcoming German attack on the Soviet Union, Operation BARBAROSSA, and the southern advance policy coming out of the 2 July Imperial Conference.

Ōshima provided MAGIC listeners with a ringside seat at the opening of

Ambassador Ōshima, in his uniform as a lieutenant general in the Imperial Japanese Army, with Foreign Minister Ribbentrop at Hitler's headquarters in East Prussia, 14 July 1941. (Source: National Archives)

Ōshima during a visit to the eastern front, 14–19 July 1941, at the Mauersee near Hitler's headquarters, Rastenburg, in East Prussia. In the picture, left to right, are Lieutenant Colonel Saigō Jugō; an unknown Japanese person, probably a valet; Heinrich Georg Stahmer, Ōshima's Foreign Ministry escort, soon to be ambassador to the Japanese-backed Wang Ching-wei government in Nanking (1942) and then to Japan (1943–45); and Ambassador Ōshima, in the uniform of a lieutenant general with service ribbons. (Courtesy of David Kahn)

Hitler's campaign to conquer the Soviet Union. "When Barbarossa commences," Hitler had predicted, "the world will hold its breath." Indeed, most American and British military analysts had serious doubts about the Russian ability to survive 1941; among the western pessimists were the two chiefs of staff, General George C. Marshall and General Sir John Dill.[16] Marshall, in particular, although cautious in his forecast, was influenced by reports from his own intelligence experts.[17] The pessimistic view of Russia's prospects was promoted by reports from the American military attaché in Moscow, Major Ivan Yeaton, and Ōshima's messages from the German side tended to give substance to the report that the "end of Russian resistance is not far away."[18]

The Germans gave Ōshima daily reports on the war, and he was kept fully informed from the outset. Ribbentrop even had a Foreign Ministry representative give Ōshima a report at the close of the first day of fighting. The U.S. Army Military Intelligence Division (MID) had Ōshima's account to

Tokyo translated two days later and made available to General Marshall. The account said that in addition to massive German units, twenty-five Rumanian and fifteen Finnish divisions were participating in the invasion and that at least 500 Russian airplanes had been destroyed.[19] In another message Ōshima revealed that "up to the night of the 23rd (the second day of fighting)," over 2,000 Russian airplanes were destroyed. "Thus, the Soviet air forces . . . were completely annihilated and the German air force has gained, already, the mastery of the air."[20] This was an ominous sign, for Marshall was very appreciative of the fact that the British had survived the Battle of Britain the previous year in part because the Luftwaffe had failed to gain mastery of the air. In Russia the tables had turned.

About the same time, a Soviet mission arrived in Washington to begin co-ordination of Soviet orders for American military aid for use in the struggle against the German invaders. On 26 July 1941, Under Secretary of State Sumner Welles and General Marshall met with Soviet Lieutenant General Philip Golikov and Engineer General Alexander Repin. It was a worried Marshall who wrote to his deputy chief of staff, Major General Richard C. Moore, on 28 July 1941, "In a telephone conversation with the President yesterday he took up the necessity of providing railroad traffic experts to assist the Russians in keeping the Siberian Railway out of Vladivostok open."[21] On the same day Marshall wrote to his G-2 saying that the secretary of war wanted estimates on the German-Soviet war: "The Secretary particularly wishes to have the possible effect of the guerrilla tactics evaluated. What is thought of the capacity of the Russians to carry out such a type of warfare? He would like to have a brief study of the present status of Russian industry."[22] Marshall knew that Ōshima's MAGIC reports would provide ample evidence that the five-week-old war was not going well for the Soviets.

Marshall's intelligence experts also knew that there was a possibility of a Japanese attack on the Soviet Union from the east. It was well known that Foreign Minister Matsuoka believed that a Japanese strike against the Soviet Union was inevitable, and if it materialized, surely such an attack would be the coup de grace to Soviet forces pitted against the warring Axis coalition. On 2 July, ten days into the invasion, Matsuoka's message to Ribbentrop was equivocal. In an English text written in cipher he maintained that "Japan is preparing for all possible eventualities as regards the U.S.S.R. in order to join forces with Germany in actively combating the communist menace." Moreover, he claimed that Japan was making military preparations, was carefully "watching development of conditions in Eastern Siberia," and was "determined . . . to destroy the communist system established there."[23] Yet an enigma about the true intent of Japanese foreign policy remained in the minds of American intelligence analysts.

They were suspicious of the reliability of information obtained from diplomatic intercepts. Some reflected the ignorance of their author, and some reflected the false reporting of informants. All diplomatic intercepts had to be studied as integral parts of a continually changing whole and had to be carefully interpreted to isolate those messages or parts of messages containing genuinely reliable information. It was not clear in early July, for example, whether Matsuoka's politely pro-Axis message to Ribbentrop would be followed by a declaration of war against the Soviet Union. After all, Matsuoka had recently angered the Germans by entering into the Soviet-Japanese Neutrality Pact, thus assuring, if the agreement were adhered to, that Russia would not be caught in a two-front war after the German attack.

However, Ōshima's intercepts formed a continuum. He was the German government's main Japanese contact in Berlin throughout most of the 1930s and had become something of a confidant of Hitler.[24] Ōshima was a particularly diligent student of the war, especially after the German invasion of the Soviet Union, so his reports were thought to be reliable and warranted close scrutiny, all the more so when his explanations, interpretations, and recommendations focused on specific events.

U.S. Army G-2 analysts were convinced that Ōshima was a good source for learning about the German side of the picture in the summer of 1941 because German leaders had no reason to deceive their long-term Japanese friend. On the ninth day of the war Ōshima flew to Hitler's field headquarters near Rastenburg, East Prussia, for a two-day visit.[25] He returned less than a week later and talked with Hitler for over five hours and inspected battlefields during a three-day tour. Ōshima was so favorably impressed with German progress in the war that he recommended to his government that Japan strike quickly at the Soviets in the east.[26] But by that point, mid-July, Foreign Minster Matsuoka, thought to be pro-German, was forced to resign. His successor, Admiral Toyoda Teijirō, advocated a southward advance rather than a move against the Soviet Union. Nevertheless, Toyoda, like his predecessor, sent assurances to Berlin. Matsuoka had assured Hitler and Ribbentrop "that you will see no change in the Imperial Government's foreign policy because of my resignation."[27] A carefully circumspect attitude toward the war in Russia remained a hallmark of Tokyo's foreign policy. However, as the Germans continued to pour eastward, it seemed increasingly plausible that the Japanese would take advantage of the opportunity to attack across the Amur River from Manchukuo, and thus break the Soviet-Japanese Neutrality Pact.

Ōshima was at his best when reporting on the German-Soviet war in 1941. One chief characteristic of the pattern of radio communications between the Japanese embassy in Berlin and Tokyo concerned the high quality

General Ōshima reviewing German troops on an airfield, probably in East Prussia in 1941. (Courtesy of Mrs. Ōshima Toyoko)

of analysis of the eastern front. During the summer of 1941, Ōshima, through exacting and enthusiastic work, continued to send Tokyo detailed reports about the gigantic sweep the Germans were making into the Soviet Union. Two months into the war, on 23 August, Ōshima again flew to Hitler's East Prussian headquarters where he talked with Ribbentrop for four hours and for another hour with Field Marshal Wilhelm Keitel.[28]

News in late August of the huge scale of destruction of Soviet forces was staggering to American intelligence analysts. Keitel, whom Ōshima had known since the mid-1930s, gave the Japanese warrior-diplomat a full report: "The total number of Soviet casualties, including wounded, dead, and captured, is estimated at between five and six million." Furthermore, Ōshima reported to his superiors that the rate of destruction of what little remained of the Soviet air power was so high that the Red air force "need no longer be taken into consideration."[29] All six parts of Ōshima's major message of 25 August were intercepted and deciphered; within three days they had been translated by naval Op-20-G and distributed to Marshall and other high-ranking military officers. Others, such as President Roosevelt, Secretary of State Cordell Hull, and Under Secretary Welles, had the opportunity to read some of the messages in 1941, although the reports they received were not always complete.[30]

American leaders knew what Ōshima was reporting, and they feared that the Russians might be defeated before the end of the year. Their fears seemed to be confirmed by the Russians themselves. On a few occasions contemporary Soviet statements, often delayed, were revealing of German effectiveness in the war, as claimed initially in Ōshima's messages. In October, for example, the Russians admitted the destruction of 5,000 planes (the size of the Soviet Air Force in June 1941), the devastation of their tank forces, and the loss of a large number of their guns, gun crews, and huge ammunition dumps. In sum, the information they received on Soviet casualties, through the Ōshima connection in the summer of 1941, was accurate, as later Soviet and western scholarly estimates have substantiated.[31]

The Japanese Foreign Ministry was extremely secretive in communications with all representatives in foreign capitals, and nothing of a specific nature was revealed about the daring southern advance policy, but the ambitious Ōshima sought more information about his government's intentions, especially those that had bearing on German-Japanese relations. However, the ambiguity of Foreign Minister Toyoda's responses left the Berlin envoy uncertain about modifications in Japanese foreign policy. It was symptomatic of the awkward German-Japanese alliance that the two governments did not coordinate strategic planning or fully apprise one another in advance of new foreign policy adventures. Toyoda's message to Ōshima at the end of July complained that Germany started "a war with Russia because of her military expediency when it was least desirable on our part."[32] Curiously, Toyoda admonished Ōshima to work in the future within the broad framework of the policy decided upon in the 2 July Imperial Conference, but from the tone of his message, MAGIC intelligence analysts still had good reason to believe that Japan would eventually join its Axis partner in the war against the Soviet Union.

Toyoda did not seem to be appreciably different from his predecessor, Matsuoka. On 31 July Toyoda wrote to the Japanese ambassadors in Berlin and Washington, D.C., with instructions for Ōshima to send the message also to the embassy in Rome, that "the Russo-German war has given us an excellent opportunity to settle the northern question, and it is a fact that we are proceeding with our preparations to take advantage of this occasion."[33] Thus, the Japanese government was determined "to bring about the success of the objectives of the Tripartite Pact." Although Toyoda's message contained the warning that "Japanese-American relations are more rapidly than ever treading the evil road," the bulk of his remarks centered on such issues as the recent Japanese acquisition of military bases in French Indo-China,

Receiving German salutes during a parade, General Ōshima is in perfect step with his German officer escort on the left, ca. 1941. (Courtesy of Mrs. Ōshima Toyoko)

the war in China, the Soviet-German war, and the fundamental spirit of the Tripartite Pact. Thus, Japan left its representative in Berlin, the host German government, and intelligence analysts in Washington in the dark about new strategic planning that would eventually result in the Pearl Harbor attack.

Throughout the summer and autumn Ōshima continued to urge Tokyo to attack the Soviet Union. "Both Führer Hitler and Foreign Minister Ribbentrop have expressed their hope," Ōshima reported on 9 August, that Japan would cooperate fully to "destroy communism at its source." The ambassador advised his government, "This coincides with our interests." He predicted that Germany would create a new Russia in Europe, and if Tokyo continued to hesitate to join Germany in the attack, "Japan will be left to cope single-handed[ly] with the problems of Communism east of the Urals and the reestablishment of order in Siberia."[34] On several occasions Ōshima repeated this plea for Japanese action.[35] (Even after the attack at Pearl Harbor Ōshima did not falter in his conviction.)[36] Tokyo remained evasive, however, and did not respond to Ōshima's entreaties, nor did the Foreign Ministry inform its ambassador of new strategic considerations.

General Marshall's G-2 experts hoped Ōshima's protests that he was woefully uninformed would result in a flow of explicit information about the strategic planning under consideration in Tokyo. On 20 August Ōshima repeated his complaints to superiors in Tokyo that he had "no clear-cut information"—rather, he had been given "merely an outline of the [government's] policy"—and he found it difficult to function effectively in Berlin. He wrote to Foreign Minister Toyoda that

> since you do not wire replies to questions I address to you, I find it impossible to know what the real intention of our government is. If in the present great crisis the right kind of diplomacy should be carried on with the officials at home and abroad acting as a unit, that the officials abroad should be well informed on the policy the government is . . . a prerequisite.[37]

No specific replies have been found to Ōshima's repeated requests for explanations "concerning our Government's real national policy," as he again complained in a message to Toyoda on 20 September:

> Ever since the principal points of our national policy were decided on July 2nd, 1941, I have been performing my duties in a fog, so to speak, not knowing a single thing about our Government's policy during this period of critical international relations. Under such circumstances, I find that I cannot perform my duties satisfactorily and my conscience does not permit my going on in this manner.[38]

Although on 8 October Toyoda explained to Ōshima the general background of Japanese-American negotiations and sent him reassurances that the Tripartite Pact remained foremost in Japanese foreign policy, Ōshima remained as uninformed as ever about Japanese strategic planning.[39] This Japanese censoring of specific information about the impending Pearl Harbor attack helped the Imperial Navy to achieve surprise in its assaults early in December.

A little earlier, quite unexpectedly, Ōshima had offered a new piece of information from Berlin which Tokyo was inordinately curious about. During a discussion on several unrelated matters with a high-ranking German official who had just returned to Berlin from Hitler's field headquarters, the Japanese ambassador was told in mid-August "that when the question of the United States came up in the course of a conversation, Hitler had said that if a clash occurs by any chance between Japan and the United States, Germany will at once open war against the United States."[40] Ōshima was convinced that the report of Hitler's point of view was genuine. Ōshima's startling disclosure in mid-August must have caused Tokyo policymakers to reconsider their reserved attitude and their initial coolness and reluctance toward Ōshima's demands for closer German-Japanese cooperation. Hitler's declaration was especially significant in light of Japanese plans for a southward advance. This was an important part of the circuitous MAGIC road to Pearl Harbor, although the picture was not complete at the Munitions Building in Washington. Curiously, this newfound dimension of the Axis coalition was revealed when Roosevelt and Prime Minister Winston Churchill met secretly to conclude a far-reaching basis for Anglo-American cooperation through the Atlantic Charter.

It appeared opportune for the Japanese Foreign Ministry to show a little more interest in the Ōshima-Hitler proposal to have Japan join the war against communist Russia.[41] By mid-August no definite decision had been reached in Tokyo about new northern *or* southern offensive operations, but the Germans from their own independent sources had strong indications that the Japanese would soon attack the Soviet Union. The fact that German intelligence reported at the end of August that the Japanese Army had abandoned plans to attack Russia at least until the spring of 1942 appears not to have undermined Hitler's determination to declare war on the United States in the event of a war between Japan and America, but the Japanese Foreign Ministry could not be certain of this. It seemed tactically prudent to cultivate Axis solidarity, primarily for the purpose of benefiting future independent Japanese policy, not for the purpose of promoting Axis strategic coordination.

Part of the problem in German-Japanese relations in the latter half of 1941 was the issue of Japanese-American negotiations. On 22 July the German ambassador in Tokyo bluntly warned the vice minister for foreign affairs, Ohashi Chūichi, that the German government "will not be favorably impressed by these negotiations. In view of the fact that of late the Russo-German war is becoming increasingly favorable to Germany, it would be well for the sake of our common interest for Japan to decide now where she stands."[42]

Ōshima had already forewarned Tokyo. Fresh from a visit to Hitler's field headquarters Ōshima reported on 17 July that "the Führer was not at all satisfied with Japan's attitude, particularly with regard to the continuation of the Japanese-U.S. negotiations."[43] Hitler believed the negotiations were contrary at least to the spirit of the Tripartite Pact, but Berlin and Tokyo had different interpretations of their obligations under the terms of the Tripartite Pact, particularly the secret addenda. In the Japanese interpretation, Tokyo was released from the ironclad obligations of political, economic, and military assistance cited in Article 3 of the published treaty.[44] Typically,

Ōshima, an unwavering champion of Hitler's views, repeatedly raised the question of Tokyo's attitude toward the Tripartite Pact.[45]

In July both foreign ministers, Matsuoka and Toyoda, had attempted to mollify the Germans with partial explanations for the conduct of Japanese foreign policy in view of "the fundamental spirit of the Tripartite Pact," but Tokyo offered the most thoroughgoing explanation only after reaching the decision to go ahead with preparations for war with the United States.[46] The new foreign minister after October, Tōgō Shigenori, worked feverishly to mend matters with Germany, since Hitler, as Ōshima first revealed, had already given Tokyo the assurance that the Japanese could expect Germany to declare war on the United States. At the outset of his tenure Tōgō believed Japan's membership in the Tripartite Pact was becoming one of several major obstacles to success in Japanese-American relations, especially as German U-boat attacks on American vessels mounted. It was clear to Tōgō that the United States expected Japan to drop out of the Axis alliance, probably something impossible for any Japanese government to do. There were still several other critical problems in Japanese-American negotiations that were far from resolved, and only hours after the task force commanded by Vice Admiral Nagumo Chūichi weighed anchor for the voyage to Pearl Harbor, Tōgō hastened to instruct Ōshima on 27 November to convey to Hitler, "confidentially and in a suitable way," the reassurance that Japanese-American "negotiations do not in any way affect the validity of the Tripartite Pact."[47] Three days later Ōshima was instructed to explain *immediately* to Hitler and Ribbentrop that since the beginning of Japanese-American negotiations "the Imperial Government adamantly stuck to the Tripartite Alliance as the cornerstone of its national policy . . . with the intent of restraining the United States from participating in the war." Since Washington insisted on "the divorce of the Imperial Government from the Tripartite Alliance . . . , [Japan] could no longer continue negotiations with the United States."[48]

The week before the attack on Pearl Harbor, Ōshima met several times with Ribbentrop who "understood fully the explanation" for the earlier Japanese-American negotiations.[49] But not until just after the German declaration of war on the United States (11 December) did Ōshima have an opportunity to explain to Hitler directly that the "negotiations were conducted within the bounds of the terms contained in the Tripartite Pact." Hitler piously "replied that before war is declared it is but natural that every peaceful overture be made."[50]

An earlier change in government that gave one of Ōshima's longtime adversaries the Foreign Ministry portfolio oddly enough resulted in a situation in which hints of a switch in Japanese strategic planning were sent to Berlin.

But it appears that these hints, another part of the circuitous MAGIC road to Pearl Harbor, went largely unnoticed in Washington.

The fall of the third cabinet of Prince Konoe Fumimaro on 18 October 1941 contributed to a climate in which war was increasingly likely. Soon afterward, General Tōjō Hideki formed a new cabinet in which he retained three portfolios for himself while giving Tōgō Shigenori the top Foreign Ministry post. While there was no bad blood between the two military men, Tōjō and Ōshima, there was considerable enmity between Ōshima and his diplomatic superior, Tōgō. Ōshima offered to resign on 19 October, not merely a pro forma act of an ambassador at the time of a change of government. In a message to Foreign Minister Tōgō, Ōshima restated his desire for more information about Tokyo's intentions because "it is essential that all of the Empire's diplomatic representatives abroad have a perfect understanding of and be in absolute harmony with the Imperial Government's policies." Ōshima maintained that because they had differed in their opinions on policy, as the Japanese ambassador in Berlin he might not be able to carry out Tōgō's policies. Therefore, he sought permission to resign: "Your ambassador feels that he should be disqualified as a public figure."[51]

Ōshima's trepidation about the new foreign minister's view on his continuance as head of the Berlin mission was not without some justification. In 1938 an open clash had developed between Tōgō, then ambassador to Berlin, and General Ōshima, then military attaché in the Berlin embassy. Ōshima, through his personal contacts with Hitler and Ribbentrop, had circumvented traditional diplomatic channels to strengthen relations with Germany beyond the scope of the 1936 Anti-Comintern Pact. Tōgō, a scholar of German literature and a distinguished career diplomat, disapproved strongly, but as ambassador he had found that under the circumstances it was impossible to control Ōshima. Within ten months of his arrival in Berlin, Tōgō had been forced to relinquish his position under intense pressure from Ōshima's supporters in various pro-Axis, promilitary quarters in Tokyo and Berlin, and Ōshima replaced Tōgō as ambassador in October 1938.[52]

Tōgō's primary concern as the new foreign minister in October 1941 was the deepening deterioration in Japanese-American relations; he had neither the time nor the inclination for vengeance. Besides, Ōshima's mission and his rapport with the Germans were probably invaluable to the Japanese at the time, especially if diplomacy failed and war with the United States ensued. It is not surprising, therefore, that Tōgō dismissed any notion of having Ōshima leave his post in Berlin, telling Ōshima at the end of October that his "position in Berlin is at present a very important one and a Chargé could not hold it down, so I want you to stay there. You know our two countries are now up against great difficulties and we could not possibly change Ambassador at this pass, so for the time being please yield your own desires to the common good."⁵³ Tōgō had witnessed Ōshima's close association with Hitler and Ribbentrop in 1938, and he knew firsthand how effective diplomatically that camaraderie could make Ōshima. Ōshima had the power to close the Axis triangle by using his unique relationships among ranking National Socialists to obtain their military commitment. Moreover, Tokyo had learned earlier from Ōshima's summary reports that Italy would follow the German lead. However, Ōshima would have to hurry before hostilities started to unfold automatically.

Significantly, it seemed necessary also to bring the ambassador in Berlin at least partially into the picture of Japanese strategic planning as the countdown to the start of war in the Pacific approached, and especially after the countdown was launched on 27 November 1941.⁵⁴ Thus, the American cryptologic intelligence community was provided with hints of new things to come through the Tokyo-Ōshima cipher communications. "It could be judged that something big was about to happen in "the South,'" one scholar quite rightly concluded later, but "the exact when, where, and how were unfortunately far more elusive."⁵⁵

The MAGIC messages to Ōshima contained only limited indications of the impending hostilities—they were indeed an elusive road. They also came piecemeal and very late in the remaining days of peace in the Pacific. Tōgō was in a hurry to smooth relations with Germany and to obtain a *formal* commitment from Hitler that Germany would become Japan's warring ally against the United States. He wanted affirmation of the idea expressed in Hitler's comment passed indirectly to Ōshima over three months earlier— that Germany would open war against the United States.

Ōshima had been sounding out the Germans. He concluded by 29 November, based on a discussion with Ribbentrop late during the previous evening, that "there are indications at present that Germany would not refuse to fight the United States if necessary."⁵⁶ Ōshima quoted Ribbentrop verbatim: "Should Japan become engaged in a war against the United States, Germany, of course, would join the war immediately. There is absolutely no possibility of Germany's entering into a separate peace with the United States under such circumstances. The Führer is determined on that point."⁵⁷ This was encouraging to Tōgō, but it would be more satisfactory if a formal declaration of war and an Axis war alliance could be announced before the surprise attack on Pearl Harbor.

Ōshima was given hints of events to come, with the hope that if he were better informed about the true intent of Japanese policy he would be more effective in efforts to win German cooperation. On 30 November, after explaining that Japanese-American negotiations had been broken off, Ōshima was instructed to tell Hitler and Ribbentrop "that there is extreme danger that war may suddenly break out between the Anglo-Saxon nations and Japan through some clash of arms . . . ; this war may come quicker than anyone dreams."[58]

Ōshima ran out of time before he could obtain Hitler's promise of a formal forthcoming declaration of war and sign the war alliance. By 2 December Ribbentrop had again expressed his government's willingness to fight the United States, but since Hitler could not be reached to arrange a joint declaration of war against the United States, Ribbentrop told Ōshima, "please do not wire this to Japan."[59] Ōshima sent the message anyhow, although it was not translated and made available to American authorities in Washington until three days after the attack on Pearl Harbor. The Führer was on the eastern front directing the final all-out attack on Moscow on 1 December and trying to stabilize German lines after the successful Russian counterattack launched on 6 December. The Japanese had no alternative but to rely on Ribbentrop's promises. Moreover, Ōshima's close association with Ribbentrop at this crucial juncture was a source of comfort to Tōgō. Ōshima radioed his foreign minister that "from my past experiences with Ribbentrop I feel fairly confident when I say that you will not be mistaken if you assume that there will be no objections" about declaring war on the United States.[60] In this instance, however, the message was available in Washington the day *before* the attack at Pearl Harbor.

"Developments are taking a fast turn and it might even be that before the official signing [of the war alliance] is completed the crash may develop," Tokyo told Ōshima the day before the attack. "Make it very clear [to Ribbentrop]," Tōgō continued, "that Japan is expecting Italy and Germany to go to war against Britain and America before this agreement is officially signed."[61]

It was not a misplaced expectation, as Tokyo was to learn shortly. On 7 December at 11:00 P.M. Berlin time, Ōshima received news that Japanese-American hostilities had started. He at once conferred with Ribbentrop, who assured the Japanese envoy that "Germany and Italy's immediate participation can be assumed to be a matter of course." "Now, while I was in the room," Ōshima interjected in an urgent message to Tokyo, "von Ribbentrop immediately passed on the gist of our conversation by telephone to [Italian Foreign Minister Count Galeazzo] Ciano."[62] Within some twelve hours Ōshima again conferred with Ribbentrop to learn that Hitler had just returned to his headquarters and was deciding how best to announce Germany's formal declaration of war. Ōshima was told also that Hitler had already "issued orders to the entire German navy to attack American ships whenever and wherever they may meet them."[63]

The hastily drafted war alliance supplemented the Tripartite Pact of 1940, but it was not ready for signing until 11 December, the day Hitler declared war on the United States in a tirade full of personal insults hurled at President Roosevelt. Signed by Ribbentrop, Ōshima, and the Italian ambassador to Berlin, Dino Alfieri, the war alliance featured an agreement not to conclude an armistice or a separate peace either with the United States or with England.[64] Declarations of war were handed to American diplomatic representatives in Berlin and in Rome shortly after 2:00 P.M., 11 December 1941.

The awkwardness of German-Japanese relations in 1941 was an indication of greater difficulties to come once Germany and Japan were in the war together and fighting against two of the main Allied powers. As it turned out, December 1941 was the high-water mark of German-Japanese military cooperation, an inauspicious sign in modern coalition warfare. Ōshima's role became more difficult as the war developed, for the often conflicting demands and expectations that his government and his host government imposed on him made it very difficult to satisfy both parties as well as his own convictions.

The Japanese were seized in November and December by concerns about the attitude of their Axis ally, Germany, not unlike the concerns that occupied German attention about Japan on the eve of the German-Soviet war and for a long time afterward. Yet each power was prepared to pursue an independent policy to the point of declaring war on its neighbor without the guaranty of ally participation. Indeed, the disharmony in the German-Japanese alliance derived from each power's refusal to subordinate selfish private goals to the common end.

After the shock of the attack on Pearl Harbor, American intelligence analysts had additional reason and many more opportunities to recognize that Ōshima had been a unique source of intelligence during the previous eleven months. Indeed, the trauma of Pearl Harbor taught Americans generally the need for intelligence, although the struggling COMINT teams had appreciated this need throughout the interwar period.[65] Opportunities were missed to make the most sophisticated use of the material supplied by Ōshima, partly because American intelligence analysts failed in 1941 to understand that Ōshima was more than merely the senior Japanese representative in Germany and in those portions of Europe controlled by Germany. They had known since the mid-1930s that the upper echelons of the German government often confided in him, but throughout most of 1941, American analysts failed to see that his ideological intimacy with Nazi leaders in the 1930s had led to special ongoing relationships with those same leaders during the stress of war. Ōshima was made privy to the most secret of Germany's wartime plans after his return to Berlin in February 1941, in part at least because he was ideologically compatible with the leaders in Berlin. William Shirer, the distinguished foreign correspondent in Berlin from 1934 to 5 December 1941, was accurate in his assessment when he wrote that Ōshima had often impressed him "as more Nazi than the Nazis."[66] In all respects, Ōshima was a unique Japanese ambassador to Germany, a warrior-diplomat who was as at home in Berlin as he was in Tokyo.

After Pearl Harbor, translations of Ōshima's messages were produced at greater speed. In scanning messages from him to Tokyo during the twenty weeks before 1 December 1941, and during the twenty-week period after 14 December 1941, one finds for the earlier test period that the average delay between the time a message was sent and the time American intelligence teams made the first translation was 4.6 days. For the second test period, starting a week after the attack at Pearl Harbor, the average delay was 2.5 days. Several factors, in addition to newfound regard for the Ōshima source per se, could have contributed to the shortening of the delays.[67] Some MAGIC analysts interested primarily in the European theater started to single out and prudently focus on Ōshima's reports, and the insight and value that SIS attributed to Ōshima's detailed reports would increase throughout the war in Europe, although other Japanese diplomatic intercepts were also carefully studied and highly valued.[68]

The secret of MAGIC intelligence was not lost after the December attack, in spite of the noise caused by congressional investigations of the Pearl Harbor attack and a growing number of revisionists. Some assertions were made by Republican campaigners during the elections of 1944 that President Roosevelt knew just before the attack that Japanese ambassadors Nomura Kichisaburō and Kurusu Saburō had been ordered to destroy one of their cipher machines in the Japanese embassy in Washington, D.C., and to deliver an ultimatum to the American secretary of state.[69] Chief SIS cryptanalyst Frank Rowlett wrote in the early 1980s that

> as I look back at all the messages and other information available to us at that time [late 1941] regarding the Japanese intentions, it becomes crystal clear to me that this message ordering the destruction of certain of Washington's codes provided the necessary evidence that the Japanese unquestionably intended to take some action which would make war between the United States and Japan a certainty. Unfortunately, Pearl Harbor was never identified in either the Japanese intercepted messages or collateral information as the point of attack.[70]

General Marshall worried that for political purposes New York Governor Thomas E. Dewey, the Republican presidential candidate, might exploit the issue of breaking the Japanese diplomatic cipher during his bid for the White House in 1944. With such a cleverly articulated campaign issue, Dewey could reasonably expect to take some votes away from his Democratic rival. But the publicity generated by using the issue would have resulted in a serious blow to the Allied war effort. Marshall had told Dewey in September 1944 that Ōshima was Washington's "main basis of information regarding Hitler's intentions in Europe," and he had asked Dewey not to reveal in the campaign the fact that American cryptanalysts had broken the Japanese PURPLE diplomatic cipher before the attack on Pearl Harbor because the Japanese were still using the same ciphers and codes in 1944. Such a revelation would cause the Japanese to change their code, thus denying vital information to the Allies.[71]

Marshall's letter to Dewey, written on his own initiative and without Roosevelt's knowledge, was an appeal to the governor's sense of judicious statesmanship in time of war. Dewey did not know in 1944 how circuitous the MAGIC road to Pearl Harbor was, but to his credit he abandoned any notion of exploiting the issue concerning Japanese secret communications for the remainder of the campaign. His prudent and selfless decision no doubt contributed to victory over Axis Germany and Japan and saved many lives. Obviously, however, it was always a struggle to protect the secret of MAGIC, particularly in the crucial months of the war between the Pearl Harbor attack and the successes enjoyed by the Allies by the fall of 1944.

2
Ōshima's MAGIC Messages in the Aftermath of Pearl Harbor

After the attack on Pearl Harbor, the United States worked feverishly to understand how the disaster had come about. Inquiries and investigations were made, and much emphasis was placed on the fact that some Japanese codes and ciphers had been broken before the attack. If there was not unanimity about what was explicit or implied in the intercepts, there was general agreement that MAGIC information contained in intercepted Japanese messages would be important in the future. Most significantly, however, PURPLE was still being used. There was good reason to believe that this main line into Japanese secret diplomatic communications would reveal much about the nature of the other side of the hill, which to a large degree in early 1942 remained otherwise very remote from Washington's observation.

International alliances and alignments set the stage for the global conflict. Soon after that infamous Sunday morning in December, the United States became part of a grand wartime coalition pitted against the Axis coalition. London and Washington embarked together upon the new dimension of World War II, although secure communications posed a problem. Soon after the alliance was formed Roosevelt prodded the army chief of staff to improve the system of communication with London. Marshall wrote to the chief signal officer on 15 January 1942 that "the ultimate desire in the President's mind is to have secret telephonic communication between Washington and London. Some of the difficulties involved were pointed out, but he desires that a study be made as to the best method for improving the communications between the two capitals." Since Marshall had been at the White House the previous night and had talked with Roosevelt about the matter, he added a more thorough explanation in a typed note: "It is rapidity that he wants, approximately a telephone conversation as nearly as possible. He and the P[rime] M[inister] hoped that it would be unnecessary to code mssages [*sic*] over a leased cable. He wanted it set up so that the messages could go back and forth approximating a telephone conversation. GCM"[1]

There was a sense of urgency produced by the incident at Pearl Harbor that helped to make the alliance solid and reasonably cooperative from the outset. The personal magnetism and compatibility of Roosevelt and Churchill also greatly aided the Anglo-American partnership. Extraordinary forthrightness was demonstrated early in the alliance. Churchill wrote to Roosevelt on 25 February 1942 with the news that British cryptanalysts had been deciphering American diplomatic communications, but since the alliance had been concluded such work had ceased. Churchill sought to alert the president to the insecurity of U.S. State Department systems. The prime minister recounted that

> one night when we talked late you spoke of the importance of our cipher people getting into close contact with yours. I shall be very ready to put any expert you care to nominate in touch with my technicians. Ciphers for our two Navies have been and are continually a matter for frank discussion between our two Services. But diplomatic and military ciphers are of equal importance, and we appear to know nothing officially of your versions of these. Some time ago, however, our experts claimed to have discovered the system and constructed some tables used by your Diplomatic Corps. From the moment when we became allies, I gave instructions that this work should cease. However, danger of our enemies having achieved a measure of success cannot, I am advised, be dismissed.[2]

No doubt Churchill's revelation prompted more concern about cryptographic security, but Marshall assured the president that the yearlong Anglo-American cryptanalytic interchange operation was entirely satisfactory.[3]

In sharp contrast to the Anglo-American coalition stood the Axis alliance, which MAGIC analysts watched develop slowly and awkwardly. In 1940 some information was gleaned by monitoring radio communications between the Tokyo Foreign Ministry and the Japanese embassy in Berlin, and American intelligence analysts were moderately abreast of general developments by the time Japan, Germany, and Italy signed the Tripartite Pact of 27 September 1940. After eighteen months of intensive work, it was at the time these three nations pledged mutual support in the treaty that SIS made the crucial breakthrough in deciphering Japanese diplomatic messages, although the Japanese always considered PURPLE to be an unbreakable cipher system. Thus, when the flow of top-priority diplomatic dispatches between

Japan and Germany increased after the pact was concluded, MAGIC decipherers of PURPLE traffic were given the opportunity to refine their skills.

For some time before December 1941, the army and navy joined forces in the operation of MAGIC, the navy processing messages bearing an odd date of origin and the army those bearing an even date. Soon after the attack on Pearl Harbor, however, the navy ceased to work on the Japanese diplomatic intercepts in order to concentrate on the study of Japanese naval systems. As Rowlett recently wrote, the army

> felt that the intelligence from the Japanese diplomatic messages, particularly those exchanged between Tokyo and Berlin, . . . would be of vital importance in the prosecution of the war. Accordingly, the decision was made by the army to expand its effort on the Japanese diplomatic messages, to insure that all Japanese diplomatic intercepts could be promptly processed and the resulting information provided to U.S. intelligence agencies. This arrangement continued until the Japanese surrendered.[4]

Thus, the U.S. Army remained completely responsible for the Berlin-Tokyo traffic.

The volume of MAGIC traffic increased enormously after December 1941, and SIS's old facilities in the Munitions Building in Washington proved to be inadequate. The building was a large, multiwinged, cement structure on Constitution Avenue, facing Twentieth Street. SIS's vault was used for the general storage of various classified documents relating to communications intelligence work, and it was neither secure enough nor sufficiently large for the storage of the secret codes. Also, because of the precedence and importance of wartime cryptologic service, SIS sought a new headquarters sufficiently isolated from the prying eyes of enemy agents and official Washington and yet convenient to the capital and to Vint Hill Farm, a proposed intelligence monitoring site near Warrenton, Virginia. Arlington Hall Junior College for Girls, Arlington, Virginia, attended by some 200 students, was selected. Under the authority of the War Powers Act of March 1942, SIS acquired the site and renamed it Arlington Hall Station in June 1942. By August SIS completed the move from the Munitions Building after the grounds at Arlington Hall had been surrounded by a double chain-link fence with an alarm and a badge system instituted to control access. Facilities were rapidly expanded, and by the end of the war the station's complement was nearly 9,000, most of whom were civilians.[5]

The increase in volume of Ōshima's intercepted MAGIC messages alone is indicative of SIS's expanding workload. During eleven months in 1941 he sent approximately 75 messages to his superiors in Tokyo, 100 messages in 1942, 400 in 1943, 600 in 1944, and 300 during the first five months of 1945. There was a nearly equal number of return messages. All of these messages varied from one to thirty pages of typed, single-spaced material. The Japanese language was one of the most difficult of the foreign languages handled by SIS translators to render effectively into contemporary English, and the most skillful translators were few and in great demand.

The Berlin-Tokyo PURPLE traffic was highly valuable as Anglo-American analysts sought to develop a comprehensive strategic view of the war. Messages from Ōshima contained much detailed tactical military data and were frequently reviewed by his service attachés before being wired to Tokyo. In the first half of January 1942, Ōshima had a two-hour interview with Hitler after which he compiled a detailed report on the German-Soviet war since June 1941. He was explicit in his concluding remarks to Tokyo: "I will carefully watch the development of the situation [on the eastern front] and report my findings to you. The local [Japanese] military and naval attachés, too, agree with these views of mine. Please pass this information along to the army and navy chiefs."[6]

Ōshima's role became more important after the alignment of the Allied and Axis warring coalitions was complete. After the Anglo-American partnership decided on the Europe First strategy,[7] some aspects of Ōshima's reports on Hitler's planning became crucial as the Allied forces planned their own moves in the weeks after Pearl Harbor. On the eastern front, for example, Ōshima remained an independent source of intelligence for the assessment of conditions on that decisive yet otherwise obscure front. His reports revealed Axis plans in North Africa, for example, where it was feared the Germans would make a harder drive in 1942, and in the Indian Ocean where, after their successes in December, the Japanese might make a new drive. Whatever developments were to materialize in the Atlantic-European-Mediterranean–Indian Ocean areas during the crucial aftermath of Pearl Harbor, it was clear to MIS MAGIC analysts that thanks to the knowledgeable and communicative Japanese ambassador in Berlin they would remain privy to German war plans.

From the outset, Anglo-American strategists were confident of their capacity to wage coalition warfare effectively, but they did not know fully the nature of their adversaries' coalition. One of their first concerns after Pearl Harbor was that the Germans and Japanese would coordinate their strategic planning and, through operational cooperation, produce a junction of Axis forces somewhere east of Suez and west of Singapore during the first half of 1942.[8] Thus, analysts of MAGIC translations eagerly sought a better understanding of the nature of the enemy coalition and of its operations.

SIS cryptanalysts provided G-2 intelligence analysts with the text of the supplement to the Tripartite Pact two days *before* it was signed in Berlin by Ōshima, Ribbentrop, and Italian Ambassador Alfieri on 11 December 1941.[9] The Axis coalition appeared ominous during the bleak weeks following Pearl Harbor. No separate armistice or peace was to be made with England or the United States, and Germany, Japan, and Italy pledged themselves "to cooperate until victory has been achieved." Thereafter, the same "close cooperation" was maintained as the Axis powers established their respective "new orders," a topic on which Ōshima had published an article seven months earlier.[10] Three days after the supplement to the Tripartite Pact was signed, Hitler ceremonially bestowed the Order of Merit of the German Eagle on Ōshima in recognition of the Japanese ambassador's services rendered in the achievement of German-Japanese cooperation and "Ōshima stood at the top of his career."[11]

Oddly enough, at the ceremony Hitler "comforted" Ōshima, explaining that it was natural for a great nation to attack a country with which negotiations were being conducted. Japan had recently been in a situation like that experienced earlier by Germany, Hitler declared. "Germany attacked Poland and Russia unexpectedly as soon as she realized that those countries did not want to conclude treaties. There was no other appropriate means," Hitler maintained. Japanese participation in the war against the Anglo-American powers "is a great help to Germany," Hitler claimed. "For in the future German submarine captains can avoid the psychological fatigue of trying to distinguish between American and British ships before attacking." He emphasized the importance of German-Japanese cooperation, and he wanted Ōshima to obtain information about Japanese naval weapons and tactics employed so effectively at Pearl Harbor so that "Germany can attack Britain with surprise."[12] Although Ōshima did not at that time report to Tokyo that conversation with Hitler, readers of MAGIC intercepts soon gained much insight into Hitler's strategic thinking from Ōshima's other reports of his frequent "business" conferences with the Führer.

Ōshima realized that as warring allies it was particularly important for Germany and Japan to coordinate planning and implement joint operations. Article 4 of the 1940 Tripartite Pact provided the machinery, the joint technical commissions. A plenary meeting had been scheduled for April 1941, but it did not take place because most of the key German officials were engaged in more pressing work at Hitler's headquarters in East Prussia. Since Germany and Japan were now in the war together, Ōshima "decided that the time had come to establish" a tripartite council. "Ribbentrop immediately agreed with me," Ōshima informed Tokyo on 18 December.[13]

American intelligence analysts learned how the tripartite council and a general commission under the council were to function. They were pleased to learn that the council would be largely ceremonial. More significantly, they had new evidence of Ōshima's important position. He and Ribbentrop could circumvent the decision-making hierarchy. Foreign Minister Ribbentrop explained to Ōshima his idea of how the council ought to work: "Even if we do apparently establish a council, I can tell you one thing, and there is no mistake about it, *just as always* you and I are going to talk the thing through and make the real decisions."[14] Thus, within two weeks of the Pearl Harbor attack, the American cryptologic intelligence community became confident that they could obtain all the significant information available about German-Japanese military cooperation by simply focusing on Ōshima.

Early in 1942, MAGIC readers were delighted to learn that the Germans planned to tell Ōshima everything, including special military intelligence. Indeed, Ōshima informed Tokyo on 7 January that Ribbentrop agreed to "supply us daily with intelligence reports" compiled by the Germans. Ōshima declared that after he carefully studied the various reports he would label and "send on any item connected with this [source of information] as 'D' intelligence reports." He warned, however, that "any leakage of these reports due to our fault would be of grave consequences, so all handling of these reports should be strictly secret."[15] Ōshima was, of course, completely unaware that this particular message would be intercepted, translated, and available for analysis in Washington by 19 January, twelve days after he sent it. American confidence in the value of the Ōshima connection was, therefore, reinforced at the outset of the new year. And although D intelligence, as Ōshima called secret information received from the German government, would probably have been given to any Japanese ambassador in wartime Berlin, its completeness, often refined and elaborated upon personally by Hitler and Ribbentrop, was owing to Ambassador Ōshima's close rapport with top German officials.

The care and thoroughness with which Ōshima gathered and reported military secrets were similar to the attention he gave to other aspects of his post in Europe. Ōshima was a realist and sometimes quite sophisticated in his assessments. He understood that "this war will continue . . . quite a long time during which communication between Europe and Asia is cut," he apprised Tokyo in a message dated 17 January 1942. He believed that "one of the special features of modern warfare is the importance of speedy and accurate observation of all political, economical, intelligence reports, occupation, propaganda, etc., which parallel actual war operations as an important element on which victory is based." Ōshima worried that the staffs of Japanese diplomatic posts abroad, especially those in Europe, would be overworked from the strain of war and that they could not be relieved by personnel who under other circumstances would arrive from the Foreign Ministry in Tokyo. He warned his superiors that "a definite plan should be laid now with the future in mind, for if we do not do so and just meet each new situation as it arises, by taking temporary steps such as switching our staff around from one office to another, we will find that in the long run it will result in lowering the quality of work of all of our offices, and interfere with our activities and thus end in great disasters."[16]

Ōshima, the senior Japanese diplomat in Europe, was concerned that when additional diplomatic responsibilities were undertaken in Europe, the Foreign Ministry would simply assign them to him. He had already been named minister to Slovakia in addition to his ambassadorial duties in Berlin.[17] And he worked hard to fulfill his responsibilities at the lesser diplomatic posts throughout much of Europe.[18] Moreover, Ōshima had long shown concern about embassy personnel. For example, after he arrived in Berlin as ambassador, he complained to Tokyo that his military staff was too large: "The number of assistant military attachés at the present time is rapidly getting too large (originally there were only four here; now by an increase of ten, we have a total of 14)." The increase was "unpleasant to the German authorities," Ōshima claimed. "Therefore, I think that it would be well to reduce the number."[19] Ōshima was sensitive to the attitude of his host government.

Ōshima's assessment of Japan's needs for embassy personnel in Europe changed dramatically a year later after he became isolated by the war. In early 1942 he made some timely and imaginative proposals to get more personnel during what he anticipated would be a long war. "Arrange for our diplomats in England . . . to be transferred here," he told Tokyo, and "the same steps could be taken for our diplomats being sent back from the United States." Although he did not receive any Japanese diplomatic personnel formerly assigned to Great Britain or to the United States, Ōshima sought more space for his staff. In March he was successful in negotiations with Ribbentrop to take over the building formerly occupied by the French next to the Japanese embassy.[20]

Ōshima was resourceful as can be seen in another of his innovative proposals for obtaining extra personnel. He wanted "to select . . . outstanding characters from our newspapermen, tradesmen, and students now in Europe, those suitable for training in his field, and to gather them in one place and to educate them in the rules of our Foreign Office, and after that have them work in our offices in Europe."[21] He no doubt increasingly employed nationals. By the time Ōshima and his official diplomatic staff surrendered

Ambassador Ōshima (right) standing at a bar in the Imperial Japanese embassy, Berlin, in 1939. (Source: National Archives)

at the end of the war, Ōshima was responsible for everyone in the European Japanese community, including many Japanese newspaper reporters.[22]

Evidence suggests that many Japanese university students caught in Germany or elsewhere in Europe by the war were not as dedicated to National Socialist Germany as Ambassador Ōshima. When the war in Europe began in the autumn of 1939 and Ōshima was still in his first tour of duty as ambassador, he tried to quiet the Japanese community in Berlin and advised Japanese students to stay, saying, "There is no need for those who planned to study for a year or two to leave Germany in a hurry."[23] A year later an unidentified Japanese university student who often visited the Japanese embassy in Berlin thought that German officials, when they told the people of Berlin to treat Poles as they would treat Jews, were beasts by Japanese standards.[24]

Emphasizing the need for German-Japanese cooperation, Ōshima spoke directly with Hitler and Ribbentrop during a two-hour meeting on 3 January 1942.[25] They discussed bringing Thailand, Manchukuo, and the Nanking Chinese government into the Tripartite Pact, a proposal with which Hitler agreed completely. All parties fully understood that the German attack on the Soviet Union the previous June had interrupted the transfer of invalu-

able supplies to Germany via the Trans-Siberian Railroad from Japan, Manchukuo, and occupied China.[26] Therefore, the Germans agreed with Ōshima's proposal to establish a Mutual Economic Aid Pact for Winning the
War to supplement the agreement of 11 December 1941. Ōshima explained
to Hitler and Ribbentrop that

> it is important for the Treaty powers to accomplish the aim of the
> Tripartite union by cooperation in exerting the full power of the
> countries in military, economic and all other ways. In addition to
> mentioning cooperation in the war along military lines in the Far
> East and Europe for the realization of this, . . . it is important that
> Japan assume the responsibility of supplying to Germany those vari-
> ous materials which Japan has in the Far East, and that Germany in
> turn . . . supply Japan with those types of equipment and various
> kinds of machinery which are needed by the Imperial Japanese na-
> tion.[27]

This information on German-Japanese cooperation was an early indication that Hitler was favorably predisposed to the points raised by Ōshima.
Readers of MAGIC messages knew that specific agreements would soon be in
place and that blockade-running ships carrying strategically important materials would be plying the seas. These blockade runners were engaged in
what was called Yanagi operations, and their vulnerability was considerable,
for they were sailing, as one historian has written, "straight into the meshes
of the Allied signal intelligence net. MAGIC (with its command of the diplomatic signals and the Japanese-German naval attaché code) and, most significantly, the British ability to read the German ENIGMA cipher contributed
intelligence about the Yanagi operations which, cumulatively but decisively,
aborted them."[28]

Ōshima's messages to Tokyo in 1942 revealed much information about
the sailing of various Yanagi ships, frequently from Bordeaux, through a
designated narrow lane in the Bay of Biscay into the open Atlantic. By the
end of March 1943, losses of Axis blockade runners were so severe that the
Germans decided to inaugurate a submarine transport service to ferry rubber and other precious materials from East Asia.[29] Ōshima's messages from
Berlin gave the first information about this decision.[30]

Tokyo's responses to Ōshima's information about blockade running also
provided MAGIC readers with an early clue about economic problems within
the Axis coalition and about how difficult it was for Yanagi operations to
have much impact on the problems. For example, a little over two months after the Pearl Harbor attack, Tokyo complained to Ōshima that after holding

a conference with the German naval attaché and other representatives from the German embassy "on the problem of landing Yanagi freight," it became clear that "the German point is that this plan [for the shipment of matériel] was made before the outbreak of war." Since the Japanese wanted mostly heavy and bulky freight from Germany, such as locomotives, vehicles, armor plate, and aircraft, and since it was no longer possible to send German goods "across Siberia, it is technically impossible for Germany to ship Japan the things she needs imperatively." This was a vital piece of information for the Allies fighting Japan, because it indicated that the dangerous surface Yanagi operations could not meet Japanese requirements for heavy equipment in the great war of attrition. Ōshima was ordered to "contact the German officials there" and to do his "best to have them carry out our wishes."[31] In the aftermath of the Pearl Harbor attack, British and American strategic fears envisioned close Axis cooperation,[32] but MAGIC intercepts from the Tokyo-Berlin traffic soon revealed that surface Yanagi operations were a failure. Moreover, Ōshima's communications revealed that submarines were to replace surface transports in future Yanagi operations. Thus, Japanese strategic command was jeopardized.

Ōshima's MAGIC messages revealed much about Hitler's strategic plans in early 1942. The menace of Hitler's capital ships caused the British constant anxiety and demanded much attention. In 1941 all available units of the Royal Navy, including several battleships and battle cruisers and two aircraft carriers, concentrated from Scapa Flow to Gibraltar to sink the battleship *Bismarck*. In 1942 the British were particularly galled by news of the successful "Channel dash" of the German battle cruisers *Scharnhorst* and *Gneisenau* and the heavy cruiser *Prinz Eugen*, which sailed on a high-speed run from Brest to safer German home waters on 12–13 February. The escape of these ships, the U-boat menace, and the interception of Italian transports carrying men and supplies were the chief concerns of Bletchley Park, home of the British Government Code and Cipher School (GC&CS) near London throughout 1942.[33] Ōshima boasted to Tokyo that the fact that the German capital ships "made their way through the Channel [in daylight] was in itself a grave threat to England's sovereignty of the seas and makes possible an attack upon the British homeland." Moreover, Ōshima reported that the ships, after their spectacular dash through the Straits of Dover, were to be "accompanied by the [battleship] *Tirpitz* and other capital ships" in preparation "for the opening of the coming campaign."[34]

Anglo-American intelligence fully understood what Ōshima meant by the "coming campaign." The group of capital ships was to attack convoys carrying valuable war supplies through Arctic waters to Russia. Within two weeks, after concluding three separate meetings with Ribbentrop, Ōshima elaborated upon Hitler's plans. The Germans were alarmed by the flow of American war supplies to the Soviet Union, and Ōshima explained that "great importance is attached to the necessity of severing this line of communications between the Soviet [Union] and the outside." Ōshima and Ribbentrop saw that "the recent movement of the *Gneisenau* and other ships through the Channel makes [this] possible."[35] At the time western Allied strategic planners could not have anticipated that the German ships of the famed "Channel dash" would be unable to make good their threat to northern convoys in 1942. Most of these vessels were damaged by mines, bombs, or torpedoes.[36]

However, another of Ōshima's early 1942 revelations about German strategic plans would continue to demand the careful attention of Anglo-American strategists. During the months following the German failure to take Moscow, when the Japanese struck at Pearl Harbor, Ōshima's intercepted messages to Tokyo provided the western Allies with much information about conditions on the Russian front. In many respects that was the decisive front of the war in 1942, yet it was a front where the Anglo-Americans had very little influence. At this point in the war, Washington and London were relegated to watching events unfold largely through Ōshima's reports. On at least three different occasions since late 1941, Ōshima's intercepted messages had steadfastly assured the western Allies that Hitler would not negotiate a separate German-Soviet peace, but there was some concern that conditions could deteriorate to the point that the Soviet Union might sue for peace.[37] At the end of January the Japanese Foreign Ministry asked Ōshima to "investigate . . . and advise us on the policies and conditions in German occupied Soviet Union."[38] Washington learned a month later that the Germans had executed or interned nearly 31,300 Latvians out of a September 1940 population of 2 million, and in Lithuania, 40,000 people out a population of nearly 3 million were executed or interned. In Estonia, 60,911 people had been interned and 11,784 executed by the Germans between June and 1 December 1941, and in German-occupied areas of the Soviet Union the carnage was even worse—about 5 percent of the population had been interned or executed.[39] The Soviet Union was taking a terrible beating, and the strategic repercussions for the western coalition would be disastrous if the Soviet Union surrendered and the European and East Asian Axis powers secured a continental linkup.

MAGIC readers knew that they could depend on Ōshima for more information about conditions in German-occupied Russia. Indeed, he concluded his January 1942 message with the note that "as reports come in I will notify you in subsequent telegrams." Soon Tokyo wanted to know to what extent the German Army of occupation had found materials and factories destroyed. At the end of March Ōshima reported that the Russian scorched-earth policy had not been very effective in the Baltic states, which were ideally suited for German peasant emigration, as a lot of horses and charcoal tractors were still available for the spring planting of crops. Damage amounted to about 25 percent of some industries—oil shale mines, electric-power plants, and paper and textile substitute industries—however, "at present these are being reconstructed," Ōshima assured Tokyo. In the Ukraine, the Russian scorched-earth policy had been more thoroughgoing, but work toward "complete restoration in the immediate future" was proceeding smoothly. Most significant, however, was Ōshima's report about German preparations for making early use of damaged Soviet oil industries: "Germany is putting a special effort into the rehabilitation of the . . . oil industry." The oil fields around Lemberg (L'vov) in Galicia "have already been restored to operation. . . . Germany is profiting by her past experience and is preparing facilities for the rehabilitation in a comparatively short time of oil fields taken over in the future."[40]

Oil was crucial to Hitler's conduct of war. Soon after the invasion of Russia the previous June, Hitler had become increasingly concerned about the threat posed by Soviet bombers from airfields in the Crimea to the Ploesti oil fields in Rumania. By December 1941, the Germans had occupied most of the industrial area between Kharkov and Rostov, and the vast oil fields in the Caucasus were not far away from the front when, in March 1942, Washington intercepted Ōshima's report saying that the Germans had been working on how to quickly restore captured oil fields to full production.

Ōshima explained the goals of the spring offensive for MIS analysts. He quoted Ribbentrop: "The occupation of the Donets [Coal] Basin, Caucasus, and other important raw material areas," indeed the entire "southern area . . . , is the area in which the opening phases of the offensive will be carried out." The Allies had long anticipated the German spring offensive on the eastern front, and delayed by an abortive Soviet attack near Kharkov in mid-May, it was finally launched in June 1942. Within a few weeks German forces reoccupied Rostov at the mouth of the Don River, and were poised, ready to advance into the Caucasus. There was a pervading atmosphere of optimism among several of Hitler's military planners. By early August the Germans captured the first of the Caucasian oil fields, but only after the Russians had set them afire. Later in the month Hitler moved his field headquarters from Rastenburg, East Prussia, to Vinnitsa in the Ukraine. It seemed that nothing was likely to prevent the Germans from conquering the isthmus between the Black Sea and the Caspian and from possibly striking south over the Caucasus into the Near East. Increasingly, however, Hitler focused on Stalingrad, and before the end of the year the sway of stalemate and attrition at Stalingrad consumed the German offensive strength everywhere, especially in the southern steppe country.

Ōshima's reports to Tokyo contained important information about another front where British forces were engaged. His observations in February 1942 about Erwin Rommel appeared especially ominous to Anglo-American intelligence. During his previous year in North Africa, Rommel had made significant gains against larger British forces with no more than three German divisions, which were usually below strength. Widely respected by his British adversaries as a classic warrior,[41] Rommel was being "reinforced," MAGIC listeners learned from Ōshima in mid-February, and his military command was being "raised in status from army corps to that of army. In addition, in a most unprecedented manner he has been freed of all the restraining influences of the High Command and given sweeping authority."[42] Although Ōshima might have unknowingly exaggerated Rommel's independence from the German High Command, the prospect that such a dynamic general was to be given free rein was threatening to the Allies.[43] Thus, Ōshima's reports at the beginning of 1942 gave forewarning of a German buildup in North Africa. After Rommel captured Tobruk on 21 June, Hitler rewarded the conquering hero by making him a field marshal, but Rommel remarked privately that he would rather Hitler had given him one more division instead of a field marshal's baton.[44] By the end of the month, western intelligence learned from one of Ōshima's intercepted messages that Rommel was "granted full discretionary powers by Hitler for his further campaign." Rommel, who was about to capture Mersa Matrûh about 100 miles west of El Alamein,[45] was urged by Hitler to continue the eastward advance and capture the Suez Canal.

It appeared possible in 1942 that the European Axis forces and the Japanese might meet, or at least sufficiently close the gap between their fighting forces so that regular aerial contact could be established. After Rommel's victory at Tobruk, the British continued their disorderly retreat, not stopping until early July when they reached a point some sixty miles west of Alexandria. The news that Rommel was so close led the British fleet to abandon its base at Alexandria and withdraw through the Suez Canal into the safety of the Red Sea. Files in British military headquarters in Cairo were hastily burned, for, as Churchill wrote after the war, "it was widely believed that Cairo and Alexandria would soon fall to Rommel's flaming sword."[46] The tide did not clearly turn against the Axis forces in North Africa until Rommel's defeat at El Alamein in October and November.

Some of Ōshima's messages in early 1942 contained the news that German and Japanese forces appeared to be coordinating military operations as a grand piece of coalition strategy, and Ōshima outlined for his superiors in

Tokyo Hitler's plans for linking up with the Japanese. Ribbentrop asked Ōshima to meet him on 17 March, when Ōshima reported that because Ribbentrop "wanted to make the German position very clear, he read from a document he had written." Ribbentrop emphasized that "Germany would eagerly welcome a Japanese invasion into the Indian Ocean whereby contact between Europe and Asia might be established." Ribbentrop said that Hitler was about to "start a new blitzkrieg to give an all out blow to Russia. At the same time Germany intends to attack through the eastern Mediterranean and Africa and also through the Caucasus and fight through to the Indian Ocean." Ōshima reported that the German foreign minister concluded the meeting with the "hope that Japan can plan to cooperate in carrying out" this scheme to establish direct contact through the Indian Ocean.[47]

The threat of Japanese thrusts into the Indian Ocean, and westward toward the Red Sea and the African coast, appeared alarmingly related to the eastward advance of European Axis forces in North Africa and in the Soviet Union. The Japanese forced the British out of Burma in May 1942 and soon consolidated control of that country, thereby eliminating a surface route over which the Chinese had been receiving supplies for fighting in the Sino-Japanese theater. At about the same time the Japanese Navy operated extensively in the Indian Ocean and established a direct link with the Germans, albeit scanty, before the Axis reverses at El Alamein and Stalingrad. Some Anglo-American strategists feared that U.S. supply lines to Russia from the south would be cut off in the summer of 1942.[48] Allied naval consultants observed that "the Persian Gulf route was faced with the triple threat of German raiders in the South Atlantic, the Japanese in the Indian Ocean, and the German armies advancing toward the Caucasus and the Caspian."[49]

The Germans were eager for the Japanese to make further gains in the Indian Ocean, but American intelligence learned that they could not expect to glean much information about specific Japanese military or naval plans from Tokyo's messages to Ōshima. Thus, Allied strategists sometimes had to act upon the assumption that Tokyo was likely to behave as Ōshima or the German government suggested. Ōshima was unable to respond to Ribbentrop's overture in March to make the necessary arrangements with the Vichy French for the Japanese to establish a naval base on Madagascar. On 17 March Ōshima complained:

> Inasmuch as I have received no information whatever from my government, all I could do was to state that I was unable to answer but that I would transmit his questions . . . to my government. . . . It is a matter of great embarrassment to me never to be able to answer Ribbentrop's questions. I earnestly hope that I may be permitted to

have an understanding of the broad outlines at least of our policies
. . . , also will you let me know whether our navy has . . . intentions
or not [to establish a base on Madagascar].⁵⁰

To the regret of MAGIC intelligence analysts and to Ōshima's considerable
consternation, the Japanese ambassador in Berlin was left in the dark and
was given no specific information about how Madagascar figured into Japanese naval plans, but the British could not afford to take a chance. The British learned from Ōshima's message of 17 March that the Japanese might
take "the Madagascar islands as a naval operation base" and that "Germany was prepared to give complete diplomatic assistance" by making certain that the Vichy French cooperated with the Japanese.⁵¹ Churchill quickly
resolved to take Madagascar because of the Japanese naval threat developing in the Bay of Bengal and the peril to Ceylon. On 24 March he wrote to
Jan Christian Smuts, prime minister of South Africa, that "we have decided
to storm and occupy Diégo Suarez, as arrival of Japanese there would not be
effectively resisted by the Vichy French and would be disastrous to the safety
of our Middle East convoys."⁵²

The Japanese sweep westward was impressive. Using five of the six air-
craft carriers he had employed at Pearl Harbor four months earlier, Vice
Admiral Nagumo Chūichi sortied into the Indian Ocean in early April 1942.
Successful air strikes on the two principal British naval and air bases in the
Indian Ocean, Columbo and Trincomalee on Ceylon; the sinking of several
British warships, including two heavy cruisers and a light carrier; and the
sinking of some two dozen merchant ships obligated the British Eastern
Fleet to retire to the western half of the Indian Ocean before mid-April. Japanese ships were unscathed and aircraft losses were light,⁵³ and although Admiral Nagumo's carrier strike force then turned back toward Japan, Japanese submarines (I-boats) continued to operate extensively in the Indian
Ocean, particularly from the Gulf of Aden southward along the African
coast to the Mozambique Channel. Five I-boats, some of them carrying
midget submarines, sailed westward from Penang, Malay, in late April. A
month later they attacked the British with midget submarines in Diégo
Suarez Bay, Madagascar, recently taken over by the British and important
because of Madagascar's proximity to major shipping lanes.

A fleet tanker was sunk, and the old battleship *Ramillies* was badly damaged. Four of the five I-boats continued to hunt in the western part of the
Indian Ocean for the next two months and easily destroyed over 100,000
tons of Allied shipping. A postwar U.S. Naval Technical Mission to Japan
concluded that the Indian Ocean was an excellent hunting ground until

April 1944, no matter whether Japanese submarines patrolled "the coast of Africa, the Gulf of Aden, or the Arabian Gulf."[54]

Establishing direct contact with the Germans was also part of the mission of the Japanese submarine sortie into the Indian Ocean. After the attack on Madagascar, one submarine of the original five, *I-30*, was reprovisioned from two auxiliary cruisers accompanying the submarine squadron. It was the first I-boat in World War II to proceed independently around the Cape of Good Hope and northward in the Atlantic Ocean to the Bay of Biscay, where it was met by German minesweepers and escorted safely to Lorient, France, in early August. With much fanfare the Japanese sailors were greeted by Grand Admiral Erich Raeder, commander in chief of the German Navy.[55]

It was a long and difficult journey, and the submarine's arrival was symptomatic of the frailty of the Axis warring coalition. In a clumsy piece of propaganda intended to offset what the Japanese called a "strategic retreat" after their disaster at the Battle of Midway (in early June), the Japanese Imperial General Headquarters brazenly announced that part of the Japanese fleet had made a thrust into the Atlantic Ocean. The Germans were not amused. Japanese diplomatic and military officers in Berlin admitted confidentially that the arrival of one Japanese Navy submarine in German-occupied France hardly justified Tokyo's proclamation, and Ōshima tried to put the best face on the awkward situation by conceding that Japanese forces had been "somewhat unlucky" in the Battle of Midway. Earlier that year Hitler had told Ōshima of his enormous respect for the Japanese Navy, saying "if I had had the Japanese fleet instead of the Italian fleet in the Mediterranean, the situation there would already have been stabilized,"[56] but after Midway the Japanese Navy was weaker. Vice Admiral Nomura Naokuni, chief of the Japanese Tripartite Commission at Berlin, judged that because of the setback at Midway the Japanese Navy would not again be able to assume offensive operations in the Indian Ocean until the spring of 1943, and other Japanese officers made similar reports at Hitler's headquarters in mid-October.[57] The failure at Midway, largely owing to U.S. naval communications intelligence successes against the Japanese,[58] forced the Japanese Navy to pursue a more defensive strategy, and major offensive operations beyond Japan's basic defense perimeter, west of Sumatra in the Indian Ocean, were unthinkable in less than nine months after Pearl Harbor.

I-30 also brought firsthand news confirming German intelligence reports that the Indian Ocean was alive with Allied shipping, largely out of convoy and without naval escort.[59] Ribbentrop complained to Ōshima that he had "reports that numerous American and British vessels have been going back and forth from southeast Africa very frequently, and that some of them, sailing on the high seas, were going to Suez, others going to Soviet Russia through the Persian Gulf, and still others making round trips to Bombay." Ribbentrop was making an official request that "the Japanese Navy send numerous submarines to that region for the purpose of attacking the above-mentioned American and British ships."[60] Again on 8 August he complained to Ōshima about the weakness of Japanese submarine operations in the western Indian Ocean: "In the imminent battle of Egypt and in the coming struggle in the Caucasus and the Near East, we should strive to join hands from our respective areas, so will you please cooperate with us in this endeavor."[61]

The sea lanes of the Indian Ocean were particularly vital to the Allies fighting in the European theater, but Japanese submariners were neither especially interested nor adroit in conducting operations against merchant shipping throughout most of the war.[62] After Midway, Japanese priorities in the Pacific Ocean and strategic necessity drastically curtailed any appreciable military cooperation with the European Axis powers, which Ōshima confirmed for the western Allies.

The Germans soon realized that they could not rely upon their East Asian partner to help them reduce the flow of Allied matériel going through the Indian Ocean, and they had no choice but to extend U-boat operations around the Cape of Good Hope and into the Indian Ocean as far as Lourenço Marques, Mozambique. This requirement coincided with the introduction into service of the new Type IXD_2 U-boat, which had greater range and endurance. The first of these U-boats arrived in the Indian Ocean (east of 20° east longitude) in October 1942, and by the end of the year five U-boats had sunk over 170,000 tons of Allied shipping.[63] More U-boats were sent to the Indian Ocean the next year, some of them operating out of Penang, Malay, and by the time Germany surrendered in May 1945, fifty-seven boats had been committed to the Indian Ocean (four were sent out twice, and *U-181* three times). They sank at least 151 ships totaling some 935,000 tons.[64]

The crucial months after Pearl Harbor were foreboding, but the tide slowly started to turn against Japan and Germany in their respective theaters and against the entire Axis coalition. In order for that coalition to have had any prospects of winning the war, or achieving a negotiated peace, genuine cooperation between the Japanese and German governments, including their military, economic, and political bureaucracies, was essential. But genuine cooperation was lacking from the outset, and Ōshima's messages continued throughout the war to reveal that happy state of affairs for the Allies.

3
The MAGIC Perspective of Strategic Change in 1942

By mid-1942, after the crucial months following the Japanese attack on Pearl Harbor, there were growing indications from MAGIC intelligence reports that the tide was beginning to turn against the Axis coalition. Anglo-American managers of the war had a new sense of strategic direction, but they also had more understanding about the eventual cost of victory. By this point in the war, MIS analysts were highly sensitive to the ongoing value of the window into Hitler's secret chambers that the Ōshima connection offered. There would be several strategic concerns that warranted special attention, and the extremely informed and communicative Japanese ambassador in Berlin was likely to reveal more significant strategic information than any other person in Germany.

The president of the United States and his advisers understood that military conditions on the German-Soviet front could be altered dramatically if the Japanese struck at the Soviets in Asia. Shortly after Germany invaded the Soviet Union in June 1941, Roosevelt told his secretary of interior, Harold Ickes, that care was needed in American foreign policy so as not to "tip the delicate scales and cause Japan to decide to attack Russia. . . . The . . . [Japanese] are having a real drag-down and knock-out fight among themselves . . . trying to decide which way they are going to jump—attack Russia, attack the South Seas . . . , or whether they will sit on the fence and be more friendly with us. No one knows what the decision will be."[1] The precision of the president's remarks suggests strongly that Roosevelt had probably been studying summaries of MAGIC traffic.

During the first full year of the German-Soviet war, several Americans responsible for making strategic decisions were not convinced that the Japanese would continue to honor their neutrality pact with Moscow and decline the German entreaty to declare war on the Soviets. It was a momentous question that deserves a careful review because of the long-range impact the Japanese decision had upon the course of World War II. For the Americans, intercepts between Berlin and Tokyo were the most important source of intelligence on this sensitive topic.

An attack on the Soviet Union by Japan would have increased the possibility that Axis forces would defeat the Soviet Union, occupy vast sections of Eurasia, and tap new sources to strengthen the Axis coalition. No doubt the concern was much greater in the second half of 1941, than in the first half of 1942, since the likelihood in 1942 of Japan's attacking the Soviet Union was probably slight, especially after the Japanese defeat at Midway in early June and the successful American landing in the Solomon Islands in August. There is some evidence that at least a significant segment of the Japanese Army was convinced as early as August 1941 that the German offensive in the vastness of the Soviet Union had failed. Therefore, far from wanting to strike at the Russians, there were some in the Japanese Army who wanted Germany to negotiate a settlement with the Soviet Union.[2] As Tokyo told Ōshima on 21 November 1941, Japan "would like to break up the policy of British-U.S.-U.S.S.R joint action. We would, therefore, welcome, if anything, peace between Germany and the Soviet Union. For the purpose of enhancing our position, we would not be opposed to mediating in a peace, if such a course is possible.[3]

Nevertheless, there was the counterpull of contemporary evidence that urged caution and fostered prudence for many months after the surprise attack at Pearl Harbor. The Japanese and Russians maintained powerful land and air forces in the vicinity of the Argun, Amur, and Ussuri rivers between eastern Siberia and Manchukuo. And if in early October 1941 Soviet master spy Richard Sorge could confidently inform his superiors in Moscow that the Soviet Union was safe from a Japanese attack for the remainder of that year, in early 1942 cautious American strategists were mindful that they had recently been surprised by the Japanese on more than one occasion. Besides, Japanese military strength had probably increased since the Pearl Harbor attack, in spite of Japan's greatly expanded military perimeter and certain naval setbacks in mid- and late 1942.

The end of the career of possibly the most successful secret agent of the war must have been interesting to American strategic planners. Sorge was arrested and his spy ring was broken up by the *Kempei* (Japanese military police), and by late October he confessed to the Japanese chief prosecutor, "I am a Communist and have been doing espionage."[4] But before the end of the month, American MAGIC intelligence analysts learned of Sorge's arrest because of "a series of Communist activities." Foreign Minister Tōgō Shigenori radioed the shocking news to Ōshima. Sorge, in Tokyo as a senior

German journalist for the influential *Frankfurter Zeitung*, had long enjoyed free access to the German embassy and the total confidence of his friend, Ambassador Ott. Ott, like his Japanese counterpart in Berlin, had been military attaché, and in 1938 he too was appointed ambassador from within the embassy. Tōgō told Ōshima that "when Sorge was arrested the amazement of Ambassador Ott knew no bounds. He called me up and frantically asked to be allowed to interview the correspondent. In view of our particular relations with Germany, I made an exception and let him talk with Sorge in the presence of police officials." Foreign Minister Tōgō then advised his ambassador in Berlin to keep the matter "in the strictest secrecy" while Japanese judiciary officials investigated the affair.[5] Thus vanished the Sorge source of information about Japanese military capabilities and intentions.

The arrest of Sorge did not reduce concern in Washington that Japan could still attack the Soviet Union. No evidence has been discovered to suggest that American intelligence sources knew of Sorge's espionage work between the time he arrived in Japan (September 1933) and the time of his arrest (early October 1941), but at least the broad outline of Sorge's views could be found in his numerous publications. Surely with the news of his arrest at least some of his published works attracted attention among American intelligence analysts. In 1940 and until his arrest Sorge published over a hundred articles in the *Frankfurter Zeitung* that focused on important Japanese, German, and international political and military concerns. Similarly, he contributed eleven major articles to *Zeitschrift für Geopolitik* between 1935 and 1939, the journal of the famous geopolitician from the University of Munich, Karl Haushofer. He also wrote for the monthly magazine *Heidelberg Geopolitik* and *Die Wehrmacht*, an official organ of the German Army. American service attachés and intelligence officers regularly read publications from Axis countries. Indeed, in the U.S. embassy in Berlin, the reading of public military publications had long been the chief means of collecting information. Since November 1938, when American Ambassador Hugh Wilson returned to Washington from Berlin, leaving a chargé d'affaires to conduct official activities, American-German relations had remained strained. German restrictions were frustrating, and they eventually closed off all contacts and travel to the American attachés.[6] Nevertheless, American military attachés in Berlin were amazingly resourceful, as Colonel Truman Smith's work in Germany (August 1935–April 1939) would suggest.[7]

It seemed that Sorge had been correct. The Japanese decided to undertake the southern advance in lieu of an attack on the Soviet Union in 1941, as Sorge had reported to Moscow. Americans were surprised by events in early December 1941, but looking ahead, there was no guarantee that after the military front stabilized the Japanese would not attack the Russians later in the summer of 1942.

It was feared in some Washington circles that the troubled year of 1942 continued to hold strategic surprises for American interests. After considering the extent of recent Japanese conquests and the increased size of the Japanese armed forces, proportionately Japan was at least as strong as it had been in 1939. That was the time of one of Sorge's prophetic published assessments of Japanese military capabilities. He wrote an article claiming that the Japanese were then strong enough to attack well beyond China; while deeply embroiled in China, the Japanese in 1939 could still expand as far as French Indo-China, Siam, Hong Kong, *and* Vladivostok, Sorge proclaimed in the renowned journal from Munich.[8]

Traditionally, most Americans held the Japanese in low regard and frequently underestimated their fighting ability. The surprise of Pearl Harbor was not readily put aside in any American assessment of Japan in 1942, yet the 1942 perspective is not easily focused for the historian. A contemporary study made by the Institute of Pacific Relations shortly after the Japanese crushing reverse in the Battle of Midway noted that

> to the important question, How strong is Japan? there can be no absolute answer. Japan's strength in the Orient is directly related to the course of the war in Europe. It is a complete mistake to regard Japan as "Hitler's stooge," as a country which is acting in obedience to Germany's orders. But Japan now has a vested interest in Germany's ability to keep the greater part of America's and Great Britain's military resources occupied in Europe for an indefinite length of time. Every American and British airplane and warship in European skies and European waters is so much clear gain for Japan.[9]

Ōshima frequently advocated an attack on the Soviet Union, and Tokyo's responses did not always seem to treat the topic unequivocally or as if it were a closed book.

Even before the German invasion of the Soviet Union, the Japanese gave the Germans considerable assurance that Japan would attack the Russians in the event of a German-Soviet war. Between June and December 1941, similar assurances were sometimes given, and MAGIC intelligence analysts had to weigh them all. But during the first seven months of 1942 the pattern of MAGIC traffic between Berlin and Tokyo on the issue of opening a Japanese-Soviet front did not change appreciably: Ōshima wanted war, and Tokyo was evasive or equivocal.

The Anglo-American planners continued to face a difficult strategic situation through most of 1942, and there was a lot of uncertainty about Axis plans and capabilities. Five weeks after the Japanese attack on Pearl Harbor, Ōshima told Hitler that Tokyo "is concentrating on the war in the South, however, Japan will be very pleased when Germany deals the Soviet a terrific blow in the spring."[10] Ōshima had compiled massive and detailed files on the war against the Soviet Union, and duplicates of these files were, for the most part, available at Special Branch, MIS, in the War Department. In January Ōshima sent Tokyo an elaborate six-page review of the first six months of the German-Soviet war, and the Japanese military and naval attachés agreed with Ōshima's assessment that the Russians would be unable to seize the initiative in 1942 and that in the end the Germans would win.[11] In this review Ōshima also cited earlier studies and reports.[12] During the first three months of 1942, MAGIC analysts knew from his intercepted messages about the nature of the forthcoming German spring offensive. It seemed possible that the European Axis powers would undertake an all-out blow to Russia and a drive through northern Africa, the eastern Mediterranean, and the Caucasus to the Indian Ocean. Some of the plans seemed to be materializing in the summer of 1942. At about the same time, the Japanese forced the British out of Burma and were making thrusts into the Indian Ocean, westward toward the Red Sea and the African coast. It appeared that these favorable Axis conditions were hardly offset by the American victory at Midway; moreover, the outcome of the costly struggles for Guadalcanal and Stalingrad would not be decided until much later in 1942.

Some two weeks after the American victory in the Battle of Midway, President Roosevelt wrote to Stalin warning that Japan might attack the Soviet Union. On 17 June 1942 Roosevelt wrote that he had "tangible evidence that the Japanese Government may be taking steps to carry out operations against the Soviet Maritime Provinces." The president promised immediate assistance should such an attack materialize, but he wanted the Soviet Union to make available suitable landing fields in Siberia. Roosevelt felt that the matter was so urgent that the operation should "be immediately initiated between our joint Army, Navy, and Air representatives in order to meet this new danger in the Pacific."[13] A month later the president again wrote to Stalin: "In the event of a Japanese attack on the Soviet Maritime Provinces, such a Siberian airway would permit the United States quickly to transfer American aircraft units to the latter area for the purpose of coming to the assistance of the Soviet Union."[14] However, before Stalin received Roosevelt's second message, he responded to Roosevelt's initial overture. The Soviet leader willingly agreed to make appropriate Siberian airfields available, but he emphasized that the purpose was to create "the Alaska-Siberia route for U.S. aircraft deliveries to the western [German-Soviet]

Front."[15] Stalin made no mention of a possible Japanese attack, and there is no evidence to suggest that in the first part of 1942 he shared Roosevelt's concern about the Japanese. However, the president's perspective was different. Slightly less than a month before the Pearl Harbor attack the previous year, Roosevelt started to receive original MAGIC material on a daily basis,[16] and events soon heightened the president's interest in MAGIC intelligence. It is likely that Ōshima's messages intercepted during the first seven months of 1942 were the chief source of the president's "tangible evidence" referred to in his letter to Stalin.

American MAGIC analysts saw Ōshima at his best in April 1942 when he skillfully reasoned with his superiors in Tokyo that it was in Japan's most profound interests to attack the Soviet Union. The previous month Ōshima had finally responded to Tokyo's suggestions made on the eve of the Pearl Harbor attack that Japan would like to mediate peace between Germany and the Soviet Union. He reported that during a two-hour meeting with Ribbentrop, the German foreign minister told him that "Germany hopes to deal the Soviet a knockout blow during this year and then come what may advance into the Near East."[17] At the beginning of another detailed six-page message dated 6 April 1942, Ōshima artfully stated in a key message to Foreign Minister Tōgō his views about "the national policy of the Japanese empire." His argument was lengthy and fairly sophisticated.

> In view of the motivating force of the war in the Far East, the primary objective of our campaign being the overthrow of England's hegemony and the establishment of our supremacy in the South, it is but natural that we should expand. We must, therefore, consider whether we are going to carry out our ultimate objectives in connection with Japan's great mission—the establishment of a New Order in East Asia. That is to say, (1) are we, in conjunction with the development of our campaign in the South, going to dispose of the Soviet and set up a complete and thoroughgoing sphere of co-prosperity; or (2) stop with the destruction of Chinese, British and American hegemonies, keeping our hands off the Soviet, and let the future bring about the solution.[18]

Ōshima knew that his latter proposition would run against the grain of traditional and widely held Japanese political attitudes on the subject of communist Russia. Japan was an original signatory to the Anti-Comintern Pact in 1936, and most Japanese leaders were strongly opposed to communism. The ambassador came from a rabidly anticommunist background, and his father, as war minister from March 1916 to September 1918, had been largely responsible for the Terauchi cabinet's announcement in August 1918 of the Siberian intervention. Indeed, over 70,000 Japanese troops had been sent to Siberia, including Captain Ōshima Hiroshi.[19] Ōshima also knew that Tokyo anxiously anticipated news of German success on the Soviet front. "Now, let us look at Germany's coming offensive against the Soviet as it affects us," the Japanese ambassador in distant Berlin continued in his 6 April message.

> It is clear that if we take the first of the two alternatives [to dispose of the Soviet], this offensive will be of great benefit to us. If the latter course is followed [keeping our hands off the Soviet], a [German] blow to the Soviet would only delay her restoration to power. . . . Therefore, to a certain extent, for us to desire an independent German-Soviet peace would not redound to our favor.

Ōshima's concluding paragraph stressed the importance that he attached to this message—never before had he been so emphatic or so insistent: "This message outlines the results of joint studies made with the military and naval attachés. Please pass this information on to the Army and Naval Ministers, [the] Chief of the General Staff and the Naval Chief of Staff."

Ōshima's persistence finally produced the information that MAGIC analysts had long awaited. Tokyo's reply came at the height of the German offensive on the Russian front, and for the first time Foreign Minister Tōgō was unequivocal. There would be no Japanese attack on the Soviet Union, Ōshima was told on 27 July 1942. MIS analysts read the news with much interest and satisfaction. Also of much interest was the Japanese admission to their Axis partner that the Anglo-American forces were "still formidable" and that Japan simply did not have sufficient strength with which to expand the war to include the Soviet Union.[20]

The message to Ōshima was carefully designed. Tōgō knew very well that Ōshima had a long history of interpreting restrictive instructions from the Foreign Ministry in Tokyo to suit his own views of the "real situation" in distant Berlin.[21] Thus, Tōgō made certain that Ōshima knew that the "no-war-with-Russia" policy did not rest with the Foreign Ministry alone. Tōgō concluded, "This telegram has been discussed and approved by the government and Imperial headquarters."[22]

Tōgō's message reached Ōshima during a ten-day tour of the Russian front. Ōshima did not take the news very well, but as a Japanese Army lieutenant general, he fully understood the pressing military strategic considerations in 1942, and he must have anticipated Tokyo's final refusal. Soon Ōshima lamented in a message to Tōgō: "But the conclusion you reach in your

Personnel in the Japanese embassy, including the attachés, were extremely popular in wartime Berlin. For example, the military attaché, Lieutenant General Banzai, was given the honor of the rank of Generalkapitän, 21 April 1942. (Courtesy of the George C. Marshall Foundation, Lexington, Virginia)

reply is that 'it would be unprofitable in view of the situation as a whole to divide the Japanese forces.' I regret to say that giving this as a basis and avoiding explicit reasons will make it impossible to obtain Germany's full acquiescence."[23] Nevertheless, he had immediate instructions to make his government's position clear to the Germans. Ōshima spent much of the morning of 30 July discussing the matter with Ribbentrop at command headquarters in the Ukraine. "Starting out suitably by saying that I was speaking on instructions from the Imperial government," Ōshima radioed to Tōgō, "I communicated to him the contents of your" instructions of 27 July. "He seemed worried about the question of our joint warfare . . . and asked me many questions on this point." As an additional disclaimer, making clear that he was carrying out the government's instructions but that he did not agree with them, Ōshima noted, "Chancellor Hitler was not there so I asked Ribbentrop to inform him concisely and clearly of the contents of your message."[24]

Tōgō's message to Ōshima was seminal in Allied relations. The initial translation was done in two segments, the first part was completed on 30 July and the second on 3 August. This is one of the few occasions during the war for which there exists clear evidence that MAGIC intelligence was given over to the Russians. President Roosevelt, an avid reader of MAGIC traffic since late 1941, wrote to Stalin on 5 August 1942 with the news that Japan had decided not to attack the Soviet Union, at least for the time being. Roosevelt did not reveal the source of his information, but he claimed that it was "definitely authentic."[25] (One wonders what Stalin thought at this time, for only about six weeks earlier Roosevelt had warned Stalin that the Japanese were going to attack the Soviet Maritime Provinces.)

Ōshima returned to Berlin to compile a full report, after observing "the progress the Germans are making in their war against the Russians," as he wired to Tokyo. He followed up on his earlier brief field reports with an incredibly detailed eleven-page military, economic, and political report on conditions in the German-Soviet war.[26] Ōshima's indiscreet communications to his superiors in Tokyo revealed to MAGIC analysts in MIS more precise information about the Soviet fighting machine and conditions generally on the Russian front than the Russians told their American and British partners in the grand Allied coalition.

The western Allies were concerned about conditions on the Soviet front and about Russian effectiveness against the Germans, but the Soviets were very secretive. Indeed, until near the end of 1942 the Russians refused to give the Americans any specific strategic or operational information concerning their military conduct, in spite of the efforts of a U.S. military mission to the Soviet Union established in October 1941. Nor were the Soviets cooperative during the visit nearly a year later of President Roosevelt's personal representative, Wendell Willkie, who was later attacked in *Pravda*.[27]

It was only after some clever maneuvering by Roosevelt that an American was allowed firsthand experience in a Soviet combat zone. In early October 1942, Roosevelt explained in a letter to Stalin that the Australian and New Zealand governments were clamoring for an immediate and all-out attack by the United Nations against Japan. If their protests were met, the Anglo-American powers would have to divert forces away from fronts where Germans were already being engaged. The president was, therefore, sending General Patrick J. Hurley, former secretary of war and then minister to New Zealand, to visit Moscow before returning to his diplomatic post in New Zealand. Roosevelt told Stalin that he wanted Hurley to learn

> through his own eyes, the most significant aspects of our present world strategy. I wish him in this way, as a result of his personal experiences, to be able to assure the Government of New Zealand and likewise the Government of Australia that . . . the best strategy for the United Nations to pursue is for them first to join in making possible the defeat of Hitler, and that this is the best and surest way of ensuring the defeat of Japan.[28]

Stalin was quick to understand the dilemma that Roosevelt had set up for him, because on the same day that Hurley, with Roosevelt's letter in hand, arrived in Moscow and met with Stalin, the Soviet leader replied to Roosevelt. Hurley, Stalin wrote, "asked for an opportunity to visit one of our fronts, in particular the Caucasus. This opportunity will be provided."[29] Within a week, then, Roosevelt sent a letter of appreciation to Stalin: "I am glad you have been so kind to General Hurley. As you can well recognize, I have had a problem in persuading the people of Australia and New Zealand that the menace of Japan can be most effectively met by destroying the Nazis first. General Hurley will be able to tell them at first hand how you and Churchill and I are in complete agreement on this."[30]

This kind of Anglo-American maneuvering with the Soviet ally was not appreciated by many top officials in Washington and London. However, the western Allies had the advantage of reading MAGIC intercepts, an alternative source for obtaining information about conditions on the German-Soviet front.

No wonder Ōshima's messages, along with all Berlin-Tokyo radio traffic, were given the highest intercept priority throughout the war. As Frank Rowlett explained, based on his wartime experience with SIS: "This meant that more than one intercept station would cover the radio circuits carrying Japanese diplomatic traffic from these cities. All Japanese diplomatic messages intercepted by all stations would be immediately enciphered and transmitted to Arlington Hall, either by landlines or radio, depending on the location of the intercept station."[31] As an unwitting informer on the most secret exchanges between Germany and its East Asian Axis partner, Ōshima provided "the Allies with highly secret and vital information throughout the war," wrote the former cryptanalyst who solved the Japanese RED machine system in the mid-1930s and whose later work was indispensable to the solution of PURPLE.[32]

Aside from offering forecasts and extensive information about military conditions on the Russian front, Ōshima provided MAGIC MIS analysts with a series of other military predictions during the year following the attack on Pearl Harbor. At the outset, shortly after Pearl Harbor, his predictions appeared ominous, and they required careful study by Anglo-American planners in light of a series of Axis, particularly Japanese, spectacular advances.

One ominous piece of information in 1942 concerned Tokyo's wishes to negotiate peace on the German-Soviet front, a topic to be discussed more thoroughly in the context of the full 1941–1945 war (Chapter 7). Fortunately, from the Allied point of view and for the welfare of the Anglo-American partnership, Tokyo was the only party that desired a separate German-Soviet peace. Stalin was always categorically opposed to a separate peace, instead seeking, soon after the German invasion, a no-separate-peace agreement with the British because he feared that Berlin and London might conclude a similar treaty. If so, additional German forces would be available for deployment to the eastern front. The Anglo-Soviet agreement, signed on 12 July 1941, included the provision that neither party would negotiate or conclude an armistice or treaty of peace except by mutual agreement.

Ōshima's intercepted messages also revealed, no doubt to western relief, that Stalin remained true to his initial pledge and was never tempted to sue for a separate peace with Hitler, no matter how devastating the German advances. It was reassuring to some Anglo-American strategists that Hitler's conditions were sweeping and unreasonable. In addition to the cession of much Russian territory, Ōshima reported in March that "peace terms would include closing of Murmansk and Archangel . . . and Stalin would balk at that."[33] Nor did Ōshima's predictions change eight months later when conditions on the Soviet front were appreciably worse for the Germans. After admitting that "the two nations appear rather at a deadlock," Ōshima expressed the fear that "it will be practically impossible for Germany to overthrow the Stalin regime." The immediate implications were clear to him.

> Judging from the present extreme situation, I must say that it is almost impossible to look for a peace settlement between Russia and

Germany or a major change in their relations. This is because Russia simply will not accept the chief German provisions—the limitation of armaments and the cession to Germany of the Caucasus and Ukraine. Therefore, I see no point at all to Japan's hoping for a Russo-German peace or trying to help it along.[34]

Two weeks later he lamented that the Soviets "have broken through the line at Stalingrad, and the German army could not hold them in check." Nevertheless, Hitler continued to refuse to change his terms, Ōshima observed, and "the German government has not considered the question [of peace]. . . . It appears that Stalin also is not giving the question of peace any consideration."[35]

Like Stalin, Ōshima was categorically opposed to the conclusion of a separate peace. MIS analysts observed his words on several occasions in 1942: "There is no possibility of . . . a separate peace"; "Germany will never carry out a separate peace"; "Germany is not only uninterested in peace but is moved to greater determination to go ahead," he advised his home government between April and October.[36]

Ōshima's predictions were greatly strengthened and gained sway in the minds of SIS and MIS officers when he also reported the attitudes and nearly verbatim words of Hitler and Foreign Minister Ribbentrop. In March, Ribbentrop told Ōshima that "Germany has no intention of making a separate peace with Stalin," and in the same month Hitler told his Japanese admirer that "as soon as good weather returns we can crush the Soviet forces completely."[37] Anglo-American strategists knew that as long as the Germans were advancing on the Russian front Hitler would predictably continue to insist on a Carthaginian peace. Therefore, German military events would eventually decide the issue of war or peace in the East. However, Anglo-American strategists were perplexed about whether a severe military setback late in 1942 would cause the German government to cease to adhere doggedly to unreasonable conditions for peace.

Only from Ōshima's intercepted messages did Anglo-American strategists learn unassailably that the German government would never conclude a separate peace. In early December, German and Japanese officials in Berlin celebrated the first anniversary of Japan's entry into the war, and Ōshima and Ribbentrop had a four-hour meeting. Ribbentrop admitted that German forces had suffered some recent setbacks, and he claimed that the Soviet breakthrough at Stalingrad occurred because "the Roumanian troops were not up to snuff, but I won't lay the blame on the Roumanians because we Germans are to blame for not supporting them better." He acknowledged that "the English and American landing in French North Africa was admittedly a success" and that "Rommel's retreat was bad news for us Germans. It was the greatest fizzle we have seen in this war. The reason why," Ribbentrop continued, "was that almost all the tanks and oil sent to withstand the British drive were sunk," but he did not really understand why Rommel's supply ships were sunk so readily.[38] Ribbentrop knew, of course, that every time ships were loaded in Naples or Taranto and sent to North Africa, Rommel was informed by ENIGMA what supplies he was to receive and when the ships would sail. Course and speed data were included in such ENIGMA messages. But the German foreign minister did not know that ENIGMA was being intercepted by the British ULTRA operation or that Ōshima's report of their four-hour meeting would be intercepted by the American MAGIC operation.[39] Nevertheless, Ribbentrop hoped "to keep Rommel supplied, but there is no guarantee that we will completely control that sea lane." The German foreign minister then confided openly in Ōshima, "What we are most worried about, to tell you the truth, is that North African situation."[40]

Ōshima, in the middle of the four-hour meeting, asked a crucial question that linked recent developments in North Africa with those on the Soviet front. Ribbentrop's answer convinced MAGIC analysts that the Germans would not sue for peace in the East. Ōshima reported his verbatim discussion with Ribbentrop to Japanese officials in Tokyo.

> Ōshima: "Your Excellency has held all along that Germany has no intention of making peace with Russia, but there is the new Mediterranean question. Aren't you also thinking of making peace with the Kremlin and concentrating your full force against Europe and America?"
>
> Ribbentrop: "Our policy toward the Soviet has never swerved. I? No, I have not the slightest intention of seeking peace myself; but on the other hand, if Stalin asks us for peace . . . , that is another matter, and I might add that I do not believe that he is thinking of this at present."
>
> Ōshima: "Well then, in case the peace question does arise, are you going to present the same terms as you have been insisting upon; namely, German obtention of the Ukraine and the Caucasus, severance of connections with the outside world, and demilitarization."
>
> Ribbentrop: "That is right."[41]

Ōshima's messages started to suggest a strategic setback for the Germans on the Soviet front, and he seemed annoyed and suspicious in late September when Ribbentrop was evasive with him. Ōshima asked if Germany could conduct a winter attack on Moscow, and Ribbentrop "avoided a candid answer," Ōshima complained to Tokyo. In the same message Ōshima reported what Ribbentrop told him about Germany's limited oil reserves. "The consumption of oil is tremendous," Ribbentrop declared, and he noted that there was barely enough for military operations. But when the Germans "get the Caucasus oil," Ribbentrop boasted, "the situation will not be as discouraging as it now looks."[42]

However, a realistic reading of events made it clear that the Germans were in serious strategic trouble. The Germans captured only a limited amount of Caucasus oil, because the oil fields were set afire by the retreating Russians and they were not held long enough by the Germans to enable the invaders to restore their production. Thus, forewarned with Ribbentrop's admission about the critical shortage of oil and the need for Caucasus oil, the reality of operational developments soon gave MAGIC analysts an idea of the new dimensions of the German strategic dilemma. In spite of a certain amount of pessimism about German military might in the bulk of Ōshima's summary of the Russian front in late September 1942, he concluded with a startling claim and outlandish recommendation: "Let me remind you," he told Foreign Minister Tōgō,

> that the defeat of Russia is essential to the establishment of the co-prosperity sphere in Greater East Asia. . . . I suppose it is our first policy to maintain neutrality with Russia, but that cannot last. Let us maintain this neutrality for a while, settle affairs in the South Seas, all the while making ready to hit the Soviet, and when next summer comes, let us join forces with the Germans and be in on the kill.[43]

This was the same sort of argument used by Japanese pro-Axis advocates when, on the eve of the conclusion of the Tripartite Pact two years earlier, they had maintained that Japan "would miss the bus" if it failed to cast its lot with the seemingly victorious European Axis powers.[44]

Increasingly, Ōshima attributed Axis setbacks to the lack of genuine cooperation between Japan and the European Axis nations. In September 1942, Ribbentrop asked Ōshima how much longer he thought the war was going to last. The Japanese ambassador prefaced his answer with important conditions, probably as much for his audience in Tokyo as for the German foreign minister. He was convinced that Germany and Japan ought to cooperate "more intimately than ever before," that they ought to "prepare for a long war," and that they must be so effective in their military operations "that the enemy cannot get the upper hand." With these premises delineated carefully, Ōshima then told Ribbentrop "that we might aim to keep fighting until the winter of 1944, by which time we should win conclusively." Cooperation within the Axis coalition was the proviso to Ōshima's prediction of victory. "As the first step," Ōshima continued, Japan "is determined to stabilize the South Seas area and, at the same time, invade the Indian Ocean. While we are doing that you Germans, just as soon as you have mopped up the Caucausus, should send forces to Iran and Iraq and join hands with us Japanese across the Persian Gulf."[45]

Here one is tempted to credit Ōshima with wholly unrealistic thinking. Although Ōshima strongly advocated that Japan cooperate with Germany by attacking the Soviet Union, he also understood that the reality of Japan's extensive commitments in the South Seas probably precluded the opening of a new front against Russia in the north, although he probably did not know of the extent of the Japanese Navy's setbacks. However, he knew that a part of the Japanese Navy was still operating in the Indian Ocean. Thus, before the turn of the tide for Germany on the Russian front, and with the precedent of Japanese naval activity in the Indian Ocean, it seemed propitious for Ōshima to advocate a different route, through the Indian Ocean, for German-Japanese cooperation.

Ōshima also envisioned cooperation between German and Japanese planners to reach well beyond the Indian Ocean. Here Ōshima appears to have given free rein to his imagination in the presence of the Nazi foreign minister. In Ōshima's scheme, the crushing blow to the Soviet Army would come with the spring and summer drives in 1943, Egypt and India would be cut off from England and the United States, and "Germany should make absolutely failure-proof preparations for an invasion of England by the summer of 1944." It was of vital importance to the Japanese that England be crushed, otherwise, Ōshima warned, the British would not "accept our terms at the time of the peace conference." The use of submarines and air raids alone would not bring England to her knees, Ōshima predicted in September 1942, therefore, Ōshima concluded in his outline for Ribbentrop, if the German invasion of England "uses *poison gas*, I think the result will be certain."[46] Ōshima put the best possible face on this strategic assessment, but within a few weeks it had to be erased completely.

Ribbentrop reported Ōshima's recommendations to Hitler at military headquarters on the Russian front. He then reported back to Ōshima: "Although the Führer also is considering various ways of bringing the war to a favorable conclusion, he is putting special emphasis on a German-Japanese junction across the Indian Ocean. After occupying the Caucasus, it is decided that there will certainly be an advance into the Middle East."[47] Thus, Ōshima unwittingly provided MAGIC readers with an elaborate strategic scheme of his and Hitler's expectations for the next two years. It was not difficult for Anglo-American planners to forecast with much accuracy the seriousness of the Axis long-range crisis. Then came MAGIC reports that Hitler was doggedly determined to take Stalingrad. It followed, then, that Hitler's fate was sealed when the Russian winter offensive was launched with enormous success on 19 November. Rumanian forces were overwhelmed immediately, and German forces soon fell back or were encircled.[48]

In addition to failure at Stalingrad, November brought more bad news for Ōshima and the Germans. As soon as Ōshima received news of the Anglo-American landing in North Africa, he telephoned Ribbentrop for a report. Ribbentrop told him that "we certainly cannot entertain any optimism over the situation there."[49] The tide had turned, and Ōshima's predictions of Germany's victory over the Soviet Union, which MAGIC analysts had once feared might materialize, were now viewed largely as the ambassador's wishful thinking.

In this setting of growing doom, Ōshima called a conference of the heads of Japanese diplomatic posts in Europe. His purpose seemed to have been to find backing for his views, for the conclusions reached in the conference bore a remarkable resemblance to his own advice forwarded earlier to Tokyo. Collaboration of Japan with the European Axis powers was the hallmark opinion. Ōshima warned his government that "if we win we must win both in the East and the West, and if we lose it must be the same." Cooperation with Germany and Italy was essential, but his panacea for victory in 1943 or 1944 was the same one he had advocated during much of the preceding two years: "establishing contact between Europe and Asia, thus making the exchange of essential materials possible. . . . Paralleling a German drive next year throughout the Near and Middle East, our Empire too should take more drastic action against India, at least engaging in actual warfare in a part of India, thus severing this member from the British colossus." Ōshima concluded this remarkable mid-November message by lecturing his superiors in Tokyo: Japan "must have faith in Germany's good intentions and in her actual strength," and Japan must stop "hiding things from Berlin."[50] The MIS summary of Ōshima's MAGIC message included the comment: "*Note*: Ōshima has long urged the foregoing views on his Government."[51]

The Tōjō cabinet had a new foreign minister, Tani Masayuki, who severely criticized Ōshima's assessments and ignored his advice about cooperation. The MIS summary of Tani's response referred to it in restrained terms as "a remarkable communication" that "challenged Ōshima's optimism about the German military situation."[52] However, the foreign minister rebuked his ambassador at the end of November and contemptuously questioned Ōshima's judgment. Tani angrily cited point after point.

As for Germany having succeeded in preparing herself for a long war through obtaining essential military materials, what about oil, as just one instance? . . . I don't see how you can say she is so prepared.

You say that Germany has weakened Russia. Well, what about Russia weakening Germany? . . . I think you would be very wrong if you imagined it impossible for the Soviet to come back with a swift blow, and that right soon. I think you had better wait a while before judging Soviet forces to be so weak.

Stalingrad hasn't fallen, has it? And the fact that the Germans were unable, with all their might, to take that city is an evil omen. . . . Now that the United States has penetrated into North Africa, a new situation faces the Reich. . . . I myself doubt if Germany could even de-militarize the Caucasus.

However you view it, Germany cannot easily get into the Middle and Near East.

Now what we want is for Germany to get ready for a long war.[53]

Ōshima seems not to have responded directly to Tani's charges. He seems to have had an amazing capacity to dismiss Tokyo's views and proceed solely within his German sphere of reference. Only in a very oblique manner, without specific reference to Tani's condemnatory communiqué of late November, did Ōshima respond nearly three weeks later. He wrote that everyone would have to wait to see what the Russians did during the winter and what effect Anglo-American military operations would have on German strategy. Nevertheless, he was convinced that the Germans would devise "a scheme for the division of their military resources and the distribution of their forces."[54]

Throughout 1942 the Ōshima-Tokyo traffic was a good measure of the war-making capacity of the Axis nations, particularly Germany, and late in the year it became clear that the strategic balance was shifting in favor of the Allied powers. Ōshima's predictions, in light of events, at times became increasingly wide of reality. MAGIC intelligence analysts understood this development, and so did Tokyo.

As far as the German-Soviet war was concerned, increasingly in the last five months of 1942 a new sense of strategic direction seemed to take hold in Washington. These were months of growing certainty, and the focus was on the crucial Soviet front. The intelligence Ōshima provided was responsible for the restoration of a sense of confidence that, as in the days of Napoleon, the Russians would be able to push the invader from Russian soil. At this point in the war the focus started to change from one centered on concern about where, when, and how the next German offensive would materialize to one concerned about how effectively the Germans might be able to resist Russian offensives. The deepest German advance into Russian territory occurred after seventeen months of hard fighting, but it would take the Russians at least another twenty-four months to push the Germans out. Thus, the new American concern about how the Russian offensives would fare was not without significance. It would be a long and costly war, and among Allied managers of war there remained a healthy respect for the resourceful German enemy. American MAGIC analysts found that the intelligence Ōshima inadvertently revealed about the Russian front was crucial in 1941 and 1942, and his reports continued to be extremely valuable until the war's end.

4

MAGIC and the Enigma
of the Eastern Front

From December 1942 onward, only a year after Japan became part of the Axis warring coalition against Great Britain and the United States, Ōshima and his government seemed to grow more remote from one another. Yet Ōshima still had much to report concerning Hitler's intentions and the war in Europe. The volume of Ōshima's messages to Tokyo in 1943 increased dramatically over the number that the ambassador initiated in 1942, and their content addressed a vast array of important issues. Significantly, the chance seemed to have passed that either Japan or Germany could have an appreciable impact on the other's theater of operations.

The Allies were starting to reverse the tide in the second half of 1942, and the path of war would soon be strewn with Allied strategic achievements. The western Allies had faith in eventual victory, and because of Ōshima's reports they had ample evidence that Hitler's capacity to continue extensive offensive operations was handicapped. Ōshima revealed in considerable detail that Axis forces were beginning to suffer from severe setbacks on the German-Soviet front, notably at Stalingrad. Other reverses occurred in North Africa, especially at El Alamein and in the aftermath of the successful Allied landings on the Algerian and Moroccan coasts, and in the South Pacific, with the Allied offensives on Guadalcanal and New Guinea, but no one among the Allied leaders believed that the war would soon be over or easily won. Indeed, as late as the end of January 1945 in Europe, U.S. Army General Omar Bradley, the Twelfth Army Group commander, believed that the war would "continue into the spring with climactic battles in July and August and an ending of the war by September."[1] Anglo-American strategic planners desperately needed evidence concerning the German and Japanese governments' most secret assessments of recent Allied gains, of Axis designs for response, and of the Axis capacity to continue the war. Intelligence specialists intimately involved with MAGIC intercepts may have felt they were standing at the center of the universe when Ōshima's messages came in. After reading them, they alerted their superiors, and the trail led quickly to the army's chief of staff (Marshall) and to Admiral William Leahy, Roosevelt's personal chief of staff.

A survey of Ōshima's messages to Tokyo from November 1942 through February 1943 offers ample evidence that in Ōshima's assessment, strategically the tide had turned against the Germans on the eastern front. His messages equaled approximately a hundred sheets of typed MAGIC intercepts, and American intelligence analysts knew that as a former military attaché to Germany, Ōshima's appraisals of military conditions were not to be taken lightly. During the four months under review, Ōshima became increasingly pessimistic about German military opportunities and capacity to deal effectively with the Russian assaults. At the same time, he had a dreaded respect for the growing strength of the Soviet Army, and he feared the Russians would be able to sustain their broad offensive. Colonel Carter W. Clarke, chief of Special Branch, MIS, queried SIS when Ōshima "forecast Hitler's failures in Russia which Col. Clarke could hardly believe Ōshima would pen."[2] The solutions to the German dilemma that he proposed in messages to Tokyo included greater Japanese cooperation with the European Axis powers and, rather shockingly at this point in the war, he advocated a Japanese attack on the Soviet Union. Soon, however, after the German collapse at Stalingrad in October, Ōshima became less loquacious about advocating Japanese direct assistance. As a translator at SIS wrote: "We begin to discern a growing uneasiness on the part of Ōshima who thereafter was not slow to admit it when Germany suffered reverses. At this time Ōshima was in a very strategic position. His advice to Tokyo became invaluable and he became envied and hated by a number of [Japanese] career diplomats in Europe."[3]

In late 1942, the Soviets reluctantly told their western Allies more about conditions on the eastern front. However, even after the Soviet Army went over to the offensive in November, Ōshima's intercepts continued to provide a different and extremely valuable perspective of conditions in the East. It, therefore, was reassuring to Allied leaders in Washington and London when they learned from Ōshima in December that German Foreign Minister Ribbentrop reported that "the war with Russia is *not* progressing as expected."[4]

Western intelligence analysts were interested in Ōshima's promise to create an intelligence apparatus intended to produce more and better information about the military capacities of the western Allies and the Soviet Union, with an emphasis on the eastern front. At that crucial point in the war Ōshima decided to hold an intelligence conference of Japanese ambassadors and ministers in Europe from "the 10th to the 28th of January 1943," the ambassador to Berlin informed his superiors in Tokyo in December.[5] American intelligence officers were delighted to have this two-week advance notice of the conference, and a few days later MAGIC specialists received the agenda for Ōshima's conference. MIS could not have wished for more. "We have worked out the following subjects to be discussed at the conference of intelligence officials," Ōshima told Tokyo on 30 December:

1. A study of the situation in Europe and Africa subsequent to the conference of ambassadors and ministers.
2. The establishment of a net to procure information on the United States and England, and the founding of an organ to study from every angle British and American military power.
3. The strengthening of mutual liaison among officials in charge of intelligence, particularly the exchange and evaluation of intelligences.
4. Bringing the [Japanese intelligence] personnel [in Europe] to full strength.[6]

Japanese intelligence officers traveled to Berlin from throughout Europe—Sweden, Vichy France, Spain, Bulgaria, Vatican City, Italy, Paris, Switzerland, Portugal, and Turkey—and, immediately after the conference, Ōshima spelled out the results of their discussions in elaborate reports amounting to eighteen pages of typed intercepts.[7] It had been decided to intensify the study of the Soviet Union's military strength by stationing Japanese intelligence officers who were Russian specialists in Germany, Turkey, Bulgaria, Sweden, and Finland. These "accredited agents" would meet in Berlin periodically, and Ōshima planned to wire their comparative reports to Tokyo. The new intelligence apparatus sought unimpeachable information about the Russians, Americans, and British by the "decoding and decipherment of enemy codes and ciphers." Little wonder then, since the apparatus was to be based in the Japanese embassy in Berlin, that Ōshima's traffic continued to receive first-rate attention among American cryptanalysts. They knew that nearly all Japanese intelligence in Europe went through Ōshima in Berlin,[8] and this level of German intelligence was not often penetrated by the British-dominated, ENIGMA-based ULTRA secrets.

While studying evidence about conditions on the German-Soviet front, MAGIC analysts soon learned that the Japanese in Berlin seemed reluctant to tell Tokyo the full story of the impending German disaster at Stalingrad. During the second week of December, Ōshima merely quoted Ribbentrop's report on the Soviet breakthrough at Stalingrad as "a tactical victory."

Thereafter, as the encircled German Sixth Army's fate became sealed, Ōshima tended to understate the precariousness of the German situation or he remained ominously silent.[9] This was a period of difficult transition for Ōshima, for he believed strongly in the invincibility of German armed forces, yet reality on the eastern front was forcing him to make painful reevaluations. Only on 25 January 1943, when the surrender of Field Marshal Friedrich Paulus and his Sixth Army was merely eight days away, Ōshima foretold what was sure to happen: "The German forces surrounded at Stalingrad," Ōshima reported to Tokyo, can no longer be kept supplied and "the danger . . . has increased immensely" that they may never be saved.[10] On the next day one of Ōshima's messages proclaimed that "the German High Command admits that the situation on the Eastern Front has suddenly become desperate."[11]

After the surrender of the remnants of the German Sixth Army on 2 February, Ōshima sent a reasonably accurate operational synopsis of the Battle of Stalingrad, the watershed of the war on the eastern front. His report, which seems to have been based largely on intelligence from one of Ōshima's German informants, concluded that "the defeat suffered by the German army at Stalingrad was the greatest disaster that has overtaken it since Napoleon defeated the Germans at Jena." Then there followed even more profound observations.

> Since Germany has been fighting Russia, Hitler and the generals have been at odds over the conduct of the war, and now the time has come for the Chancellor to stop and think, because he knows how much criticism is being heaped on his head. The German military insists that a general, well versed in military strategy, be put at the head of the general command, that the Chancellor and the general staff be in agreement on strategy, and that the military be given more freedom—a certain amount of independence.
>
> The military [officers] say that it is not that they want to quarrel with Hitler, but winning the war is the first consideration. The Chancellor understands this and will, in all probability, willingly give in. It is rumored that a number of the generals who had been in disgrace will soon be brought out [of obscurity and placed] on the staff again and that Field Marshal Keitel will be moved [out of the position of chief of the Armed Forces High Command]; however, so far there seems to be no certainty as to these matters.[12]

In spite of gross underestimates of Hitler's will and power to persevere at all costs, there were expressed here shades of dissatisfaction that would eventually lead to the attempt on Hitler's life seventeen months later. This intercept contained evidence that the German war machine was not monolithic; one can only speculate that Allied strategists hoped that Hitler would continue to direct the war personally and that he would keep his most capable generals on the perimeter without authority or prerogative.

As conditions on the eastern front worsened for Hitler's forces, MAGIC analysts observed renewed German efforts to persuade the Japanese government to declare war on Moscow. A Japanese attack in the eastern Asiatic part of the Soviet Union would inevitably reduce Soviet military strength on the German-Soviet front. Although by the preceding August 1942 American strategic planners were convinced from a study of the Berlin-Tokyo traffic that the Japanese would not attack the Soviet Union, it remained instructive for the Americans to watch MAGIC intercepts in early 1943. Most informative was the fervor with which Hitler and Ribbentrop pursued their threadbare scheme for Japanese involvement in the German war against the Soviet Union. Japanese entry was a forlorn German hope, and reporting on his two-hour conference with Hitler on 21 January, Ōshima quoted Hitler as having said:

> Now I don't want you to think that I am weakening in my conviction that we will win, but the first question we have to face is disposing of the Soviet Union. It is clear that if, in order to destroy the striking power of Russia, you Japanese would, from the East, take a hand and help us out, it would be very advantageous in getting this job off our hands. But after all, the Japanese officials who understand their national resources better than anybody else must make this decision.[13]

Hitler no doubt understood, particularly with the disaster of Stalingrad at hand, that Japan would never initiate an attack on the Soviet Union. Ōshima had some evidence of this from a private talk with the German foreign minister. The obsequious Ribbentrop elaborated upon his Führer's suggestions. "As for the Soviet Union," Ribbentrop said to Ambassador Ōshima,

> you Japanese know better than anyone else whether or not you can afford to attack her. That is something for you to decide after calculating your strength. I know well enough that if, after Japan attacked Russia, she did not win quickly, all Siberia would become an air base for the United States; so we Germans would be loath to criticize your policy of concentrating on England and the United States. I just wanted you to understand that.[14]

Nevertheless, two days later, on 26 January, Ōshima begged his government to cooperate with the Germans, if at all possible. "I now once again plead that you most seriously consider attacking the Soviet Union," Ōshima wired Foreign Minister Tani Masayuki.[15]

Tani was, of course, unmoved by Ōshima's entreaty in early 1943 (as he had been in November 1942), and his reply was firm. He extensively reviewed for Ōshima Japanese intelligence assessments on conditions in the Soviet Union, and American strategic planners learned much about the fighting capacity of the Soviet armed forces by reading this first-rate review. Initially, the Japanese diplomatic traffic was between the Japanese ambassador in Kuibyshev on the upper Volga (some 500 miles east of Moscow) and Tokyo, and the raw intelligence data on the Soviet Union sometimes underwent elaborate analysis before Tokyo sent it to Ōshima in Berlin.[16] Thus, American analysts had an opportunity to study any Tokyo additions and refinements to the data before Ōshima received them in Berlin. In this instance, Americans must have viewed Tani's concluding remarks to Ōshima with mixed feelings. "Now the Soviets scarcely ever speak of help from England and the United States or of a second front. They say, 'We ourselves, alone, can whip those Germans anytime.' This attitude is general throughout the Soviet [Union] and it is something we cannot afford to lose sight of."[17] However, this was only a mild irritation in the Washington-Moscow alliance which was often plagued with suspicion and misunderstanding. In fact, Stalin continually harped on the need for a second front and complained of delays in opening one.

The turn of the tide on the German-Soviet front placed Japan in an increasingly awkward position. It was clearly in Japan's interest to continue to adhere to the terms of the Soviet-Japanese Neutrality Pact signed in Moscow in April 1941. The pact stipulated that if an attack by a third power were made on one party, the other signatory would remain neutral; moreover, the territorial integrity of Manchukuo and the Mongolian People's Republic would be respected. Although there was some Japanese debate about breaking the pact after the German attack in June 1941, discussion subsided predictably when the Soviet Union failed to collapse. Later Japanese foreign ministers sought to remain carefully neutral, especially after Tokyo realized that the defeat of Germany was inevitable.

The intelligence garnered from the Kuibyshev-Tokyo-Berlin MAGIC intercepts was important to American and British understanding of what was occurring in the Eurasian scope of the war. Early in 1943, western Allied strategic planners had an opportunity to study the full range of Foreign Minister Tani's intelligence reports on the Soviet Union that he sent to Ōshima. In their MAGIC ringside seat Anglo-American analysts witnessed Ōshima hand-ing over the information to the Germans, and Tokyo's activity in this regard was clearly in violation of the spirit if not the letter of the Soviet-Japanese Neutrality Pact. On the other hand, the Americans and British, without telling their Soviet ally of conditions behind German lines, continued to learn from MAGIC intercepts. Thus, they quiescently watched events unfold on the eastern front throughout the spring of 1943.

Tani knew that Ōshima was soon to meet with Hitler and Ribbentrop and intended for the Germans to see the new Japanese reports on the Soviets. The message was classified as "strictly secret," and Ōshima was told to "please send a copy of this message to all our ambassadors and ministers in Europe." The source of the intelligence was made clear to Ōshima at the outset: "From the last of February to the last of March Secretary Kōta [?] and civilian expert Takehisa Shimizu made a trip through Russia and on the basis of their studies and observations they sum up the present situation in the Soviet Union as follows."[18] Ōshima was given this very sensitive information for the purpose of convincing the Germans to modify their policy. Even if the Germans did not see that the tide had turned against them on the eastern front, the Japanese intelligence report made it clear that the Soviets viewed the struggle over the long haul and that time was against the Germans.

> The Soviet [Union] has been fighting the Germans now for nearly two years, and although it is true that both materially and militarily she has suffered considerable losses, by her policy of concentration of essentials and particularly of moving heavy industries to safe places, her essential industries, particularly her military industries, are now estimated to be about 70% of what they were when the Russo-German war broke out. . . .
>
> Apparently the transference of factories and installations to the East is now about complete and the Ural industrial area is remarkably well organized and prepared. Sverdlovsk and Chelyabinsk, both cities, are beehives of activity.[19]

Ōshima appreciated the sensitive nature of the information Foreign Minister Tani had placed in his hands, and he had no doubt about its strategic importance.

He also had no doubt about how to treat the information, for three days later he readily reported to Tokyo that the strictly secret "summary of the Russian situation" was given to Ribbentrop. Ōshima met with Ribbentrop at the German foreign minister's mountain villa Fuschl during the morning of 18 April.[20] Ribbentrop was particularly intrigued by "the 'psychological aspects' mentioned at the end of your summary," Ōshima explained to Tani. Ōshima continued: "Ribbentrop requested that I present to Hitler personally my views on German policy toward occupied areas."[21] The Japanese suspected that the people's growing bitterness and enmity were owing to the wrongdoings and frightful mismanagement by German administrators in the occupied areas. Moreover, the Germans were guilty of doing enormous harm to the anti-Bolshevist cause and unwisely creating additional hostility to their invasion of the Russian homeland[22] Later, during the afternoon of 18 April, Ōshima and Ribbentrop traveled to the Berghof, Hitler's retreat on the Obersalzberg in Bavaria, to meet with Hitler. Field Marshal Wilhelm Keitel also sat in on the meeting. Ōshima handed Hitler a sophisticated piece of Japanese reflection.

> 1. The war aims have been well driven home and the determination of the people may be called unshakable. All the people cry, "Let us slay the German invader!" You get the impression that the whole Soviet nation in its fury is welcoming another attempt by Germany to come back.
> 2. The successes of the Red Army during the past winter's drive and the annihilation of the 6th German Army in Stalingrad have given an impetus not easily stopped. They say, "Look, we have plenty of food and materials and can give the Germans two blows for [their] one." The Soviet officials call their present battle against Germany the struggle for the fatherland and the peculiarly vicious propaganda of the Bolsheviki—lus[c]ious, vitriolic and full of hate—is rampant. Indeed the propaganda of the leaders seems to have succeeded in making the home front well nigh impregnable, and the bloodthirstiness of the Soviet masses may be adjudged insatiable.[23]

Ōshima was quite eloquent in his delivery before Hitler, and he personally elaborated upon Tokyo's assessment.

> Stalin has had considerable success in carrying out the war aims which were to be achieved within Russia itself. The Russian people, on the whole, seem to be imbued with the idea that the fight against Germany is a war of peoples. Therefore, although the outcome of the war will naturally be decided by force of arms, the implementation of plans for the alienation of elements within Russia would have no little effect upon its course.

"As Field Marshal Keitel . . . well knows," Ōshima continued, while I was in office here as Military Attaché [1934–1938], I carried on joint investigations with Admiral Canaris concerning measures to be taken inside Russia. We arrived at the conclusion that in view of the diversity of nationalities within Russia, the emancipation of these peoples should be made our leading slogan. On the basis of Germany's policy in the eastern occupied areas, wouldn't it be possible for Germany to consider political strategy toward Russia from this viewpoint?[24]

Hitler, of course, was not persuaded by Ōshima's argument. Since Ōshima had been introduced to Hitler eight years earlier, the two men had met many times. Certainly since 1935 Hitler met more frequently with Ōshima than with any other foreign representative, and their meetings were always extremely cordial and congenial. Hitler never displayed any of his notorious outbursts when meeting with Ōshima, and their meetings were often marked by much candor. Ōshima's questions and comments were sometimes pointed or even brutally frank, but he rarely pressed or queried Hitler for more thoroughgoing responses than the Führer wished to provide. Ōshima, perhaps in deference to the German head of state, always appeared to be satisfied with Hitler's usually dogmatic statements, and in this instance also, Ōshima simply reported to Tokyo that "Hitler, after looking through the papers I had presented to him, replied: 'Your idea sounds plausible enough. However, the fact is that the most effective way is to weaken morale on the battle front by military offensive. There is danger that political schemes would have just opposite results.' "[25] Thus, with Hitler's pronouncement the matter was dropped, and there was no further discussion at this particular Hitler-Ōshima-Ribbentrop-Keitel meeting.

If Ōshima did not press Hitler on this occasion, neither did he forget his argument about the expedience of actively working to foster antibolshevism, especially in the areas of the Soviet Union occupied by the Germans. In May, he again raised the issue with Ribbentrop, concluding explicitly, "I think you should lose no time in giving guarantees of independence to the Ukraine and the three Baltic nations."[26] Citing Manchukuo as an example, Ōshima further explained to the German foreign minister that at the outset a puppet government would be necessary in order to bring the areas in line with German desires. Like Hitler, however, Ribbentrop rejected Ōshima's advice, saying that the scheme was impossible.

Ōshima probably planned to raise the subject again with Hitler, with whom he thought in late May he would soon meet. However, because of Hitler's rapid and unpredictable movements, particularly between his headquarters closer to the eastern front and Berchtesgaden, Ōshima was unable to arrange a meeting for several weeks.[27] Nevertheless, Hitler wanted to see Ōshima as soon as possible, because Ribbentrop had told him that Ōshima had instructions from the new Japanese foreign minister, Shigemitsu Mamoru, "to go straight to Hitler."[28] Ōshima and his superiors in Tokyo were alarmed by new reports of the deteriorating German position on the eastern front.

Ōshima had a special piece of Soviet intelligence to present directly to Hitler. Ribbentrop had already been given a four-hour briefing by the Japanese when the ambassador, accompanied by Major General Okamoto Kiyotomi, visited the German foreign minister at his estate at Fuschl, outside Salzburg, on 19 May. Okamoto explained the results of his survey completed during a recent 5,000-mile trip through the Soviet Union. He had crossed into Russian territory from the small frontier town of Manchouli[29] in extreme western Manchukuo on 10 March and entered Turkey from the Transcaucasian and renamed Armenian town of Leninakan on 30 March 1943. His survey was similar to an earlier one made between the Afghanistan border and Kuibyshev although much more extensive and sophisticated.

It was a remarkable trip—by ship across the Caspian Sea but otherwise entirely by rail through the huge country. The Japanese traveled first on the Chinese Eastern Railroad to the Trans-Siberian Railroad, arriving in Chita on 11 March; they were in Irkutsk two days later, and in Novosibirsk on 16 March. The Japanese delegation, which included Hidaka Shinrokurō, Japanese ambassador designate to Rome,[30] then turned southward on the Turkish-Siberian Railroad and arrived in Alma Ata on 20 March, in Tashkent on 21 March, Ashkhabad on 24 March, and Krasnovodsk on 25 March. They then crossed the Caspian Sea to Baku, arriving on 28 March, and then proceeded to Tiflis on 29 March, and finally arrived in Leninakan on 30 March. It was then easy for Okamoto to make his way through neutral Turkey and then to Berlin.

The Japanese had planned carefully and took full advantage of their unique opportunity to spy on the Soviet Union. Everyone in the delegation, including Ambassador Hidaka, took notes on what was seen from the train windows and around various railroad stations and platforms. Surveillance of the Japanese by Soviet plainclothes security agents was not very thorough—usually only two GPU (Gosudarstvennoye Politicheskoye Upravleniye, State Political Directorate) officials assigned to each railroad car full of Japanese. Only on one occasion, near the end of the trip in Georgian SSR, were the Japanese closely watched when ten GPU men rode in the same car. The head of the Japanese delegation, General Okamoto, reported that "the shades of our car windows were most firmly pulled down, allowing no glimpse of the outside, so I presume something of a military nature requiring the utmost secrecy was going on."[31] Generally, the shades were not drawn, but whenever one of the two GPU agents with the Japanese attempted to interfere, other Japanese not then under surveillance were on the lookout for sensitive Soviet information. As Okamoto summarized, because there was "an unusually large number of people in our party, this was of great advantage to us both in making observations and in exercising precaution toward the GPU men."[32] Once out of the Soviet Union, notes were compared and coordinated for the final reports.

The Japanese trip yielded significant information on the warring capacity of the Soviet Union. General Okamoto was responsible for compiling extensive reports from the observations made by his sizable party of Japanese Army and Foreign Ministry officers, and Ōshima took the final intelligence reports directly to Hitler. (A few months later in 1943, another major general, this one in the U.S. Army, traveled over some of the same railway with a list of Soviet items on which intelligence reports should be obtained for the United States. It is likely that the American "inspection" list was designed more precisely because of the earlier MAGIC reports of Okamoto's observations.[33]) Ōshima also sent the full reports back to Tokyo, providing the same sweeping Soviet intelligence to the western Allied strategic planners that the ambassador and Okamoto would later explain to Ribbentrop on 19 May and much later to Hitler personally.[34]

The final Okamoto intelligence reports were divided into three main categories: (1) observations of railway shipping in the Soviet Union, (2) observations about military factors along Soviet railways, and (3) description of construction in areas along the railways.

1. *Observations of railway shipping in the Soviet Union.* The Japanese were meticulous in their reports on Soviet railroad shipping.[35] Trains were counted throughout the trip, and the reports included the time of observation, the direction the train was traveling, number of cars, type of cargo, and the rolling stock standing on side tracks. The richness of the reports can readily be seen in the eastbound railroad traffic near Tashkent on 21 March 1943. One military freight train was observed carrying ten fighter planes and six old trucks, and there were six train cars of molybdenum ore, ten cars of iron ore, and five cars of cotton and sugar beets. Also observed were two coal trains, two limestone trains, seven petroleum tank-car trains with about ninety-five cars each, two passenger trains, and one troop train carrying about 150 soldiers. Other trains were transporting heavy metal pipe and oil-drilling equipment.

There was much evidence of the shipment of large quantities of oil. On the Caspian Sea, for example, "between Krasnovdsk and Baku," Okamoto reported to Tokyo, "petroleum is ferried in tankers of the 5,000-ton class. In

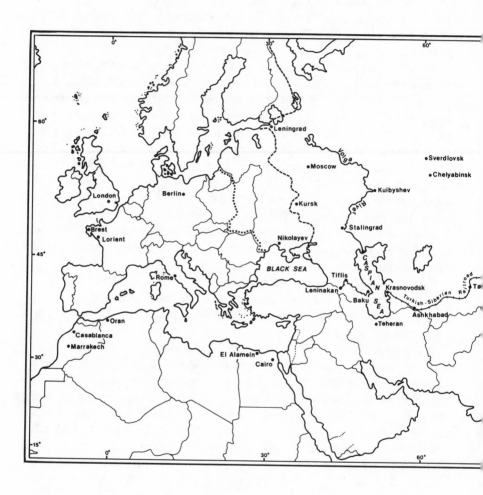

Railroad route traveled by the Okamoto delegation, March 1943

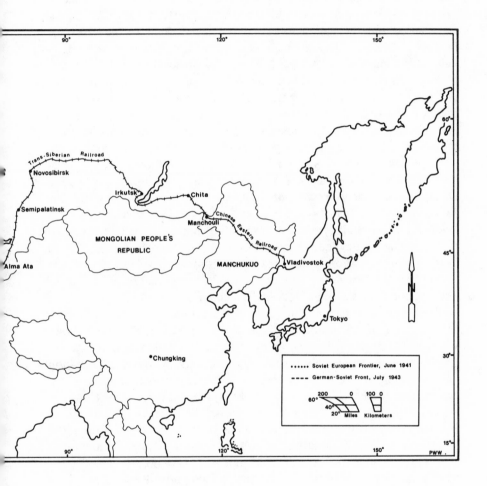

the port of Baku there are also some smaller ones, and we saw at least 8 tankers. At the first port we boarded the *Daghestan* [also *Dagestan*] (of about 2,000 tons) which towed a smaller vessel on which were about 20 tank [railroad] cars." Their ship was lightly armed with two small-caliber cannons on the bridge and two forty-millimeter machine guns on the stern. Wartime restrictions became more stringent as the Japanese traveled westward, and during the night before the party reached Baku on the west coast of the Caspian Sea, General Okamoto reported that "all lights were extinguished in a blackout and all was tenebrous till we docked."

Anglo-American strategic planners were reassured by news in the MAGIC intercepts that there was an enormous volume of Soviet rail transport and evidence of Soviet staying power, of strategic strength and economic recovery. Traveling westward, the Japanese found that the closer to the war zone their trains moved the more activity they observed. Okamoto recorded, "as we approached Krasnovodsk on the 4th day . . . rolling stock increased tremendously." MAGIC analysts at MIS also saw operational evidence in Okamoto's intelligence reports of American aid to the Soviet Union. The Japanese reported that "west of Ashkhabad trains loaded with American lend-lease in particular caught the eye." One military freight train carried "74 new small six-cylinder trucks—about 2/3rds Studebakers and 1/3rd General Motors." Another train was transporting "70 new Ford trucks" and several freight trains were "loaded with wooden boxes marked with English lettering and clearly containing American manufactured goods."[36]

The heavy rail traffic required careful organization and constant repair. Most of the railroad, with the exception of the Siberian trunk double railway line, was single track along which new shunting stations with one or two tracks were built at intervals of some ten kilometers, and every other station had two shunting tracks. Work crews were frequently seen, and the system was kept in good repair. Extra locomotives were kept in reserve along the railway, especially in the mountainous areas. The Japanese estimated that Russian diesel locomotives had much less traction power than the older steam engines. But locomotives generally were not in very good condition. "We saw . . . piles of discarded locomotives," Okamoto wrote. "If the wheels and chassis were satisfactory, [many locomotives] were kept on the job regardless of [war] damage. In some cases wooden barrels were used instead of [the original metal] tank" on the steam locomotives.

Soldiers were everywhere, and they were given priority over civilian passengers. Warm food was available to them, for example. "Quite a few [soldiers] were front bound after furloughs," Okamoto estimated. Furthermore, "the wounded and sick were very numerous and at the railway stations the thumping of many crutches could be heard."

Thus, Okamoto presented a picture of much success, if hardship, in connection with railway shipping in the Soviet Union. It was a day-by-day depiction of recovery and promise with clear and convincing evidence that the tide had turned far to the east of the front, deep within the Soviet Union. In a protracted war of attrition, Anglo-American strategic planners could hope for no better news about the secretive Russians in the Allied wartime coalition.

2. *Observations about military factors along Soviet railways.* Japanese observations of military factors along the railway in the Soviet Union were perhaps of greatest interest from an Anglo-American point of view, but Tokyo and Berlin were also extremely interested.[37] The chief Japanese concern centered on rumors of growing Soviet military strength in eastern Siberia, but there was no basis for such rumors. General Okamoto concluded that "throughout the whole course of the present journey the impression made upon us was that the districts of Eastern Russia were very calm and quiet. . . . We think that at present Russia has no plan to intensify her strategical measures against us." Two days earlier he had made the same assessment: "I can at present detect no indications whatsoever that they [the Russians] are planning to attack Japan."[38]

Soviet strength to carry on the war against the invading European Axis powers was the immediate concern, and although Okamoto's assessment was prudently cautious, it is evident that he believed the tide had turned against the Germans. The Japanese were convinced "that the strength of the Russian army is not yet exhausted by any means." Furthermore, Okamoto observed: "Weighing the height and depth of the Soviet ability to fight Germany, I say it is not yet materially weakened and at present . . . [the Soviets] are endeavoring to improve the organization and equipment of Red troops. . . . I can safely say that the fact that a second line is being placed and held in reserve around Tashkent, to forestall a German invasion of western and central Asia, proves this."[39]

Okamoto believed that the second line of reserve forces around Tashkent deep in Asiatic Russia was chiefly concerned with the German-Soviet front, particularly to the degree that the front in European Russia extended into the Caucasus. His perspective was unique, and he provided the Germans, British, and Americans with a window into the vast wartime strategic reserve of the Soviet Union. The densely populated and heavily cultivated regions around Tashkent could support large military forces, but regions as far west as the Caspian Sea "are extensive and boundless uninhabited deserts in which no considerable military forces could presumably be maintained."

The details of Okamoto's military reports substantiate his conclusions about the recovery and staying power of the Soviet Union. On 24 March, "while at a standstill at Ashkhabad a freight train drew up from the east bearing submarine sailors, possibly bound for the Caspian." During the next several days the Japanese delegation saw "powerful submarines" of a "light 1,000-ton" class in the Caspian Sea.[40] There were also two monitors and a 2,000-ton troop transport "equipped with small caliber cannon and machine guns, and full of sailors." The transport and an escort vessel "sailed for parts unknown," but the Japanese had "strong suspicions that considerable shifting of troops" was taking place.

The Japanese also carefully reported on every aviation enterprise observed, including the condition of airstrips, the number and types of aircraft on various airfields, defense installations, and warehouse, hangar, and barracks facilities. For example, four airfields were observed near Alma Ata in the rugged high country deep in Asiatic Russia. In the same report, General Okamoto mentioned a "2nd field (about 4 kilometers north of Alma Ata station). One Douglas passenger plane [probably a Lend-Lease C-47 Dakota, a military version of the DC-3 airliner] and about 40 single seater, slow training planes of uncertain type, a wireless station and three two-storied barracks [were noted by the Japanese]. One plane [was] taking off, landing, and taking off again."

Several Douglas C-47s were also seen on Soviet airfields within the craft's flying range to Chinese airstrips. Some members of the Japanese delegation speculated, since the famous workhorse aircraft played a major role in keeping the Nationalist forces of Chiang Kai-shek supplied, that Moscow was in this way maintaining contact with the Kuomintang government at Chungking. The Japanese were aware that Stalin had sold Chiang Kai-shek small quantities of arms before the Soviet-Japanese Neutrality Pact was concluded in April 1941,[41] but now, two years later when the Soviets were gaining the upper hand in the war against the European Axis powers, the Japanese were increasingly watchful for signs of any change in Soviet attitude toward their official policy of neutrality with Japan.

Finally, the Japanese reported on military conditions near the Turkish border. They observed that there were practically no military installations on the Turkish side, but "the Russian defense facilities, surveillance, emplacements bristling with guns, and artillery units filled us with awe and made us shudder." Here, then, was ample evidence that the earlier schemes of a few Axis strategists were merely pipe dreams. Almost solely out of wishful thinking, they envisioned a German-Japanese linkup, the entrance of Turkey into the war on the Axis side, and a combined attack through Armenian and Georgian SSRs, over the Caucasus Mountains to join other Axis forces advancing eastward in European Russia. An appreciation of the magnitude of Soviet military prowess weighed heavily on the many strategic planners in

Tokyo who cherished their neutrality with the Soviets while they increasingly viewed their Axis partnership with the Soviet Union's enemy as a mixed blessing.

3. *Description of construction in areas along the railways.* More than ever, while traveling across the breadth of the Asiatic Soviet Union, the Japanese had an opportunity to understand something of the enormous commitment the Soviets had made to victory over their Axis enemies. The strategic dimensions of the struggle were most prevalent in Okamoto's delineations of material construction and sacrifice for the cause of victory.[42] There were large tractor stations, agricultural warehouses, and oil storage tanks from the Altai Mountain districts to the vicinity of Semipalatinsk. There "were quite a number of large three-storied buildings brightly lighted with electric lights," large factory chimneys, and "continuous" suburbs. The Japanese "somehow . . . felt thrilled at the sight." Around Alma Ata there were several large oil storage tanks and "a few large factories under construction," and some factories were "carrying on operations in oxygen autogenous welding at night."

Agricultural conditions improved dramatically around the oasis of Tashkent where there was evidence of raw cotton, sugar beets, and piles of wire and scrap metal along the railway. Okamoto claimed that "agriculture is most fully developed along the whole railway line running through Soviet Central Asia. Rich farming continues through the region with raw cotton as the main crop." The Soviet agricultural irrigation systems also impressed the Japanese.

The average workers with whom the Japanese talked during the long trip were weary of war and of the food shortages and long hours of work, but life had also been difficult before the war. The populace was subservient to authority and seemed resolved to toil for victory. Moscow's propaganda also played an important role. Okamoto explained:

> The catchwords which were pinned up in the [railway] stations have a very earnest quality about them. They deal with the advancement of scientific technique, the benefits of war strength, and the increase of education. Among these they [Soviet authorities] have interspersed slogans to arouse the people to war against Germany, and exaggerating [Okamoto declared] the cruelty of the German leaders (especially Hitler and Goebbels) and the barbarisms of the German invading army, and by using base and vulgar cartoons, they hope to arouse the antipathy against the Germans into an uproar.[43]

Moreover, Soviet propagandists displayed the portraits and names of their heroes and extolled "the Russian style of co-prosperity to the skies." Only in two places during the entire trip did the Japanese delegation "see any posters advocating an alliance between Russia, England, and America."

While MAGIC cryptanalysts were decrypting Okamoto's intelligence reports about the railways from Manchouli in Manchukuo to Leninakan in Armenian SSR, Anglo-American strategic planners were studying another elaborate report on the military resources of the Soviet Union. The report that Foreign Minister Shigemitsu forwarded to Ōshima was based on a recent study made by the Japanese ministries of war, navy, and foreign affairs. More strategic and comprehensive in nature, Tokyo's conclusions coupled with Okamoto's assessments provided General Marshall, Admiral William D. Leahy, and others in Washington with a remarkably thorough and sophisticated estimate of Soviet military resources.

The Tokyo report made its purpose clear at the outset: "We have estimated as follows the Soviet Union's power to fight."[44] In the area of human resources, the Japanese estimated that Soviet losses between June 1941 and April 1943 amounted to approximately, 8.8 million (consisting of 3.5 million prisoners and 3.4 million dead and 1.9 million wounded who cannot be rehabilitated for return to the battlefield). The Soviets could mobilize a reserve force as high as 4 million soldiers and still maintain the indispensable war production for such a vast mobilization, and recruits entering the Soviet Army in 1944 were expected to number from 1 million to 1.2 million. The Japanese suspected that the quality of these recruits would be a little lower, but "the quality of military leadership is fully equal to that of political leadership" in the Soviet Union. "By and large we do not believe that the quality of the Red Army has been materially lessened."

The Japanese were convinced that by April 1943 the efficiency of munitions plants had been restored to from 60 to 70 percent of what it had been before the German invasion and that Soviet factories were producing 1,450 aircraft and 1,400 tanks each month. The transfer of factories was complete, and full production capacity would soon be reached; thereafter, the Japanese expected efficiency of operation to continue to increase.[45] Thus, "with the number of soldiers on hand, Russia is fully as able to combat Germany as she was last year."

As far as food resources were concerned, the most recent harvest fell short of the Soviet annual consumption by 4,530,000 kilotons, the Japanese Tokyo report estimated. But the Soviets had 7 million to 10 million kilotons of cereals in storage, so there would be no shortage in the interim before the new harvest. As for petroleum reserves, the Japanese believed that the Russians had 20–25 million kilotons of petroleum stored in tanks. The Tokyo study also had claimed that rail transport could not keep up with increased military production, but the estimate was modified in light of Okamoto's reports. The Okamoto spy group offered an in-depth survey that showed how effectively the Soviets were dealing with their transportation difficulties.

The Japanese estimates of the amount of Anglo-American aid arriving in the Soviet Union were low. Moreover, the Japanese wrongly claimed that the amount of aid would not exceed the early 1943 rate of about 3.5 million kilotons of matériel a year. American lend-lease aid to the Soviet Union was a particularly delicate and embarrassing topic for the Japanese. Nearly 50 percent of lend-lease shipments entered the Soviet Union via Siberia, much of it by air but also much of it by cargo ship over the Pacific route to eastern Siberian ports, especially Vladivostok. Japan did not blockade shipments to Soviet ports because the Soviet Union, although at war with Japan's ally, Germany, was neutral in the war between Japan and the United States. (Moreover, as discussed earlier, by 1943 Japan was jealously protective of the Russo-Japanese neutrality.) However, Washington feared that Tokyo's policy might change and American vessels bound for Soviet ports would be intercepted whenever it suited Japan's convenience, so after the attack on Pearl Harbor, this awkward arrangement was modified. In a somewhat un-real contrivance 15 American ships were transferred under lend-lease to the Soviet flag in November and December 1942, 125 by mid-1945.[46]

Japan's estimate of the Soviet Union's power to fight ended ominously: "The Stalin regime, through able management and careful mobilization, has rallied all resources of the state to combat Germany. The army and the people are firmly behind Stalin and the war consciousness is running high." In another message to Ōshima of the same date as Tokyo's estimate of Soviet strength (28 April 1943), Foreign Minister Shigemitsu wrote tersely and pro-foundly, "The Imperial Japanese government, seeing the results of this year's drive, fears, and very much fears, that Germany may lose all her self-reliance and that in the meantime America and England will be left free to strengthen their striking power and finally to launch a great offensive."[47] Coupled with Okamoto's reports, Tokyo wanted Ōshima to use the two Jap-anese studies to impress on Hitler the necessity of concluding peace with the Kremlin.

Three months elapsed before Ōshima had a chance to talk with Hitler, and by the end of July, Foreign Minister Shigemitsu's forecasts had been partially overtaken by events. There was no need to report in detail on the conclusions reached in Japanese studies on the Soviet Union made over three months earlier—no doubt Hitler had had a report from Ribbentrop af-ter the foreign minister's meeting with Ōshima and Okamoto on 19 May. In spite of the great Soviet victory over the Germans in the recent Battle of Kursk, the Führer remained as obstinate as ever. Ōshima suggested to Hitler in their meeting of 30 July that Germany "adopt the policy of making peace with Russia." Absolutely out of the question, Hitler responded. "Why, don't you know that if I did [make peace with the Soviets, they] would beyond any peradventure of doubt reach out, clasp hands with the United States, and squeeze you Japanese to death between them!"[48] Moreover, Mussolini had just been forced to resign, and Italy's continuance in the war was problematic. Hitler's closing comments to Ōshima were absurd and revealing of his depths of recklessness. Ōshima reported to Tokyo:

> In conclusion Chancellor Hitler said to me, "That Italian situation is utterly lamentable, but in any case we won't worry too much since our neighbor is all right in peace, but weak in war. What an Ally! If we had only had you Japanese in the position of Italy we would have already surely won this fight. Ah, well, it only goes to show that the only *Soldatenvölker* left in this world . . . [are] the Germans and the Japanese. We strong Japanese and Germans are separated by 10,000 kilometers, it is true, but taking the long view, this is marvelous, I should say, or call it divine providence. From now on we are going to overcome every difficulty before us and there shall be no fear of a clash of interest—absolutely none. We must stick closely together during war, and in the future we are going to have occasion to work in very intimate unison."
>
> I replied, "The Japanese government feels exactly as you do." I told him that a number of times.[49]

There was no more compelling evidence that the tide had turned on the German-Soviet front than that provided by the MAGIC intercepts of Japanese communication transmissions between Berlin and Tokyo, and Ambassador Ōshima was pivotal in this network. The ambassador's enciphered messages to Tokyo conveyed his considerable military and political knowledge about the war in Europe, and they faithfully reflected his conversations with Hitler and the German war council. On the other hand, Tokyo responded to Ōshima with its own insightful analysis.

The appointment in April 1943 of Shigemitsu Mamoru as the Japanese foreign minister, a post he would hold until April 1945, also highlighted Ōshima's role. Shigemitsu was a distinguished career diplomat who had been ambassador to the Soviet Union (1936–1938) and ambassador to Great Britain (1938–1941), and he knew Ōshima and the European diplomatic community firsthand. Shigemitsu was convinced that the Germans would eventually be defeated in the East, and his Foreign Ministry messages to Ōshima frequently included Japanese intelligence reports on the Soviet Union. While maneuvering diplomatically through Ōshima and within the confines of the Axis alliance after the Italian defection, the Japanese continued to urge the Germans to disentangle themselves from the Soviet Union so that Germany and Japan could concentrate on the defeat of Great Britain and the United States. Berlin, however, would not make peace with Moscow. As Shigemitsu lamented in his 1931–1945 memoirs, "Meanwhile Hitler continued to talk of victory to Ōshima, . . . [and] I continued anxiously to watch the progress of the German war."[50] So were Anglo-American readers of the MAGIC intercepts, who studied carefully the weighty Berlin-Tokyo dialogue.

5

MAGIC Intelligence during the President's Travels in 1943

The sophistication of MAGIC intelligence and the growing reliance on it created a special problem when the president and his chief advisers were overseas for extended periods. The restraining factor in conveying MAGIC or ULTRA intelligence to the president and his party was not the availability or performance of communications equipment or facilities; rather, it was a zealous concern for the protection of the source, the high-grade cryptographic systems of the enemy that had been solved. There was grave danger that the Japanese and Germans would change their ciphers if they suspected their cryptographic systems were compromised. This was Marshall's fear, indeed his nightmare since PURPLE was broken in the fall of 1940. Thus, the extraordinary travel plans of the president brought to the forefront the problem of communications and the distribution of MAGIC intelligence. A classic hellish intelligence dilemma manifested itself: Crucially secret information about the enemy is of little use unless it reaches the appropriate authorities and can be acted upon.

General Marshall read individual MAGIC messages and used them in a variety of ways. At the end of December 1941 he wrote a memorandum to Brigadier General John C. H. Lee in which the chief of staff declared at the outset, "I notice in MAGIC 26941 a very interesting statement."[1] In another instance in late 1942 Marshall cleverly sought MAGIC assistance to see if a certain piece of information were sent to the European Axis powers. He explained to his assistant chief of staff, G-2, that he had recently attended a dinner where there were many Latin American military attachés and representatives. Marshall spoke very frankly at the dinner, thinking

> that it could do no harm in friendly Latin America and that I would take the risk on the Argentine fellow—whom I do not trust at all. I

don't know that there was any particular detail that would be really harmful to us if it leaked out, provided it did not reach the Italians and Germans today or tomorrow. . . .

I wish you would watch for communications [from the Argentine embassy in Washington] to the Argentine during the next few days, commencing this morning [13 November 1942], to see if any report is attempted.[2]

Occasionally, when pursuing special points Marshall would have Arlington Hall send him particular intercepted messages. He asked his intelligence officers for special assistance on 15 March 1942:

Please have Colonel Bratton look over MAGIC and see if he finds any reference to the *Queen Mary*. I have a dim recollection that her stop in Rio was reported in MAGIC. If this is the case, I would like a little statement of the report from MAGIC with an indication of the hazard we are submitting to, lack of control of such communications out of Brazil, a statement of the quotation from the report from Rome of the sinking of the *Queen*.

Added to this should be a statement that she actually is carrying 9,000 troops.[3]

Attention to details in MAGIC was often seen in Marshall's memoranda. However, the burden of his office weighed so heavily on him that he usually had time only to study the summaries.

As suggested earlier, not long after the Pearl Harbor attack it became apparent that the event had been foreshadowed in Japanese diplomatic traffic. The secretary of war, Henry Stimson, concluded that the MAGIC traffic should be studied more thoroughly and that the job could best be done by a lawyer with experience in handling and presenting large legal cases involving complicated facts. Alfred McCormack, a distinguished member of the New York bar, was therefore appointed special assistant to the secretary of war on 19 January 1942. Special Branch, MIS in the War Department, where McCormack served as a colonel, was assigned the task of following diplomatic material and evaluating it for intelligence purposes. McCormack also started to produce a daily summary of the messages instead of circulating the messages themselves.

The operations of Special Branch were severely handicapped at the outset. In particular, getting imaginative people of absolutely first-class ability and suitable training was extremely difficult in the pressing wartime conditions of 1942. By mid-1942, Special Branch had succeeded in assembling only twenty officers, one enlisted person, and eighteen civilians. Eight additional officers and thirty-seven more qualified civilians were found and employed in the MIS operation by early 1943.

By late 1942 the MAGIC Summary system became more reliable and sophisticated. In compiling the MAGIC Summary, Special Branch carefully prepared daily publications in which the most important information was gleaned from each day's batch of messages. This was to make essential information readily available to the people who needed it, without overwhelming them with the tremendous mass of daily intercepts. The summaries were not intended to offer editorial comment beyond the minimum necessary to identify a person, place, or situation with an appropriate backdrop or reference.

Creating the summaries was an involved process. Morale of Special Branch, MIS, personnel was high and the department had a reputation for hard work. Rank played no part, and it was not unusual for enlisted men and women to replace officers in particular jobs. Special Branch was in effect divided into sections concerned with either order of battle or diplomatic and related matters. Deciphered and translated messages from Arlington Hall Station were screened initially as they arrived in the Pentagon. They were then channeled to the appropriate area desk, and

> each message was accompanied by a notation: either "write" or "note." Messages marked "note" were read by the desk officer and then were placed in a file. Being aware of the content of these messages was extremely important because frequently the messages could only be understood in the light of previous messages. Messages marked "write" were written up by the desk officer and then presented to the editors [of the MAGIC summaries]. The writing could involve a good bit of work because obviously the messages translated in Arlington Hall would not be in the King's English and might well be un-understandable. Also, of course, there was a problem of what part of the message could properly be omitted. The object was to write a passage that could be quickly read and also would be understandable.[4]

Thus, such a digest was correlated with background information, earlier evaluations, and conclusions that specialists arrived at through systematic and coordinated study of large quantities of intercepts.[5]

Periodically the editors of MAGIC summaries would call for a major study on such topics as the effectiveness of the Japanese fishing industry or the amount of rice the Japanese exported from Korea. These special studies also required careful examination of the vast files of earlier messages and incorporated collateral sources (such as the *New York Times*). The War Department's Special Branch, taking what the cryptanalysts and translators sent from Arlington Hall Station, played a vital role in separating the wheat from the chaff.[6]

Remarkably sophisticated work in Japanese materials was done at Arlington Hall Station. One SSA (SIS before 1 July 1943) translator in B-1-D, Japanese diplomatic translation (B for B building, 1 for wing one, D for diplomatic messages) wrote that "the work was difficult and exciting—frightening is not too strong a word."[7] The Japanese language program for communications intelligence specialists was extensive and included historical and cultural dimensions with such excellent instructors as Edwin O. Reischauer.[8] There were also a few former missionaries who had lived in Japan, and by late 1942, after repatriation, they were serving as Japanese language instructors and translators at Arlington Hall. Among them was Andrew Nathaniel Nelson, who later published a distinguished Japanese *kanji* dictionary.[9] The "un-understandable" English that occurred sometimes in their translations was often the failure of some Special Branch intelligence officers to appreciate the uncertainties of the complex Japanese text of the deciphered messages. Moreover, few of the translators could genuinely master the Japanese language and all of its nuances.[10] Often the messages covered a wide variety of subjects, thus requiring their translators to master a very large vocabulary, and the Japanese authors were often classically educated and therefore composed their messages in a grammatical style that was extremely complex and difficult for American translators to understand. One student in 1943 in the SSA language program recalled recently that "there were intensive classes in grammar, reading, *kanji* study, conversation—day and night, indeed. We lived Japanese: saw Japanese movies, ate Japanese food at restaurants in Washington, studied Japanese economy and history."[11] The Japanese language students labored long hours to become more efficient and saw themselves as part of a team engaged in a grand international struggle to defeat fascism. Their practice translations were not of elementary textbooks but of crucial enemy communications, giving them a well-defined sense of mission and purpose.

One translator recalled that during the war he was working with John Hurt, who joined SIS in 1930. Hurt

> was going over one of my translations with me [when] we were interrupted by a messenger from A[rlington] H[all] Information & Liaison. Hurt read the note which was handed to him, turned to me, and said, "Will you please excuse me for a minute, corporal? I have to

answer a question for Mr. Churchill." Heady stuff for a then somewhat naive Midwesterner! (Churchill was in Washington consulting
with President Roosevelt at the time.)[12]

Another wartime Japanese-translator remembered "that when Churchill
was in Washington word would sometimes come to get out this or that message, perhaps to discuss with FDR or with other American leaders something that he had read at home."[13] Cryptanalysts and translators at Arlington Hall had ample evidence that in the daily drama of the war years
their work was receiving much attention in the highest councils of the Anglo-American governments. Thus, clearly the evaluation of MAGIC intelligence was not restricted to MIS; there is evidence that only the translators at
Arlington Hall, not the Special Branch intelligence officers in the Pentagon,
could answer certain questions.

It is clear that there was an elaborate procedure for processing information derived from Japanese Foreign Ministry ciphers before refined intelligence was available to the strategic managers of the war. The procedure was
intended to be swift, thorough, and safe, and to make MAGIC intelligence
available to high-ranking officials, but the material was so sensitive and security measures were so intricate that some people who needed the secret information for making decisions did not always receive it in a timely fashion.

As long as key officials who needed MAGIC intelligence were in Washington, D.C., or nearby, the handling of the special intelligence and its dissemination to the War Department, to certain other executive departments, and
to the president directly was routine and thought to be a reliable procedure.
However, the MAGIC trail leading to the president is difficult to document
completely.[14] MAGIC material was only loaned to the White House, and couriers usually retrieved it. The snippets of MAGIC material at the Hyde Park
Roosevelt Library, for example, are there by accident, although it is clear
that they have been declassified. The head of the navy's Op-20-G, Laurence
Safford, described the navy's distribution procedure in 1941:

> Lieut. Commander A. D. Kramer, USA, in command of my Trans-
> lating Section, segregated and cross-referenced all messages, and
> briefed the Director of Naval Communications (Rear Admiral Leigh
> Noyes), to the Director of Naval Intelligence (Rear Admiral T. S.
> Wilkinson), the Officer-in-Charge of Far Eastern Section ([Office of
> Naval Intelligence] ONI) (Commander A. H. McCollum), and the
> Assistant Chief of Naval Operations (Rear Admiral R. E. Ingersoll).
> Important messages were also shown to Director War Plans Division
> (Rear Admiral [Richmond K.] Turner). The most important mes-

sages, as designated by the Assistant C.N.O., were shown to the Chief of Naval Operations (Admiral H. R. Stark) and the Secretary of the Navy (the Honorable Frank Knox). The message files were then turned over complete to the Naval Aide to the President (Rear Admiral J. R. Beardall) who took them to President Roosevelt and returned them to Kramer. The Secretary of State (the Honorable Cordell Hull) and the Under Secretary of State (the Honorable Sumner Welles) were also shown these messages, Colonel [Rufus] Bratton, U.S. Army, being responsible for delivery. On one occasion the President read the Japanese Ambassador's secret report of a private audience with him. He was much impressed and commented, as he read the translation, "Yes, I said that"; "That is correct, he said that"; etc. I do not recall whether this was in Kramer's presence or told to Kramer by Admiral Beardall. After that, President Roosevelt never doubted our decryptions or translations.[15]

Summaries were frequently taken to the White House and there handed directly to Rear Admiral Wilson Brown, the president's naval aide since February 1943. They were soon picked up by an MIS courier and destroyed after Roosevelt had a chance to review them. By the beginning of 1944, Marshall had summaries bound daily in a "black book" for convenience of reading and for greater security in handling. Sometimes two or three of these books were produced by Special Branch in a single day. MAGIC summaries also received much attention in Marshall's morning staff meetings. The chief of staff meetings usually included General Henry H. Arnold, among other air officers, and always included Marshall's assistant chief of staff, Intelligence (G-2), Major General George V. Strong (March 1942—February 1944), and Major General Clayton L. Bissell, later in the war.[16]

In spite of elaborate preparations, the president had only limited access to MAGIC intelligence when he was away from Washington, as he so frequently was after 1942, and until 1944, this failure to distribute MAGIC intelligence speedily and completely was the Achilles' heel of the system. There was enormous concern at the highest levels of the U.S. wartime government for the safeguard of the MAGIC and ULTRA secrets. Soon after the Americans broke PURPLE, authorities in Washington started to provide the British with MAGIC intelligence, and in February 1941, two representative of SIS and two for Op-20-G visited Bletchley Park to give the British two PURPLE machines with current keys, plus the three-letter keying code, and techniques of solution.[17] Eventually, the British gave Washington new intelligence, with the special security classification ULTRA, which they obtained by breaking the German ENIGMA system. The British, however, sometimes felt that American security was not stringent enough, although Marshall and Ernest J. King were particularly sensitive to the problem of security. In 1944, Marshall wrote to Douglas MacArthur in Australia specifically about Japanese UL-TRA, the classification that Americans also applied by mid-1942 to information obtained from reading certain Japanese ciphers in the Pacific theater. Marshall explained that there "is the grave danger that the whole structure may collapse if a single blunder in the handling of ULTRA in any theater leads the enemy to suspect that his high-grade cryptographic systems are being read."[18] MacArthur (general headquarters, southwest Pacific area), in particular, was notoriously casual, especially from the navy's point of view, in protecting the ULTRA source.[19]

There were many infractions throughout the war that threatened the MAGIC-ULTRA secret. Less than a year after the Pearl Harbor attack Admiral King was outraged over the dangerous exposure of signal intelligence. He explained in a testy message to Admiral Chester W. Nimitz, commander in chief of the Pacific Fleet, that an "Associated Press release . . . dated Pearl Harbor, 15 September [1942] contains summary of carriers remaining in Jap[anese] navy. So far as is known here only possible source of this information is ULTRA. Investigate."[20] Similarly, there were stories appearing in such newspapers as the *Washington Times-Herald* and the *Chicago Tribune* that alarmed navy secretary Frank Knox. He recommended that indictments under the Espionage Act be obtained against the newspapers and certain correspondents.[21] Interior Secretary Harold L. Ickes suggested to the president, perhaps with tongue in cheek, that the ships carrying newsprint from paper mills in Canada to the *Chicago Tribune* "be requisitioned by the Army or the Navy" or perhaps the Canadian government could "be encouraged to shut off this news-print at the source, on the ground that when it gets to this country it is put to a use that is of aid and comfort to the enemy."[22] Under these circumstances army and navy authorities found it difficult to devise a system for the safe, thorough, and speedy distribution of MAGIC and ULTRA intelligence to the commander in chief and his party when they were abroad.[23]

By the time of the Casablanca Conference (code name SYMBOL), 14–23 January 1943, communication equipment intended for the president's use was reasonably sophisticated at the White House and in Casablanca. There were direct War Department—White House telephone and teletype printer circuits as well as identical communication equipment (an Electric Code Machine [ECM Mark II] produced by the Teletype Corporation in Chicago, a strip cipher, and a double transposition cipher system in the War Department and the White House. During Roosevelt's trips in the first half of 1943, messages intended for a specific person in the presidential party were enciphered in the Map Room and taken to the White House Telegraph Room. There they were sent by direct printer circuit to the War Department and thence to a prearranged point in the president's travel itinerary.[24] By this time there was also a Signal Corps railroad car included as part of the president's private train for travel within the United States. Moreover, additional radio links were established in Casablanca, running to London and other points in Africa, and the special radio channels carried 450 enciphered messages during the sixteen days the communication facilities were in operation for the conference.[25] As explained in the series *United States Army in World War II*, the Signal Corps had to provide unlimited communications facilities for the president and his party, frequently on short notice, so that they could maintain, with perfect security, "unbroken contact with their advisers at home and with their military commanders the world over."[26]

MAGIC Summaries were not normally inserted verbatim into messages sent to Roosevelt when he was out of the country, because the summaries frequently contained lengthy passages quoted directly from the original intercepts and would jeopardize the security of an American cryptographic system. Although snippets of MAGIC were sometimes sent to the president, the source of the information was disguised. The name "Colonel Boone" at the beginning of an enciphered message was used as a code term meaning that MAGIC was the source of the guarded language and abbreviated information that followed. Examples can be found among the president's communications when he was away from Washington during most of January 1943 for the Casablanca Conference. At that time the White House Map Room forwarded UTAH messages to the president's naval aide, Captain John L. McCrea, who gave them directly to Roosevelt. UTAH was McCrea's code name during the trip. (Messages for others associated with the trip had different code names; COOPER messages, for example, were intended specifically for Michael Reilly, head of the president's secret service protection detail. Messages were numbered serially throughout the trip.) Captain McCrea had received 106 ciphered messages during the journey to Casablanca when near the end of the conference trip he received UTAH 107 of 28 January 1943. It included an example of disguised MAGIC intelligence reported to the president: "From Colonel Boone XX Jap[anese] Ambassador Berlin imploring his government consider attack on Russia and at least effect closer war plans liaison with Germany."[27] This brief extract came from a six-page MAGIC Summary.[28]

However, the MAGIC source of information included in McCrea's UTAH messages was not always thoroughly concealed. Carelessness can be observed in UTAH 76 of 21 January 1943: "Colonel Boone's *magic* showed convoy leaving Truk to arrive Shortlands twenty-fourth."[29] In UTAH 53 of 17

January 1943, the Japanese source in Berlin was referred to as "Ambassador Yamaguchi in Berlin." Although part of the UTAH text of this message was within quotation marks, an examination of the original MAGIC intercept and the MAGIC Summary reveals that the passage was, in fact, paraphrased, not identical, and reproduced verbatim within the quotation marks, as once assumed.[30] Nevertheless, the source of the information in this particular UTAH message is easily discernible. These weaknesses or infractions were quickly detected; investigations were not infrequent and regulations were adjusted to make them more stringent and to tighten security. Reliable security arrangements for all of COMINT, not only MAGIC, were a recurring problem for MIS throughout the war, and it was always more acute amid the demands of presidential trips abroad.

Not only was the distribution of MAGIC intelligence important, but the contents of particular MAGIC messages from Ōshima late in 1943 were of special importance to Anglo-American strategic planning. At the time the western Allies were preparing to return to the Continent. To Churchill, in particular, Ōshima made a difference.

British strategic planners were more apprehensive about OVERLORD, the cover name of the plan for invasion of northwestern Europe, than were Pentagon planners. In particular, the British prime minister—perhaps because of memories of the carnage of frontal attacks during World War I, perhaps because of other motivations—emphasized a more predictable and less costly Mediterranean strategy over the anticipated hazards of a cross-Channel assault. London feared that Hitler's Atlantic Wall and his *Festung Europa* were indeed formidable. At the Casablanca Conference in January 1943, Churchill and Roosevelt agreed that it was impossible to launch OVERLORD that year, and they at least tacitly agreed that the cross-Channel operation would be launched in the spring of 1944. Indeed, at the TRIDENT Conference held in Washington five months after Casablanca, the British and Americans agreed on a target date of 1 May 1944.

The British outline plan for OVERLORD (125 pages) explained the decision for selecting the Caen area, between the River Orne and the base of the Cotentin Peninsula, as the best site for the landings. The outline also confirmed the findings of an earlier study that an attack on the Pas-de-Calais would be strategically unsound.[31] (In time Ōshima's messages revealed that the Pas-de-Calais was exactly the spot on the French coast where Hitler predicted the forthcoming Allied landings would occur.) Nevertheless, in the autumn of 1943 Churchill remained unenthusiastic about the coming of OVERLORD. At the Teheran Conference near the end of 1943, however, Stalin angrily insisted on a second front in western Europe, and the strong Soviet-American endorsement giving priority to OVERLORD assured primacy for the operation in the strategic planning of the Grand Alliance. Churchill yielded to his two powerful Allies, yet he knew that in "our supreme adventure in France . . . , terrific battles were to be expected, on a scale far greater than anything that we had experienced before."[32]

MAGIC information of great consequence in the early planning of OVER-LORD was being intercepted during the second week of November 1943, as Roosevelt and Churchill were leaving on the first leg of their long journeys for meetings with Chiang Kai-shek in Cairo and with Stalin in Teheran. (Roosevelt sailed from Hampton Roads, Virginia, shortly after midnight on 13 November in the new battleship *Iowa*—Churchill, in the World War I battle cruiser *Renown*, sailed from Plymouth on the afternoon of 12 November.) Ambassador Ōshima had recently completed a thorough inspection tour of German fortifications along the French coast, and on 9 November he started to radio a series of messages to Tokyo in which he described German defenses in detail. The full picture was not immediately clear when parts of the messages started to reach the U.S. Army's Signal Security Agency (SSA) during the evening of 11 November. Although other important pieces arrived within two days, the finishing touches were not available and integrated into Ōshima's long composite message until a month later, 9 December.

The Arlington Hall group was frequently called upon to handle important intercepts as quickly as possible. The cryptanalysts and translators were the first to recognize crucially important material as it started to reach their desks, and they responded with enthusiasm. Ōshima's Atlantic Wall inspection messages reaching Arlington Hall Station in late 1943 created an enormous stir. A veteran translator recalls that occasion. He

> was on duty when that report on the inspection trip began to come in from the signal corps intercept stations around the world. . . . When I picked up the first intercept, I was not sure what I had because it was not part one. But within a few hours as . . . [more] of the message came in the magnitude of what was in hand was apparent. I could scarcely contain my excitement, but working, as I was, late at night, it was not until morning that my superior officers, alerted by me, alerted in turn the appropriate "higher headquarters"—Special Branch in the Pentagon . . . and, I was told, General Marshall's office and the Map Room at the White House headed by Admiral William Leahy. I remained on duty throughout much of the day, continuing to translate along with colleagues who pitched in to complete the work. (I was too electrified to go to sleep!) In the end we produced what was veritably a pamphlet, an on-the-ground description

of the north French defenses of "Festung Europa," composed *dictu mirabile* by a general.[33]

The general, Ambassador Ōshima, compiled a notable set of plans of Hitler's Atlantic Wall. Various cryptanalysts and translators at Arlington Hall saw Ōshima's message, as did Colonel Carter W. Clarke, chief of Special Branch, MIS, and his deputy chief, Colonel McCormack. But Ōshima's virtual blueprint was not available before President Roosevelt left the country, taking with him a large entourage of the highest ranking military officers and strategic planners for work at the Cairo and Teheran Conferences.

The president left the White House at about nine-thirty on the evening of 11 November and proceeded in an automobile cavalcade to Quantico where the party boarded the presidential yacht *Potomac*. Besides the president, his immediate party included Harry Hopkins, Rear Admiral Wilson Brown (naval aide), Major General Edwin M. Watson, Rear Admiral Ross McIntire (surgeon general), and Admiral William D. Leahy, chief of staff to the commander in chief. The yacht sailed to the mouth of the Potomac River and into the Chesapeake Bay, where the next morning the party boarded the newly commissioned USS *Iowa*, commanded by Captain John L. McCrea, former naval aide to the president. Some sixty officers in the joint staff organization were already aboard, and U.S. chiefs of staff Generals Marshall and Henry H. Arnold and Admiral Ernest J. King sailed down the Potomac on King's flagship, the gunboat *Dauntless* (PG-61), some ten hours ahead of the president.

Security was particularly tight for the president's trip to the Cairo (code named SEXTANT) and Teheran (EUREKA) conferences because of newfound concerns over the security of MAGIC. Moreover, Roosevelt and his party were well within enemy striking range, and it was known that earlier the Germans had penetrated some American ciphers. While steaming eastward in the *Iowa* in late 1943, Leahy kept a journal in which he noted that "the Nazis apparently were completely unaware of the prize target now within range of their planes as well as their U-boats. Conceivably the course of the war might have been changed if the enemy could have . . . killed the president." During the return trip, on a side trip to Malta, Leahy recorded that "we all felt that if the Germans knew of this particular flight they would make a desperate effort to shoot down the president of the United States."[34]

Leahy remembered that North Africa was a hotbed for intrigue and espionage, and, in particular, that the previous year Lieutenant General William H. E. Gott was killed in North Africa. Gott was flying in an unescorted Bristol Bombay transport aircraft, preparing to assume command of the British Eighth Army, when he was ambushed by six Messerschmitt 109f fighter planes between Alexandria and El Alamein on 7 August 1942.[35] Moreover, Leahy, Marshall, and some others in the president's Cairo-Teheran party were painfully aware of the fact that in 1941 the Germans had obtained the Black Code and superenciOLpherment tables used by American military attachés. Thus, the American military attaché in Cairo, Colonel Frank Bonner Fellers, to whom the British had freely given secret military information, inadvertently informed the Germans of important British secrets. His encrypted reports to Washington were intercepted and teletyped to Berlin, where the information was decrypted, translated, and sent back to Erwin Rommel's field headquarters in North Africa—sometimes within a few hours of the original message. A specialist on the history of cryptography, David Kahn, has estimated that Fellers's intercepted messages "provided Rommel with undoubtedly the broadest and clearest picture of enemy forces and intentions available to any Axis commander throughout the whole war."[36] (Nevertheless, Fellers's revelations were relatively modest from late 1941 to July 1942 when compared to Ōshima's revelations about the Axis forces in Europe from February 1941 until the German surrender in 1945.) Shortly before Gott was killed, Fellers was recalled to Washington and the American code was changed.[37]

Evidence to date suggesting that the Germans knew in advance of Gott's flight and that the encounter was calculated is not conclusive. However, the Germans could have learned a lot because Eighth Army cipher systems were slow and clumsy, untrained communication staffs were employed, and plain if guarded language was used at times. Nevertheless, increased radio traffic frequently associated with the travel of VIPs might have alerted the Germans, for the route along which Gott was shot down was considered to be so safe that no fighter escort had been provided for Churchill's plane when he flew safely along the same route two days earlier.[38] Thus, no escort was thought to be necessary for Gott.

When Admiral Leahy originally recorded his fears in December 1943 that the president could be shot down, he was also mindful that nine months earlier Admiral Yamamoto Isoroku, commander in chief of the Japanese Combined Fleet, was shot down and killed by American aircraft, an operation possible only because Japanese encrypted communications were being read by U.S. Navy cryptographers. Japanese encrypted radio messages detailing Yamamoto's flight path and itinerary to Bougainville, within range of U.S. Army fighter planes on Guadalcanal, were intercepted by the Combat Intelligence Unit at Pearl Harbor four days before Yamamoto's flight. Leahy obviously knew about the targeted kill of Yamamoto; indeed, Roosevelt personally approved the ambush beforehand and sent congratulations to the successful American pilots afterwards.[39] There was considerable fear that the intercept of Yamamoto's plane would alert the Japanese to the danger that their signal communications were insecure. In the aftermath of the Yamamoto affair, American handling of high-grade cipher intelligence vacillated between dangerous exposure of MAGIC-ULTRA in the Pacific theater and over-restrictive distribution of it elsewhere.[40]

These anxieties about security heightened concern about communications with the presidential party in late 1943. Control of communications was highly centralized for the Cairo-Teheran trip, and the president's naval aide outlined procedure for the director of naval communications the day before the party left Washington in November.

> During his absence from the city the President directs that any radio despatches for him sent by Naval Communications shall first be cleared through the White House Map Room (Colonel L. Mathewson, U.S.A., in charge). The purpose of these instructions is to control the amount of radio traffic sent to the President through a single agency. Colonel Mathewson has been given authority to decide what shall be sent by radio and what shall be sent by pouch.[41]

The procedure and communications equipment were much more elaborate for the Cairo-Teheran conferences than for the Casablanca Conference eleven months earlier. Indeed, while Roosevelt was on the presidential yacht *Potomac* for the brief cruises to and from the *Iowa*, at the beginning and end of his 17,442-mile journey, a navy lieutenant accompanied him to decipher messages from the White House Map Room. The state-of-the-art cipher machine used aboard the *Potomac* was the navy ECM Mark II system, introduced in 1940 and used throughout the decade. White House instructions of 11 November 1943 were explicit. The following cipher system publications were detailed for use during the presidential yacht leg of the journey:

> Navy Presidential wheels 1471
> ECM key list 1149(C)
> Operating instruction for ECM-1100(B)
> Rotating external indicators will be used on every message as indicated in Rotating Indicator List 1465(U)[42]

The sophisticated navy ECM Mark II system was also used while the president was aboard *Iowa*, which dropped Roosevelt and his party off at Oran, Algeria, and picked them up again nineteen days later at Dakar. But in spite of elaborate communications facilities, White House instructions emphasized that excessive communications could endanger the safety of the presidential party.

Traffic must be held to the minimum and no messages are to be sent by any individual, agency or department of the Government until they have been released by the White House Map Room [Colonel Mathewson]. . . .

The Map Room will send to the President only messages from the Prime Minister, Marshal Stalin and Generalissimo Chiang Kai-shek and urgent government business. . . .

Traffic must be held to the absolute minimum. . . .

Duplication of information should be avoided as the information of any one passenger will be made available to all passengers. The Navy expects that they will be able to transmit all essential information to Naval Commands in less than one hundred (100) words daily. While facilities exist for a far greater load, the safety of the party will be unduly jeopardized by too long transmissions. . . .

Traffic to Army commands embarked [on the *Iowa*] should be transmitted in Navy [cipher] system to prevent disclosure of Army personnel on a Navy ship. . . .

The ship will not break Radio Silence except in a real emergency.[43]

Similar precautions were adhered to when the army assumed responsibility for the transmission of all messages after the presidential party disembarked in North Africa.

Efforts to centralize communications in the White House Map Room and to reduce traffic proved effective. Colonel Mathewson held the rein tightly and cipher communication with the president was not as extensive on the Cairo-Teheran trip as it was during the earlier and considerably shorter Casablanca trip. An example is found in the traffic of Roosevelt's naval aides, who usually received ciphered messages intended for the president. Indeed, a tabulation of the Map Room—naval aide communications reveals that Captain McCrea received an average of 5.1 messages daily during the Casablanca trip and Rear Admiral Brown's daily messages averaged 3.7 during the Cairo-Teheran trip.

There exists a surprisingly complete outline of communications with the presidential party during the trip to Cairo and Teheran. Map Room outgoing messages were numbered serially and used the word WHITE, and messages originating with Roosevelt and members of his party were called BLACK and also numbered serially. The serial numbers were enciphered within the text of the messages, and code words were used for the names of people and places associated with the conferences. For example:

Almond	Chiang Kai-shek
Apple	Admiral King
Beech, Maple, or Spruce	the President
Bear	Moscow
Camel	Cairo
Cedar	Admiral Leahy
Cherry	General Arnold
Dog	Casablanca
Hickory	USS *Potomac*
Holly	USS *Iowa*
Lime	General Eisenhower
Lion	Washington, D.C.
Locust	Map Room
Mouse	Teheran
Peach	General Marshall
Plum	Prime Minister Churchill
Pony	Norfolk, Virginia
Poplar	Captain McCrea
Redwood	Premier Stalin
Tiger	London
Walnut	Admiral Brown

Thirty-five additional code words were included on the list, of which there were only four copies.[44]

No evidence has been found in the Roosevelt Library to substantiate the possibility that the president had any reliable knowledge of Ōshima's inspection of Hitler's Atlantic Wall while Roosevelt was on the Cairo-Teheran trip, and it appears unlikely that he learned about it until later. Unlike communications during the Casablanca trip, the president's messages in November and December 1943 contain no Colonel Boone type of phrases to disguise information derived from MAGIC. Nor has any reference to Ōshima's inspection been found in the WHITE or BLACK messages.

It also seems that couriers did not take Ōshima's full inspection report to the president while he was abroad. Unlike earlier arrangements for the Casablanca Conference, a detailed courier service was established on 9 November to reach Cairo during the November and December conferences. Material intended to go in the pouch for the presidential party was delivered to the secretary of the Combined Chiefs of Staff in the Public Health Building or to the War Department Classified Message Center in the Pentagon. Colonel Mathewson iterated the pervasive concern for security in the first pouch of

14 November: "I have deliberately refrained from putting these Prime [Minister?] messages on the air for reasons which I believe to be sound. Thinking it well however to have them in the President's hands as soon as you reach Oran I have arranged to have this first pouch meet you there. Subsequent pouches will of course proceed direct to Cairo as prearranged."[45]

The first pouch reached the presidential party on 20 November when the *Iowa* arrived off Oran. There were ten additional pouches, the last of which was made up on 14 December and taken aboard the USS *Potomac* for the rendezvous with the president two days later. Shortly before the rendezvous the president recorded in his personal handwritten diary that "the little 'Potomac' has loomed 6 miles ahead at the mouth of the River and at 4:30 I will transfer to her. . . . And tomorrow we should get to the Navy Yard in Washington at 9:30 & soon afterwards I will be at the W.H. & using the telephone. So will end a new Odyssey."[46]

However, on 16 December the president was given the blueprint to Hitler's fortifications along the northern French coast. Just sixteen days earlier Roosevelt had written in his diary: "The conferences have been going well—tho' I found I had to go along with the Russians on military plans. This morning the British came along too, to my great relief." German defenses were discussed extensively, and Roosevelt agreed with Stalin that the invasion could be launched successfully in the spring of 1944. The president was not altogether comfortable with his decision, but near the end of his journey he found the linchpin to his Odyssey waiting for him in the Map Room pouch aboard the *Potomac*.

The lists of contents for the Map Room pouches did not usually identify the contents in detail, and there was no specific reference to MAGIC intelligence in the lists. Nevertheless, the evidence is clear that the president received Ōshima's inspection report. There were seventy-four pieces of mail carried by the courier service, many of them personal letters for various members of the presidential party or items requiring Roosevelt's attention, such as court martial cases, changes recommended in U.S. Navy regulations, and, in one instance, a recommendation of the Legion of Merit for a Brazilian naval officer.

The president was probably aware that Ōshima had made a trip along the French coast. In one of the earlier pouches a MAGIC-based summary dated 22 November 1943 included a fleeting reference: "On his trip along the French coast Ōshima also witnessed two German blockade runners about to depart from the vicinity of Bordeaux."[47] Ōshima was cited by name in another context in this thirteen-page summary, but no additional information about the inspection tour was included in this document. However, a cover sheet attached to the summary indicates that Roosevelt received the actual reports, not just the summaries. A memorandum from Major Frank T. Hurley to one Captain Freseman—on stationery with a War Department General Staff letterhead—stated explicitly that General Marshall had requested that Hurley deliver the attached MAGIC *reports* for the information of the president and Admiral Leahy.[48] Marshall was with the presidential party at this time; thus, it is possible that he had left standing instructions in the Pentagon to have such MAGIC-based special summaries, not the usual daily MAGIC summaries, forwarded to Roosevelt.

Ōshima's sixteen-page report and some additional intelligence material were addressed directly to the president and included in the final pouch. The MAGIC envelope in Map Room Leather Pouch Number 11 was listed as a "Brown Manila Envelope Addressed to the President from War Department, Office of the Chief of Staff, Washington." Thus, Ōshima's report finally made its way into the hands of the president.

Since this was the first pouch of mail the party had received since leaving Africa on 9 December, the president was very busy reading of new matters after his transfer from the *Iowa* to the presidential yacht late on the afternoon of 16 December. The log of the trip kept by a navy lieutenant of the presidential party read simply: "7:00 P.M. The president worked on official mail that had been brought down via the *Potomac* by Lieutenant (jg) R. H. Myers, U.S.N.R. (Map Room watch officer). There were no Congressional matters included in this mail."[49] It is clear, therefore, that Roosevelt did not see the results of Ōshima's inspection until after the evidence had been in the hands of other American authorities for some thirty-five days. Ironically, in a technical sense he had been close to major portions of Ōshima's messages initially when his motorcade was en route to Quantico to meet the USS *Potomac* on the evening of 11 November. At that time the president and his top advisers passed close to Arlington Hall Station, where cryptanalysts were working on Ōshima's intercepts, and still closer to the Pentagon.

The evening before the *Potomac* docked at the Washington navy yard at 8:50 the following morning, Roosevelt read Ōshima's complete report and then attached the following note, which a White House secretary soon typed for the file: "Show the attached to Admiral Leahy and ask him to return it to Admiral Brown for file when he has finished with it. F. D. R."[50] Admiral Leahy signed his initials ("WDL") on the first page of Ōshima's report and again on Roosevelt's covering memorandum; Rear Admiral Brown wrote only on the memorandum, "File WB."

Nine days earlier Roosevelt left Churchill in Cairo on 7 December, and the next day the prime minister received from a courier the British summary of Ōshima's inspection reports, "MI 14 Report on the Visit of the Japanese Ambassador in Berlin to the German Defences in France."[51] British Military

Intelligence evaluated the Japanese ambassador's report (MI 14 did not mention Ōshima by name) as "a reasoned and well considered document." Churchill, fresh from extensive debates with Roosevelt and Stalin on the feasibility of OVERLORD in the following spring, recognized immediately the significance of Ōshima's intercepted messages. With a copy of the blueprint of Hitler's coastal fortifications in hand, Churchill must have felt reassured about his earlier decision to go along with his ally and friend, Roosevelt. The decision for the cross-Channel invasion in 1944 took on new promise for Churchill. Therefore, as substantiated in the British official history, on 8 December an optimistic Churchill instructed his intelligence people to make certain that Ōshima's report was "shown to the president" as soon as possible (not until 16 December, as it turned out).[52]

On the volition of Marshall's G-2 staff one might assume that Ōshima's inspection report would have been forwarded under any circumstances to the president. Yet, Colonel Mathewson was in charge, and he clearly decided otherwise. Furthermore, Ōshima's full report was not available in Washington until near the time the president was scheduled to start his return trip. It is clear that British Military Intelligence was initially responsible for getting the report into the president's hands, a fact confirmed on the American side. The routing and work sheet addressed to the chief, Signal Security Agency on 14 December 1943 contains the following note:

> 1. On Saturday, 11 December, Lt. Compton, speaking for Special Branch, advised the undersigned [Lieutenant Colonel Earle F. Cook] that the Prime Minister had requested that messages SSA 101671, 101709, and 104453, of which copies are appended hereto [see Appendix 1], should be presented to the President of the United States.
>
> 2. This information on the copies of messages is furnished in view of the fact that the request from the Prime Minister represents the attachment of considerable importance to these translations.[53]

In spite of Colonel Cook's convoluted writing, he recognized the importance of Ōshima's report, if only because of Churchill's keen interest.

There is good reason to believe that an unusually large number of military officers studied Ōshima's report very carefully after the president passed the material to Admirals Leahy and Brown. It is commonplace in the armed services for efficient officers to study documents that they know their superiors have seen and initialed. Ōshima's report was, in fact, destined to become a hallmark in the planning for OVERLORD.

Some indication of the nature and scope of Ōshima's inspection is appropriate here, although a more thoroughgoing discussion appears in Chapter 6. It is likely that Ōshima expressed interest in the German defense installations, thus Hitler authorized an inspection tour. Ambassador Ōshima, usually in the uniform of a lieutenant general with service ribbons, frequently inspected and visited German military forces. During his inspection tour of German defenses on the Atlantic coast of France between 24 October and 1 November 1943, Ōshima was accompanied by embassy secretaries Uchida Fujio and Ushiba Nobuhiko as well as an assistant military attaché, Lieutenant Colonel Nishi Hisashi, a highly capable liaison officer to the German supreme command, the Oberkommando der Wehrmacht (OKW). Ōshima's visit focused on defenses within the Brest-Bordeaux-Paris triangle, but the Japanese warrior/diplomat discussed the whole gamut of defense preparations with various German general officers, including Supreme Commander West, Field Marshal Gerd von Rundstedt. And Rundstedt's chief of staff, Lieutenant General Günther Blumentritt, gave Ōshima a detailed briefing on German defenses from the Netherlands to the French Mediterranean coast.[54] Ōshima's report to Tokyo included the order of battle of all German armies engaged in coastal defense. According to a prominent historian of British wartime intelligence, who as a Cambridge University undergraduate in 1941 was recruited as a cryptanalyst by the Government Code and Cypher School at Bletchley Park, the first comprehensive decrypt to throw direct light on German preparations to defend the French coast came in "a telegram from the Japanese Ambassador in Berlin following a tour of the defences in October."[55]

Anglo-American cryptanalysts discovered confirmation of Ōshima's estimates in the description of the Atlantic Wall by Colonel Itō Seiichi, a Japanese military attaché attached to the headquarters of the German OKW West. Japanese military attaché cipher systems were solved by November 1943 when Itō's report to his military superiors in Tokyo was intercepted.[56]

Of considerable interest to Churchill were the forces of the Seventh Army defending the long coastline from the River Seine to the Loire, including the Normandy beaches. Ōshima reported that there were only eight divisions in Colonel-General Friedrich Dollmann's Seventh Army, most of which were understrength. Churchill was especially interested in the German ability to reinforce fixed coastal divisions, and Ōshima provided him with a reliable estimate. Such reinforcements were mobile divisions that were part of the general reserve. "Divisions from the general reserve were dispatched to the Eastern Front," Ōshima declared. The number varies according to circumstances, Ōshima explained, but in November 1943 the Germans had fifteen mobile divisions available—six infantry, four armored, and five mechanized. About nine additional divisions could be sent in the event of an Anglo-American landing, but they were mostly in training and understrength.

At Teheran, little more than a week before reading Ōshima's report, Churchill explained to Stalin the minimum conditions under which OVERLORD could be launched: "There should not be more than 12 mobile German divisions behind the coastal troops and . . . German reinforcements for sixty days should not exceed 15 divisions."[57] Although Ōshima's information made OVERLORD seem more feasible to Churchill, the margins remained very tight. It did help that Stalin promised to time his general offensive along the eastern front to coincide with Anglo-American landings in France. Thus German forces could not be easily transferred to the western front. The western Allies had six months to prepare for OVERLORD while they enjoyed the assurance of continued Soviet pressure from the east and knowledge of the status of German defense preparations.

Ōshima and other members of his embassy staff inadvertently provided Arlington Hall Station and MIS with updated information. Embassy attachés made at least one additional inspection of Hitler's Atlantic Wall before June 1944, and they sent annexes to Tokyo in military codes and ciphers that were also being read by Anglo-American cryptanalysts.[58] Similarly, several of Ōshima's messages to Tokyo in the first five months of 1944 further discussed German preparations. A postwar MIS study concluded that the principal intelligence contributions obtained from diplomatic ULTRA and reported in the MAGIC Summary included (1) the "detailed reports of Japanese officials in Europe who made inspection trips through German coastal defenses in France," and (2) "accounts of German strategy before and after the June 1944 landings, as outlined to Japanese officials by Hitler, Ribbentrop and various Wehrmacht and Foreign Office officials."[59]

The margin for success on the Normandy beaches was narrow, but MAGIC and Anglo-American cooperation made the difference. The hazards to the security of signal communications as well as the importance of signal intelligence received enormous attention throughout World War II, perhaps a legacy of the surprise and disaster of 1941. The Pearl Harbor attack came when American cryptanalysts were reading some of Japan's ciphers with reasonable accuracy and speed but still trying to break other systems. Congressional, army, and navy investigations into the Pearl Harbor warning and decision continued through much of the war, and also there was always the haunting question concerning the security of one's own national ciphers. Even the most trusted of American allies, the British, were not allowed to operate the U.S. Navy ECM Mark II system or the U.S. Army equivalent, SIGABA. (Adaptors were developed so that messages could be exchanged in cipher between the American ECM-SIGABA units and British TYPEX electric cipher machines.) At the same time, encrypted enemy messages were yielding increasingly vital information. Clearly, then, in the Anglo-American conduct of the war a quicker and less costly Allied victory depended on full cooperation of U.S. cryptanalytic services with Bletchley Park and the continuous flow of MAGIC and ULTRA intelligence to Anglo-American armed forces. Churchill was correct, OVERLORD was carried out by a very narrow margin, but MAGIC was essential to its success.[60]

6
The MAGIC of OVERLORD and the Surprise of the Ardennes

A combination of unusual circumstances kept Ōshima's inspection reports of late 1943 out of the hands of key Allied military commanders. The reports, because they were specific in content, pertinent to Allied planning, and extremely timely, were one of Ōshima's most significant contributions to the Allied side. News of Ōshima's inspection of a considerable portion of the Atlantic Wall and of German defense plans (see Appendix 1) arrived in Washington and London not long after Allied leaders at the Quebec Conference (August 1943) had approved the choice of western Normandy as the site for invasion. Ōshima's reports were a great intelligence windfall for the Allies as they entered the second stage of planning for the largest amphibious operation ever undertaken, and there was a great possibility that future intercepted messages would contain updates. Dwight D. Eisenhower, whom the president, while he was still in Cairo in early December 1943, had named supreme allied commander, took early stock of Ōshima's inspection reports when he first learned of them, probably during a meeting with Churchill at the end of 1943.

A reconstruction of the travel itineraries of key Anglo-American leaders suggests that both the president and Eisenhower learned of the reports before the chief of staff, but Churchill was the first, as discussed in the previous chapter. Marshall, who wanted to visit MacArthur in the southwest Pacific, quietly left the presidential party in Cairo, flying secretly to Ceylon and Port Moresby, around the globe, and arriving back in the United States shortly before Christmas.[1] Like the president when he was en route home from the Cairo and Teheran conferences and to protect the security of MAGIC, Marshall was not one of the first to see Ōshima's Atlantic Wall inspection reports, although obviously his G-2 staff in Washington was. But it was Marshall who acted swiftly and decisively once he had the blueprint of Hitler's coastal fortifications before him.

Marshall immediately summoned Eisenhower, who at first seemed annoyed by the urgent entreaty. Writing in his wartime memoirs published three decades before the declassification of ULTRA and MAGIC materials, Eisenhower complained that while he was hard at work making detailed preparations to leave his post as commander in chief, Allied Force Headquarters in the Mediterranean, and to go to England around 10 January to assume command of OVERLORD,

> I received a Christmas telegram from General Marshall. He urged me to come immediately to Washington for short conferences with him and the president . . . before undertaking the new assignment. I protested, on the ground that time was vital and that, moreover, I could accomplish little by a visit to Washington until I had been in London at least long enough to familiarize myself with the essentials of the problems there. General Marshall did not agree. He advised me to "allow someone else to run the war for twenty minutes," and to come on to Washington. Strictly speaking, my commanders were the Combined Chiefs of Staff but, realizing General Marshall's earnestness in the matter, I quickly cleared the point with the British side of the house and made ready to leave for the United States.[2]

Eisenhower wrote to General Walter Bedell Smith on 30 December that "the insistance from the War Department that I go to the United States is so great that I must make the trip."[3] Marshall then said that he was "delighted" Eisenhower was returning. Presumably the Combined Chiefs of Staff knew about Ōshima's reports and, no doubt, would have informed Eisenhower after the supreme Allied commander arrived in London. It is also likely that Marshall knew about Churchill's instructions to his intelligence people to make certain Roosevelt personally saw Ōshima's startling material, but that was no assurance that Eisenhower would be given the full COMINT picture as soon as Marshall thought necessary or as he specifically wanted explained to Eisenhower.

Churchill seized the opportunity, in spite of his illness and exhaustion, to confer privately with Eisenhower before the supreme commander's return to Washington. In response to Churchill's urgent message to meet him in Marrakech, Morocco, where the prime minister was recuperating, Eisenhower joined him on the afternoon of 31 December. Their conference lasted several hours, and Eisenhower did not leave until shortly before 5:00 A.M. on New Year's Day, flying to the Azores, then to Bermuda, and arriving safely in

Washington shortly after 1:00 the next morning. It was a long and grueling flight, but within hours, early in the afternoon, Eisenhower was off to see Marshall at the War Department.

Churchill discussed many issues with Eisenhower to which the general could later refer publicly in his memoirs—the Anzio operation and questions concerning command structure in the Mediterranean, for example. Of course, Eisenhower was not permitted to refer to MAGIC or ULTRA in his wartime memoirs published in 1948. Nevertheless, Eisenhower clearly knew about Ōshima's inspection tour, and it is likely that Churchill apprised him.

The prime minister took much delight in telling select people about Allied success in solving enemy cipher systems, and in late June 1942, Churchill was the first to tell Eisenhower about the ULTRA secret.[4] Churchill was reasonably certain that Eisenhower did not know about Ōshima's reports by the end of December, for on the strict "need to know" criterion there was no reason why Eisenhower should have seen them.

It is likely that Ōshima's crucial reports were not only at the heart of Churchill's urgent message for a conference at Marrakech, but they were equally important in Marshall's urgent Christmas telegram to Eisenhower. Undoubtedly there were other important matters to be discussed, otherwise, Eisenhower's rejoinder—that he be allowed a little time in London, before visiting Washington, to familiarize himself with problems there—would have been persuasive to Marshall.[5]

On 2 January 1944, Eisenhower met Marshall and very likely discussed Ōshima's revelations in strategy conferences with chief of staff and G-2 staff officers in the Pentagon.[6] It was immediately clear that Ōshima had a good understanding of the larger picture of the German defense scheme and could report with confidence about the completeness of German preparations and plans for reinforcement. In spite of the fact that Ōshima had not visited the specific fifty-mile stretch of coast intended for invasion, the Caen-Cotentin area from the River Orne well into the Cotentin Peninsula, his impressions and views and the details of his actual tour gave Anglo-American planners a new perspective for working on the task before them. When Eisenhower arrived in England to assume command in mid-January, Ōshima's material served as an effective backdrop for updating, revising, and confirming estimates in Plan OVERLORD of July 1943.

Ōshima confirmed several earlier Allied estimates. In early 1943 Allied intelligence had estimated that the Atlantic Wall fortifications and troop disposition were particularly strong in the area of the Strait of Dover. Ōshima confirmed this. Eisenhower and his staff were also reassured by the news that the Germans continued to believe that the Pas de Calais would ultimately be the main site of the invasion. Any landing elsewhere, including the Caen-Cotentin area in western Normandy, would be a feint, Ōshima reported. Thus, units of the German Fifteenth Army focused on the defense of Calais were not to be diverted and used as reinforcements to smash Allied landings on the Normandy beaches. Intercepts of Ōshima's messages for the next five months continued to confirm this aspect of German defense strategy.

Ōshima also gave Allied intelligence analysts cause to rethink their earlier estimates. Ōshima cited thirty-one German coastal defense divisions while contemporary British intelligence, MI 14, estimated that there were twenty-eight divisions plus two unidentified divisions.[7] Similarly, MI 14 believed that 26 percent of the coastal defense divisions were at full strength with three regiments each; Ōshima claimed 33 percent. However, taking a cue from Ōshima's report that the other divisions were being brought up to full strength, MI 14, having investigated the matter more closely, admitted "there is some indication that personnel are being provided to form the third regt."[8]

A few claims in the report were discounted by the Allies, not on the assumption that the Germans were deliberately giving Ōshima false information, but because they thought he perhaps misunderstood his German guides. It was also possible that inaccuracies occurred in the reports during the elaborate process of encipherment, interception, and deciphering; transmission around the globe; or preparation of the final versions in English of Ōshima's original Japanese words. In one part of Ōshima's reports American analysts deleted a paragraph concerning the alleged authority of the German naval command over army batteries because the transmission was garbled and so imperfect that the accuracy of the translation could not be guaranteed. In another instance British intelligence believed that the immediate transfer of two airborne divisions from Italy was unlikely and that Ōshima probably erred in his reference to automatic grenade throwers with a firing rate of 120 rounds per minute. Nevertheless, MI 14 was convinced that Ōshima's report was "a reasoned and well considered document."[9]

Other aspects of Ōshima's reports helped Eisenhower and OVERLORD planners to develop a clearer picture of German defense measures and of what sort of conditions the D-Day assault forces were likely to encounter. Eisenhower, writing publicly of the planning for OVERLORD after his arrival in England on 14 January 1944, made several oblique references to the wealth of information he had about German preparations to defend the French coast against an Allied invasion.[10]

There is a remarkable similarity between some of Ōshima's summary remarks in Appendix 1 and an official history (*Omaha Beachhead, 6 June–13*

June 1944) published originally by the War Department in September 1945. Ōshima reported the following on 10 November 1943:

> All the German fortifications on the French coast are very close to the shore and it is quite clear that the Germans plan to smash any enemy attempt to land as close to the edge of the water as possible. . . . Were the enemy successful in making a partial landing, crossfire from mutually supporting defense posts and the appearance of mobile forces would annihilate the invaders. This scheme of lateral firepower and mobile units is the basic concept behind Germany's defense in the West. . . . Camouflaging has been carried out very thoroughly. . . . The important feature of the defense lines is that they are not arranged in one continuous and connected line but are arranged to enable even the smallest unit to operate independently. In other areas strongpoints have been constructed in large numbers all along the coast, the gaps between these strongpoints being closed by obstacles (mainly land mines). Each strongpoint is equipped with various types of arms . . . , [but] the principal feature of these weapons is that they all can be concentrated to fire on one object at the same time, whether at sea or on land.

The U.S. Army official history, prepared in part in the field by a historical unit attached to the First Army and published only fifteen months after the Normandy landings, confirmed generally the accuracy of Ōshima's report.

> Enemy firing positions were laid out to cover the tidal flat and beach shelf with direct fire, both plunging and grazing, from all types of weapons. Observation on the whole Omaha area, and flanking fire from cliff positions at either end, were aided by the crescent curve of the shore line. . . . Each strongpoint was a complex system made up of elements including pillboxes, gun casemates, open positions for light guns, and firing trenches, surrounded by minefields and wire. . . . The heavier guns were sited to give lateral fire along the beach, with traverse limited by thick concrete wing-walls which concealed the flash of these guns and made them hard to spot from the sea.[11]

The elaborate preparations made by the Germans caused Allied planners to rely heavily on deception operations. Indeed, the July 1943 proposal for Operation OVERLORD stated that "in order to contain the maximum German forces away from the Caen area diversionary operations should be staged against other areas such as the Pas de Calais and the Mediterranean Coast of France."[12]

By late 1943, Ōshima provided evidence that the Germans remained confident that Calais would be the site, but the Allies remained fearful that their various deception operations would not always be convincing to the Germans and that the Caen-Cotentin sector in Normandy would somehow replace Calais in German preparations for invasion.[13] Reports from commando forays on the French coast or from the French Resistance and secret agents were of some assistance. So was aerial reconnaissance. The Ōshima connection, however, was much more reliable for the early detection of any sudden change in German strategic thinking in preparation for the invasion. Unlike any of the other sources, Ōshima had direct access to the top German military leaders, including Hitler himself.

Ōshima was always greatly concerned about German military problems and frequently involved himself by taking sides in debates or offering opinions. In this instance he was an early supporter of the idea that the main landing would be in the Pas de Calais. Before Roosevelt saw the full inspection report, Ōshima met with Ribbentrop to thank him for helping to arrange the recent tour. During their ensuing conversation Ōshima hypothesized on 8 December that the Anglo-Americans would not "start right off the bat by making such an invasion across the difficult English Channel." Rather, they would first "establish a bridgehead on the Normandie or Bretagne peninsula. If they did this," Ōshima continued, "they could say they were fulfilling their promise to Russia and if they succeeded they could then attempt a full-fledged expedition over . . . the English Channel."[14]

Seven weeks later, in another conversation between these two longtime associates, Ribbentrop seems to have taken at least part of Ōshima's earlier hypothesis and introduced it as an idea of his own. (Ribbentrop frequently used this procedure to win Hitler's favor, Gordon Craig has written, and the technique "was to be the foundation stone of his career.")[15] Ribbentrop said to Ōshima on 23 January: "Doesn't it look like the appointment of Eisenhower, etc., and all this boastful propaganda is a kind of camouflage? Still, in view of their relationship with Russia, England and America can't get away without doing anything at all. Even though it be not a large invasion, I think they will have to carry out one that they may call, in their propaganda, a second front."[16] The same day Hitler told Ōshima during a private meeting that "beyond any doubt the most effective area [for the main landing] would be the Strait of Dover," but such a difficult landing would be postponed because the enemy was not strong enough. "On the other hand, along the Bordeaux coast and in Portugal the defenses are relatively weak, so this zone might be a possibility."[17]

Ōshima did not meet again with Hitler for several months after January, thus his reports were usually less specific about the invasion than previously. Although not specifically reassuring that the German High Command continued to believe that the Pas de Calais would be the chief landing site, Ōshima's reports in February, March, April, and the first half of May were reassuring because they tended to ignore Normandy as a possible landing site. Most of his general reports suggested the time more often than the site of the forthcoming landing. On 24 April, Ōshima told Tokyo that "in regard to the Anglo-American invasion, there is strong expectation that it will take place during the present week; however, if it does not, that will indicate that it may be delayed for several weeks."[18] Three days later he reported that "everyone has a deepening conviction that the Second Front is almost here and a tense atmosphere can be detected in the articles of the press."[19] But exactly one month before the actual landing at Normandy, Ōshima reported that since periods considered most suitable for landing operations, namely the end of April and the beginning of May, have "passed, there is now [a] strong body of opinion [which holds] that operations in question will be postponed another 2 or 3 weeks."[20]

Two weeks later Ōshima had more positive news for the Allies. Although the invasion was "not far off," Ōshima reported to Tokyo on 19 May, it seemed that the site of the landing could possibly be in Dalmatia, Norway, or southern France.[21] The next day Ōshima said that he personally believed that the invasion could come from the Kattegat to Göteborg, Sweden. However, Ōshima admitted that "General Alfred Jodl [chief of operations staff, Armed Forces High Command (OKW)] told me that he does not think as I do."[22] It was reassuring to the western Allies that their various deception operations were sowing confusion in the enemy camp. Whatever uncertainty Ōshima had recently presented from the "other side of the hill" about the site and time of the forthcoming invasion, his last revelation at the end of May, on the eve of D-Day, held much promise. He had another private meeting scheduled with Hitler.

By May, Eisenhower's G-2 Division was probably better tuned and more appreciative of the Ōshima connection than it had been previously. Eisenhower failed initially in efforts to have his G-2 in the Mediterranean, British Major General Kenneth W. D. Strong, transferred with him to be chief of intelligence at Supreme Headquarters, Allied Expeditionary Force (SHAEF). Strong, a blunt, hardy Scot, enjoyed direct access to Eisenhower, with whom he had an outstanding rapport, and his chief of staff, Lieutenant General Walter Bedell Smith. After several requests from Eisenhower and Smith, the War Office agreed to transfer Strong, and he became chief of intelligence at

SHAEF on 25 May 1944, five days before Ōshima's crucial report became available for study.

It is of considerable consequence that Strong knew Ōshima. Strong was a British military attaché in Berlin in 1938, and although Strong was considerably junior to Ōshima, he was aware of Ōshima's unprecedented promotion within the Japanese embassy in October, from military attaché to ambassador. Strong was also familiar with Ōshima's astonishing entrée to Nazi officialdom, and news of Ōshima's meeting with Hitler on the eve of the Normandy landings alerted Strong to the probability that major revelations were forthcoming.[23]

Such major revelations were on Strong's desk on 30 May 1944. Strong and Eisenhower were reassured that Hitler continued to believe that Calais would be the site of the major landing. Ironically, Hitler, who had wavered in his predictions about where the main assault would come, finally settled firmly on the Pas-de-Calais area. Ōshima's revelations about Hitler's thoughts were astonishing and extremely valuable for the Allies to have on the eve of D-Day. Planners of OVERLORD could not have hoped for more. Nearly a year before they had concluded that Pas-de-Calais was "an unsuitable area in which to attempt our initial lodgement on the Continent." The British outline plan pointed out emphatically, however, that the conclusion was reached "without prejudice to the importance of the Pas de Calais area as an objective for feints and diversions."[24]

On 27 May Ōshima had a two-hour private meeting with Ribbentrop at the latter's estate near Salzburg, and later the same day the Japanese envoy had a similar meeting with Hitler at the Führer's Berghof.[25] In a special wire Ōshima quoted for his superiors in Tokyo Hitler's words verbatim, noting that Ribbentrop's views concerning "the problem of the second front" were the same as Hitler's and that, therefore, he wanted "to avoid repetition."[26]

Speaking of the Second Front, Hitler said, "I believe that . . . [sooner or later] an invasion action will be carried out against Europe. On the British Isles there are already about eighty divisions of men gathered together, I believe. (Actually among them there are a mere eight divisions of real fighting men that have experience in actual warfare," [Hitler added.] I [Ōshima] then asked, "Does Your Excellency believe that these Anglo-American forces are fully prepared to invade," and Hitler answered, "Yes." I waited for a moment and went on: "I wonder what ideas you have on how the Second Front will be carried out," whereupon Hitler answered, "Well, as for me, judging from relatively ominous portents, I think that diversionary actions will take place against Norway, Denmark, the

southern part of western France, and the coasts of the French Mediterranean—various places. After that, after they have established
bridgeheads on the Norman and Brittany Peninsulas and [have] seen
how the prospect appears, they will come forward with the establishment of an all-out Second Front in the area of the *Straits of Dover.*[27]

Significantly, by this point in the war, Anglo-American cooperation in the
field of signal intelligence was at a high mark. Thus, the Führer's words
could be analyzed and placed effectively in the broad context of theater intelligence.

Postwar intelligence assessments emphasized the importance in knowing
what Hitler thought. A précis concerning former German military intelligence was drawn up by the U.S. Headquarters, Berlin District, and Headquarters, First Airborne Army. Dated 4 October 1945, it started rather predictably with a quotation from Clausewitz: "By 'intelligence' we mean every
sort of information about the enemy and his country—the basis, in short, of
our own plans and operations."[28] Clausewitz's warnings about the short-
comings of intelligence were not cited. However, the G-2 summary was quite
accurate in the discussion of "Adolf Hitler and the Intelligence Problem."

No discussion of German intelligence would be complete that did
not take into account the personality of Adolf Hitler. All important
strategic decisions were made by Hitler personally up to 1941, thereafter, he also made all important operational decisions. Intelligence,
to influence the course of the war, had to influence Hitler. . . .
Hitler arrived at most of his decisions as to enemy intentions
through his intuition and not by the objective processes of intelligence.[29]

Thus, Ōshima's material was available, and it provided Eisenhower with up-
to-date, firsthand evidence that Hitler's intuition continued to be the basis
for his estimates of how the invaders would behave. Ōshima cleared away
many of the fearsome apparitions held by OVERLORD planners. Here, then, as
Clausewitz explained theoretically, was a reliable intelligence report that
bridged "one of the great chasms between *planning and execution.*"[30]

In all of the uncertainties of intelligence encountered during the preparation for OVERLORD, none was more admirably overcome than those Ōshima
addressed in his messages to Tokyo. Much of the importance of Ōshima lay
in his spreading out the whole picture of "the other side of the hill," some of
which was already reconstructed from the whole gamut of more traditional
intelligence sources. But of all the valuable information gleaned from Ōshi-

ma's messages, one piece is unique. Ōshima seemed to know the precious truth about an otherwise unfathomable matter: How Hitler's forces would react to the invasion at Normandy. Eisenhower and his lieutenants learned from Ōshima what attitudes and stubborn beliefs Hitler held about the coming invasion before it was too late to take advantage of the Führer's errors.

Anglo-American joint work and cooperation in the field of COMINT had long been in the making. Although several American signal intelligence officers had been sent to the United Kingdom earlier in the war, considerable trans-Atlantic negotiation and inevitable delay prevented thoroughgoing cooperation for some time. As noted earlier, even though Anglo-American confidence grew gradually, neither country released *all* ULTRA or MAGIC intelligence to the other unless, as a recently declassified NSA publication states, "the action would benefit itself either directly, or indirectly, by the uses to which the other would put the assistance."[31] As a result of a new Anglo-American intelligence agreement of 17 May 1943 (see Appendix 3), by late 1943 the number of American SIGINT personnel stationed in the European theater of operations, U.S. Army (ETOUSA) increased sharply and a Special Project Group was organized to learn how to produce ULTRA. In March 1944 Marshall carefully explained security regulations governing the dissemination of British ULTRA intelligence to Eisenhower (see Appendix 4). American ULTRA officers worked at Bletchley Park, and by 1 July 1944, Americans were producing the daily composite called the MAGIC European Summary, 90 percent of which was based on inclusive Special Intelligence, the most important of intelligence categories. The decrypts of Ōshima's messages also fell into this category. Ōshima's special wire about his second front conversation with Hitler reached Eisenhower on the same day, 30 May, that the main cryptosystem in use by the commander in chief, Army Group B, Field Marshal Erwin Rommel, became readable at Bletchley Park. Rommel's forces were in the crucial area extending from the Netherlands to southwestern France. Thus, Special Intelligence, in which MAGIC figured heavily, was largely assimilated in the maze of Bletchley Park cryptographic languages and commonly referred to simply as ULTRA. ULTRA afforded the Anglo-American command a good understanding of what the Germans expected, especially by 1944.[32]

From 1944, when the system of special security officers [SSOs] was established in the European theater of operations to provide field commanders with enemy signal intelligence, the various SSOs in ETO headquarters received daily MAGIC summaries. These arrived by top secret pouch, but the SSOs also received *cable* messages (not less secure radio messages) giving the substance of priority items and concerns of immediate importance.[33]

The Battle of Normandy, which lasted from 6 June to 24 July 1944 according to a report on ULTRA intelligence for the First U.S. Army, and the Battle of Northern France (25 July to 14 September 1944) were undertakings in which reliable information about the enemy's intentions was of utmost importance. An American ULTRA report of 21 May 1945 concluded that "the divisions the enemy sent to stop us only became engulfed in our offensive. It mattered not what we did, provided we did something." The weight and speed of Anglo-American attacks were appreciated by the Germans "too little and too late." Yet this report also concluded that the enemy "did not have the means to carry out his intentions."[34] In fact, the enemy did have the means, but indecision about concentrating German forces and particularly armor units, especially during the first week after D-Day, compelled a piecemeal commitment of forces as they arrived in the battle area already dominated by superior Anglo-American forces.

Hitler was chiefly responsible for the German failure in June, and in the aftermath of the Normandy landings Ōshima continued to inform Tokyo of the full range of Berlin's policy. Since the invasion of the Soviet Union, Ōshima had been assigned a special contact officer whose job it was to keep the ambassador fully informed when there was no opportunity for Ōshima to confer directly with Hitler or Ribbentrop. Thus, Ōshima's intercepted reports served the Allies as a barometer of the Führer's thinking in the days of potential crisis immediately after the beachheads were established. On 7 June, Ōshima wired news to Tokyo that the first wave of five or six enemy divisions had landed at Normandy, but that fact did not preclude the possibility that large-scale Anglo-American landings would take place elsewhere.[35] The next day he reported that the Germans told him "it is uncertain whether they [U.S.-British forces] will later attempt a landing in the Calais-Dunkirk area."[36] And on 9 June he claimed that German forces "are now on their guard against landings in the Calais and Saint Malo regions."[37]

Ōshima continued to report faithfully on German indecision. He was told by a Foreign Ministry official on 11 June, "After we Germans clearly see what the enemy's real plans on the Norman peninsula are and after we have let as many of them as will come ashore, we intend to slap them off at one blow."[38] The rhetoric of this official report to Ōshima was strikingly similar to what MAGIC-ULTRA analysts knew Hitler had said privately to Ōshima two weeks earlier on 28 May. Near the end of the crucial period following the initial landings, Ōshima unwittingly informed the Allied command that "in the Northern France area there are many (? harbors ?) where the enemy has been expected to make landings; special vigilance is being maintained in these areas, particularly between Dieppe and Boulogne."[39] This was clear and reassuring evidence to Eisenhower that Hitler still feared other major landings and continued to refuse to give Field Marshals Rundstedt and Rommel freedom of action.

The field marshals wanted to draw reserves from coastal areas not immediately threatened by invasion in order to launch a large-scale, concentrated counterattack at the decisive point of the Anglo-American assault. There were four static and reserve divisions and one attack infantry division along the coast between Dieppe and Boulogne; moreover, there were several divisions inland, including two powerful panzer divisions.[40] But Hitler clung to his strategy of a static defense, exhorting the German soldiers to fight harder. No withdrawals or evacuations were permitted for whatever tactical or strategic reasons, and the Führer's generals who differed with him were soon replaced.

Perhaps not altogether surprisingly, therefore, in early July Eisenhower continued to enjoy good news from Ōshima about Allied deception operations. They still held sway with Hitler. A month after D-Day the Japanese ambassador reported that "after the taking of Cherbourg [26 June], it is a matter of course for the enemy to launch an attack for the purpose of expanding the bridgehead, but Germany is still waiting for Patton's group to engage in a second landing operation in the Channel area."[41]

Three weeks later, near the end of July, Germany was still waiting for Patton, in spite of the fact that Patton had been replaced on 14 July 1944 as commanding general of the notional First United States Army Group (FUSAG) in England. Patton was the linchpin to this deception scheme, named Operation FORTITUDE, for the flamboyant Patton was greatly respected, indeed feared, by the Germans.

The threat of FUSAG fooled the Germans longer than the Allies had expected.[42] Again, it was Ōshima who provided evidence of this fact. On 23 July he learned in a three-hour conference with Ribbentrop that the foreign minister did not believe the Patton landings were "very far off." The ambassador then said to Ribbentrop: "I have been told that the German Supreme Command expects the army groups under Patton to make a landing in Northern France very soon, and that their policy is to direct their operations against Normandy after they have first knocked out this landing." A confident Ribbentrop replied: "No matter when the troops under Patton make a landing, the German army is fully and infallibly prepared to meet such a situation."[43]

The Allies were unduly optimistic in light of the naked intelligence they were receiving from Ōshima about Hitler's incompetent direction of the war, but there was also uncertainty. There was a chance that German military professionals would be given control of the war, and if so, the end of the series of Allied gains since D-Day was probably not far off. Or perhaps the

Third Reich was about to collapse. Then came the attempt on the Führer's life.

At first the attempt was seen as another sign that perhaps the war would soon end. A U.S. First Army after-action report addressed the issue of "morale, for it was hoped that the July 'putsch' would have repercussions among the [German] troops" in the west.[44] However, the 20 July attempt failed, and there would be no change in leadership. Moreover, the Nazi swift, sweeping, and criminal retribution strengthened German resolve to see the war through to a bitter conclusion. This was also the conclusion of the First Army G-2 on 24 July. The American intelligence analyst saw no evidence that the Hitler government would be overthrown by internal revolution or by revolt of German field armies. The defeat of German armies in the field was the only thing that would force the downfall of Hitler.[45]

Indeed, the first conclusive evidence to reach Washington that the attempt had failed came from Ōshima. Ōshima's message to Tokyo, sent some seven hours after the attempt on Hitler's life, lacked the traditional identification number of the broadcast, "evidence, perhaps," so the Arlington Hall SSA specialists concluded, "of considerable perturbation at the Japanese embassy." Ōshima declared that "At 2000 on today the 20th, Vice Minister Steengracht told me that he had been in direct telephone communication with Foreign Minister Ribbentrop at High Command Headquarters, who had told him to tell me that Hitler is absolutely all right and was not hurt at all."[46] Within the hour Ōshima telephoned Gustav Adolf Steengracht to express his "deep concern" and to seek more information, but no additional details were immediately available. Nevertheless, American intelligence analysts were reassured by Ōshima's second message that the Japanese ambassador, and thus they, would soon be given "the facts [as soon as they] become clear."

Ōshima concluded his second wire with a specific recommendation to the Japanese foreign minister: "Since this is a grave plot against the sovereign of a friendly country, I think it would be proper for you to send a personal telegram of sympathy."[47] War leaders in Berlin, Washington, and London soon had before them the personal telegrams to Hitler from the most prominent of Japanese authorities. First came Emperor Hirohito's message written in French originally: "Having just learned that Your Excellency was fortunately able to escape without serious accident the outrageous attempt on his life of which he was the victim, I hasten to express to you my deepest sympathy and my most sincere congratulations."[48] Prime Minister Koiso Kuniaki's message to Hitler expressed a kind of Axis solidarity that was hauntingly fatalistic.

With regard to Your Excellency's recent injury, the President and the members of the newly appointed Imperial Japanese Cabinet wish to express their sincere regard for Your Excellency's well being. Whatever difficulties the Imperial Japanese Government may face, we are thoroughly determined to push forward the present war side by side with our Axis allies. We are convinced that the final victory we are planning will be ours.

Moreover, the injury received by Your Excellency, which resulted from the recent ill-advised plot, was fortunately slight, and we offer our heartiest congratulations on Your Excellency's safety, and send you herewith our warmest sympathy. The spectacular escape is surely an act of God, and should be considered an omen of victory. We wish Your Excellency success in battle all the more because of this event.[49]

Allied leaders soon gleaned from a series of Ōshima's messages the awful story of Nazi retribution against the German Resistance movement. Colonel Graf Claus Schenk von Stauffenberg "brought the bomb" and "the man behind the scenes and the center of this plot, it would seem, was the former Chief of Staff, Colonel-General [Ludwig] Beck," Ōshima reported the day following the attempt.[50] Stauffenberg was executed, his confederates were arrested, the Department of Communications was guarded, and Berlin "returned to normal," Ōshima confidently reported on the afternoon of 21 July.[51] Soon followed Ōshima's strategic assessment.

The Germans' basic strategy of attempting to extricate themselves from a two-front war and using every effort to regain occupied territories is still unchanged. In order to extricate themselves from the two-front war, in theory it could be considered desirable to make a political compromise with one or the other of their enemies, but it is clear that from a practical standpoint it would in the present situation be equally undesirable to [? make peace ?] with either the Anglo-Americans or with Russia, and there is absolutely no basis for believing that the German leaders have any such intention.[52]

Anglo-American cryptanalysts had a comprehensive picture of the thinking of Hitler's government. The 29 July edition of the Magic Diplomatic Summary, which Marshall and other top Allied strategic leaders read daily, best pulled together all of the troubling and complex aspects of the German war in the West. Again, Ōshima was the author of this remarkable contemporary document by the SSA analysts at Arlington Hall Station titled "Ambassador Ōshima's Views of Germany's Situation after His 23 July Talk with von Ribbentrop."

> The attempt on Hitler's life is the most serious occurrence for Germany since the outbreak of the war. Of course, it has been apparent that ever since the Nazi regime seized power there has been discord between the traditional Prussian General Staff group and the radical Nazi party element. However, there was no occasion for it to come to the surface in face of the steady success of Nazi policy and the gratifying progress of the war. More recently the war situation has deteriorated to the point of producing such an event as that which has just occurred.
>
> At first my colleagues [in the Japanese embassy] and I were very anxious about the revolt, especially because of the issuance of fake orders, etc. The German leaders, too, were disturbed. However, within a few hours the situation had returned to normal, certainly a happy outcome for this unhappy event.
>
> Judging from the information which has . . . so far been made available, the group of rebels was not very large. It consisted of General Beck, several high ranking officers close to him, and a group of staff officers who admired that clique. Apparently they had almost no connection with the officers and men at the front. By taking the sort of measures carried out at the time of the 30 June 1934 incident [the Roehm purge], it will be possible for the Nazis to eliminate with one blow the faction which is causing the trouble. However, since this incident involves the Army we cannot be too optimistic. In my opinion, it will almost inevitably have unpleasant domestic and foreign repercussions.
>
> By destroying the last groups opposing them, however, the Nazis will be able to strengthen their ——— [two words missing] home front. From our own point of view, I might point out that this rebel faction was inclined to be quite pro-Anglo-American, and its elimination should contribute to the strengthening of cooperation between Japan and Germany. . . .
>
> Although Germany has received hard blows both within and without, the fighting spirit of the German leaders is high and they will continue to exert their best efforts to bring the present war to an end with a clear-cut victory.[53]

Ōshima's assessment was correct. Hitler consolidated military control even more in his own hands, as Ōshima's individual messages during the previous week suggested. The German combat soldier was too busy trying to stay alive to be influenced by news of the failure of a plot against Hitler, and the officer corps remained overwhelmingly loyal to him. There was no disaffection within the German armed services or within the German-Japanese warring alliance, so Ōshima's future intercepts would remain important to Anglo-American forces in Europe.

Since early June Allied tactical operations on the Continent had had a devastating effect on the enemy, as the continual assaults prevented German forces from getting fully set before the next assault came. And Hitler's increased direction of the war in June and July further aided Anglo-American forces in carrying out their objectives. After D-Day they were able to retain the initiative and avoid setbacks.

Hitler specifically ordered important coastal ports to be held "to the last man, to the last cartridge," but Cherbourg and Granville had already fallen. At the end of July American troops seized Avranches and Pontaubault at the base of the Cotentin. Thus, St. Malo, Brest, Lorient, and St. Nazaire, the principal ports of Brittany, were threatened. With the dramatic breakout into Brittany, St. Malo was captured by mid-August, and the other three fortress ports were encircled by U.S. troops and isolated. Brest fell in mid-September, but the German garrisons in Lorient and St. Nazaire held out and finally surrendered at the end of the war. The pace of war and the movement of German forces back toward the Rhine caused unabashed Allied optimism. The Breton ports were increasingly remote from the front, and there was not enough time to repair and rehabilitate their often badly damaged harbor and dock facilities. (Brest was thoroughly demolished by the time the German garrison surrendered.) Nor were the ports of Brittany any longer essential because larger and less-damaged ports seemed to be within reach, including Rotterdam and Amsterdam.[54]

German forces seemed to be in disarray. The liberation of Paris and the opening of the port of Marseilles on the Mediterranean came near the end of August, and pursuit to the German border was near at hand. In view of these rapid conquests in German-occupied France, Allied cryptanalysts read Ōshima's general assessment of 18 August with much interest. Ōshima declared that in Berlin there was much concern because of the sudden new military developments in northern and southern France.

> All the newspapers too have been reporting . . . [these developments] in detail, but since the American forces broke through in the neighborhood of Avranches, even the Germans, it seems, have ceased to give an explanation of the new turn in the war situation. Among the commentators too there are very few who seem to harbor

any hopes for the future, and many of them do nothing more than make simple excuses. Therefore, a large number of articles have appeared on diplomatic problems, in which, beginning with the Polish question, they reveal the failure of the enemy's diplomacy and attack the ambition which the enemy has for world political domination. Nevertheless, these articles cannot avoid revealing the fact that the writers are in low spirits. However, the intensification of the general mobilization within the country reflects the poignant nature of the war situation and this is not only receiving the serious thought of the government authorities but the support of the people in general, so that a new development is gradually taking place.[55]

The message contained a hint that the Germans had some new strategy in mind. Such a general assessment was helpful to Allied strategic planners, but Ōshima's additional specific reports and insights to Hitler's thinking would be more significant.

More specific reports arrived soon, yet their import seems to have been missed by Anglo-American commanders. Ōshima had already reported on 16 August that the Germans planned to undertake a major offensive in the West,[56] and on 21 August Ōshima wired Tokyo with the news that one of Ribbentrop's vice ministers had told him that it would be possible to launch a large-scale offensive in the West in about two months. There could be as many as 125 divisions involved.[57] Arlington Hall translated this message on 23 August, but there is no record of who on the American side saw it. However, on the British side it is clear that it "was sent to the Commands by GC and CS on 24 August."[58]

After early June 1944, the coordinated East-West offensives into German-occupied territory brought alarming new pressures upon the Berlin government. The Allies wondered how Hitler would react to the two-front war if, as Ōshima reported earlier, there was absolutely no chance of Germany making a political compromise with either the Anglo-Americans or the Soviets. The Allies had long been aware of Hitler's propensity for developing new and possible revolutionary weapons as a panacea for Germany's military woes. Hitler was boastful of new weapon systems, especially in view of increased military might of the Allied coalition and the specter of defeat that loomed before the Third Reich. The powerful V-2 rockets were of particular concern to the British. Ōshima had already reported in general terms in late July about a series of new weapons German scientists were developing, and on 9 August Albert Speer, minister of armament and war production, and Field Marshal Erhard Milch, with special permission from Hitler, met with Ōshima and his embassy staff for nearly five hours.[59] Soon followed Ōshima's extensive reports on German production of weapons, munitions, and materials from subsidiary war industries.[60] It was now crucial to have advance warning not only about German military developments but also about Hitler's intentions as the invading forces prepared to penetrate the Reich.

However, Anglo-American cryptanalysts were also mindful that Ōshima had not met personally with Hitler since their conference on the eve of the Normandy landings. Ōshima's reports to Tokyo based on his conversation with Hitler had been most reassuring to Eisenhower in the first week of June, but now what possible surprises did Hitler have up his sleeve? Thus, it was with much anticipation that Bletchley Park and Arlington Hall read Ōshima's requests in late August to obtain a private meeting with Hitler.[61] Finally, good news came on 5 September. In a message marked Extremely Urgent, Ōshima told Tokyo that he had "left for High Command Headquarters on the 3rd, had an interview with Foreign Minister Ribbentrop and then one with Chancellor Hitler on the 4th, and returned to Berlin on the 5th. I am wiring a gist of the interviews separately."[62]

The rapport that Ōshima and Hitler long enjoyed contributed to the frankness of this meeting at the Führer's East Prussia headquarters in early September. It was their last meeting, as it turned out, but in spite of his recent military setbacks, Hitler continued to show trust and confidence in his Japanese comrade, in whom he had confided since the mid-1930s.

Hitler's assessments and assertions might have served as a signal to Anglo-American strategic planners that the war in the West was not going well. German reverses had enabled the conspirators to lash out in the 20 July incident, and thereafter, while the purge was extending even to the lowliest of those involved, the military situation in the West reached a critical moment when a fighting retreat was successfully carried out but only with grave difficulty. It was necessary to withdraw most of the forces to the West Wall, even from the Antwerp area, leaving behind several hundred thousand garrison troops and their equipment in the coastal fortifications of the Brittany ports, Bordeaux, and elsewhere. But the line was to be stabilized by launching a counterattack with forces being massed southeast of Nancy.

Hitler also planned a large-scale offensive. "It was his intention," Ōshima said in summarizing Hitler's words on 5 September 1944, "as soon as the new army of more than one million now being organized was ready, to combine them with units to be withdrawn from the front in every area and, waiting upon the replenishment of the air forces which is now in progress, to take the offensive in the West on a large scale."[63] Hitler anticipated that this build up would take place under the cover of rainy weather in September and October, when the Allies would not be able to make full use of their superior air power. Thus, the large-scale offensive in the West would take place "after the beginning of November," said Hitler in early September in reply to Ōshima.[64]

The cover of rainy weather was particularly effective for six weeks after 1 November, giving Hitler a special opportunity to assemble massive forces for an offensive. The U.S. Army in World War II historical series notes that in the northern and eastern areas of France, "the month of November [1944] would bring a total of 7.2 inches of rain, as contrasted with a normal fall of 3.0 inches during this month."[65] Another problem was that Allied planes were frequently grounded because of bad weather through much of November and during the first half of December.[66]

Hitler had long hankered for a large-scale offensive in the West, indeed since August, one of the major German participants in the Battle of the Ardennes wrote after the war, but long *before* the MAGIC and ULTRA secrets were revealed to the public.[67] The Führer attached high hopes to this offensive, with Antwerp as the ultimate objective. It was crucial to recapture Antwerp before the Allies could clear the channel into the port and bring to bear against the German offensive their superiority in soldiers and materials. Therefore, Hitler insisted that the offensive be launched no later than the final week of November. Eventually, however, he abandoned his intentions and relented to the arguments for postponement of his field generals, and the launch date was fixed for 10 December, then 14 December, and finally 16 December.[68]

In spite of a considerable amount of activity in preparation for the attack in mid-December, especially during the second week of that month, the offensive caught the Allies by surprise. The volume on the Ardennes offensive in the U.S. Army in World War II series concludes that the incident was a gross failure by Allied ground and air intelligence.[69] And even an old hand in the service of the Office of Strategic Services during the war, former CIA Director William Casey, claimed that "nobody expected an attack in the Ardennes."[70]

Not to have been more alert to the likelihood of the Ardennes offensive by mid-December 1944 was also a gross failure by Allied signals intelligence. ULTRA revealed more about the coming of the Battle of the Bulge, as the Americans dubbed the confrontation, than has been generally assumed. Although Hitler never suspected that the Anglo-Americans were at this time reading his military enciphered messages, the Führer ordered radio silence in all matters related to the Ardennes offensive.[71] Yet Hitler's orders were not followed in every case, and many disclosures came from intercepted German ENIGMA messages, especially as they related to some Panzer Corps and Luftwaffe units.

The best account of signal intelligence revelations about the coming of the Ardennes offensive is in the British official history of intelligence in the war.[72] Its conclusion about the failure of intelligence is candid: "It is not a misuse of hindsight to hazard the judgment that the British COS [Chiefs of Staff] and the JIC [Joint Intelligence Sub-Committee] made a fundamental mistake."[73] COS and JIC agreed with most German generals about the limitations of Germany's military capabilities. Therefore, the Anglo-Americans concluded that an ambitious offensive would not be launched, but they discounted the rift between Hitler and his generals and disregarded Hitler's propensity to control German military strategy. It is also probable that a more thorough and systematic study of Ōshima's messages would have helped intelligence analysts to foresee events in the West more accurately.

Ōshima's advance warnings concerning the Ardennes offensive are not given adequate attention in the otherwise comprehensive British official history of intelligence. The oversight is not unlike the mistake made by Anglo-American analysts of ULTRA-MAGIC intercepts during the five months before the Ardennes offensive. In the chapter titled "The Allied Autumn Offensives and the German Counter-Attack" of the official history, only five of Ōshima's reports are cited. They are the messages thought to have bearing on Allied suspicion that Hitler was planning and preparing for a large-scale offensive in the West.[74] In Table 6.1 the American MAGIC translations of Ōshima's messages corresponding to the five cited in the British official history are indicated by three Xs (XXX) in the Implied and Expressed columns. Yet there were many more of Ōshima's messages transmitted from Berlin (16 August to 15 December 1944) that have particular significance to the coming of the offensive. This becomes evident through a systematic culling of nearly 16,000 SRDJ numbers during the five-month period.

A clear pattern was developing in those months, pointing to the increased probability of the Ardennes offensive, made thoroughly credible if Allied analysts had been more appreciative of the profound connections Ōshima had in Hitler's government. In this regard the British authors of the official volume judiciously observe the following in a note:

> In a commentary written at the request of the DMI [director of military intelligence] not long after the German offensive had faltered GC and CS remarked that the "Japanese are less critical than some in believing what they are told" and added later, with particular reference to the decrypt of 10 September [the deciphered date—see note 63], that the long delay since its receipt had made the Ambassador's information seem to be out-dated.[75]

Table 6.1. Ōshima's Messages Referring to the Coming of a Large-Scale Offensive in the West, August–December 1944

Transmitted from Berlin	Intercepted	Received at Arlington Hall	Translated	Implied[a]	Expressed[b]	Explicit[c]
16 Aug	17 Aug	17 Aug	17 Aug		X	
18 Aug	20 Aug	20 Aug	23 Aug	X		
21 Aug	22 Aug	22 Aug	23 Aug		XXX	
5 Sept	6 Sept	6 Sept	7 Sept		XXX	
6 Sept	7 Sept	7 Sept	7 Sept		X	
9 Sept	10 Sept	10 Sept	11 Sept	X		
25 Sept	26 Sept	26 Sept	28 Sept	X		
26 Sept	28 Sept	28 Sept	29 Sept	XXX		
26 Sept	28 Sept	28 Sept	30 Sept	X		
11 Oct	12 Oct	12 Oct	17 Oct	X		
12 Oct	13 Oct	13 Oct	13 Oct	X		
24 Oct	25 Oct	25 Oct	26 Oct	X		
30 Oct	31 Oct	31 Oct	31 Oct	X		
6 Nov	7 Nov	8 Nov	11 Nov	X		
10 Nov	11 Nov	11 Nov	13 Nov	X		
11 Nov	12 Nov	12 Nov	13 Nov	X		
16 Nov	19 Nov	19 Nov	19 Nov	X		
16 Nov	18 Nov	18 Nov	18 Nov	X		
16 Nov	?	19 Nov	19 Nov		XXX	
16 Nov	18 Nov	18 Nov	18 Nov	X		
17 Nov	19 Nov	19 Nov	20 Nov	X		
22 Nov	23 Nov	23 Nov	23 Nov		XXX	
24 Nov	27 Nov	27 Nov	28 Nov	X		
2 Dec	3 Dec	3 Dec	4 Dec	X		
11 Dec	11 Dec	15 Dec	22 Dec			X
14 Dec	15 Dec	15 Dec	16 Dec			X
15 Dec	18 Dec	18 Dec	19 Dec		X	
15 Dec	19 Dec	20 Dec	2__? Dec		X	

Sources: NSA, RG 457, SRDJ Nos. 67849-84556, 16 August–15 December 1944.

[a]Ōshima suggests that the Germans have intentions of resuming the offensive as soon as possible.

[b]Ōshima states that a German large-scale offensive is planned for late 1944.

[c]Ōshima is confident the large-scale offensive will soon begin and mentions the Aachen area.

Thus, Arlington Hall first, and then Bletchley Park had pertinent information from Ōshima but failed to evaluate it accurately or early enough to prevent surprise in the Ardennes. It was not fortuitous that Ōshima's most revealing statements (those in the Expressed column of Table 6.1) transmitted in August, September, and November were contained in reports about his recent interviews with Ribbentrop and Hitler. Allied analysts knew this, but the awareness suffered from the counterpull and weight of what has been called the "besetting tendency in intelligence to become too wedded to one view of enemy intentions."[76] There was indeed a continuum of intelligence pointing to the crucial offensive, but it was not perceived until too late.

Those errors in judgment were quite different from the mishaps of the eleventh hour. Ōshima's last four messages cited in Table 6.1 were not available in translation until after the German offensive was launched at dawn on 16 December, even though the two most explicit messages, still in the Japanese PURPLE cipher, had arrived at Arlington Hall Station several hours earlier on 15 December. The enormous volume of foreign cipher traffic received by SSA and the overworked pool of Japanese linguists precluded the completion of a translation of one of Ōshima's Explicit messages until some fifteen hours after the start of the German offensive; the other was not translated at Arlington Hall until 22 December.

Ōshima must have transmitted his first report on "the offensive of the German army in the region south of Aachen" with some satisfaction on 19 December. The attack achieved "full and complete surprise," he proclaimed to his superiors in Tokyo. Ironically, this was only because his earlier warnings were not fully assimilated and analyzed in an Allied composite of his messages.[77] On balance, however, Ōshima seemed subdued in his coverage of the offensive. As an army officer he understood that the attack was no more than an attempt to make a strategic adjustment along the western front and that only at the tactical level could it be called an offensive operation. He seems to have acquired a greater respect for the fighting capacity of Anglo-American forces since the Normandy invasion. By 23 December he confined his reports to the stories carried in German newspapers, adding that his official contacts in Berlin maintained a circumspect attitude and feared that the Soviets would soon launch a large-scale offensive.[78] Ōshima's lackluster reports forecast the turning point in the Ardennes during the evening of 26 December, when military initiative passed from German to American hands.[79]

Ōshima's reports about the western front remained pedestrian in tone until he met with Ribbentrop in a three-hour conference on 7 January 1945. Afterward his reports appeared briefly more optimistic, if also unrealistic. The only hint about any failure came in his message of 11 January, when he admitted that the Ardennes attack did not reach the level of a powerful tactical offensive because new troops were not fully organized and replenishment of the Luftwaffe was not completed.[80]

The significance of the western front was soon overshadowed by new developments in the East. The long-anticipated Soviet attack commenced on 12 January; thereafter, Ōshima's reports concentrated on conditions in the East.[81] It seems that Ōshima's primary concern was starting to shift. The evident, if not spoken, German failure in the West held new meaning for Ōshima. This was mainly because of the massive Soviet offensive from East

Prussia in the north to Budapest in the south. Since the Normandy landings in June the Allies were starting to close in on Germany. Now in mid-January the two very strong fronts were much closer to Berlin. It was not difficult for Ōshima to conjecture that Germany would soon be overrun. In that event Japan would be left alone to face the combined strength of the seasoned, fresh-from-victory Allied forces. Ōshima was fearful that Japan would also have to face the Soviet Union if, as Ōshima probably suspected, opportunists in the Kremlin were interested in broadening Soviet gains by honoring their commitment within the Allied warring coalition.

In Ōshima's view, events in Europe in the second half of 1944 had taken an increasingly ominous turn. The faith in Hitler and the Third Reich Ōshima had held since the mid-1930s was being rapidly dispelled by the beginning of 1945. Yet his PURPLE messages continued to be read with keen interest at Arlington Hall and Bletchley Park, so he remained an important source of information, although the information he provided probably was not as strategically important as it had been earlier when Allied power was less developed.

7

MAGIC and the Question of a German-Soviet Separate Peace

The western Allies understood the extreme importance of the eastern front, and they were concerned about the possibility of a German-Soviet rapprochement. In chapter 3 the topic of a separate peace was introduced in the context of 1942 strategic changes; the intent here is to examine the topic through the entire war.

A mere 150 days after the German invasion of the Soviet Union in June 1941, and two weeks before the Japanese attack at Pearl Harbor, Germany's East Asian Axis partner, Japan, sought to mediate the German-Soviet conflict. The first Japanese offer was made on 21 November 1941; the last was made in early 1945. The Japanese were nothing if not persistent. American and British intelligence analysts watched delivery of these proposals and sought to understand the reasons and conditions surrounding the repeated Japanese overtures made through their embassies in Berlin and Moscow. MAGIC intelligence was the most contemporary and detailed source of evidence on this important wartime question.[1]

It was always in Japan's interest to effect a German-Soviet peace. Such a peace was essential in order to deflect attempts by London and Washington to get Stalin to enter the war against Japan. Significantly, throughout Japan's quest for peace on the eastern front, the Japanese had to weigh the relative values of their neutrality pact with Stalin and their military pact with Hitler. The ever-changing nature of the fortunes of war added greatly to the balance and complexity of the Japanese task, although the merits of the neutrality arguments were convincing.

Not surprisingly, the British and Americans were concerned that a separate peace would perhaps be negotiated and that the closing down of the German-Soviet front would free enormous German military force to be redirected against the western democracies as had happened late in World War I.

At no time after June 1941 did the Germans have less than two-thirds of their army on the eastern front, and most of the time four-fifths of their army was committed there. Officials in Washington had to weigh various contingencies and often circulated studies and position papers concerning their Soviet ally. One such paper in the summer of 1943 was titled "To Determine the Proper Course of Action for the United Nations in the Event Russia and Germany Effect a Compromise Peace in July or August 1943."[2]

It is sometimes difficult for people studying World War II to appreciate how precarious the German-Soviet front was and how decisions there could easily have had wide-ranging repercussions, if not decisive impact on the very outcome of the war. What is even more difficult to fathom are the circumstances in which exasperated Anglo-American intelligence analysts had to watch, anxiously and yet silently, the reactions of Hitler and Stalin to various Japanese overtures. Western policymakers were mindful that these bitter totalitarian rivals had surprised the world by signing the nonaggression pact on the eve of the European war in 1939. Yet during the war years western policymakers were permitted only to watch what the protagonists were discussing about the possibility of a separate peace. They were not permitted to act whatsoever upon the secret information. Otherwise, the MAGIC secret would surely have been jeopardized.

Some Japanese strategists were alarmed on the eve of the attack on Pearl Harbor that their German ally had not yet forced the Soviets to capitulate. The longer the Soviets were able to hold out, the more awkward the April 1941 Japanese-Soviet Neutrality Pact became for the Japanese. Logically, therefore, the Japanese launched new endeavors to obtain a certain amount of tranquillity with their northern Soviet neighbor before opening hostilities in the south. Thus, Germany's failure to win the war against the Soviets by late 1941 created a serious dilemma for the Japanese.

The Japanese foreign minister communicated directly with the Japanese ambassadors in Moscow and Berlin on the matter of a possible separate peace, and Anglo-American forces intercepted the complete dialogue. Nevertheless, the full traffic with Moscow has not been declassified, and only certain pieces of evidence can be cited at this time, although all of the Berlin side has been declassified and is available to researchers. Significantly, Tokyo's overtures for a separate peace went through Ōshima and then to the German government, so Arlington Hall was always abreast of developments.[3]

The first reference to the possibility of mediating a German-Soviet rapprochement was made in a sophisticated message from Foreign Minister Tōgō in Tokyo to Ōshima in Berlin. Ōshima was initially instructed only to "keep an eye on developments" while bearing in mind Tōgō's assessment in the third week of November 1941:

> It may be that Germany would prefer to avoid being faced with a long term resistance by the U.S.S.R., so that she—Germany—may transfer her entire fighting forces to some other part. On the Soviet side, it seems possible that sentiment for peace may develop when she views the situation from the standpoint of reconstruction.
>
> Our relations with the United States may have considerable effect on our southward program, depending, of course, on what turns those relations take. In other words, our relationship with Great Britain and the United States has a great bearing on the future of our national greatness. . . .
>
> We would like to break up the policy of British-U.S.-U.S.S.R. joint action. We would, therefore, welcome, if anything, peace between Germany and the Soviet Union. For the purpose of enhancing our position, we would not be opposed to mediating in a peace, if such a course is possible.[4]

Here, then, lay the seeds for the destruction of the Allied coalition even before America's entry into the war. From the outset, the Military Intelligence Division in the War Department watched developments on the crucial German-Soviet front, where London and Washington had so little influence.

The three chief Axis powers were at war with the United States by mid-December 1941, and Italy and Germany were also at war with the Soviet Union, but Japanese-Soviet neutrality remained a stumbling block in Axis relations. Therefore, Tokyo remained eager to learn about the status of the German invasion of the Soviet Union and would, in time, step up efforts to mediate a peace. As a top secret ULTRA U.S. Navy study in late December 1944 concluded: "Indeed, the only limit to her [i.e., Japan's] activities in this direction is her desire to do nothing that will impair her relations with Russia. To maintain the status quo in the matter of these relations seems to be the guiding principle of her foreign policy, and it is in the light of this principle that her efforts to help Germany extricate herself from her war with the Soviet Union must be examined."[5]

Ōshima's initial response to the question of a separate peace was a single sentence buried in a long message reporting the gist of a recent two-hour discussion with Ribbentrop. The two diplomats touched on many different subjects related to the establishment of the "new world order," and in March 1942 Ōshima reported only that "Germany has no intention of making a separate peace with Stalin, hence there is no way of settling the Soviet problem save by force of arms."[6] Although this brief statement must have been reassuring to Washington and London, American intelligence analysts continued to peruse MAGIC intercepts for a more thoroughgoing explanation. Within three weeks it came.

Four months had passed since Tōgō had instructed Ōshima to "keep an eye on developments." In April 1942, after the ambassador and the embassy's military and naval attachés completed comprehensive studies about the German-Soviet war, Ambassador Ōshima forwarded the results to Tokyo. In a 1,500-word message, he recounted German-Soviet relations since 1940, German military advances since June 1941, and Hitler's plans for administering European Russia; he concluded that Hitler would only accept Moscow's unconditional surrender and that there was no possibility of a separate negotiated peace.[7] Within two days a MAGIC Summary titled "Ambassador Ōshima's View on Separate German-Soviet Peace" was read by Major General George V. Strong, Marshall's assistant chief of staff, Intelligence (G-2), in the War Department.[8]

The Japanese embassy in Berlin, without much encouragement from Tokyo, continued during the remainder of 1942 to report that the German government was not interested in a separate peace.[9] Near the end of October, however, the new foreign minister (17 September 1942 to 20 April 1943) in the Tōjō cabinet, Tani Masayuki, sent Ōshima a piece of hearsay from Tokyo: "On the evening of the 23rd of this month, several members of the Russian Embassy in Tokyo came to the Tokyo offices of TASS and said, 'Soon there will be an armistice between Germany and Russia.' They all drank a toast with beer and talked very plainly about it."[10] Nevertheless, Foreign Minister Tani did not give the story any credence and told Ōshima that it was being forwarded to him for general information purposes only.

Time was running out for the Japanese, and the new foreign minister was convinced that a German victory in the Soviet Union was no more likely in late 1942 than it had proved to be the previous year. Furthermore, Foreign Minister Tani worried increasingly about maintaining cordial relations with the Soviet Union, in the spirit of the April 1941 neutrality pact. The urgency of such a policy became clearer while the Japanese were starting to suffer setbacks in the Pacific (for example, at Midway and Guadalcanal); while they were embarrassingly obligated to allow American lend-lease matériel for the Soviet Union to reach Vladivostok;[11] and while Hitler's immoderate leadership in the European war started to unnerve some leaders in Tokyo who were otherwise firmly committed to the Axis coalition.

By the end of November, however, Ōshima's explanations and optimism about Germany's lot in the war started to alarm the new foreign minister. Thus, Tani took up the subjects of a separate peace and Ōshima's assess-

The newly constructed Japanese embassy on Tiergartenstrasse was officially opened on 25 January 1943. Thoroughly rebuilt and expanded in the late 1980s, it is now the Berlin headquarters for a Japanese-German center, Japanisch-Deutsches Zentrum Berlin. (Photograph by the author)

ments with a vengeance. In what MIS and compilers of the MAGIC Summary called an incredible rebuff to Ōshima, Foreign Minister Tani "challenged Ōshima's optimism about the German military situation."[12] This remarkable document, a critical analysis, is worth extensive quotation from Tani's original message of 28 November 1942.

> From: Tokyo
> To: Berlin
> November 28, 1942
> #903 (Two-part message complete)
>   Strictly secret.
>   1. *German-Soviet war.*
>   a. As for Germany having succeeded in preparing herself for a long war through obtaining essential military materials, what about oil, as just one instance? All Germany has taken is Maikop. I [Tani] don't see how you [Ōshima] can say she is so prepared.

b. You say that Germany has weakened Russia. Well, what about Russia weakening Germany? Furthermore, I believe that Russia still has plenty of soldiers and munition plants. I think you would be very wrong if you imagined it impossible for the Soviet to come back with a swift blow, and that right soon. I think you had better wait a while before judging Soviet forces to be so weak.

c. Let the Germans take Grozny [a major oil center]; let them take Tuapse [a Black Sea shipyard facility and coastal oil refinery terminus with pipelines from Grozny]; and let them take them this winter. Stalingrad hasn't fallen, has it? And the fact that the Germans were unable, with all their might, to take that city is an evil omen. You may say that Germany will head for the Near East after demilitarizing the Caucasus, but now that the United States has penetrated into North Africa, a new situation faces the Reich, and it is very doubtful if Germany can follow her preconceived plan of strategy. I myself doubt if Germany could even demilitarize the Caucasus; but even if she did, I think we would have slight chance of penetrating into the Near East.

2. *Warfare against England and the United States.*

a. Even though it might be possible for Germany to get passage through Turkey instead of securing the Caucasus, there are many, many considerations she would have to face. Turkey is neutral, and so long as she sticks to that policy, it will be to Germany's advantage not to invade her. However you view it, Germany cannot easily get into the Middle and Near East.

b. I believe that Germany will put up a stiff fight for Tunis and I believe that she will probably succeed, but if she doesn't, things will be bad. When we consider this, in connection with the effect it will have on Italy, it gives us pause and makes us think. If worse comes to worst, in order to stabilize the situation in Italy, German troops will have to take over there.

3. *Germany's power to wage war.*

I believe that it would be an exaggeration to say that Germany is exploiting the production power and the man power of Europe to the limit. I do not believe that she has been using every possible resource. Even if we assume that she can already use the raw materials of the Caucasus, as I said, the only doubtful point is the one concerning petroleum. I do not believe that it would be possible for Germany, considerably and quickly, to expand her productive power, even though she has secured the Ukraine.

4. Now what we want is for Germany to get ready for a long war.

We believe that we are justified in saying that gradually she is suc-
ceeding, but she is a long way from ready. She faces a much harder
job than she did when the war first began, and she has a much
longer road to tread than she thought she did. I hope that she will realize these things and get ready to expend her all in our common effort.

Page 2

#58955   Japanese Inter. 12/13/42 (92)
ARMY   Trans. 12/16/42 (A-e)[13]

Ōshima responded in mid-December with his impressions formed after a
four-hour discussion with Foreign Minister Ribbentrop. Although Ōshima
tried to put a good face on his assessment, his impressions could not have
been very reassuring to Tani. Quite the contrary. Ōshima recognized that the
war was "no pushover for the Germans," that "with the landing of united
nations troops in North Africa it is clear that the Reich will have to fight on
two fronts," and "that the overthrow of the Red regime could not be
counted on." Nevertheless, the Japanese envoy in Berlin was confident
"that our joint warfare in Europe and Asia is strengthening our superior
grip on the situation," and he felt "sure that next year the attack on Russia
will be through the Caucasus to the Near and Middle East."[14] Thus, it is
clear that MAGIC provided SIS and MIS teams with detail about the warring
government of Germany and its attitude to a possible separate peace, but
much the same can be said for the Soviet side of the equation.

Although the exact evidence in the full sweep of appropriate MAGIC messages dealing with Moscow remains largely classified, NSA did declassify a
few snippets of evidence concerning the Moscow connection in the early
1980s. They show that the Japanese Foreign Ministry sought to negotiate a
German-Soviet peace by working through its ambassador in the USSR, Satō
Naotake.

Satō's PURPLE traffic from Moscow to Tokyo was highly significant and
similar to Ōshima's PURPLE traffic from Berlin to Tokyo, although obviously
there was a great difference in the types of information to which each Japanese ambassador had access. (In the second half of 1942 the diplomatic
corps was moved out of Moscow and temporarily located in Kuibyshev.)
Arlington Hall Japanese translators sometimes developed a feeling for the
personalities and temperaments of the two ambassadors, Ōshima and Satō.
Ōshima was close and even ideologically committed to Hitler and the Nazi
inner circle; he was not a favorite at Arlington Hall. Yet Satō was highly regarded among several American translators because his messages showed
much human warmth, understanding, and compassion. Indeed, it was occa-

sionally rumored within Arlington Hall, stupidly so, that such admiration for the enemy was perhaps reason to question the translator's interpretation of certain nuances in some Japanese messages. Similarly, those translators who had lived and studied in Japan, sometimes as translators, were occasionally victims of conflicting emotions when they translated messages describing bombing devestation of their former Japanese communities and the death of their friends.[15] Nothing comparable to Ōshima's arrangement in Berlin existed for Satō in Moscow. Nevertheless, Tokyo's effort to play the role of the mediator in the German-Soviet war through the obscure Satō-Moscow connection was likely no less diligent than we know it was for the thoroughly documented Ōshima-Berlin connection.

Several different foreign cipher systems were being read by SIS and SSA during the war, and those systems were all included under the cover name MAGIC. There is little doubt that the dedicated and brilliant cryptanalysts at Arlington Hall also solved at least certain Soviet systems and that G-2 was "reading the mail" of an American ally. It is clear that intelligence about the Soviet Union reached Washington in Ambassador Satō's intercepted PURPLE messages. Furthermore, after mid-1941, when Matsuoka was no longer foreign minister, Tokyo sought to protect its increasingly fragile policy of neutrality with the Soviet Union. It feared that a victorious Moscow in the European war would then lash out at Japan. Prudence therefore dictated that Tokyo learn as much as possible about Moscow's intentions. Japanese cryptanalysts were trying to solve Soviet codes and ciphers, and the extent to which their successes were communicated in Japanese systems already solved by U.S. cryptanalysts is the extent to which Washington (and probably London) gained additional intelligence about the Soviet Union. The stakes were high during the war years, and failure to be informed about the intentions of an ally with checkered past policies or a potential adversary would not be tolerated in any modern national intelligence agency in a world at war.

As one would expect, the published firsthand accounts of various wartime participants have only generally referred to Japanese overtures to Moscow to conclude a separate peace. One former member of the Japanese Foreign Ministry cited overtures on three occasions (in September 1943 and in April and September 1944) in an early postwar publication.[16] The Soviet refusal to consider the matter of a separate peace was quick and decisive. In his still earlier memoirs, Secretary of State Cordell Hull publicly acknowledged these wartime Japanese efforts and expressed his relief and great satisfaction with the Soviet rebuff to the Japanese. Hull cited the Soviet government's envoy in Washington, Andrei A. Gromyko, as the source of this information, not MAGIC.[17] Safeguarding the MAGIC secret remained extremely important long after the war, and in this instance Hull could easily use the Gromyko cover. (Unlike the British, the Soviets were never officially let in on the MAGIC secret by the U.S. government during the war, although MAGIC-based information was sometimes passed on to the Soviets without revealing the source.)[18]

Secretary Hull not only knew through MAGIC about the 1943 and 1944 Japanese overtures, he also knew about the initial Japanese conversations with the Soviets in 1942. Foreign Minister Tōgō believed "that Japan should work to restore peace between Germany and the U.S.S.R." Thus, he stated publicly after the war that before resigning from office on 1 September 1942 he had "instructed Ambassador Satō—then evacuated, with others of the diplomatic corps, from Moscow to Kuibyshev—to visit Moscow from time to time to prepare the ground so that he could undertake mediation immediately upon receipt of instructions to that effect."[19] Nevertheless, MAGIC documentation remains restricted with reference to the Satō-Moscow connection.

Much of that information has been obliterated in the declassification process. However, buried in the center of one of the special research histories (SRHs) declassified by NSA in 1983 is ample evidence to establish the connection. The document, SRH-252, is titled "A Version of the Japanese Problem in the Signal Intelligence Service (Later Signal Security Agency), 1930-1945" by John Hurt. The author, a remarkably skilled Japanese linguist who joined Friedman's unique team of cryptanalysts in 1930, compiled this 218-page study shortly after the war. Hurt based his study on highly classified contemporary materials and his own private Japanese files. In a particularly significant appendix, titled "Prologue and Commentary on Four Groups of Selected Messages," Hurt quotes verbatim from MAGIC messages and comments in detail about relevant circumstances. Thus Hurt, who had a keen sense of history and of the Japanese personalities in this wartime cryptographic drama, understood Satō's role and provides the key for the modern researcher.

Satō's appointment as ambassador to Moscow attracted much attention at SIS and MIS. It was claimed that his diplomatic position in Moscow in 1942 was comparable with the position of Ambassadors Nomura Kichisaburō and Kurusu Saburō in Washington, D.C., on the eve of the Pearl Harbor attack.[20] Intelligence analysts deduced that a careful study of Satō's PURPLE traffic could reveal information perhaps missed earlier in the Tokyo communications with the two Washington ambassadors, and many MAGIC analysts greatly respected Satō, not only because he showed such human warmth and understanding, but also because he was remarkably sophisticated in his wartime analysis.

Ambassador Satō was angered by the reception he received in Moscow at the outset of his tenure. He had long sought an audience with Stalin, but Foreign Commissar Vyacheslav Molotov stalled and claimed that Stalin was too busy to meet with the Japanese ambassador. Satō replied hotly that if Molotov thought that

> "Stalin is busy, what do you think Premier Tōjō is? It is simply the custom in Japan as everywhere else for the chief of state upon request to grant an audience to a foreign ambassador." Molotov retorted that Russia has no such precedence and that Stalin is simply too busy.
>
> In conclusion Satō, deeply hurt and in this respect typical of all Japanese, concludes "Stalin has seen [British Ambassador Archibald Clark] Kerr when he presented his credentials and so if the Russians do not grant me this interview it will delight London and Washington to see Stalin discriminate against us."[21]

It is significant that Japanese language translators at Arlington Hall, particularly Hurt, saw a deeper meaning in this initial meeting of Molotov and Satō on 14 April 1942. Foreign diplomats found Premier Stalin, president of the Council of People's Commissars of the Soviet Union, generally inaccessible, and they were often frustrated in their dealings with lesser Soviet functionaries who seldom were empowered to engage in constructive discussion on even minor matters, the American chargé in Kuibyshev complained in February 1942. Indeed, the newly appointed American ambassador, Rear Admiral William H. Standley, arrived in Kuibyshev on 7 April 1942 and presented his credentials, not to Stalin whom he did not see for some time, but to Mikhail Ivanovich Kalinin, president of the Presidium of the Supreme Council of the Soviet Union. The date was 14 April, the same day Satō met with Molotov.[22] But in the instance of Satō's meeting, John Hurt, knowing that Satō was usually a mild-mannered man and well controlled, concluded that the Japanese ambassador would not have reacted so strongly unless he realized that he was being deliberately snubbed by Stalin. Stalin probably did not want to meet with Satō directly, preferring to be as elusive as possible and thereby avoiding any direct and possibly embarrassing entreaty for peace from Satō. Significantly, MIS sought SIS assistance in interpreting such subtleties in Japanese messages.

Soviet policy toward Japan was in a state of flux throughout the war. There was a continuous succession of small changes depending largely on Moscow's relations with the Anglo-American governments and on the status of the Soviet Army in front of the German invaders. As early as December

1941, during negotiations started when British Foreign Secretary Anthony Eden visited Moscow, Stalin toyed with the idea of going to war against Japan.[23] The Soviet premier wrote to Churchill on 30 March 1942 and had a long talk with the new British ambassador, Sir Archibald Clark Kerr, of whom Satō was very jealous. Stalin was convinced "that our joint work will proceed in an atmosphere of perfect mutual confidence."[24] By that time there was very little chance that Stalin would agree to Japanese mediation, but it was not in his interests to reveal his intentions to anyone—Tokyo, London, or Washington—at that time. This was one reason why the Ōshima-Berlin connection was so important to American strategic planners and analysts as they studied Hitler's attitudes. Yet until the end of 1942, Ambassador Kerr continued to fear "a possible peace between Hitler and Stalin if we" British fail to live up to Churchill's promise to Stalin to establish a second front in 1943.

Churchill's closest military adviser, General Sir Alan Brooke (later Field Marshal Viscount Alanbrooke), did not agree with Ambassador Kerr.[25] And it appears that the new Japanese foreign minister, Shigemitsu Mamoru (20 April 1943 to 22 July 1944), from the outset of his tenure lined up on the same side as the British field marshal. Shigemitsu was under no illusion that Japan would be able to mediate peace between Germany and the Soviet Union. Moreover, since the Soviet Army had assumed the offensive and was strikingly successful at every turn, Moscow was taking on a threatening attitude toward Japan, and Shigemitsu was convinced that Stalin would eventually denounce the neutrality treaty.[26] Thus, with a complex progression of events increasingly favorable to the Soviet Union, Stalin was finally ready, by the end of October 1943, to reveal his true intentions to Secretary Hull. Stalin made "a statement of transcendent importance," Hull wrote in his memoirs. "He astonished and delighted me by saying clearly and unequivocally that, when the Allies succeeded in defeating Germany, the Soviet Union would then join in defeating Japan."[27]

Expediency played no small part in the conduct of Soviet wartime diplomacy, and the fate of Soviet-Japanese relations was increasingly tied to the consequences of the war. Furthermore, in the latter part of the war Stalin was no doubt posturing and increasingly vying for strategic position in the postwar world.

Ambassador Satō's reports of his earliest conversations with Foreign Commissar Molotov in April 1942 clearly set forth the urgency of Japanese concerns and of Soviet indifference. Satō suggested that the ultimate outcome of the European war was much in doubt and that the effectiveness of U-boats off the eastern coast of the United States would severely reduce the amount of lend-lease matériel reaching the Soviet Union. Therefore, the

Japanese ambassador hinted that it would be prudent to negotiate with Hitler sooner rather than later. Molotov emphatically denied Satō's assertions and quickly changed the subject to an extremely embarrassing topic for the Japanese envoy. A coy Molotov explained that

> Mr. Matsuoka formed a nonaggression pact with us on his way back to Tokyo from Berlin [only one year ago]. Both Ambassador Tatekawa [Yoshitsugu] and Foreign Minister Matsuoka himself told me that you Japanese knew nothing about the coming German attack on Russia beforehand. I don't believe you Japanese knew anything about it at all. They even said that Germany's attack on us was contrary to Japan's plans and that Japan had no part in it. But what I don't understand is this: Mr. Matsuoka stayed in Berlin for a long time. He talked with Hitler, Goering and Ribbentrop often and long. You see how things have turned out. No, it is all beyond me.[28]

John Hurt, the Arlington Hall author of this postwar study, had translated many MAGIC intercepts in April 1941, and he recognized the deception immediately. He had evidence that Molotov knew that the Japanese foreign minister "had been advised somewhat in detail about the German attack on Russia more than two months beforehand."[29] Satō, who was not in the diplomatic service the previous year, claimed to know little of the circumstances leading to the neutrality pact, and although Satō could not get Matsuoka's version because the former foreign minister was ill, he told Molotov that he would query former Ambassador Tatekawa, Satō's predecessor in Moscow, and report back to Molotov. Satō axiomatically declared that "this is a strange war. You are on one side and we are on the other. We see only one side of each other's faces."[30] Although they warned each other to adhere strictly to the terms of the neutrality pact, Molotov and Satō ended their conversation on a friendly note. Yet there remained a threatening undertone that future relations were inescapably tied to the fortunes of war. Significantly, American and British intelligence officers knew all of this.

Ōshima's reports from Berlin were no less foreboding for the prospects of peace on the eastern front. The Japanese Foreign Ministry, the army, and the navy continued to watch in late 1942 for an opportunity to effect a German-Soviet rapprochement, in spite of information that Germany was completely "uninterested in peace" (see note 9). However, by early 1943 Japanese concern was heightened because, as the foreign minister wrote to Ōshima, "we look at the results of last year's German-Russian fighting along with the recent resistance on the part of the Russians."[31] Therefore, Ōshima was ordered to do his utmost to influence the German leadership to consider a negotiated peace. Yet there remained the hint that Japanese foreign policy could not be held up or tied to the diminishing prospects that a German-Soviet rapprochement might yet materialize.

Near the end of January 1943, Ōshima replied with sureness. Although "the German High Command admits that the situation on the Eastern Front has suddenly become desperate," Ōshima confessed, "German leaders have a deep determination to fight the war through. . . . They have determined never to compromise with either the Soviet or England or the United States—never!"[32] Thus, Hitler's obstinacy referred the issue to the judgment of battle during the third summer of the war on the eastern front.

July 1943 brought news of the staggering defeat for the Germans at the Battle of Kursk and the resignation of Mussolini in Italy. It took Tokyo a while to assess the full impact of these disasters and to consider modification of Japanese policy toward the war in Europe, but at the outset Ōshima sounded the alarm to the Germans and to his own government. "I am afraid throughout this upheaval," he said to a German Foreign Ministry officer whom Ribbentrop had assigned to the Japanese embassy to keep Ōshima supplied with information. "Italy is shaping a government that will cordially shake hands with the Anglo-Saxons and start peace talks right off the bat." The German liaison admitted that Italy would probably "drop out," but because "Italian forces were never any good" and the Germans "had to keep bolstering Italy with men, arms, and planes," the loss of this ally will help Hitler "to fight this war to the end."[33] However, this false optimism was soon exposed and hastened by Mussolini's complete debacle and rescue by Hitler in September. These were ominous signs for Tokyo and the Axis coalition generally.

The communications between Foreign Minister Shigemitsu and Ambassador Ōshima throughout September 1943 were heavily dominated by discussion concerning the Italian surrender, the new Badoglio government's "betrayal," and Mussolini's survival.[34] There seemed to be an almost embarrassed silence about the question of a separate peace. Tokyo was preoccupied with news of the immediate disaster in the European Axis coalition and did not broach the topic of a German-Soviet rapprochement, and only on one occasion during the month did Ōshima report the vague and not altogether unusual rumors of a rapprochement.[35]

A sort of artificiality seemed to characterize Tokyo's treatment of the new alignment in Europe. Emperor Hirohito sent Mussolini, "Head of the Italian Fascist Republican Government," a congratulatory telegram "on the occasion of the third anniversary of the establishing of the Tripartite Pact," and Foreign Minister Shigemitsu sent a similar message.[36] Finally, by the beginning of October, Ōshima was hard put to reduce Tokyo's suspicion about

The former Japanese embassy (right) at 24–27 Tiergartenstrasse, Berlin, and the former Italian embassy in the background (to the east) as they appeared in 1991. (Photograph by the author)

the frailty of the new German-backed Mussolini regime. And Ōshima explained, probably to the bewilderment of Tokyo and certainly to the amazement of American cryptographic eavesdroppers, that Mussolini expected to raise "a trustworthy Italian army" of 200,000–300,000 troops; moreover, Ōshima continued, "we may expect wonderful results therefrom for the Germans."[37] This total lack of realism indicates that Ōshima failed to understand the extent of the Italian debacle, and in an editorializing endnote, SSA compilers and analysts were quick to observe that "this message shows a very evident war fatigue and requires almost paranoiac rationalization to translate into English, which permits of no such vagaries of grammar and rhetoric. For a military man like Ōshima is supposed to be, this is almost unbelievable, but is nevertheless true." On the same day this incredible message was sent, 2 October, Ōshima "left Berlin for the Führer's Headquarters on the Eastern front," he informed Tokyo upon his return to the German capital.[38] Ōshima's additional reports on the Italian debacle were insignificant and limited to the rhetoric of Ribbentrop and Hitler. Thus, Foreign Minister

Shigemitsu, quite understandably, remained stoic about the Italian situation.

Ōshima's reports on the attitudes of German leaders concerning a possible rapprochement were more candid, if no less ominous. American intelligence analysts now saw a different aspect of Ōshima. He was baiting. He was frank with Ribbentrop. The Japanese envoy reminded Ribbentrop that in the summer of 1941, soon after the invasion of the Soviet Union, he and Hitler had told Ōshima that the German "object was to give the Red army a terrific defeat, break Russia up into small nations, and render her ineffective; but now," Ōshima continued, "I consider it impossible to do anything like that." Therefore, Ōshima advised rhetorically, "why not soften down your terms in dealing with Russia and stress knocking out the Anglo-Americans . . . don't you think you could reconsider this matter?" Ōshima noted that Ribbentrop, "changing his tone and not bristling with his usual antagonism when this subject was broached," said that he regarded the question of peace as "a serious matter" and that he was "going to think about it."[39]

However, it was clear that there would be no change in German policy, for Hitler continued to hold fast. Hitler told Ōshima that he thought "it the best policy to first slap at the American and British forces as soon as we get a chance now, and then turn again on the Soviet."[40] There was no hint in Hitler's comments that he had altered his opinion that the German-Soviet front must be decided by force of Germans arms, as Ribbentrop explained to Ōshima earlier in the day, 4 October. Yet Ōshima's description of Hitler's disposition and attitude is more telling. For the purpose of comparison Ōshima noted that Ribbentrop "was not yet completely well" because he had pneumonia and more recently, during the celebration of the anniversary of the Tripartite Pact (27 September), "he caught cold and had to go to bed." On the other hand, "Hitler was sprightly in both body and soul. While explaining the military situation he was very calm, but once he got started on Badoglio's betrayal and his vituperations against American and British forces, he slapped the top of his desk with his hand and spoke in his frank old style with boundless enthusiasm."[41]

As badly as Ōshima wanted to see a German-Soviet peace materialize, he knew that as long as Hitler remained resolute in his no-peace-negotiations stance, Ribbentrop's so-called conciliatory attitude was of no consequence.

In fact, Germany had probably already ruled out the possibility of concluding a peace treaty with the Soviet Union considerably before Molotov first agreed formally to the unconditional surrender policy, together with an agreement to refuse a separate peace, in the Four Power Declaration at the end of the October 1943 Foreign Ministers Conference in Moscow.[42] At the time, however, most American foreign policymakers were busy with immediate wartime needs, and they probably were not tuned finely enough to take full advantage of this particular MAGIC informational coup. Had they known assuredly, and from the outset, that Hitler would *never* agree to a compromise on the eastern front, American foreign policy could have been less conciliatory to Stalin.

Japanese officials in Berlin realized that an in-depth analysis of the war was essential at this critical stage. Thus, Ōshima and his military and naval attachés concluded a thorough study after the ambassador's meetings with Ribbentrop and Hitler. Their analysis was forwarded to Tokyo some nineteen months before the eventual German surrender in May 1945. There appeared to be little hope for a German-Soviet rapprochement, although Tokyo, and belatedly Ōshima, advised that one good way for Hitler to achieve an opportunity to strike at the West more effectively would be to settle the war in the East politically. Yet "right now the war is gradually growing into a darkly earnest phase," Ōshima noted, and he felt very fatalistic. He concluded rather prophetically, "Whether or not we are to win or lose this war, of course, depends on how well both Japan and Germany fight it out together."[43]

The topic of a possible rapprochement was infrequently and then only fleetingly raised in the Ōshima-Shigemitsu exchange of messages during the remainder of 1943. Ōshima reported verbatim what Ribbentrop told him during their meeting on 25 November: "At the present time we are not considering any compromise peace with the Soviet Union. Our new strategy in the war is to completely paralyze the strength of the Soviet forces."[44] Two weeks later Ōshima again conferred with Ribbentrop, but the subject of a separate peace was not raised at all.[45] Ōshima's reports about German tenacity came as no surprise to Shigemitsu.

Japanese officials in Tokyo could easily deduce from some of Ōshima's other reports that Germany was losing the war—such deductions must have been foreboding. Ōshima's messages in late November, for instance, were not reassuring when they described the damage caused by powerful air attacks against Berlin. "Although it was a perfect carpet-bombing pattern," one report read, "tremendous damage resulted also from the spreading of fire by high winds and incendiary bombs. . . . Right now, the 23rd, fires are rising everywhere. . . . Foreign Minister Ribbentrop called at the embassy in person to make kind enquiries."[46] And Ōshima soon reported on the damage caused by the bombing raids on the following two nights. "The embassies and legations of Denmark, Croatia, Spain, and Italy were damaged. The others were partially or completely destroyed. Besides myself," Ōshima proclaimed, "the only people [of the diplomatic corps] who are now staying in Berlin are the Bulgarian Minister and Italian Ambassador."[47] Ōshima

The fifteenth-century Pomeranian Arnim palace as it appeared in 1991 near Boitzenburg, a two-hour drive north of Berlin. The middle wing with the square tower was rented by the Japanese and used for embassy purposes in 1943 while the Allies were bombing Berlin. (Photograph by the author)

moved most members of his staff and the Germans employed by the Japanese embassy to Boitzenburg, 100 kilometers north of Berlin, where he had obtained a rental option on the middle wing of the Arnim palace. The lease had been signed in October as a precautionary measure. However, Ōshima himself and certain administrative staff and clerical assistants divided their time between the Japanese embassy on Tiergartenstrasse and Boitzenburg. Later, shortly before Christmas, most members of the Boitzenburg group returned to the embassy in Berlin after the bomb damage had been repaired.[48]

Ōshima did not know at the time that the November attacks on Berlin were only the beginning of a great air onslaught that would last until March 1944. Most of the sixteen major attacks were guided by radar, carried out under heavy cloud cover. Not until March was the weather clear enough over Berlin for Allied aircraft to obtain reliable photographic evidence of the bomb damage; meanwhile, Ōshima's intercepted messages to Tokyo were useful in the Allied assessment of bombing effectiveness.[49] Reading intercepted enemy signal traffic was an important way of determining the effectiveness of Allied strategic bombing.[50] Indeed, Edwin Reischauer, a liaison officer between Special Branch and Arlington Hall, wrote that "the most accurate reports on the results of Allied bombing in Germany . . . came from the messages to Tokyo of the Japanese ambassador in Berlin."[51] Reischauer left the Japanese language program at Arlington Hall, and by the fall of 1943 he was responsible for deciding which intercepted messages were important enough to be transmitted immediately by secret telephone from Arlington Hall to Special Branch in the Pentagon.

The broad strategic implications for the Axis coalition were clear to Foreign Minister Shigemitsu, yet he was helpless to react in any but the most pedestrian of ways. He wrote to Ōshima a week after the massive bombing of Berlin that he felt

> deep sympathy for the material and spiritual horror suffered by the members of your staff during the recent bombings. I wish to make up, even though only partly, for their material losses by presenting them with some cash. So, will Your Excellency please distribute to all sufferers an average of 2,000 yen each. You may use your own judgment in the exact amounts according to the extent of damage done individuals.[52]

And so the bombing, which Churchill sought in "making the German people taste and gulp each month a sharper dose of the miseries they have showered upon mankind," reminded the Japanese partner that the alternatives to devastation and total defeat were rapidly diminishing.

Hitler remained unyielding in his attitude toward Stalin, and once Ōshima reported this early in the new year, 1944, Tokyo chose not to pursue peace. Furthermore, Shigemitsu knew that discussion of peace always quickened rage and anxiety in Hitler, so Ōshima was careful when near the outset of the new year, on 22 January 1944, he had a working lunch with Ribbentrop at Hitler's headquarters in East Prussia. Later in the day he met with Hitler for an hour and a half. Both Germans told their Japanese confidant that a separate peace would be impossible to arrange.[53] Only the verdict of the battlefield would resolve the dilemma, but the Japanese saw little promise in this course.

By mid-1944 Tokyo started to foresee the day when Japan would be the sole surviving Axis power to fight against the overwhelming strength of the Allied coalition. Thus, coming three days before the Allied landings at Normandy, Ōshima's prophesy was not without significance: "I can see where it is going to be very hard for Germany to wage war from now on."[54] News of the successful landings and the rapid development of the second front confirmed the Japanese envoy's worst fears, and the attempt on Hitler's life the next month was symptomatic of a certain amount of unrest. Some Japanese viewed it as possibly a warning that Hitler's government was in as much trouble at home as his armed forces were in the field.

There was an enormous outpouring of Ōshima-Tokyo traffic about the attempted assassination.[55] Very soon Ōshima started to offer plausible explanations that were of interest to MIS analysts. He reasoned that the traditional and highly professional Prussian officer corps had long been dissatisfied with Hitler's government, but steady success of Nazi policy and the gratifying progress of the war had not permitted it to act until now.[56] Ōshima also sent a message from Berlin to Foreign Minister Shigemitsu saying that "the resignation of our cabinet together with the attempted assassination of the German chancellor struck here like a bolt from the blue."[57] (Prime Minister Tōjō, in office since 18 October 1941, was obligated to step down on 22 July 1944. The new cabinet headed by Koiso Kuniaki retained Shigemitsu as foreign minister.)

In these dire circumstances Tokyo suddenly renewed its campaign for a German-Soviet peace. In an ironic twist of events, Ōshima suggested to Shigemitsu that "it appeared that the conspirators' ideological tendency was for peace with Russia," yet he knew that those same anti-Hitler forces were being pursued with a vengeance.[58] Foreign Minister Shigemitsu explained to Ōshima that "with the European situation abruptly coming to a head," he should "go at once to the High Command and make a statement to Foreign Minister Ribbentrop" about the utmost importance of peace.[59]

The fatalistic Ōshima went to the High Command headquarters and had interviews with Ribbentrop and Hitler on 4 September 1944.[60] Ribbentrop admitted "that although there had been rumors to the effect that Germany was already sounding out Russia through contacts in Stockholm, these were absolutely nothing but rumors. In an important matter such as this, it would not be possible to do anything without receiving permission from Hitler."[61] Ōshima soon talked directly with Hitler and again was told that there was no possibility of a negotiated peace. Hitler remained fully in control.

Ōshima suggested possible terms for negotiations. Since the Soviet Union had already restored its 1940 western border, maybe if Germany were to guarantee that frontier, Stalin "would make peace with Germany in order to undertake postwar rehabilitation immediately." Ōshima had already pointed out to Hitler that the Soviet Union had suffered great losses in the fighting and that there were many conflicts of interest between the Russians and the Anglo-Americans. Hitler explained to his longtime Japanese confidant that he had "made it a point to study carefully the policy and plans of our enemy Stalin. Both he and I are leaders of dictatorial states. Therefore, I

believe that I understand well his way of thinking. Hence, I am of the opinion that as long as Stalin is not faced with the weakening of his own country,
he will not accept [an overture for negotiations]." Ōshima had already made
the following point to Ribbentrop, and he now tried to draw out Hitler by
boldly stating that "according to what you told me in 1935 [i.e., nine years
earlier], it was Germany's intention to split up the Soviet Union into several
small states, and I believe that this was Germany's original objective at the
outbreak of the Russo-German War. However, at present don't you think
that it is utterly impossible?"

Hitler admitted that although such treatment of the Soviet Union might
have been possible "throughout 1941 and 1942," it probably was no longer
possible because of the development of a number of hitches in the war. Finally, Ribbentrop said to Ōshima, in Hitler's presence, "that if the Japanese
should sound out Russian opinion directly, the enemy would think that it
had been requested by the Germans, and would conclude that Germany was
showing the white feather. Consequently, he desired that this also be avoided
in the future." There could be no doubt, peace was not an option for
Hitler's Germany, short of unconditional surrender. Ōshima reluctantly
concluded that a rapprochement was "impossible," and some Japanese were
starting to suspect that their options for ending the war were likely to be
equally limited.

Japan pushed harder than ever for a German-Soviet rapprochement as it
became more obvious in Tokyo that time was running out for both Axis
powers. Clearly, Ōshima was not making progress with Hitler; thus, the Japanese Supreme Council for the Conduct of the War (Saikō Sensō Shidō
Kaigi) wanted to send a special envoy to Moscow in order to convince Stalin
that it was in his best interest to conclude a peace treaty with Hitler. The sophisticated Ambassador Satō in Moscow was piqued by Tokyo's tactics. He
explained in a message that at such a critical point in the war it was most important for Japan to back off from the intermediary role, to allow the course
of the European war to decide the matter, and to work to promote cordial
relations with Moscow and to demonstrate Japanese sincerity and commitment to the Neutrality Pact. Satō declared that during the past two and a
half years he had "been able to get the Russians to maintain their neutrality,
thus giving our Empire the opportunity to devote all its efforts in the
south." Yet Japanese relations with the Soviet Union would inevitably deteriorate if Tokyo continued to strive for the German-Soviet rapprochement.
As the Japanese diplomat in Moscow said, "For the sake of our prestige we
do not want to ask too often and get a refusal every time." Satō then pointed
out that "in dealing with a problem such as peace between Germany and
Russia, it has become clear both from the interview which Ōshima had with

Hitler recently and from the talk which I have just had with Molotov that both Germany and Russia have rejected any efforts along that line [i.e., peace]."

Eventually, Satō offered to resign his post in Moscow if Tokyo insisted on an alternative policy,[62] but Japanese policymakers, particularly Foreign Minister Shigemitsu, became more appreciative of Satō's wisdom and deferred to his judgment. Shigemitsu was not so trusting of the traditionally pro-Nazi Ōshima and his judgment, yet the Japanese envoy in distant and increasingly isolated Berlin could only be left to his own resources.

Finally, after a mid-November meeting with Ribbentrop, Ōshima reported to Tokyo what must have been regarded by Shigemitsu as an eleventh-hour admission of doom. Ribbentrop said to Ōshima:

> I do not think that Stalin will consent to peace negotiations so long as he has no doubts as to his own actual power. . . .
>
> The tone of Stalin's recent speech also would indicate that he feels his strength. Furthermore, his calling Japan an aggressor nation in that speech, coming just before the presidential election, was intended to give Roosevelt his support on the side, and in addition to that, might be regarded as a gesture toward England and America. At the same time Stalin doubtless wanted to make a show both at home and abroad that his country has come to occupy a very strong position.[63]

Indeed, it was a jubilant and confident Marshal Stalin who congratulated President Roosevelt on his reelection. Stalin had good reason to assert in his congratulatory message sent to Washington on 9 November that the Allied powers will "round off the struggle against the common foe and ensure victory in the name of liberating mankind from Nazi tyranny."[64]

Japan was having difficulty maintaining the status quo with the Soviet Union and went out of its way to obtain reassuring statements from the Kremlin regarding Japanese-Soviet neutrality should Hitler's Germany collapse. Furthermore, Ambassador Satō was instructed to request an explanation of Stalin's reference to Japan as an aggressor. Tellingly, Tokyo was forced to accept the lame explanation that "Marshal Stalin's remarks were made from a theoretical point of view and only deal with past history."[65]

Japan, painfully conscious of the rapidly deteriorating military situation for the Axis powers, wanted to keep Germany in the war against the Anglo-American powers as long as possible. Some modus vivendi between the Soviet Union and Germany would enable Germany to concentrate all of its efforts in the West. Most significantly, however, Tokyo considered a peace between Germany and the Soviet Union to be essential to frustrate attempts by the Anglo-Americans to induce Stalin to enter the war against Japan. Indeed, Ōshima's messages even in 1945 continued to raise the question of a possible German-Soviet rapprochement.[66] In the end, however, Foreign Minister Shigemitsu had to be satisfied with maintaining the very precarious status quo, in which, as a wartime U.S. intelligence study concluded, "Japan's friends are Russia's enemies and Russia's friends are Japan's enemies."[67]

This was a nightmare that had long haunted the Japanese, and it became worse during the last few months of the war in Europe. Until 8 August 1945, Tokyo sought desperately to make peace with Moscow's friends before Russia could join them in warring against the sole remaining Axis power. However, at 5:00 P.M. on 8 August 1945 (Moscow time), Molotov summoned Satō to give him a statement which concluded with the affirmation that "the Soviet government declares that as of tomorrow, that is of 9 August, the Soviet Union will consider it is in a state of war with Japan."[68]

8
Magic and the End
of the Third Reich

In early January 1945 Soviet forces launched a massive offensive westward from the banks of the Vistula. Soon the German nightmare came true—the "Bolshevik hordes" arrived on German soil—and within a few weeks units of the Soviet Army reached the Oder River, within as little as fifty miles of the battered city of Berlin. In the west, after recovery from Hitler's Ardennes offensive, the Allies struck back in early January, pushing into Germany and across the Rhine at Remagen on 7 March. The German capital was caught between the rapidly advancing Allied fronts, and Berliners realized that their beloved city was doomed. Yet morale remained remarkably high among the Berliners, and the machinery of government in the beleaguered city still functioned surprisingly well until heavy Soviet artillery was set up and the systematic shelling began on 20 April, continuing throughout much of the rest of April. Encirclement of Berlin was completed on 24 April, and collapse was near. On 2 May the city surrendered to the Russians.

Ōshima, who had long chronicled the war and included his own analysis in reports to Tokyo, continued to reward MAGIC intelligence analysts in their ringside seats as the melodrama of the disintegration of the Third Reich unfolded. In this final chapter of MAGIC intelligence inadvertently given to the Anglo-Americans by Hitler's Japanese confidant, Ōshima easily measured up to the standards of his earlier revelations.

It was clear to Anglo-American intelligence analysts that the war in Europe was drawing to a close, and while they might not expect revelations as significant as those in Ōshima's earlier messages, it was assumed that the Japanese ambassador would adhere to his time-honored practice and continue to report. There was, for example, the battle for Berlin itself.

Although the battle for Berlin has been widely researched,[1] the siege itself is unique in the long history of siegecraft because never have such immediate and elaborate enemy reports about conditions inside the defender's camp been available. Traditionally, contemporary military assessments have had to be drawn from other sources, such as the commander leading the attack, and those views could be modified by stories from spies slipping through the lines, interrogation of enemy captives, or aerial photographic reconnaissance. And for the historian of World War II, long after the fall of the Third Reich, Berlin diarists have occasionally published their personal impressions of municipal life during the siege.[2] But in the last months of the war in Europe, British and American strategists, not Russian commanders outside of Berlin, received regular reports from inside the old capital. They described living conditions and what precisely was occurring during the gradual destruction of the once exuberant city. These detailed reports were compiled by Ōshima, and they were as considered and revealing as his earlier intercepts.

Ambassador Ōshima's searching MAGIC reports were based on more than personal impression, and, unlike the observations of the diarists, they have the crispness and urgency of the immediate conditions in the dying city. Material was submitted to him by a large embassy staff, including three counselors, a first secretary, several second and third secretaries, and many service attachés. The ranking Japanese military officers in the embassy were a lieutenant general and a rear admiral. Since February 1941, Ōshima had been the senior Japanese official in Europe, and an increasingly large number of Japanese nationals—diplomatic personnel, newspaper correspondents, bank and commercial officials, for example—sought refuge in Berlin and came under Ōshima's jurisdiction as other European cities were overrun by Allied armies. These Japanese nationals brought with them news of conditions in formerly German-occupied territory, and Ōshima included their reports in his messages to Japan. Moreover, Ōshima's longstanding sources of information, Ribbentrop, high-ranking German military officers, and other top government ministers, continued to confide in the Japanese ambassador as the Allied ring tightened.[3]

During the increasingly hopeless conditions of the opening months of 1945 Ōshima wrote detailed messages describing living conditions in Berlin. One such report of 8 March focused on the topics of transportation, public services, air attacks, communications (especially with foreign countries), morale, availability of food, and housing. Ambassador Ōshima sent the following message to Foreign Minister Shigemitsu in Tokyo on 8 March 1945; it was intercepted on 9 March, and on the same day it was received by the U.S. Army Signal Security Agency (formerly Signal Intelligence Service) at Arlington Hall. It was deciphered and translated on 10 March 1945. Ōshima explained that "the following is a summary of recent living conditions in

Berlin." He then outlined his assessment for Shigemitsu.[4] First, with regard to transportation:

> 1. Except immediately after large air raids, the S-Bahn [electric train service to the suburbs] has been running on practically all of the lines, but the U-Bahn [subway system] has quite a few places within the city at which the trains make connections by means of shuttle runs with the lines running from the central sections of the city to the suburbs. The streetcar lines in the city are very slowly repaired and they are extremely irregular. For that reason their practical use has been greatly reduced. With the exception of the "rush hours" [expressed in English] in the early hours of the morning and in the evening, traffic facilities have been reduced to half, so there is very great confusion, and, as previously reported, after half past nine or ten o'clock practically all the lines stop running.
>
> 2. The use of benzene for civilians has been more and more restricted. Places like my office have been receiving no more than 200 liters [about 53 gallons] per month, but beginning with this month [March] even that has been stopped. Therefore, many people are now purchasing benzene with coffee on the black market for use in both official and private cars. However, because of the stringent conditions, it has gradually become more difficult to purchase anything on the black market. And particularly because traffic connections with foreign countries have become more difficult, as described later on, obtaining coffee has also become quite a problem.

Nevertheless, Ōshima had reported on 22 February that since the German trains were almost entirely occupied with the transport of troops, "we have begun to evacuate the Japanese (nationals) by automobile and to buy provisions for the siege."[5] Ōshima's five-part message continued:

> 3. It is also true that the barricades [expressed by the English word] are obstructing traffic within the city. They are constructed in a number of sections of the city, but most of them are centered around the area of the Wilhelmstrasse [about 10 blocks from the Japanese embassy]. They are from 2 to 3 meters high and from 1 to 2 meters thick; made of debris and bricks, the barricades are built by prisoners of war, convicts, the Volkssturm, and women.
>
> 4. Restrictions on the use of gas and coal have been intensified in every household; furthermore, recently electric current has been frequently cut off as an economy measure. Often there is virtually no

electric power from sundown to bedtime, which makes it difficult to [words missing—?maintain proper temperature?] in homes, and it is impossible to use the radio or to show movies. The result of all this is to rob the people in general of their recreation.

As late as May 1944 Berliners could be entertained in the twenty theaters and 114 cinemas still in operation.[6] However, the last wartime performance of the Berlin Philharmonic Orchestra took place on the afternoon of 12 April 1945, and electricity was turned on specifically for the occasion. Albert Speer, minister of armaments and munitions, wrote that he "ordered Brünnhilde's last aria and the finale from *Götterdämmerung*—a rather bathetic and also melancholy gesture pointing to the end of the Reich." Then came Beethoven's *Violin Concerto in D major* and finally the program for Berliners huddled in overcoats in the unheated Philharmonic Hall concluded with a performance of Bruckner's *Symphony No. 4 in E flat* (the *Romantic*).[7] Ōshima continued:

Furthermore, in the houses of the general public cardboard has been used to replace window panes broken by the constant air attacks, so that electric light is needed even in the daytime. When the electric power is cut off, some of the retail stores have to close, which frequently makes it difficult for citizens to purchase daily necessities. This situation has caused a sharp increase in the demand for candles, but it is practically impossible to get them in Berlin. Moreover, when the air raid signals are sounded, the electric current is always turned on so that people can hear the radio announcements. On Sundays the current is turned on all day and special efforts are made to provide facilities for recreation and laundering on those days.

A month earlier, 4 February, Ōshima had reported to Tokyo that because the Russians had occupied Upper Silesia it was necessary to place restrictions on the use of coal, and the advance of the Russians resulted also in restrictions being placed on the use of gas and electricity. Since there was severe cold at the time, many inconveniences and restraints were placed on every family, and very heavy restrictions were also placed on transportation agencies inside and outside the city. The use of charcoal-burning buses, for example, was virtually discontinued. "The developments of the last two or three weeks have placed a very heavy burden, material and moral, on the ordinary German." Nevertheless, Ōshima maintained, the people as a whole were maintaining extraordinary composure, "and one can find no symptom

. . . that a state of political disorder existed or that the Germans had lost their fighting spirit."[8]

5. As another measure to save electricity, the use of telephones has been greatly restricted. Although up to now government offices, foreign diplomatic missions, and hotels have not been affected, the privilege of making calls on home telephones has been suspended in many places and it is only possible to receive calls at home. Furthermore, the recent large-scale air attacks on the central part of Berlin have left many areas without telephone service, thus considerably hindering the activities of my office [in the Japanese embassy].

On 10 February Ōshima reported that as a result of the recent Allied bombing, "the central agencies of the government were temporarily paralyzed" and it was "impossible to communicate by telephone with the government office section."[9]

6. Hotels and restaurants, for example, have been greatly damaged by the continuous air attacks, and the authorities are providing special facilities for their restoration. Nevertheless, there are many traffic problems in the city and in general there is great confusion. Contact between members of my staff and the Germans has been made more difficult by the restricted transportation facilities, and eating and drinking in restaurants at night is practically impossible because of the air raids and the transportation restrictions.

After a large air raid carried out by American planes in early February, Ōshima reported that among the great hotels completely destroyed by fire or heavily damaged were the Esplanade, Excelsior, and Fürstenhof; surviving at the time was the Adlon.[10] Ōshima's message went on to give information about air attacks:

7. Recent air attacks over Berlin have not been as heavy as those of 3 and 26 February, but air attacks on central Saxony have been so extensive that they have often caused air raid alarms to be sounded in Berlin as well. Then, too, there are frequent so-called nuisance attacks. Most of them come at about 10:00 P.M. and last an hour or so, but sometimes they occur for an hour before dawn, beginning about 3:00 A.M. Although they are called "nuisance attacks," recently at least 40–50 Mosquito planes have participated—the usual number is 60–80—dropping two-ton bombs and attempting to destroy resi-

dences with aerial mines. A large number of bombs have fallen in the neighborhood of my office [at 24–27 Tiergartenstrasse], but usually the explosions have broken only window panes. On the whole damage from "nuisance attacks" has not been particularly great, but since the attacks come every night it is difficult to overcome a feeling of annoyance. Furthermore, subways and streetcar lines, for example, are often damaged.

Ōshima inspected the damage firsthand. After the attack on 3 February, one Berliner saw the foreign minister and the Japanese ambassador "wandering about among the ruins, surrounded by a crowd of people and being greeted with the Nazi salute by those in uniform. Ribbentrop was wearing uniform, while Ōshima was wearing a leather jacket and a deerstalker. Both were carrying stout walking-sticks."[11] After the bombing raid on 26 February Ōshima told Tokyo that "a great many bombs fell in the Tiergarten area . . . but this office was not damaged. The embassy officials are all unhurt, and so far (6:00 P.M. on the 27th) we have had no reports of injuries to Japanese residents." Later, on 19 March, he told Tokyo that "a large bomb exploded in the doorway of the Italian embassy next-door to this office (on the east), and in addition bombs fell in the Tiergarten area, but there was no damage to our building though doors and windows were damaged by concussion."[12] Several weeks later, on 11 April, a few days before Ōshima left Berlin, he reported that "with regard to the plight of victims, they are taken care of by cooperation of local administration agencies, the police, and various other agencies, with the Party as the focal point. For example, immediately after a heavy air raid, emergency Kartenstellen are set up in the necessary places, and the necessary functionaries dispatched there. These Kartenstellen are organized . . . (for) provision of temporary cash, food ration tickets, clothing ration tickets, (and) temporary dwellings."[13]

8. As for communications with the outside world, practically the only air route still open is the one to Sweden, which has four flights weekly. Air connections with Spain are irregular and unreliable; air mail service to Switzerland on the government line via Basel is often suspended. Recently first-class and express trains [to Switzerland] have been discontinued; one must go by ordinary trains and make a number of transfers. Because of the danger of air attacks, a circuitous route has to be followed; thus, the trip requires 2 or 3 days. Therefore, traveling to Switzerland is also irregular and one is often delayed.

Trips [are difficult and] do not have the value that they had in the past. When couriers make trips [to other countries], the baggage which they can take with them is very limited, and it is impossible for them to carry on their business as they have in the past. Moreover, there are many difficulties in making telephone connections with other countries. It often happens that telephone connections are suspended for days at a time.

On 19 February Ōshima reported that "airplane connections between Berlin and Lisbon are irregular, but flights are still made 5 or 6 times a month." On the other hand, American intelligence had a different report: "On 15 February the U.S. Military Attaché in Madrid reported that, according to a fairly reliable source, Lufthansa service between Germany and the Iberian Peninsula was being cut to two round trips a month because of the German gasoline shortage."[14]

In these conditions it is natural that various inconveniences are experienced in carrying on the business of my office and in the official and private lives of the members of my staff. On the other hand, in order to avoid misunderstanding, I would like to add the following points:

(a) There is a large number of foreign laborers in Berlin, but even Russian prisoners of war are continuing to do their work as in the past. It is difficult to discover any evidence of unrest. The theft of food, liquor, and tobacco, for example, does not equal [the higher rate of] the past, and we hear nothing about any increase in burglaries and major crimes. Recently posters in the streets announced that a number of deserters under a certain sub-lieutenant had been shot, but the story that a large number of deserters and foreign laborers have hidden in the ruins of Berlin is nothing more than empty propaganda.

"The life of the citizens generally goes ahead calmly somehow or other," Ōshima had reported earlier in March.[15] However, several weeks later, on 22 April, after the Soviet systematic shelling of the city had taken place for nearly 48 hours, a Swedish newspaper correspondent in Berlin observed that chaos was taking hold of the city and "in the streets more and more prisoners of war and foreign workers are wandering about completely unguarded."[16] Ōshima's message continues:

(b) As a result of the present emergency, some items of food have become unobtainable and there are temporary shortages of other commodities due to transportation difficulties; on the other hand, there are supplies of commodities such as vegetables and items which can be preserved for a long time, such as sausage and hard bread. Although there have been various restrictions on the use of food ration coupons, as I have previously reported, the principle has been maintained in spite of many difficulties that the people shall be able to purchase necessary food articles at officially established prices by means of those coupons and, therefore, a minimum stability in living conditions has been attained.

(c) The destruction of residences by the continuous air attacks, together with the influx of refugees from the East, has greatly aggravated the housing problem. Consequently, when a large-scale air attack at one blow produces a large number of homeless persons, the task of housing them is not an easy one, as can well be imagined. Yet, to cite recent instances, the homeless who swarm the streets on the day of an air attack disappear into the shadows the next day. This demonstrates the organizing efficiency of the leaders and proves that their administrative ability is functioning as usual. Recently there has been some relaxation of the ban on travel and permission has been granted for women with children under ten to leave Berlin, a move doubtless designed to ease the housing problem.

Nearly a month earlier, in mid-February, Ōshima had reported that "refugees from the East are pouring in at present from every direction, and it seems that even the Germans have considerable difficulty in providing shelter for such a large number of strangers and family members."[17] Ōshima wrote on 11 April that "the total population of Berlin is 3 to 4 million. (Berlin's population in December 1940 was 4,358,911.) Originally about 1,200,000 were removed by resettlement, but later with the influx of refugees from the occupied territories and the East, about 500,000 were added. At present unemployed women with children are being advised to resettle. This is not a step toward defense of Berlin, but is intended to protect the children from the habitual air raids. Up to the present child victims of raids are very few. They do not come to 10% of those killed."[18]

Ōshima's observations in early 1945 nearly completed the wartime story of Hitler's Germany, and MAGIC intelligence analysts were relieved that the end was in sight. Although these intercepts with news of the living conditions in Berlin were interesting, they were of no particular strategic importance, unlike hundreds of his other MAGIC intercepts received since early 1941.

Nevertheless, Ōshima's observations and the significance of his intercepts reached beyond the rubble of Berlin during the final days of the Third Reich. From within an increasingly desperate city he saw the end of the society with which he had been so closely associated for the past eleven years, but perhaps more significantly, he saw into the future and reflected on what obviously lay in store for his native Japan.[19]

For some time Tokyo had been nervous about the possibility of Germany's defeat because it was clear that Japan would be left alone to face the combined Allied strength, including, in all likelihood, the Soviet Union's forces fresh from victory in Europe. At the end of January 1945, the vice chief of the Japanese Army General Staff predicted that "if the progress of the European situation permits, Russia is very likely to commence armed warfare against Japan in the latter half of this year." At the same time he predicted "that by this summer or autumn the worst will have come to Germany."[20]

American COMINT produced a series of studies in the first half of 1945 that carefully analyzed Japan's dilemma. The reports of Japanese diplomats, particularly from Ōshima in Berlin and Satō in Moscow, figured prominently in the study of 12 February 1945, which concluded that there was a "possibility that the Soviet Union might even take active steps to support the Anglo-Americans in their war against Japan."[21]

The Japanese were under no delusion about the seriousness of conditions in the German capital. Thus, at the beginning of February, the ranking military attaché at the Japanese embassy in Berlin, Lieutenant General Komatsu Mitsuhiko, began on his own authority to burn some secret cryptographic materials and to take other prearranged security measures in anticipation of the possible fall of Berlin. Also in the first week of February Ōshima recognized that "Berlin will be hemmed in before long," and he started to burn duplicates of secret code documents because he feared that it might become necessary to dispose quickly of all secret materials, especially if in the final Soviet assault Berlin were taken by storm. Near the end of February Ōshima reported to Tokyo that there was great "danger of Berlin becoming a battlefield," and by 5 March he feared "that the abandonment of Berlin may take place after another month." By the end of March he was convinced that it was absolutely impossible for Germany to continue large-scale operations for very long.[22] However, from the point of view of Propaganda Minister Joseph Goebbels, "the Japanese in Berlin, even including those in the embassy, have become very defeatists."[23]

Ōshima sent his wife to the safety of the high Alps on 26 March, to Hotel Mozart at Bad Gastein about fifty miles south of Salzburg. He himself remained in Berlin for three additional weeks. (Already, fearing the advance on Berlin of Soviet forces, the nuncio and Spanish, Portuguese, and Irish diplomatic missions proposed to the German Foreign Ministry that they be evacuated to southern Germany. Ribbentrop agreed on condition that each mission leave at least one official in Berlin in order to maintain contact with the ministry.) On 13 April 1945, Ōshima met with Ribbentrop, with whom he had worked so closely for nearly ten years. It was the end of their society, and perhaps it was with a touch of nostalgia that he said to the foreign minister: "I do not wish to be treated in the same manner as other diplomats merely by reason of the great danger from the ravages of war and bombings. I should like to make my prime object the maintenance of close contact with the German High Command and government to the very end."[24]

As it turned out, that was the last time Ōshima saw Ribbentrop, for late on the evening of 13 April Alexander von Dörnberg, the Foreign Ministry chief of protocol, telephoned Ōshima with the news that Hitler had just decided all foreign diplomatic officials then in Berlin, with the exception of skeleton staffs, were to leave immediately. Before the ambassador and nine members of his staff left Berlin on the afternoon of 14 April to join other Japanese nationals already at the mountain resort site of Bad Gastein, Ōshima was able to reach Ribbentrop by telephone. An important conversation followed, and reports of it attracted the attention of American intelligence officers.

Ōshima, as well as the U.S. Army G-2 analysts, wanted to know what the German host government was going to do. Ōshima reported to Tokyo that Ribbentrop said that "it was planned to transfer the German High Command and government to the south after they had watched developments a little longer."[25] By the next day this message from Ōshima had been intercepted, deciphered, and translated, and Marshall was informed immediately. The MIS evaluators added the following statement to the MAGIC Diplomatic Summary: "Ōshima's messages contain no indication of where in 'the south' the German Government will be located. However, it seems unlikely that Bad Gastein would have been picked for the diplomatic corps if the Government were not planning to settle in the same general area."[26] Little wonder, then, that the possibility of a final suicidal stand by some force of Germans in the Alpine or National Redoubt could not be easily discounted.[27] Thus, in the uncertainty of the final days of Hitler's Third Reich, Ōshima's last conversation with Ribbentrop renewed fears that a higher price might yet be paid for victory in Europe.

American COMINT operations had always sought Japanese enciphered messages for what intelligence they might contain, but after Ōshima left Berlin a peculiar twist occurred. Americans had never seen the sophisticated Japanese Cipher Machine, Type B system. The deciphering of hundreds of thousands of PURPLE messages during the war was accomplished by American-made analog machines, and several analog machines existed at the time of the Pearl Harbor attack. "There were more machines available than were needed," Rowlett wrote recently. Many more were built—it required in some instances no more than three days to construct a single analog.[28]

An unusual opportunity seemed to be in the making, in spite of the American assumption that the Japanese would attempt to destroy the embassy's cipher machines. On 14 April Ōshima left ten members of his staff behind to run the embassy—a counselor, a secretary, four clerks, one interpreter, one telegraphic official, and two student secretaries. This rather junior team of Japanese officials lived for the next two weeks in a reinforced concrete underground air-raid shelter in the embassy compound at 24–27 Tiergartenstrasse, less than two kilometers from the Reich Chancellery or the Reichstag. Capable of accommodating about forty people, the shelter also protected portraits of the Japanese Imperial family (many of which had come from Japanese diplomatic missions in Axis areas of Europe occupied by 1945 by Allied forces). A guard was assigned to watch over the portraits. The shelter also contained a PURPLE cipher machine, which Ōshima had left orders to destroy when the occasion arose. But time was running out, and the Japanese and the United States both knew that Soviet artillery was already shelling the city, low-flying Soviet bombers were causing much destruction, and soon howling rockets with fiery trajectories would also be showering the center of Berlin. Moreover, massive tank and infantry units were about to storm central Berlin and the Tiergarten, the last defense line of the German forces in the city.[29] Thus, from the embassy's air-raid shelter at 10:00 P.M. on 21 April, Counselor Kawahara Shun'ichirō reported to Tokyo (via Stockholm) in a "very urgent" message that "the battle line is very near, and shells have already begun to fall within the city."[30] Indeed, Soviet systematic shelling had started the day before. Therefore, Kawahara was going to destroy his high-grade cipher machine and burn all code documents as soon as possible—communications thereafter would be by means of the prearranged memory code. (American cryptanalysts soon had evidence that Kawahara was no longer using the PURPLE machine, for the last Japanese messages from Berlin—via Bern on 30 April 1945 employed a less sophisticated code.)

There was much pressure from the Soviets. On the day Kawahara planned to destroy the embassy's PURPLE machine (22 April), a Swedish correspondent telephoned the following report to his newspaper in Stockholm:

> Berlin . . . is living through its last hours in an atmosphere of confusion and panic. Russian and German pilots engage each other in ceaseless dogfights over the roofs of the city, while the air is filled

with the thunder of Russian guns and the thud of their shells, which have already fallen right in the centre of Berlin in the Unter den Linden, the Potsdammer Platz, and the Leipziger Strasse. The air is filled, too, with desperate Nazi orders, threats, and appeals, to a population that's either panic-stricken or sunk in complete apathy. . . . This . . . is probably the last time I shall be speaking to you before the fall of Berlin.[31]

By 24 April the chief German air connection with the outside was severed when the Russians occupied Tempelhof; thus trees in the Tiergarten were cut down and bronze lamp standards were removed for an improvised airstrip. On the same day most of the remaining low-firing German guns were moved into the Tiergarten, bordered on the south side by the Japanese embassy, or nearby larger city squares. The Japanese embassy, then, was located within the German final defense perimeter where the crude airstrip and a certain concentration of German strength served as a focal point for Soviet firepower. Because of acute military crisis and enormous destruction between 22 and 30 April, conditions deteriorated rapidly and chaos reigned around the Japanese embassy.

The Japanese were caught in the crossfire, and Anglo-American intelligence assumed that the Japanese were largely confined to their small underground air-raid shelter in the garden courtyard behind the embassy building. On 8 May, the day the Wehrmacht surrendered unconditionally to the Soviet Army in the building later occupied by the Berlin-Karlshort Museum (Kapitulationsmuseum), American COMINT reported that the whereabouts of Counselor Kawahara and his group from the Berlin embassy were unknown.[32] Hoping that conditions had prevented the Japanese from being thorough in efforts to destroy their equipment, American intelligence officers knew approximately where to search for the remains of an original Japanese Cipher Machine, Type B system. Indeed, substantial pieces of a PURPLE machine were later found buried in the floor of the underground air-raid shelter. There were three main pieces which were almost identical, approximately 8" x 8" x 8" in dimensions, and a fourth component which was slightly smaller. When these pieces were examined by American cryptanalysts, "the electrical wiring was essentially intact. . . . The main damage was to the mechanical parts, some of which were broken or bent out of their original shape."[33]

It is possible, although not likely, that Japanese cipher equipment in Berlin was at one point included among target items for recovery by a Target Investigation Committee (TICOM) team. If so, the operation would have occurred soon after Ōshima went south to take refuge in the Alps. Such an

This major piece of the Japanese PURPLE *machine was recovered by the U.S. Army from the Japanese embassy, Berlin, not long after the German surrender in May 1945. (Source: National Security Agency Museum)*

Anglo-American team reportedly planned to parachute into the center of Berlin to recover German cipher intelligence, but the expedition was canceled when it was realized that the Russians were about to enter Berlin and that much of German cipher operations had been moved out of Berlin to the north or to the south of the beleaguered city. Since SSA's several different PURPLE analog machines had worked efficiently for over four years, the recovery of parts of an original PURPLE machine would have had little more than curiosity value and certainly was not worth the risk of a dangerous TICOM operation. Moreover, such an operation would have jeopardized the security of MAGIC, which still promised more information about the Soviet Union. However, TICOM teams did retrieve several German cipher machines in the south as well as a Soviet system that the Germans had.[34] Similar teams commandeered German centers where atomic, U-boat, aircraft, rocket, and biological warfare research was conducted and many leading German scientists were also taken.[35]

Since no TICOM operation occurred in Berlin, components of the PUR-

PLE machine cryptographic system were obviously recovered by another means. Soon after the German surrender, U.S. Army units arrived in Berlin as part of the occupation forces, and routine searches of various buildings, including the former Japanese embassy, were conducted to recover any items which might be of intelligence interest. Not knowing exactly what they had found in the air-raid shelter but suspecting that the buried items were probably of some significance, an army search team recovered the Japanese materials and had them photographed. "Copies of the photographs were routinely distributed to U.S. military organizations in the hope that a positive identification would result," Frank Rowlett wrote. In a few weeks the pieces arrived in Washington, were turned over to the Signal Corps, "and soon thereafter," Rowlett continued, they "were delivered to my office at Arlington Hall Station on the suspicion that they might have some cryptographic purpose since they did not appear to be parts of conventional communications equipment."

Rowlett's interest quickened. What a marvelous opportunity for him after having labored on Japanese cryptographic systems so intensely for fifteen years. His own account in response to the author's questions best serves the historical record.

When I first looked at the items it was apparent to me that they had to be the cryptographic components of a cipher machine, possibly the Japanese PURPLE machine, but it would require further examination to establish that they were indeed parts of the PURPLE device. I excitedly called Leo Rosen, Robert Ferner and Al Small, all of whom had been deeply involved in the recovery of the PURPLE device, to my office to examine the items and to assist in the needed detailed examination. Needless to say, this examination was enthusiastically started without delay.

It took us less than an hour to establish that the items were truly components of the Japanese PURPLE machine. However, we wanted to make a complete comparison of the wiring we had recovered by cryptanalysis with the original wiring to determine the degree of accuracy we had achieved. Since this involved checking each of the several hundred connections on the original components with each of our corresponding recoveries, at least a couple more hours were required to complete the examination to our satisfaction. It was most gratifying to all of us to find that of the several hundred connections involved, we found only a single discrepancy—one pair of connections had been interchanged either by an erroneous recovery or by a clerical error in recording its recovery.[36]

Of all the PURPLE machines used in Japanese diplomatic missions around the world, particularly in neutral countries and in Japan up to August 1945, no complete machine survived the war. Only the pieces of the PURPLE machine from Berlin survive as evidence of the high-grade PURPLE system that was so well regarded and yet mastered by American cryptanalysts.[37]

The pieces of the embassy's PURPLE machine, which Ōshima had been so familiar with since February 1941, arrived in the United States before the former ambassador. They, in a sense, closed one chapter in this saga, and Ōshima's surrender and later encounter with then Major General Maxwell D. Taylor closed another. Taylor, commanding the 101st Airborne Division, moved his headquarters from Berchtesgaden, where he had become weary of the stream of Allied military tours in May and June, to the more remote resort town of Bad Gastein. The site for the new division headquarters was to be Hotel Mozart, occupied by Ōshima, his wife, some members of the embassy staff, and a few Japanese journalists since the closing days of the war. Taylor and his chief of staff, Colonel Gerald J. Higgins, drove to Bad Gastein in late June to break the news to Ōshima. Higgins, in response to the author's questions, described the encounter with the former ambassador.

> The Japanese embassy personnel had monopolized the entire hotel, although they needed only a small part of it for actual accommodations. Taylor approached the desk and asked the individual on duty—in English—to see the ambassador. A phone call was made, but when no appearance was made [by Ōshima] Taylor again requested the ambassador's appearance. No response was made to Taylor, but a side remark was made to another Japanese—in their language. Taylor exploded and addressed the duty officer in their native language in no uncertain terms. The effect was electrifying—everybody in the lobby [twenty to thirty Japanese] jumped up from their chairs, the duty officer grabbed the phone, and in a very short time the ambassador came hurrying down the stairs, trying to adjust his clothing as he came. Again, Taylor spoke in Japanese, and the ambassador quickly agreed with his request, everybody taking off for their rooms in a hurry [to prepare to move to another hotel]. I was afterward approached by one of the retinue who spoke English and was asked where Taylor learned to speak their language so effectively. "He told us off in 'kitchen' Japanese—he sure knew how to make a point in our language." (I found out later that the duty officer's remark was to the effect that the ambassador was taking a nap and had said to let the American "cool his heels.")[38]

Waiting at Le Havre, France, to sail aboard the USS West Point *to New York, Ōshima (eighth from right) is seen here with former embassy members and Japanese nationals on 3 July 1945. (Source: National Archives)*

However, Ōshima and his party did not remain in Europe long after this incident, but were taken to Salzburg, then flown to Le Havre, France, where they boarded the USS *West Point*, a troop transport converted from the liner SS *America*, and arrived in New York on 11 July. Ōshima was interned near Washington, D.C., and interrogated before being moved to a nineteenth-century resort hotel near Bedford, Pennsylvania. There he and a group of about 150 Japanese internees received news of the bombing of Hiroshima and Nagasaki and of Japan's decision to surrender. Later they were moved to Seattle, Washington, where Ōshima boarded a ship for Japan.

Ōshima was always stoic about his role during the war and about his fate afterward. Arrested at his home in Chigasaki and jailed in Sugamo Prison on 16 December 1945, Ōshima was indicted on several counts in April 1946 and tried as a war criminal at the International Military Tribunal for the Far East. Found guilty of overall conspiracy against peace on 12 November 1948, he was sentenced to life imprisonment. In a far different international situation from that he had known in the 1930s and early 1940s, he was paroled from prison in December 1955 and granted clemency in April 1958. He died at the age of eighty-nine in Chigasaki, Japan, on 6 June 1975, never knowing that his mail had been read in Washington and London the whole time he was in Berlin during the war.[39]

On 12 November 1948, Chief Justice Sir William Webb (Australia), president of the International Military Tribunal for the Far East, read the judgment of the court against Ōshima Hiroshi, age 62: The verdict of guilty on Count 1 resulted in a sentence of imprisonment for life. (Source: National Archives)

Ōshima left behind him an enormous intelligence legacy. One popular writer of COMINT in World War II has correctly observed that Ōshima "reported [to Tokyo] *everything* he was told."[40] But Ōshima's frequently perceptive assessments went beyond what he was told. Although he did indeed forward to Tokyo the German account of the coming of the invasion of the Soviet Union, for the next forty-two months his own assessments of nearly all dimensions of the complicated eastern front were highly valued from the Anglo-American perspective. He speculated during the Axis glow of success in the opening months of 1942 about what he thought was destined to happen in the war. Yet after midyear MAGIC intelligence analysts were reassured of an eventual Allied victory when they studied the disparity between some of Ōshima's realistic reporting on actual military conditions and his longstanding and well-known aspirations for an Axis new world order.

Ōshima appeared completely trustworthy to the Nazis, and only he could get close enough to Hitler to learn firsthand what the Führer was thinking. Throughout the war Ōshima revealed the Führer's thoughts and plans for future military "surprises" before it was too late for the Anglo-Americans to take advantage of his errors and military secrets. Ōshima clearly indicated when Hitler lost the strategic initiative, but his detailed analysis of the war also made it clear that the price of victory would be very costly. One shudders to estimate what the cost in time and human life would have been were it not for the Ōshima connection and MAGIC. Speaking of ULTRA in the larger SIGINT sense at an international conference of cryptologists in 1978, Harold Deutsch said that "in virtually all of the important encounters, ULTRA played a vital and perhaps decisive role." Reporting on this unique conference, David Kahn continued by observing that Deutsch then "asked rhetorically, if ULTRA was so important, why didn't it end the war sooner? His answer: 'It did end sooner.' "[41]

The war ended sooner in Europe because of the Ōshima connection, and Eisenhower and his staff fully appreciated the importance of Ōshima's connection to OVERLORD. Not surprisingly, it was later a grateful Eisenhower who came back from Europe after Hitler's defeat. On 11 February 1946 he visited Arlington Hall Station for a tour of the installation and to meet and to thank the Army Security Agency people who had worked to solve the Japanese codes and ciphers and provided his earlier campaign in Europe with vital information about the Germans.[42] Frank Rowlett, who guided Eisenhower, Marshall's successor as chief of staff, around Arlington Hall Station, wrote that the famed general fresh from victory in Europe "expressed to [Lieutenant] General Hoyt Vandenberg, [assistant chief of staff, G-2], his desire to extend his personal thanks to the individuals who had produced information on the German fortifications along the coast of France which he felt was vital to the success of the Allied invasion in June 1944. General Vandenberg accordingly made arrangements for General Eisenhower to visit Arlington Hall Station."[43]

Eisenhower's successor as chief of staff in November 1947, Omar N. Bradley, was given a similar tour of Arlington Hall Station on 20 February 1948, but for Bradley "we included a visit to Vint Hill Farm," the monitoring station built near Warrenton, Virginia in 1942. "He also," Rowlett wrote, "expressed his gratitude for the information from the Japanese diplomatic intercepts which had been provided to him."[44] Lieutenant General Stephen J. Chamberlin (assistant chief of staff, G-2) and Secretary of the Army Kenneth Claiborne Royall accompanied Bradley.[45] Eisenhower had also wanted to visit Bletchley Park to thank its signal intelligence people for their enormous assistance in the recent European campaign, but he had been unable to make that visit. However, he sent a letter of appreciation to Major General Sir Stewart Menzies, chief of the secret service (see Appendix 2).

The precedent that the Japanese ambassador in Berlin established as a

General of the Army Dwight D. Eisenhower, chief of staff, visits Arlington Hall Station, 11 February 1946. Left to right, General Eisenhower; Lieutenant General Hoyt S. Vandenberg, assistant chief of staff, G-2; Brigadier General W. Preston Corderman; Colonel Frank B. Rowlett; and William F. Friedman. (Courtesy of Wallace R. Winkler)

diplomat who became a vital source of information through the marvel of COMINT was not lost on Anglo-American cryptologic intelligence communities. Ambassador Satō, who arrived at his post in the Soviet Union fourteen months after Ōshima arrived in Berlin, served well the interests of Anglo-American intelligence, and Ōshima's fourteen-month precedent helped to focus attention on the new Japanese ambassador in Moscow. Satō inadvertently filled some gaps that western Allies found in their information about the Soviet side of the Russo-Japanese war. Although the Satō connection no doubt paid off in handsome intelligence dividends in the 1942–1944 period, the declassified record remains murky until the passing of Nazi Germany had become obvious.

Ōshima's intelligence legacy outside of Germany was profound. By 23 April 1945, when Ōshima had already fled from Berlin, a COMINT study con-

cluded that a recent Soviet diplomatic charge against Japan was very effective. Contrary to the terms of the April 1941 Neutrality Pact, Japan had
been helping Germany, Molotov maintained. Therefore, the Soviets abrogated the pact and obtained, American analysts deduced, "a 'Damocles'
sword' with which Russia may legally and blamelessly cut the remaining
bonds at her discretion."[46] By the time of the next major COMINT study (21
May 1945), Hitler had committed suicide and Germany had officially surrendered. The study succinctly summarized Japan's dilemma, although with
a goodly amount of poetic license: "If, as reports have it, German announcement of the death of Nazism's chief protagonist was accompanied by
the massive strains of Wagner's requiem, 'Twilight of the Gods,' it is to the
less decorous if more modern jangle of "Don't Fence Me In" that Nippon,
now a lone ranger astride a white horse, jogs dolefully toward the last round-
up."[47]

The studies cited here as COMINT products were not army works but in
fact navy Op-20-3-G50, Pacific Strategic Intelligence Section, Commander-
in-Chief, United States Fleet and Chief of Naval Operations. They were classified top secret ULTRA and produced in only five or six copies each. They
were addressing a rapidly changing international climate. A new approach, a
new perspective was assumed in the navy analysis, for as early as the first
study in this series (January 1945), the focus was on Japan, the sole remaining foe of the grand alliance. Obviously, with the demise of Hitler's Germany and Ōshima's passing from the scene of MAGIC prominence, the focus
of navy intelligence concentrated on Tokyo, and particularly on the Mos-
cow-Satō-Tokyo link. It is not surprising, therefore, that another study in
this series cited Satō's warning of 7 April that the Soviet Union "would attempt to coerce Japan into adopting 'a policy of obsequiousness based on
fear.' "[48]

American intelligence relied heavily on Satō's PURPLE intercepts to watch
developments as the inevitable defeat of Imperial Japan drew nearer and to
better understand the growing assertiveness of the Soviet Union. It was in
this context that the long-recognized humanism of Ambassador Satō came
to the forefront among American MAGIC intelligence analysts. On 9 May
Satō warned that the Soviet Union was "planning to seize the power of life
and death over Japan,"[49] but he thought the Soviet Union might not have to
declare war but "might seek to gain her ends by offering to act as mediator."
Therefore, Satō concluded prophetically, "if, backed by their vast power, the
Russians were to succeed in effecting such a peace for the benefit of the Anglo-Americans ('now paying a tremendous price on Okinawa . . .'), they
would achieve without effort an international position surpassing that of
their allies, a point which will not escape the eagle-eyed Stalin."[50] The Soviet

price for services as mediator revolved around the dissolution of the Treaty of Portsmouth of 1905, Satō forecasted, including the return to Russia of southern Sakhalin and the return of Manchukuo to Chinese rule. There was an overriding assumption seen in Japanese diplomatic traffic, however, that the Soviets would attack the Japanese when it suited the Kremlin. As an American intelligence analyst rather whimsically concluded on 18 June 1945, there is "ample evidence that in her present straits Japan is a ready prospect for tornado insurance from the northwest, and expects that the premium will be computed at 'emergency rates'—this despite desperate hopes that Russia 'will let Japan and America fight it out.' "[51]

Moreover, the Japanese themselves had solid evidence that the Soviets were preparing to invade Manchukuo. Like Ōshima in the summer of 1943, Satō used PURPLE to send military intelligence reports to Tokyo. Dated 20 June 1945, Satō summarized the observations of two Japanese couriers who had recently made trips from Manchouli to Moscow while maintaining an eighteen-hour daily watch: "During the period 9–16 June, a total of 166 eastbound military trains were seen. They were established to have been carrying about 120,000 troops as well as military equipment including self-propelled guns and rocket guns, 1600 trucks, 30 tanks (apparently American) and a number of 'Joseph Stalin' heavy tanks. In addition, 250 eastbound tank-cars were observed."[52] In early July Satō had another report about the uninterrupted flow of Soviet military strength eastward on the Trans-Siberian Railroad. In one eight-day period "there were 2,932 cars carrying troops."[53]

Satō was a realist. He warned Tokyo that if the Soviet Union were to embark on a course of "positive intervention" in the Pacific war, "we would have no choice but to reach a decision quickly and, resolving to eat dirt and put up with all sacrifices, fly into her [Soviet] arms in order to save our national structure." By July he concluded that "the peace proposal which I advocate means the acceptance of the enemy's conditions, provided our national structure is maintained. . . . I must therefore insist that we are required to bear every sacrifice for the existence of the State."[54] When Satō's words reached Arlington Hall, Rowlett, sometimes called to his office at 2:00 A.M., found that of all his experiences as a cryptologist, the translations of these MAGIC intercepts were the most rewarding.[55]

Early August brought more desperate words from Ambassador Satō. On 4 August he told Foreign Minister Tōgō:

> Regardless of whether we are able to get the good offices of the Russian Government for the termination of the war, the fact is undeniable that the 3-Power Declaration of 26 July already provides a basis

For a "profound contribution to the security of the United States," Frank B. Rowlett (between Mrs. Edith Rowlett and President Lyndon B. Johnson) received the National Security Medal from the president on 2 March 1966. The citation mysteriously added that Rowlett had applied his "creative energy to a wide range of the most complex technical and technological problems." (Courtesy of Henry F. Schorreck)

for ending the Greater East Asia War. . . . If Japan's resolution to seek peace is communicated to the United Nations even one day sooner, the degree of amelioration will be (? affected ?) to that extent, whereas if there is dilly-dallying by government and military in bringing this resolution to fruition, then all Japan will be reduced to ashes and she will not be able (? to avoid ?) following the road to ruin. . . . It is already clear in advance as to what the peace terms will be, even without looking at the example of Germany, and we must resign ourselves beforehand to (? giving up ?) a considerable number of war criminals. However, the state is (? now on the verge of ?) ruin, and it is entirely inevitable that these war criminals make the necessary sacrifice to save their country as truly patriotic warriors.[56]

The sooner the war ended the better, not only from Satō's point of view, but in the Anglo-American view as well.

Appendix 1
MAGIC Messages Concerning a Visit of the Japanese Ambassador in Berlin to the German Defenses in France

[The first message concerning Ōshima's inspection tour was not included in the collection of documents given to the president on 16 December 1943.]

From: Berlin (Japanese Ambassador)[1]

To: Tokyo (Ministry of Foreign Affairs)

Sent: 23 October 1943 (intercepted 24 October, received 25 October, translated 26 October)

I was invited by the German government to inspect conditions in France and the fortifications along the Atlantic coast. Therefore, I should like to make an official tour, beginning tomorrow, the 24th, accompanied by Embassy Secretaries Uchida and Ushiba and Assistant Military Attaché Lieutenant Colonel Nishi for a period of ten days. Please approve.

Gottfriezen [sic][2] and two officers attached to the Headquarters of the National Defense Army will accompany us on this trip. Arrangements have been made so that we will be able at all times to maintain contact with the German Foreign Office and with the German Army Command.

[Beginning of material seen by the president on 16 December 1943]

Ambassador Ōshima to Tokyo[3]

Sent: 9 November 1943 (intercepted 9 November, received 11 November, translated 11 November)

On the morning of the 3rd I returned from my trip of inspection and I will wire you separately what I saw and my opinions about German defenses. The trip itself was in general as follows:

1. On the 24th, accompanied by Secretaries Uchida and Ushiba and Lieutenant Colonel Nishi, I went directly from Berlin to Brest by way of Paris. We arrived at Brest on the morning of the 26th and inspected the defenses there and along the neighboring coast. That night we put up at Le Bourg d'Iré. On the 27th we observed the defenses around Lorient and the coast southward. That night we stopped at La Baule. We observed night maneuvers and on the 28th inspected St. Nazaire and its neighboring defense encampments. We put up at Nantes that night and on the 29th returned once again to Paris. There we were feted by Field Marshal Gerd von Rundstedt; his chief of staff kept telling us about the military situation . . . [undetermined number of missing lines in this intercept]. Early on the morning of the 30th we left Paris for Bordeaux where we inspected the coastal defenses and watched two blockade runners carrying out maneuvers. That evening General Johannes Blaskowitz, commander of the 1st Army, gave us a dinner. On the 31st we left Bordeaux and headed for La Rochelle and observed the coast along the way. We inspected the defenses in the neighborhood and spent the night there. On the 1st, we left Bordeaux and went to Poitiers. We left there the same day.

2. From Brest to Nantes we were escorted by General Wilhelm Fahrmbacher, commander of the 28th Army, who is completely responsible for the defense of that region. At La Rochelle we were guided by General Gallencamp, who is responsible for defenses there; he commands the 80th Army Corps. Also, when we were inspecting harbors, men in charge in the Army, Navy, and War Services explained everything to us, and when we were wined and dined we always had the chance to talk with the right people—those who could answer our questions.

Ambassador Ōshima to Tokyo[4]

Sent: 10 November 1943 (intercepted 11 November, received 11 and 12 November, translated 12 November)

1. All the German fortifications on the French coast are very close to the shore and it is quite clear that the Germans plan to smash any enemy attempt to land as close to the edge of the water as possible. The forts around naval bases, built in excellent and effective positions, defend the coasts, and even the smallest forts are invested so that they can hold out independently for a very long time. They are supported with large Reserve Units which can be moved to the central theater. Defense is thorough from the army groups

down to the regiments, which are directly in charge of defending the coasts. Were the enemy successful in making a partial landing, crossfire from mutually supporting defense posts and the appearance of mobile forces would annihilate the invaders. This scheme of lateral firepower and mobile units is the basic concept behind Germany's defense in the West. Furthermore, in order to avoid needless damage to fortifications and losses in men and matériel by the shelling and bombing from the enemy and to attain the maximum effect from a minimum number of soldiers performing defense work, even individual machine gun nests are, without stint, strengthened with ferroconcrete. However, at the same time the German defenders have the capacity to counterattack when the enemy attempts an invasion. Moreover, camouflaging has been carried out very thoroughly and everything possible has been done for the protection of tanks—practical experience gained since the war began has served the Germans well. This overall scheme is similar to defenses evident at the West Wall behind the Franco-German border, but the quality of the Atlantic Wall fortifications is ever so much better.

2. The whole coast fortified by the Germans is very vast and, now particularly, when we have evidence of the high quality of the [enemy] air strength, should the enemy gather together a powerful fleet and attempt to land, it cannot be expected that the invaders could be stopped everywhere along the line. Nevertheless, even if some of the enemy succeeds in getting ashore, it would not be easy for them to smash the counterattack of the powerful German Reserves, who can rally with lightning speed. I think that we may well calculate that even though the American and British forces, for a short time, establish a bridgehead, under the present circumstances it would be utterly impossible for them to form any new second front in France of any consequence. In spite of the fact that the areas which I have just inspected are areas regarded as . . . [missing term in this intercept] the way they are so efficiently prepared deepens this feeling of confidence. Moreover, the Germans are actively expanding the engineering work. When one realizes what a good job has been done, together with what the Germans are still doing and going to do, we can see what a hard time the enemy would have.

3. What pleased me most on this tour was the morale and military spirit of the soldiers. Just to give you an example, the older veteran officers of the last war always treated the higher-ranking, younger officers with great kindness and spoke well of them. The soldiers garrisoning the fortresses, already past forty, treated the weapons they had been given with care and confidence. I could see from many examples how cheerfully they carried out their military responsibilities. Everywhere I engaged in easygoing chats with the soldiers. . . .

4. I am not able to give you much of a general picture concerning the effect of Anglo-American air raids. The streets of Lorient and St. Nazaire were destroyed up to 90 percent and in other important ports not only were the metropolitan areas damaged, but also the harbor installations. We actually saw that. However, the fact that submarine bunkers stood as firm as a rock and the fact that the buildings housing the German command received hardly any damage raise doubts about enemy bombing ability and policy. Why on earth should the Americans and British not strike submarine bunkers? Why on earth did they not strike other important German facilities while they were under construction? The Germans told me that it was a damned good thing that the bombings of Lorient scared off so many useless Frenchmen from the forts. . . . Last April the flood gates at St. Nazaire were destroyed by an attack, but the inconvenience was short lived; new and powerful concrete flood gates have now been fitted.

5. In connection with an Anglo-American attempt to establish a second front, the enemy hopes that the French will cooperate and is doing everything possible to wheedle French resistance. Therefore, the peace and order of interior France and the way the people think will have a great effect on whether the United Nations invasion succeeds or not. From what the Army and SS leaders told me and from my own impressions, I think that the French have recently been encouraged by events to engage in more active opposition (sabotage of railways and murders, for example), stimulated mainly by Communists and British agents. This is much more evident than it was when I made a trip of inspection during the autumn of 1941. In general, however, the French are still apathetic and, while they are cooperating only reluctantly in the German war effort, there will not be enough resistance put up by the French to hinder Germany in carrying out effective countermeasures in the event the Anglo-Americans attempt an invasion.

Ambassador Ōshima to Tokyo[5]

Sent: 10 November 1943 (received 9 November) [*sic*]

1. The Strait of Dover area is given first place in the German Army's fortification scheme and troop dispositions, and Normandy and the Brittany peninsula come next. Other parts of the coast are regarded with less significance. Although the possibility of an Anglo-American landing on the Iberian Peninsula, followed by a crossing of the Pyrenees, is not altogether ruled out, no special defences have been constructed for this area. Instead, mobile forces are held in reserve at Narbonne and other strategic points, and

these are prepared to hold the mountain passes in the Pyrenees should an emergency arise.

Disposition of German Forces

2. Field Marshal Gerd von Rundstedt in Paris has a dual role. As Commander in Chief of Army Group D he controls the forces in the Netherlands (headed by General Friedrich Christian Christiansen), the 15th Army (General Hans von Salmuth), the 7th Army (General Friedrich Dollmann), the 1st Army (General Johannes Blaskowitz), and the 19th Army (General von Bodenstern). At the same time as Supreme Commander of the Armies in the West, he controls the forces commanded by the Chief of the Military Governor in Belgium and France (Generals Alexander von Falkenhausen and Heinrich von Stülpnagel, respectively), the 3rd Air Fleet (Field Marshal Hugo Sperrle), and Naval Group West (Admiral Theodor Krancke).

The coastal defense divisions are distributed as follows:

a. Netherlands Defense Army (covering the Netherlands down to the mouth of the Rhine)—4 divisions.

b. 15th Army (covering the area extending from the mouth of the Rhine to west of Le Havre)—9 divisions.

c. 7th Army (extending thence to the southern bank of the Loire)—8 divisions.

d. 1st Army (extending thence to the Spanish border)—4 divisions.

e. 19th Army (covering the French Mediterranean coast)—6 divisions.

One-third of these divisions have three regiments each and the remaining two-thirds have two regiments each; the latter, however, are being gradually brought up to full strength, that is, three regiments each. The coastal defense divisions have a static role, but divisions which constitute the general reserve are shared by other fronts. For example, two divisions from the general reserve were recently sent to the Eastern Front. The size of this general reserve varies according to circumstances, but at present it is made up as follows: six infantry divisions, four panzer divisions, five motorized divisions. In addition three reserve panzer divisions are being sent from Germany, two airborne divisions from Italy, and a number of infantry divisions from other fronts. These infantry divisions, however, have suffered heavily and require rest and refit on arrival in France. Some divisions are under the direct control of the Army Group and are distributed along the lines of communication in such a way that they can be rushed anywhere by vehicle (in the Netherlands by bicycle) at short notice. The forces under the Military Governors are garrison troops and consist of 25 battalions in Belgium and 17 regiments in France.

Recruit training schools for various branches of the armed forces have been moved from Germany to France and they are now busy with the work of training. There is a cadre unit which maintains a constant flow of tank troops for twelve independent tank battalions (Tigers and Panthers). There are also ten depot divisions training recruits sent to France, and several field divisions are now being formed from among their ranks. These are not, however, under Field Marshal von Rundstedt's command; they come under General Friedrich Fromm in Germany.

The total number of German forces under the Supreme Commander of the Armies in the West, including naval and air forces, is 1,400,000.

Coastal Defense Support

In areas around the principal harbors and naval bases which I inspected (viz Brest, Lorient, St. Nazaire, La Rochelle, and Bordeaux) defense works have been specially strengthened and fortified zones have been established to meet attack by land, sea, and air. Each of these zones is under a fortress commander with unified control over all three services.

The fortified zones surrounding naval bases conform for the most part to established principles of fortification. The important feature of the defense lines is that they are not arranged in one continuous and connected line but are arranged to enable even the smallest unit to operate independently. In other areas strongpoints have been constructed in large numbers all along the coast, the gaps between these strongpoints being closed by obstacles (mainly land mines). Each strongpoint is equipped with various types of arms and normally has 3-weeks supply of food so that it can conduct an independent defense. Running all the way behind the permanent line of fortifications is a series of field works being constructed as support positions.

The caliber of heavy naval guns in use in the areas I inspected range from 36 centimeters to 17 centimeters, but 15 and 12 centimeter eight-barrelled mortars are also used. There are 12, 10.5, and 8 centimeter anti-aircraft guns as well as a large number of anti-tank guns of various calibers. Although the small arms include a large number of captured weapons (French, Belgian, Czech, Russian, and Dutch) most of the weapons are of new design. The strongpoints are equipped with weapons of the latest design, including automatic hand grenade throwers (which throws at a rate of 120 per minute) and flamethrowers installed in casemates. The principal feature of these weapons is that they all can be concentrated to fire on one object at the same time, whether at sea or on land. For example, the anti-aircraft and anti-tank guns can be fired on warships at sea, and the fortress guns can be fired at tanks. (I was greatly impressed by this feature of German firepower during a practice night firing at La Baule when all guns fired out to sea together.)

Responsibility of Command

The Western Naval Command comprises the area which extends from the mouth of the Rhine to the Franco-Spanish border (excluding, however, the Netherlands, which comes under a separate naval command) and the Mediterranean. This area is divided into three sections, namely the English Channel, the Atlantic, and the Mediterranean (which includes the coast of the Italian Riviera as well as the coast of Southern France). Each of these sections is under the command of a naval chief, who in turn has two or three sea commanders under him. A sea commander is responsible for naval operations and defense in the waters assigned to him. He is obligated to cooperate with the Army during land action.

The Army Group Commander, in addition to commanding his own Army Group, exercises control over the naval and air forces, the forces of the Military Governors, and those of the TODT [labor] Organization in his defense zone, not only in the actual conduct of operations, but in the various preparations for defense. Unit commanders below the rank of Division Commander have power to command only in operational matters which concern their units directly.

The fortifications were begun in April 1942.[6] Locations were decided by the garrison commanders in their respective areas, designs were made by military fortification experts, and construction was carried out by the TODT Organization. The fortifications were completed in June or July of this year, but, as I already stated, the Germans are now strengthening them. Since, apart from a small number of Germans, the workers used by the TODT Organization have been mostly foreign, chiefly French, secret information about the fortifications leaks out to the enemy, as even the Germans realize.

[End of material seen by the president on 16 December 1943]

Appendix 2
Letter from Eisenhower to Major General Sir Stewart Menzies

JFG/fns (prepared by ?)[1]

12 July 1945

Dear General Menzies:

I had hoped to be able to pay a visit to Bletchley Park in order to thank you, Sir Edward Travis, and the members of the staff personally for the magnificent services which have been rendered to the Allied cause.

I am very well aware of this immense amount of work and effort which has been involved in the production of the material with which you have supplied us. I fully realize also the numerous setbacks and difficulties with which you have had to contend and how you have always, by your supreme efforts, overcome them.

The intelligence which has emanated from you before and during this campaign has been of priceless value to me. It has simplified my task as a commander enormously. It has saved thousands of British and American lives and, in no small way, contributed to the speed with which the enemy was routed and eventually forced to surrender.

I should be very grateful, therefore, if you would express to each and everyone of those engaged in this work from me personally my heartfelt admiration and sincere thanks for their very decisive contribution to the Allied war effort.

Sincerely,

/s/ Dwight D. Eisenhower

Major General Sir Stewart G. Menzies
            KCMG, CB, DSO, MC
The War Office
Whitehall
London, SW1

Appendix 3
Intelligence Agreement between the United States and Great Britain

May 17, 1943[1]

Agreement between British Government Code and Cipher School and U.S. War Department concerning cooperation in matters relating to:

U.S.	British
Special Intelligence A	Special Intelligence
Special Intelligence B	Y Intelligence
TA Intelligence	Y Inference

A distinction is made in nomenclature and procedure in handling intelligence derived from the solution of enemy high grade and that obtained from low grade codes and ciphers. The preservation of secrecy in regard to either category is a matter of great concern to both countries and if the highest degree of security is to be maintained, it is essential that the same methods should be pursued by both countries at every level and in every area concerned, since a leakage at any one point would jeopardize intelligence from these sources not in one area only but in all theaters of war and for all services.

[Three lines not declassified]

(1) Both the U.S. and British agree to exchange completely all information concerning the detection, identification and interception of signals from, and the solution of codes and ciphers used by, the Military and Air forces of the Axis powers, including secret services (Abwehr).

(2) The U.S. will assume as a main responsibility the reading of Japanese Military and Air codes and ciphers.

(3) The British will assume as a main responsibility the reading of German and Italian Military and Air codes and ciphers.

(4) Both countries agree that special security regulations shall apply to Intelligence obtained from decoding telegrams in enemy high grade codes and ciphers.

(5) Both countries agree to use their most secure codes and ciphers for transmission of the decodes of enemy signals and transmission of technical cryptanalytic data.

(6) British or U.S. Commanders-in-Chief, Military or Air, will receive all Special Intelligence necessary to them for the conduct of their operations from either British or U.S. centers as may be mutually agreed. Liaison officers will be appointed as desired for facilitating this. They will be given full access to all decodes.

(7) The distribution of intelligence from the sources in question will be governed by the fundamental principle that distribution will be restricted to the minimum and will therefore be confined solely to those who require to receive the intelligence for the proper discharge of their duties.

(8) All recipients of Special Intelligence A, whether British or American officers, shall be bound by the same regulations, the regulations (Appendix B [not declassified]) now in force in the theaters of war where British forces are operating to be accepted at the present time. If at a later date either country wishes to modify them in the light of further experience then this may be done by mutual agreement.

(9) The extension to officers of a knowledge of the existence of such intelligence shall be confined to as limited a number as possible and restricted to the levels of command in conformity with the above mentioned regulations. Great stress is laid on the principle that Special Intelligence A should not be intermingled in reports with general intelligence from other sources. If, however, it becomes imperative to do so, the whole must be treated as Special Intelligence A and given the same strictly limited distribution. Under no circumstances is it permissible to pass Special Intelligence A in a code or cipher which can be read by other than the authorized recipients.

(10) Although Special Intelligence B is not subject to the same stringent regulations as Special Intelligence A, since the two are closely connected, it is essential to maintain a high degree of secrecy in the handling of Special Intelligence B also. In any action taken upon such intelligence and in any documents or telegrams based upon it, it is essential that its origin be disguised and that the codes or ciphers used for its dissemination be absolutely secure.

(11) All intelligence available from decodes shall be made available to Liaison Officers, and if they deem necessary it will be exchanged between Lon-

don and Washington. These Liaison Officers will be specially appointed and given full facilities for this purpose.

(12) British and U.S. will notify one another without delay, giving full particulars, when either has information from any source indicating the compromise of any code or cipher used by the other. Action on such information will be most carefully considered in order not to compromise the source and if possible mutual agreement in such action will be sought.

[Four lines not declassified]

(14) Each country shall inform the other of the employment and scope in each joint theater of war of their Signal Intelligence (Y) units in the field.

(15) This agreement or the appendices thereto may be supplemented or modified from time to time governing any special feature for which either party wishes to make special provision.

(16) Definitions:

(a) *Y Service or Signal Intelligence Service.* The British, U.S. Army, and the U.S. Navy services concerned with intercepting, decoding, interpreting, classifying and dissemination of enemy [word or words in twelve spaces not declassified] communications, and the use of D/F and other specialized apparatus for establishing locations and identities of enemy transmitters.

(b) *Special Intelligence A.* Certain ciphers are placed in a special category, owing to their importance and difficulty of solution. The intelligence derived from these ciphers is known as Special Intelligence A. Such material is treated with most stringent security measures. Special Intelligence A is confined to a very strictly limited number of the most highly placed officers and is mainly of strategical importance.

(c) *Special Intelligence B.* Intelligence derived from the solution of lower grade ciphers. Such ciphers may under certain circumstances be upgraded to the "Special A" class. The dissemination of Special Intelligence B is wider though always treated as British Most Secret—U.S. Secret. Special Intelligence B may be used tactically.

Appendix (A)

Special Provisions Regarding Work on German Machine Ciphers

[Three lines not declassified]

This agreement provides that:

(a) All desired intelligence from this source will be made available to the War Department in Washington.

[Three lines not declassified]

(d) Transmission of intelligence to Commanders-in-Chief in the field will be accomplished by special routes and staffs who will maintain a watch over the use of the intelligence to guard against compromise of the source.

(1) U.S. liaison officers will be appointed at G.C. & C.S. to examine messages and summaries and select those desired for transmittal to Washington for G-2 or the Theater Commanders. All decoded material will be made available to those officers. Decodes giving information regarding Order of Battle will be handled as at present, i.e., through U.S. liaison officers in War Office and Air Ministry, respectively.

(2) Decodes or summaries to be passed to Washington through existing British channels.

[Approximately thirteen lines not declassified]

(7) Special Intelligence from this source will be passed to Commanders-in-Chief in the field through the Special British units provided for this purpose. The officer in command of these units will have direct access to the Commander-in-Chief and advise as necessary on the security aspect of handling and using this intelligence. Where an American officer is Commander-in-Chief, an American officer, properly trained and indoctrinated at Bletchley Park, will be attached to the unit to advise and act as liaison officer to overcome difficulties that may arise in regard to differences in language.

(8) The Director of the G.C. & C.S. will have the final decision when matters of security are involved in intelligence items (gossip) and as to what is passed to Commander[s]-in-Chief in the field.

[Remaining 40 per cent of page 173 and the whole of pages 174–175 not declassified]

Appendix 4
Letter from Marshall to Eisenhower

War Department
The Chief of Staff
Washington, D. C.

March 15, 1944[1]

Dear Eisenhower:

You are undoubtedly aware of the supreme importance which the War Department attaches to intelligence known as "Ultra." This intelligence is secured by the British from reading German enciphered radio communications.

The attached Tab sets forth the basis upon which German "Ultra" intelligence is made available to American field commands. Please give this matter your personal attention, and take all necessary steps to insure that the security regulations governing the dissemination of "Ultra" intelligence are meticulously observed. The arrangements described in the attached Tab are to be fully carried out.

Faithfully yours,

/s/ G.C. MARSHALL

General D. D. Eisenhower,
Supreme Headquarters,
    Allied Expeditionary Force,
London, England.

1. A large volume of high important military and air intelligence is derived by the British from reading German radio communications enciphered

in high-level German cipher systems. This type of intelligence is known as "Ultra" intelligence.

2. The basis upon which German Ultra intelligence is made available by the British to the US War Department and to American Field Commands in active theaters is governed by an agreement made in June 1943[2] between the US War Department and the responsible British organization.

3. The British organization which produces Ultra intelligence is the Government Code and Cipher School, the Director General of which is Brigadier Sir Stewart Menzies, [a line of censored material].

4. Administration of the agreement of June 1943 is controlled by the British . . . [27 spaces censored] . . . through Brigadier Menzies, and by the US War Department through the A.C. of S., G-2.

5. To carry out the agreement of June 1943, and to assist in and supervise the dissemination of Ultra intelligence to American Commands in the European Theater, a detachment of MID, the title of which is MID, War Department, London, has been detailed for service in the European Theater. This detachment is under the direct control of the A.C. of S., G-2, and the Commanding Officer of the detachment is the representative of the A.C. of S., G-2, on all matters relating to or affecting Ultra intelligence in the European Theater.

6. Security regulations governing the dissemination and handling of Ultra intelligence within the European and Mediterranean Theaters have been approved by the US War Department . . . [35 spaces censored] . . . and will become effective on 1 April 1944.

7. Under the agreement of June 1943 and the security regulations of 1 April 1944, the basis of disseminating Ultra intelligence to American Commands in the European Theater is as follows:

a. Ultra intelligence produced by G.C. & C.S. (including the component of the US Signal Corps at G.C. & C.S.) is disseminated to Field Commands only by means of special communication channels established and controlled by the Director General, G.C. & C.S.

b. Communications between Field Commands which discuss or mention Ultra intelligence must be passed only over the above special communication channels.

c. American officers participate at G.C. & C.S. in the selection of Ultra intelligence for dissemination to the Field Commands and in the preparation of the messages in which the Ultra intelligence is so disseminated. These officers are attached to MID, War Department, London.

d. The receipt and distribution, at the Field Commands, of messages containing or relating to Ultra intelligence, is handled by Special

Liaison Units furnished and controlled by the Director General, G.C. & C.S. The personnel of these units includes American officers attached to MID, War Department, London.

e. The Special Liaison Units distribute Ultra intelligence messages only to officers at the Field Commands who are listed as entitled to receive Ultra intelligence. The eligibility of officers for listing as authorized Ultra intelligence recipients is governed by the security regulations of 1 April 1944. The Director General, G.C. & C.S., and the Commanding Officer of MID, War Department, London, administer the provisions of the agreement relating to admission of American officers in your theater to the list.

f. One or more American officers assigned to MID, War Department, London, will be detailed to each American Field Command, which receives Ultra intelligence. These officers will be subject to the administration and discipline of the Command to which they are detailed. They will *work under the control of the G-2 or A-2 of the Command* as part of his staff. They will have had a period of training at G.C. & C.S., and, if possible, with operational commands in the Mediterranean Theater, and this training will be directed toward equipping them to use Ultra intelligence effectively and securely. *Their primary responsibility will be to evaluate Ultra intelligence,* present it in useable form to the Commanding Officer and to such of his senior staff officers as are authorized Ultra recipients, *assist in fusing Ultra intelligence with intelligence derived from other sources,* and give advice in connection with making operational use of Ultra intelligence in such fashion that the security of the source is not endangered. *If at any time the flow of Ultra intelligence* is not sufficient to occupy fully the time of these officers, *they may be used for other related intelligence assignments.*

8. The Commanding Officer and the G-2's and A-2's or all American Field Commands in your theater, which receive Ultra intelligence, will take all steps necessary to insure that the requirements of this letter and of the security regulations of 1 April 1944, are fully carried out. In order to safeguard the continued availability of this enormously important source of intelligence, it is vital that these security regulations be meticulously observed, and that all personnel entitled to handle or receive Ultra intelligence take all possible precautions in connection with its handling and use. When operational action is taken on the basis of Ultra intelligence, the utmost care must be taken, by means of proper cover, to insure that the action does not reveal or in any way suggest that this source of intelligence is at our disposal.

9. It is of particular importance that:

a. Ultra intelligence be transmitted to the Field *Commands only by those special channels mentioned in* paragraphs 7a and b above, and that communications discussing or mentioning Ultra intelligence be transmitted *only by those channels*;

b. *Ultra intelligence be discussed orally only with* personnel of the field commands who are listed as authorized recipients of Ultra intelligence; and

c. Full facilities and opportunity be extended to the MID, War Department, London, officers detailed to Field Commands in order to enable them to perform their duties fully and effectively. The Commanding Officer, MID, War Department, London, and his principal assistants, will *visit the field commands as occasion requires to consult with the G-2's or A-2's on methods of handling and using* Ultra intelligence and on the scope and method of servicing Ultra intelligence from G.C. & C.S. to the field commands.

10. *The contents of this letter will be communicated* to the Commanding Officers and G-2's or A-2's of all American Field Commands in your theater which receive Ultra intelligence.

Notes

Preface

1. Here and throughout this book, Japanese proper names appear according to traditional practice in Japan, i.e., with the family names first. In reference notes and the bibliography, however, the names of Japanese authors are cited as they appear on the title pages of their published works. Long vowels are indicated by the use of a macron, e.g., Ōshima, but such a mark is omitted in the case of well-known place names, e.g., Tokyo.

2. There is no index for the individual translations of this massive collection of diplomatic messages. For the summaries, available in fourteen reels of microfilm, the best index is David Wallace, comp., *The MAGIC Documents: Summaries and Transcripts of the Top-Secret Diplomatic Communications of Japan, 1938-1945* (Frederick, Md.: University Publications of America, 1982).

Introduction

1. Records of the National Security Agency, "The Friedman Lectures on Cryptology," SRH-004, National Archives, Washington, D.C., Record Group 457, p. 179 (hereafter cited as NSA, RG 457, with filing designations).

The U.S. Army's Signal Intelligence Service (SIS), founded in 1930, experienced several changes in name from 19 June 1942 until 1 July 1943—for example, Signal Intelligence Service Division, Signal Security Division, Signal Security Branch, Signal Security Division, and Signal Security Service (see NSA, " 'History of the Signal Security Agency,' Volume One, Part I, 1939-1945," SRH-364, pp. 021-23.) From 1 July 1943 to 14 September 1945, the SIS was called the Signal Security Agency (SSA). Thus, for the convenience of the reader, only two wartime names are used in this book: SIS before 1 July 1943, and SSA afterward.

2. Frank B. Rowlett to author, 14 February 1989. Thomas Parrish, *The ULTRA Americans: The U.S. Role in Breaking the Nazi Codes* (New York: Stein and Day,

1986), p. 56 suggests that Major General Joseph O. Mauborgne (chief signal officer, 1937–1941) also referred to his cryptanalytic team as "magicians."

3. Peter Calvocoressi, *Top Secret Ultra* (New York: Pantheon Books, 1980), p. 103.

4. Frank B. Rowlett to author, 8 November 1990.

5. Carter W. Clarke to Frank B. Rowlett, 23 December 1983; I am obliged to Rowlett for a copy of Clarke's letter. See also Omar N. Bradley and Clay Blair, *A General's Life* (New York: Simon and Schuster, 1983), pp. 237–38.

In the considered opinion of several U.S. intelligence specialists, General Clarke, who in January 1949 became chief of the Army Security Agency (successor to the SSA on 5 September 1945), was one of the greatest intelligence officers in American history. To cite only one of his contributions, without his efforts after World War II, the United States would probably have established three separate service cryptologic organizations—which would have competed with each other and served only the military establishment—instead of the National Security Agency (NSA), which serves all agencies of the U.S. government. NSA, created by an executive order during the Truman administration after the National Security Act of 1947, is responsible for all signals intelligence, whether it be obtained by communications, radar, electronic means, foreign instrumentation signals, radiation, telemetry, lasers, or nonimagery infrared.

6. NSA, RG 457, "The Achievements of the Signal Security Agency in World War II,"SRH-349, p. 21.

7. Ōshima Hiroshi to author, 21 November 1966 and 7 May 1971.

8. See Carl Boyd, *The Extraordinary Envoy: General Hiroshi Ōshima and Diplomacy in the Third Reich, 1934–1939* (Washington, D.C.: University Press of America, 1980), pp. 159–62.

9. International Military Tribunal for the Far East (1946–1948), Exhibit 507 (hereafter cited as IMTFE).

10. *New York Times*, 13 December 1939, p. 1.

11. Interviews with Ōshima Hiroshi, 14 November 1959 and 10 March 1962 (hereafter cited as Ōshima Interviews, 1959 and 1962). These extensive interviews were conducted by leading Japanese scholars of the Nihon Kokusai Seiji Gakkai (Japan Association on International Relations) for the production of *Taiheiyō sensō e no michi: kaisen gaikō shi* [The road to the Pacific War: A diplomatic history of the origins of the war]. Originally recorded on tape, these reels are in the custody of the National Institute for Defense Studies, Japan Defense Agency, (Bōeikenkyūjo Senshibu) in Tokyo.

12. Ibid.

13. Suzuki Kenji, *Chūdoku Taishi Ōshima Hiroshi* [Ambassador to Germany, Ōshima Hiroshi] (Tokyo: Fuyō Shobō, 1979), pp. 209–11.

14. See, for example, Ōshima Hiroshi, "Doitsu gaikō no rinen" [The idea of German diplomacy] , *Bungei Shunjū* (January 1940)—an English translation of Ōshima's article appears in IMTFE, Exhibit 3516-A—and "Katte kabuto no o wo shimeyo" [After winning, keep the string tight on your helmet], *Bungei Shunjū* (April 1940): 8.

15. Ōshima interviews, 1959 and 1962.

16. Suzuki, *Chūdoku Taishi Ōshima Hiroshi*, pp. 209–10.

17. Ibid., p. 224. See also John W. M. Chapman, ed. and trans., *The Price of Admiralty: The War Diary of the German Naval Attaché in Japan, 1939-1943*, 3 vols. to date (Ripe, E. Sussex: Saltire Press, 1982–), 2:350, 353.

18. NSA, RG 457, "'A Version of the Japanese Problem in the Signal Intelligence Service (Later Signal Security Agency), 1930–1945' by John B. Hurt," SRH-252, pp. 029–127.

19. Henry F. Graff to author, 11 May 1988. After the war Professor Graff taught in the Department of History at Columbia University.

20. The term "cryptologic intelligence community" is intended to include in this book both the people involved in the solving or breaking of codes and ciphers (cryptanalysts) and those intelligence specialists involved in evaluating, integrating, and disseminating the translated material provided by the cryptanalysts. The line between the two cryptologic groups and their activities was at times blurred in the case of PURPLE because of the nuances of the Japanese language and the considerable linguistic and Japanese cultural sophistication of some of the SIS translators, who were sometimes cryptanalysts as well.

21. NSA, RG 457, "'The Undeclared War, History of R. I., 15 November 1943,' by L. F. Safford, Capt., U.S. Navy," SRH-305, p. 4.

22. See Wayne G. Barker, ed., *The History of Codes and Ciphers in the United States during the Period between the World Wars, Part I, 1919-1929* (Laguna Hills, Calif.: Aegean Park Press, 1979), pp. 49–74. This and the work cited in note 25 are edited versions of parts of various signal intelligence histories, especially SRH-361.

23. See ibid., pp. 90–111, and Herbert O. Yardley, *The American Black Chamber* (Indianapolis: Bobbs-Merrill, 1931), pp. 250–305, 312–17.

24. Cf. Yardley, *The American Black Chamber*, p. 370. It seems possible that Stimson was merely reacting to the attitude he knew President Hoover held on the matter of reading the secret diplomatic messages of foreign governments, yet there remains some debate on this point. See Barker, ed., *The History of Codes and Ciphers, Part I, 1919-1929*, pp. 130–33, 160–61, and Louis Kruh, "Stimson, the Black Chamber, and the 'Gentlemen's Mail' Quote," *Cryptologia* 12:2 (April 1988): 65–89.

25. Wayne G. Barker, ed., *The History of Codes and Ciphers in the United States during the Period between the World Wars, Part II, 1930-1939* (Laguna Hills, Calif.: Aegean Park Press, 1989), pp. 7–15, 56.

26. Ibid., pp. 8–12.

27. NSA, RG 457, SRH-305, p. 8.

28. Ibid., p. 13.

29. David Kahn, "The Intelligence Failure of Pearl Harbor," *Foreign Affairs* 70:5 (Winter 1991–1992): 144.

30. Barker, ed., *The History of Codes and Ciphers, Part II, 1930-1939*, p. 80.

31. My interpretation of army-navy cooperative work on Japanese diplomatic cipher systems is based on the William F. Friedman Cryptologic Collection, Box 1, Folder 16: Correspondence, Frank B. Rowlett and John Toland, 1980–1982, George C. Marshall Research Library, Lexington, Virginia (hereafter cited as GCMRL, followed by the appropriate collection, box, file, or folder identification).

32. Barker, ed., *The History of Codes and Ciphers, Part II, 1930-1939*, p. 17.

33. NSA, RG 457, SRH-305, p. 22.

34. Ibid., SRH-349, pp. 13–19.

Chapter 1. *Ōshima and the* Magic *Road to Pearl Harbor*

1. NSA, RG 457, No. SRDJ 008564, 20 December 1940.

2. On 17 February when Ōshima arrived on the 1:46 P.M. train at the Friedrichstrasse railway station in Berlin, the German Foreign Ministry entourage there to greet him was headed by State Secretary Ernst von Weizsäcker since Ribbentrop was not in Berlin at the time. See "Botschafter Ōshimas Ankunft in Berlin," *Ostasiatische Rundschau* 22:2 (1941): 43–44.

3. Joseph Goebbels, *The Goebbels Diaries, 1942–1943*, ed. and trans. Louis P. Lochner (Garden City, N.Y.: Doubleday, 1948), p. 181.

4. "Botschafter Ōshima beim Führer / L'ambasciatore Ōshima ricevulo del Führer," *Berlin-Rom-Tokio* 3:3 (1941): 13. See also NSA, RG 457, SRDJ No. 009917, 22 February 1941 and SRDJ No. 009941, 24 February 1941.

5. NSA, RG 457, SRDJ No. 009858, 18 February 1941. The message was translated on 20 February 1941.

6. Ibid., SRDJ No. 010682, 26 March 1941.

7. Ibid., SRDJ No. 011906, 27 May 1941; emphasis added. This message from Matsuoka refers to his earlier conversations with Hitler and Ribbentrop. Occasionally, parts of Magic messages were garbled and could not be fully deciphered; in such cases American cryptanalysts sometimes inserted their parenthetical estimate with a question mark. In this instance it is logically Manchukuo.

There is no doubt that Matsuoka learned something about the forthcoming German attack on the Soviet Union during his trip, but it is not altogether clear when exactly Washington learned of it through Magic. Ruth R. Harris claims that the secret was revealed about 1 April as a result of Matsuoka's report of a conversation he had with Hermann Göring ("The 'Magic' Leak of 1941 and Japanese-American Relations," *Pacific Historical Review* 50:1 [February 1981]: 83).

The Magic intercepts that I have seen are not so explicit. It is true that Matsuoka's itinerary included lunch with Göring on 29 March (SRDJ No. 010683, 26 March 1941), but none of the messages from Matsuoka while he was in Europe in late March and early April specifically mentions the coming war. Quite the contrary. The following report is typical: "On the 29th there was a luncheon in Field Marshal Goering's suite, and he and I had a long talk. . . . I am not going to wire you any special accounts of these conversations because I want to tell you the details when I get back to Tokyo" (SRDJ No. 010701, 30 March 1941; see also SRDJ No. 010725, 27 March 1941; SRDJ No. 010702, 30 March 1941; SRDJ 010828, 5 April 1941; and SRDJ No. 010829, 5 April 1941). However, it is clear that the Ōshima-Matsuoka radio traffic starting in late May confirmed the coming of the German-Soviet war.

8. NSA, RG 457, SRH-252, p. 30. See also Warren F. Kimball, *The Juggler: Franklin Roosevelt as Wartime Statesman* (Princeton: Princeton University Press, 1991), pp. 23, 209–10 n. 5.

9. NSA, RG 457, SRDJ No. 012127, 4 June 1941. See also SRDJ No. 012027, 5 June 1941; SRDJ No. 012039, 4 June 1941; SRDJ Nos. 012034–35, 4 June 1941; and

SRDJ Nos. 012036–37, 4 June 1941. The navy translation copy of the last message, concerning "the salient points" raised during Ōshima's interview with Ribbentrop, includes the following handwritten marginal comment: "*Extra copy* requested by army." As discussed in the Introduction, the two services had "a special exchange when anything of particular importance came up," and in the context of the road to Pearl Harbor there is evidence of how the army-navy arrangement on PURPLE worked in practice.

10. Ibid., SRDJ No. 012129, 6 June 1941.

11. Ibid., SRDJ No. 012080, 7 June 1941.

12. Ibid., SRDJ Nos. 012323–24, 18 June 1941.

13. Nobutaka Ike, trans. and ed., *Japan's Decision for War: Records of the 1941 Policy Conferences* (Stanford: Stanford University Press, 1967), pp. 78–90.

14. Ōshima was informed of the "gist" of the decisions reached in the 2 July Imperial Conference in a Foreign Ministry circular marked "national secret" of the same date. He was told in part that the government would "take measures with a view to advancing southward in order to establish firmly a basis for her self-existence and self-protection." However, Foreign Minister Matsuoka concluded that "although every means available shall be resorted to in order to prevent the United States from joining the war, if need be, Japan shall act in accordance with the Three-Power Pact [concluded in September 1940] and shall decide when and how force will be employed" (see U.S. Department of Defense, *The "Magic" Background of Pearl Harbor*, 5 vols. in 8 [Washington, D.C.: Government Printing Office, 1978], 2-App.: A-56–57).

15. NSA, RG 457, SRDJ No. 013823, 31 July 1941.

16. Ronald Lewin, *Hitler's Mistakes* (New York: William Morrow, 1984), p. 117. A notable exception to the Imperial General Staff's estimate of the impending Russian collapse was that held by then Major General Frank Noel Mason-Macfarlane, head of the British Military Mission to Moscow, where he arrived in early July 1941. Returning to London, via Stockholm, briefly in late August he "found it extremely difficult to shake the conviction which the Government shared with the War Office that Russian resistance was bound to crack. . . . [Nevertheless,] in the middle of October events at the front seemed to justify the gloomy predictions of the War Office" (Ewan Butler, *Mason-Mac: The Life of Lieutenant-General Sir Noel Mason-Macfarlane* [London: Macmillan, 1972], p. 138).

17. Forrest C. Pogue, *George C. Marshall*, 4 vols. (New York: Viking, 1963–1987), 2:72.

18. Yeaton's report of 10 October 1941 is quoted in Robert E. Sherwood, *Roosevelt and Hopkins: An Intimate History* (New York: Harper and Brothers, 1948), p. 395. Just before getting out of Moscow, a famed correspondent wrote with much uncertainty about the city's future; see Alexander Werth, *Moscow '41* (London: Hamish Hamilton, 1942), pp. 236–41.

19. NSA, RG 457, SRDJ No. 012430, 22 June 1941.

20. Ibid., SRDJ No. 012503, 24 June 1941.

21. GCMRL, George C. Marshall Papers, Box 65, Folder 37: Directives—Deputy Chief of Staff, April-September 1941.

22. Ibid., Folder 51: Directives—G-2, 1941.

23. NSA, RG 457, SRDJ Nos. 012722–23, 2 July 1941. See also John W. M.

Chapman, ed. and trans., *The Price of Admiralty: The War Diary of the German Naval Attaché in Japan, 1939–1943*, 3 vols. to date (Ripe, E. Sussex: Saltire Press, 1982—) 2:491, 558, 619n, 622n.

24. Ōshima's tour of duty as ambassador in Germany from February 1941 until May 1945 was his third official tour, for he was first assigned to Germany as an assistant military attaché from May 1921 until February 1923. (He was then assigned to Vienna where he served in the Japanese legation as military attaché for twenty-one months.) During his first major tour of duty in the 1930s, Ōshima held two successive posts in Germany, military attaché from March 1934 to October 1938 and ambassador thereafter until December 1939. Thus, Ōshima lived in Berlin for nearly twelve years between 1921 and 1945, and in German-speaking Austria for an additional twenty-one months.

25. NSA, RG 457, SRDJ Nos. 012724–25, and 012766, 2 July 1941.

26. Ibid., SRDJ No. 013149, 17 July 1941, and SRDJ No. 013539, 19 July 1941.

27. Ibid., SRDJ No. 013396, 24 July 1941.

28. Ibid., SRDJ No. 014351, 24 August 1941.

29. Ibid., SRDJ No. 014440, 25 August 1941. The remaining portions of this message are more detailed; see SRDJ Nos. 014441 and 014414–18. Since this message originated on an odd date, it was translated by the navy, and different parts became available in Washington on 27 and 28 September 1941.

30. See Harris, "The 'Magic' Leak of 1941," 77–96.

31. The exact number of Russian human losses will never be known, but Ōshima's contemporary estimates were probably not far off. The Russians themselves manipulated the figures during the Soviet-German war. In a speech in November 1941, Stalin declared that the Germans had killed only 350,000 Russians by the end of October, 378,000 Russians were missing, and 1,102,000 had been wounded. Until after Stalin's death in 1953, the Kremlin never admitted to more than 7 million battlefield dead in World War II. In 1957, Nikita Khrushchev admitted that the fatalities suffered were close to 12 million; later analysts of Soviet census estimated that 30 million Russian military and civilians were killed.

It is clear that the most harrowing aspect of this devastation was the suddenness with which it developed in the first four months. By the end of October the Germans occupied territory inhabited by 40 percent of the population of the USSR (see Louis Fischer, *The Road to Yalta: Soviet Foreign Relations, 1941–1945* [New York: Harper and Row, 1972], pp. 1–2, 33–34). Soviet army strength on the front fell from 4.7 million men in late June to 2.3 million by the end of July (see John Erickson, *The Road to Stalingrad* [New York: Harper and Row, 1975], pp. 159, 210, 225–26, and B. H. Liddell Hart, *History of the Second World War* [London: Cassell, 1970], pp. 157–70).

32. U.S. Department of Defense, *The "Magic" Background of Pearl Harbor*, 2-App.: A-114.

33. Ibid.

34. NSA, RG 457, SRDJ Nos. 013924, 014285, 9 August 1941.

35. See, for example, ibid., SRDJ Nos. 015717 and 015741, 11 October 1941.

36. Ibid., SRDJ No. 018113, 23 December 1941.

37. Ibid., SRDJ No. 014323, 20 August 1941.

38. U.S. Department of Defense, *The "Magic" Background of Pearl Harbor*, 3-App.: A-422.

39. Ibid., A-142-44.

40. NSA, RG 457, SRDJ No. 014100, 14 August 1941. Technically, in the secret addenda to the Tripartite Pact, Germany did not give Japan a unilateral promise of military assistance in the event of a war between Japan and the United States; rather, the German obligation was contingent upon an initial attack launched by the United States, a country not mentioned specifically in the treaty or its addenda.

41. Chapman, *The Price of Admiralty*, 2:558, 617-18n. Hitler appears to have accepted the estimate of German Army intelligence that the Japanese would capture Vladivostok by November 1941.

42. NSA, RG 457, SRDJ No. 013390, 24 July 1941.

43. Ibid., SRDJ No. 013149, 17 July 1941.

44. See the splendid work by Hosoya Chihiro, "The Tripartite Pact, 1939-1940," in *Deterrent Diplomacy: Japan, Germany, and the USSR, 1935-1940*, ed. James William Morley (New York: Columbia University Press, 1976), pp. 191-257.

45. See, for example, NSA, RG 457, SRDJ No. 013923, 9 August 1941, SRDJ Nos. 015817-18, 1 October 1941, and SRDJ Nos. 017117-20, 29 November 1941.

46. See U.S. Department of Defense, *The "Magic" Background of Pearl Harbor*, 2-App.: A-114, and ibid., SRDJ No. 012723, 2 July 1941. See also note 14 above.

47. U.S. Department of Defense, *The "Magic" Background of Pearl Harbor*, 4-App.: A-384.

48. NSA, RG 457, SRDJ Nos. 017114-15, 30 November 1941.

49. Ibid., SRDJ No. 017596, 9 December 1941.

50. Ibid., SRDJ No. 017776, 13 December 1941.

51. Ibid., SRDJ No. 016002, 19 October 1941.

52. See Carl Boyd, *The Extraordinary Envoy: General Hiroshi Ōshima and Diplomacy in the Third Reich, 1934-1939* (Washington, D.C.: University Press of America, 1980), pp. 64-72. Tōgō was transferred to Moscow where he arrived as the newly appointed ambassador on 29 October 1938.

53. U.S. Department of Defense, *The "Magic" Background of Pearl Harbor*, 4-App.: A-329.

54. Robert J. C. Butow, *Tojo and the Coming of the War* (Stanford: Stanford University Press, 1961), p. 343.

55. Ibid., p. 357.

56. NSA, RG 457, SRDJ No. 017118, 29 November 1941, translated in Washington on 1 December.

57. Ibid., SRDJ Nos. 017119-20, 29 November 1941, translated in Washington on 1 December.

58. Ibid., SRDJ No. 017112, 30 November 1941, translated in Washington on 1 December 1941.

59. Ibid., SRDJ No. 017503, 2 December 1941, translated in Washington on 10 December 1941.

60. Ibid., SRDJ No. 017323, 3 December 1941, translated in Washington on 6 December 1941.

61. U.S. Department of Defense, *The "Magic" Background of Pearl Harbor*, 4-

App.: A-391. Dated 7 December, Tokyo time, this message was translated in Washington on 9 December 1941.

62. NSA, RG 457, SRDJ No. 017377, 8 December 1941, translated in Washington on 8 December, that is, within twenty-four hours of the date of origination.

63. Ibid., SRDJ No. 017471, 8 December 1941. The copy of this message published in U.S. Department of Defense, *The "Magic" Background of Pearl Harbor*, 4-App.: A-392, claims that the translation is not dated, but a handwritten marginal note on the copy in the National Archives makes it clear that the translation was made on 9 December 1941.

64. See NSA, RG 457, SRDJ Nos. 017469–70, and 017487–88, 8 December 1941, translated in Washington on 9 December 1941. See also Bernd Martin, *Deutschland und Japan im Zweiten Weltkrieg: Vom Angriff auf Pearl Harbor bis zur deutschen Kapitulation* (Göttingen: Musterschmidt-Verlag, 1969), pp. 44–45.

65. David Kahn, "The United States Views Germany and Japan," in *Knowing One's Enemies*, ed. Ernest R. May (Princeton: Princeton University Press, 1984), 501.

66. William L. Shirer, *The Rise and Fall of the Third Reich: A History of Nazi Germany* (New York: Simon and Schuster, 1960), p. 872.

67. Weather conditions around intercept radio stations in the Canal Zone and Hawaii, and between the intercept stations and the decipher and translation centers, were important variables. Other factors also influenced the interception, deciphering, and translation of these messages. For example, regard for MAGIC intelligence in general increased after the attack at Pearl Harbor, additional translators (always in critically short supply) no doubt toiled longer hours, and more attention was given to the organization and efficiency of the operation.

68. Thomas Parrish, *The Ultra Americans: The U.S. Role in Breaking the Nazi Codes* (New York: Stein and Day, 1986), p. 197.

69. The White House learned on 1 December that Japanese diplomats in London, Manila, Singapore, and Hong Kong were ordered to destroy their cipher machines immediately. A similar order for the Japanese embassy in Washington was intercepted and translated by 3 December (see NSA, RG 457, SRH-305, p. 27). The long fourteen-part Japanese ultimatum of 6–7 December 1941 is found in SRDJ Nos. 017336–49. It was translated on the same two days.

70. GCMRL, William F. Friedman Collection, Box 1, Folder 16: Correspondence, Frank B. Rowlett and John Toland, 1980–1982.

71. Pogue, *George C. Marshall*, 3:471.

Chapter 2. Ōshima's MAGIC Messages in the Aftermath of Pearl Harbor

1. GCMRL, George C. Marshall Papers, Box 65, Folder 35: Directives—Chiefs of Arms and Services—Chief Signal Officer, 1942. This note was probably written in longhand by Marshall on the original sent to the chief signal officer. The body of the text in this chief-of-staff archival copy is a typed carbon version, but the note enclosed in quotation marks was typed anew.

2. Louis Kruh, "British-American Cryptanalytic Cooperation and an Unprece-

dented Admission by Winston Churchill," *Cryptologia* 13:2 (April 1989): 126. This letter from Churchill to Roosevelt is from the Franklin D. Roosevelt Library.

3. Ibid., 132–33.

4. Frank B. Rowlett to author, 5 February 1987.

5. Association of Former Intelligence Officers, "Arlington Hall: Monument to Intelligence," *Periscope* (Spring 1987): 4–5.

6. NSA, RG 457, SRDJ No. 019005, 18 January 1942.

7. "Europe First" (or "Germany First") was the basic strategic concept that the principal military effort of the United States and Great Britain was to be exerted in the Atlantic and European areas in order to produce the early defeat of Germany. A strategic defensive policy was to be implemented in the Pacific, while at the operational level the U.S. Navy was to be deployed offensively against the Japanese (see Maurice Matloff and Edwin M. Snell, *Strategic Planning for Coalition Warfare, 1941–1942* [Washington, D.C.: Office of the Chief of Military History, 1953], pp. 32–62, 97–119). Ralph Bennett calls the Europe First decision "the single greatest decision of the Second World War—at any rate apart from the dropping of the atom bombs on Japan" (Ralph Bennett, "Intelligence and Strategy: Some Observations on the War in the Mediterranean, 1941–45" [Paper delivered at the Intelligence and Military Operations Conference, U.S. Army War College, Carlisle Barracks, Pennsylvania, 23 April 1986], p. 3). The Europe First strategy was initially agreed upon in American-British staff conversations in Washington, 29 January through 29 March 1941, and readily concurred with by Roosevelt and Churchill during their Washington meetings (the ARCADIA Conference) from late December 1941 until 14 January 1942 (see Winston S. Churchill, *The Second World War*, 6 vols. [Boston: Houghton Mifflin, 1948–53], 3:706; Churchill's colorful account of his visit to the United States is on pp. 662–706).

8. Matloff and Snell, *Strategic Planning*, pp. 189–90, 200.

9. NSA, RG 457, SRDJ Nos. 017469–70 and 017487–88, 8 December 1941, translated in Washington on 9 December 1941.

10. Ōshima Hiroshi, "Neuordnung des Fernen Ostens, Neuordnung Europas," *Die Aktion: Kampfblatt für das Neue Europa* 2 (June 1941): 341–42.

11. Suzuki Kenji, *Chūdoku Taishi Ōshima Hiroshi* (Tokyo: Fuyō Shobō, 1979), p. 235.

12. Ibid.

13. NSA, RG 457, SRDJ No. 017925, 18 December 1941.

14. Ibid., SRDJ No. 017926, 18 December 1941; emphasis added.

15. Ibid., SRDJ No. 018990, 7 January 1942.

16. Ibid., SRDJ No. 018978, 17 January 1942.

17. Ibid., SRDJ No. 009911, 17 February 1941; SRDJ No. 009916, 22 February 1941; and SRDJ No. 010795, 26 March 1941.

18. See, for example, ibid., SRDJ No. 021143, 26 March 1942, and Joseph Goebbels, *The Goebbels Diaries, 1942–1943*, ed. and trans. Louis P. Lochner (Garden City, N.Y.: Doubleday, 1948), p. 181. According to Goebbels, Ōshima made an extensive tour of Slovakia and Eastern Europe, and he "spoke extremely eloquently in favor of Axis policies" during visits to Bucharest and Budapest.

19. NSA, RG 457, SRDJ No. 010022, 22 February 1941.

20. Ibid., SRDJ No. 020671, 9 March 1942.

21. Ibid., SRDJ No. 018979, 17 January 1942.

22. Suzuki, *Chūdoku Taishi Ōshima Hiroshi,* p. 244.

23. See Carl Boyd, *The Extraordinary Envoy: General Hiroshi Ōshima and Diplomacy in the Third Reich, 1934–1939* (Washington, D.C.: University Press of America, 1980), p. 124, quoting from *"Berurin nikki"* [Berlin diary], Records of German and Japanese Embassies and Consulates, 1890–1945, National Archives Microfilm Publication T-179, roll 73.

24. Ibid., p. 139n.

25. NSA, RG 457, SRDJ No. 018530, 4 January 1942.

26. Ronald Lewin, *The American Magic: Codes, Ciphers and the Defeat of Japan* (New York: Farrar Straus Giroux, 1982), p. 206. Citing the Chief Customs Bureau of the Soviet Union as his source, Lewin claims that during the first five months of 1941 Germany received over 212,000 tons of Japanese commodities via Russian rail—rubber, oils and fats, foodstuffs, minerals, chemicals, and drugs. In return Japan received heavy machinery, vehicles, locomotives, armor plate, and aircraft.

27. NSA, RG 457, SRDJ No. 018535, 4 January 1942. See also SRDJ Nos. 018530–31 and 018536–39 of the same date.

28. Lewin, *The American Magic,* p. 205.

29. See NSA, RG 457, "Blockade-Running between Europe and the Far East by Submarines, 1942–44," SRH-019, and Martin Brice, *Axis Blockade Runners of World War II* (Annapolis: Naval Institute Press, 1981), pp. 126–34. See August Karl Muggenthaler, *German Raiders of World War II* (Englewood Cliffs, N.J.: Prentice-Hall, 1977) for a good account of raiders that often assisted the operations of blockade runners.

30. NSA, RG 457, SRDJ Nos. 33,664–65, 31 March 1943. Ōshima reported an interview with Field Marshal Fritz Erich von Manstein in which the German officer said that "Germany regards it exceedingly urgent that effective liaison be made between Japan and the Reich, and as it has recently . . . [become] too hot for Yanagi ships, we think we are going to use submarines. . . . We can convert [large, older model U-boats] into shipping subs . . . and use them to get essential raw materials, particularly rubber, from Greater East Asia." Ōshima recommended to his superiors that they "take a cue from the Germans, revamp our old craft and carry on all our communications with Germany under the water. The sooner we get on a purely submarine basis, the better, I believe."

31. Ibid., SRDJ No. 019982, 20 February 1942.

32. See, for example, Ladislas Farago, comp. and ed., *The Axis Grand Strategy: Blueprints for the Total War* (Harrisburg, Pa.: Telegraph Press, 1942), pp. 537–65.

33. William F. Clarke, "Bletchley Park, 1941–1945," *Cryptologia* 12:2 (April 1988): 94.

34. NSA, RG 457, SRDJ No. 019781, 14 February 1942.

35. Ibid., SRDJ Nos. 020190–91, 28 February 1942. Ribbentrop also suggested that these German capital ships would be effective against a possible Anglo-American "campaign against Norway."

36. The two German battle cruisers struck mines during the "Channel dash." Furthermore, the *Gneisenau* was hit during a heavy bombing raid at Kiel before the end of February and was devastated by fire. It was never properly repaired and remained in the Baltic. The *Prinz Eugen* was torpedoed by a British submarine (also

before the end of February), and extensive repairs required nearly eight months to complete. Unsuccessful in at least two attempts to run the Kattegat and Skagerrak en route to northern Norway in early 1943, it too remained in the Baltic and was allotted to the United States in 1945 for use in the Bikini atom bomb tests the next year. Only the *Scharnhorst* of the three famed "Channel dash" vessels emerged, in 1943, in an attempt to intercept convoys north of Norway. There it was sunk (72°25' N, 28°00' E) with great loss of life in a running battle with superior British units on 26 December 1943.

37. NSA, RG 457, SRDJ No. 016845, 21 November 1941; SRDJ No. 020696, 17 March 1942; and SRDJ Nos. 021456–61, 6 April 1942. Hitler's continuous refusal to negotiate a separate German-Soviet peace is discussed in chapter 7.

38. Ibid., SRDJ No. 019748, 31 January 1942.

39. Ibid., SRDJ Nos. 019997–98, 21 February 1942.

40. Ibid., SRDJ Nos. 021352–53, 31 March 1942.

41. Basil Liddell Hart wrote that "until I delved into Rommel's own papers I regarded him as a brilliant tactician and great fighting leader, but did not realise how deep a sense of strategy he had. . . . It was a surprise to find that such a thruster had been so thoughtful, and that his audacity was so shrewdly calculated. . . . He became the hero of the Eighth Army troops who were fighting against him—to such an extent that it became their habit, when wanting to say that someone had done a good job of any kind on their own side, to describe it as 'doing a Rommel.' " (See B. H. Liddell Hart, ed., *The Rommel Papers* [New York: Harcourt, Brace, 1953], p. xv).

42. NSA, RG 457, SRDJ No. 019782, 14 February 1942.

43. See, for example, Liddell Hart, ed., *The Rommel Papers*, pp. 187, 191.

44. Ibid., p. 232.

45. NSA, RG 457, SRDJ No. 024202, 26 June 1942.

46. Winston S. Churchill, *The Second World War*, 6 vols. (Boston: Houghton Mifflin, 1948–53), 4:393. See also B. H. Liddell Hart, *History of the Second World War* (London: Cassel, 1970), p. 283.

47. NSA, RG 457, SRDJ No. 020696, 17 March 1942.

48. T. H. Vail Motter, *The Persian Corridor and Aid to Russia* (Washington, D.C.: Office of the Chief of Military History, 1952), p. 31.

49. Robert Greenhalgh Albion and Jennie Barnes Pope, *Sea Lanes in Wartime: The American Experience, 1775–1942* (London: George Allen and Unwin, 1943), p. 306.

50. NSA, RG 457, SRDJ Nos. 020697–98, 17 March 1942.

51. NSA, RG 457 SRDJ No. 020698, 17 March 1943.

52. Churchill, *The Second World War*, 4:227. See also Ronald Lewin, *The Chief: Field Marshal Lord Wavell, Commander-in-Chief and Viceroy, 1939–1947* (New York: Farrar Straus Giroux, 1980), pp. 202–3.

53. See Paul S. Dull, *A Battle History of the Imperial Japanese Navy, 1941–1945* (Annapolis: Naval Institute Press, 1978), pp. 104–11.

54. Reports of the U.S. Naval Technical Mission to Japan, 1945–1946, *Japanese Submarine Operations* (Washington, D.C.: Operational Archives, Naval Historical Center, microfilm reel JM-200-1, report no. S-17 [February 1946]), p. 117; see also p. 114. After 1942 Japanese submarines did not concentrate on the destruction of Allied shipping in the Indian Ocean; see Carl Boyd, "The Japanese Submarine Force

and the Legacy of Strategic and Operational Doctrine Developed between the World Wars," in *Selected Papers from The Citadel Conference on War and Diplomacy, 1978,* ed. Larry H. Addington et al. (Charleston, S.C.: Citadel Press, 1979), especially pp. 29 and 38n, and *Submarine Operations in Second Phase Operations, April–August 1942,* pt. 1, *Japanese Monograph No. 110,* Military History Section, Headquarters, Army Forces Far East, 1952 (Office of the Chief of Military History), pp. 5–9, 12–14, 37–39.

55. See Mochitsura Hashimoto, *Sunk: The Story of the Japanese Submarine Fleet, 1941–1945,* trans. E. H. M. Colegrave (New York: Henry Holt, 1954), pp. 73–74, and Bernd Martin, *Deutschland und Japan im Zweiten Weltkrieg: Vom Angriff auf Pearl Harbor bis zur deutschen Kapitulation* (Göttingen: Musterschmidt-Verlag, 1969), pp. 141–48. After exchanging materials, *I-30* set out on the long return journey, arriving at Singapore in October. Leaving Singapore for Japan, the submarine struck a British mine and sank.

56. NSA, RG 457, SRDJ No. 021073, 24 March 1942.

57. Martin, *Deutschland und Japan im Zweiten Weltkrieg,* pp. 147–48. The Battle of Midway was disastrous for Japan—four Japanese aircraft carriers and a heavy cruiser were sunk. Imperial General Headquarters went to great lengths to conceal the truth, yet the United States promptly announced to the world the results of the battle, accurately naming the ships damaged and sunk (see "Authors' Preface," in Mitsuo Fuchida and Masatake Okumiya, *Midway: The Battle That Doomed Japan* [Annapolis: U.S. Naval Institute, 1955], pp. xiii–xv).

58. See Carl Boyd, "American Naval Intelligence of Japanese Submarine Operations Early in the Pacific War," *Journal of Military History* 53:2 (April 1989): 169–89.

59. Allison W. Saville, "German Submarines in the Far East," United States Naval Institute *Proceedings* 87:8 (August 1961): 81–82.

60. NSA, RG 457, SRDJ No. 024182, 26 June 1942.

61. Ibid., SRDJ No. 025818, 8 August 1942.

62. Boyd, "The Japanese Submarine Force," pp. 27–40, and Boyd and Akihiko Yoshida, *History of Imperial Japanese Navy Submarine Operations in the Second World War* (Annapolis: Naval Institute Press, forthcoming).

63. See Karl Doenitz, *Memoirs: Ten Years and Twenty Days,* trans. R. H. Stevens (Annapolis: Naval Institute Press, 1990), pp. 238, 294–95, and Jürgen Rohwer, *Axis Submarine Successes, 1939–1945,* trans. John A. Broadwin (Annapolis: Naval Institute Press, 1983), pp. 264–66.

64. Saville, "German Submarines in the Far East," p. 91. See also NSA, RG 457, "U. S. Navy COMINCH [Commander in Chief, United States Fleet Admiral Ernest J. King], Radio Intelligence Appreciations Concerning German U-boat Activity in the Far East (January-April 1945)," SRH-232.

Chapter 3. The MAGIC Perspective of Strategic Change in 1942

1. Quoted in Robert Dallek, *Franklin D. Roosevelt and American Foreign Policy, 1932–1945* (New York: Oxford University Press, 1979), p. 273.

2. Gerhard Krebs, *Japans Deutschlandpolitik 1935–1941: Eine Studie zur Vorge-

schichte des Pazifischen Krieges, 2 vols. (Hamburg: Gesellschaft für Natur- und Völkerkunde Ostasiens, 1984), 1:582–83, 591.

3. NSA, RG 457, SRDJ No. 016845, 21 November 1941.

4. Quoted in Gordon W. Prange, *Target Tokyo: The Story of the Sorge Spy Ring* (New York: McGraw-Hill, 1984), p. 462. An especially solid work on the Sorge spy ring is Chalmers Johnson, *An Instance of Treason: Ozaki Hotsumi and the Sorge Spy Ring*, expanded ed. (Stanford: Stanford University Press, 1990).

5. U.S. Department of Defense, *The "Magic" Background of Pearl Harbor*, 5 vols. in 8 (Washington, D.C.: Government Printing Office, 1978), 4-App., A-341.

6. Charles B. Burdick, *An American Island in Hitler's Reich: The Bad Nauheim Internment* (Menlo Park, Calif.: Markgraf, 1987), pp. 5–7.

7. Truman Smith, "Air Intelligence Activities, Office of the Military Attaché, American Embassy, Berlin, Germany, August 1935–April 1939 (163 pp.), with Special Reference to the Service of Colonel Charles A. Lindbergh, Air Corps," on microfilm at the Yale University Library, New Haven, Conn. Smith summarized the successes of his office:

1. By November 1939 the office of the military attaché in Berlin reported to Washington both the existence and the approximately correct characteristics of all German combat planes. . . . 2. The Berlin office listed and located all German aircraft assembly plants which were in operation in November 1938. It described with reasonable accuracy these plants and estimated their 1938 production rate and floor space with only small margins of errors. 3. The military attaché office listed and located all important German aircraft engine plants in existence up to November 1938, with the exception of one or two in Austria. . . . . 4. All German Luftwaffe units which were in existence in November 1938, with three or four exceptions, were reported to the intelligence division of the General Staff. The location of these units was given correctly as well as the type of airplane with which they were equipped at that time. Those units still unidentified by the attaché office in November 1938 were in most cases reported by Major Vanaman to Washington prior to the outbreak of war. 5. The Berlin office reported to G-2 the bulk of airfields in operation as of the end of 1938. Some airfields in the Rhineland (in which attachés were forbidden to travel by motor) and in East Prussia (which was seldom visited) were never located. 6. The office correctly estimated and reported the principal technical strong and weak points of Luftwaffe equipment. 7. During the expansion of the Luftwaffe between 1935 and 1939 the office estimates of its personnel strength were reasonably close at all times. 8. The office stressed again and again the considerable difficulties the Luftwaffe was encountering, from 1935 to 1939, in acquiring efficient officer personnel of all grades. 9. The office listed and located many parts and instrument factories of the German air industry. . . . 10. The office stressed, from the autumn of 1937 on, the basic fact that the Luftwaffe was designed for close support of the German armies in Europe, rather than as a long range air force constructed primarily to bomb objectives far behind the front

lines. It pointed out also the failure of Germany to build four-engined bombers other than prototypes.

In listing the above successes and partial successes, it must again be emphasized that not one penny of money for espionage was given to the Berlin military attaché's office. [pp. 154–56].

8. Richard Sorge, "Die japanische Expansion," *Zeitschrift für Geopolitik* 16:8/9 (August-September 1939): 622.

9. William Henry Chamberlin, *Modern Japan* (St. Louis: Webster Publishing, 1942), p. 47.

10. NSA, RG 457, SRDJ No. 019093, 15 January 1942.

11. Ibid., SRDJ Nos. 019000–5, 18 January 1942.

12. The long, intricate paper trail of intercept files is worth explaining in this instance. In the report cited in note 11, Ōshima referred to German plans in late 1941, telling the Foreign Ministry in Tokyo that his account was "in my Nos. 1064 and 1066. On August 23rd [1941], Foreign Minister Ribbentrop and Field Marshal Keitel explained this to me." In a footnote to this January 1942 intercept, SIS, still in the Munitions Building at the time, crossreferenced Ōshima's earlier messages: Ōshima's No. 1064 was not available at SIS, but his No. 1066 (in six parts, complete) was on file in Washington as SIS's Nos. 21521 and 21575. The report concerned "the German-Soviet war as described personally by Marshal Keitel." Thus, Ōshima's No. 1066 of 25 August 1941 became SIS's Nos. 21521 and 21575 of 27 and 28 August 1941. These, in turn, became SRDJ (Individual Translation, Japanese Diplomatic Messages) Nos. 014414–18, 014440–41, declassified by NSA on 1 December 1978, and now in the National Archives.

13. Stewart Richardson, ed., *The Secret History of World War II: The Ultra-Secret Wartime Letters and Cables of Roosevelt, Stalin, and Churchill* (New York: Richardson and Steirman, 1986), p. 36.

14. Ibid., p. 41.

15. Ibid., pp. 42–43.

16. Ted Morgan, *FDR: A Biography* (New York: Simon and Schuster, 1985), p. 606.

17. NSA, RG 457, SRDJ No. 020696, 17 March 1942.

18. Ibid., RG 457, SRDJ Nos. 021456–61 (the full message), 6 April 1942.

19. See Suzuki Kenji, *Chūdoku Taishi Ōshima Hiroshi* (Tokyo: Fuyō Shobō, 1979), pp.46–47, 56–57, and Walter Voigt, "Begegnung mit Hauptman Ōshima," *Das Deutsche Rote Kreuz* 7 (1943): 32–33.

20. NSA, RG 457, SRDJ Nos. 025150–54, 27 July 1942.

21. As discussed briefly in Chapter 1, for about ten months in 1937–1938, Tōgō, a distinguished career diplomat, was ambassador in the Berlin embassy where Ōshima had been military attaché since 1934. To Tōgō's and the Foreign Ministry's consternation, Ōshima was involved in political as well as military discussions with the Germans. Indeed, before Tōgō arrived in Berlin, Ōshima negotiated the Anti-Comintern Pact with Ribbentrop in 1936, and after a heated embassy shakeup, Ōshima replaced Tōgō as the Japanese ambassador to Germany in October 1938.

22. NSA, RG 457, SRDJ No. 025154, 27 July 1942.

23. Ibid., SRDJ No. 025160, 29 July 1942.

24. Ibid., SRDJ No. 025293, 2 August 1942.

25. U.S. Department of State, *Foreign Relations of the United States, Diplomatic Papers, 1942*, 7 vols. (Washington, D.C.: Government Printing Office, 1960–1963), 3:616, and Richardson, ed., *The Secret History of World War II*, p. 45. Similarly, the British prime minister gave Stalin selected ENIGMA-deciphered German intelligence. At the end of September 1942, for example, Churchill wrote to Stalin that the "Germans have already appointed an Admiral to take charge of naval operations in the Caspian. They have selected Makhach-Kala as their main naval base. About twenty craft including Italian submarines, Italian torpedo boats and mine-sweepers are to be transported by rail from Mariupol to the Caspian as soon as they have got a line open. On account of the icing-up of the Sea of Azov the submarines will be loaded before the completion of the railway line." Churchill added that this information came "from the same source that I used to warn you of the impending attack on Russia a year and a half ago. I believe this source to be absolutely trustworthy" (see Martin Gilbert, *Winston S. Churchill*, vol. 7, *Road to Victory, 1941–1945* [Boston: Houghton Mifflin, 1986], 235–36).

26. NSA, RG 457, SRDJ Nos. 025429–39, 8 August 1942.

27. W. Averell Harriman and Elie Abel, *Special Envoy to Churchill and Stalin, 1941–1946* (New York: Random House, 1975), p. 295. The attack in *Pravda* came fifteen months after Willkie's visit and the publication in *Life* magazine of a story about his concerns regarding Moscow's attitude toward the liberated eastern European countries (see Alexander Werth, *Russia at War, 1941–1945* [New York: E. P. Dutton, 1964], pp. 768–69, and Alexander S. Cochran, Jr., "Other Front in the Mediterranean, 1943: The Role of Operational Intelligence and Strategic Planning for Coalition Warfare" [Paper delivered at the Soviet-American Relations during World War II Symposium, Hyde Park, N.Y., 21 October 1987], pp. 17–37).

28. Richardson, ed., *The Secret History of World War II*, pp. 49–50.

29. Ibid., p. 57.

30. Ibid., pp. 57–58.

31. Frank B. Rowlett to author, 11 September 1987.

32. Ibid., 28 March 1987. By December 1941, U.S. monitor and intercept stations had been established at Fort Hancock, N.J.; Fort Scott, Presidio of San Francisco; Fort Sam Houston, Tex.; Post of Corozal, Panama Canal; Fort Shafter, Territory of Hawaii; Fort McKinley, Philippines; Fort Hunt, Va.; Amagansett, N.Y.; Cheltenham, Md.; Jupiter, Fla.; San Juan, Puerto Rico; Bainbridge Island, Wash.; Guam; and Corregidor, Philippines (see NSA, RG 457, "Expansion of the Signal Intelligence Service from 1930–7 December 1941 by William F. Friedman," SRH-134, p. 26, and ibid., "U.S. Navy Communication Intelligence Organization, Liaison and Collaboration, 1941–1945," SRH-197, pp. 8–9). Several additional stations were commissioned in 1942–1945.

33. NSA, RG 457, SRDJ No. 020696, 17 March 1942.

34. Ibid., SRDJ Nos. 028743–44 (the only available parts of this message), 14 November 1942.

35. Ibid., SRDJ No. 028761, 28 November 1942.

36. Ibid., SRDJ Nos. 021457, 021459, 6 April 1942, and SRDJ No. 34354, 13 October 1942.

37. Ibid., SRDJ Nos. 020696, 17 March 1942, and SRDJ No. 021174, 28 March 1942.

38. Ibid., SRDJ No. 028951, 12 December 1942.

39. The British made certain that each convoy en route to North Africa saw an aircraft which was sent up for the purpose of being spotted; then warships intercepted and attacked the convoy. This was one of several deceptive schemes used to confuse European Axis forces and to protect the ULTRA secret. Harold C. Deutsch has noted, however, that "Rommel's resources were so overstrained that ULTRA or no ULTRA, he would scarcely have succeeded in reaching the delta or Suez." ("The Influence of ULTRA on World War II," *Parameters* 8:4 [December 1978]: 13. See also, Roger J. Spiller, "Assessing ULTRA," *Military Review* 59:8 [August 1979]: 13-23, and Williamson Murray, "ULTRA: Some Thoughts on Its Impact on the Second World War," *Air University Review* 35:5 [July-August 1984]: 52-64).

40. NSA, RG 457, SRDJ No. 028952, 12 December 1942.

41. Ibid., SRDJ No. 028955, 12 December 1942.

42. Ibid., SRDJ Nos. 026913-14, 21 September 1942.

43. Ibid., SRDJ No. 026619, 23 September 1942.

44. Suzuki, *Chūdoku Taishi Ōshima Hiroshi*, pp. 209-10.

45. NSA, RG 457, SRDJ Nos. 026634-35 (the full message), 22 September 1942.

46. NSA, RG 457, SRDJ No. 026661, 25 September 1942; emphasis added.

47. Ibid., SRDJ No. 026662, 25 September 1942.

48. See Earl F. Ziemke, *Stalingrad to Berlin: The German Defeat in the East* (Washington, D.C.: Office of the Chief of Military History, 1968), pp. 37-65.

49. NSA, RG 457, SRDJ No. 028077, 9 November 1942.

50. Ibid., SRDJ Nos. 028266-67 (the full message), 14 November 1942.

51. NSA, RG 457, MAGIC Summary, SRS 786, 24 November 1942.

52. Ibid., SRS 809, 17 December 1942.

53. NSA, RG 457, SRDJ Nos. 029010-11, 28 November 1942.

54. Ibid., SRDJ No. 029308, 18 December 1942.

Chapter 4. MAGIC and the Enigma of the Eastern Front

1. Hansen diary, 29 January 1945, Chester B. Hansen Papers, Archives, U.S. Army Military History Institute, Carlisle Barracks, Pa.

2. NSA, RG 457, "'A Version of the Japanese Problem in the Signal Intelligence Service (later Signal Security Agency), 1930-1945' by John B. Hurt," SRH-252, p. 86.

3. Ibid., p. 164.

4. Ibid., SRDJ No. 029044, 15 December 1942; emphasis added.

5. Ibid., SRDJ No. 029790, 23 December 1942.

6. Ibid., SRDJ No. 029692, 30 December 1942.

7. Ibid., SRDJ Nos. 030731-32, 030939-50, 031105-6, and 031589-90, 28-29 January 1943.

8. Ibid., SRDJ No. 31968, 22 February 1943, and SRDJ No. 32550, 1 March 1943.

9. Ibid., SRDJ No. 028951, 12 December 1942.

10. Ibid., SRDJ No. 030790, 25 January 1943.

11. Ibid., SRDJ No. 030560, 26 January 1943.

12. Ibid., SRDJ Nos. 031514–15, 5 February 1943.

13. Ibid., SRDJ No. 031266, 24 January 1943.

14. Ibid., SRDJ Nos. 031305–6, 24 January 1943.

15. Ibid., SRDJ No. 030561, 26 January 1943.

16. In October 1941, the Foreign Affairs Commissariat as well as foreign embassies and missions accredited to the Soviet Union moved from Moscow to Kuibyshev. In Kuibyshev, as an eyewitness observed, "the foreign embassies in most cases were housed in what had been before the revolution the houses of wealthy merchants" (see Valentin Berezhkov, *History in the Making: Memoirs of World War II Diplomacy*, trans. Dudley Hagen and Barry Jones [Moscow: Progress, 1983], p. 155).

17. NSA, RG 457, SRDJ No. 031059, 5 February 1943. See also SRDJ Nos. 031071–72, 1 February 1943, an intelligence report in which Foreign Minister Tani described conditions in the Soviet Union between Kuibyshev and the Afghanistan border. In SRDJ Nos. 32389–90, 9 March 1943, Tani sent Ōshima a copy of the intelligence report from the Japanese ambassador in Kuibyshev on "conditions in Russia for February." Thus, the Japanese provided the Anglo-American powers with a lot of information about Soviet warring capacity.

18. Ibid., SRDJ Nos. 34430–32, 16 April 1943.

19. Ibid., SRDJ No. 34430, 16 April 1943.

20. Ibid., SRDJ No. 34204, 15 April 1943, and SRDJ No. 34848, 19 April 1943.

21. Ibid., SRDJ No. 34433, 19 April 1943.

22. A rich contemporary view is Alexander Werth, *Moscow '41* (London: Hamish Hamilton, 1942), pp. 254–68.

23. NSA, RG 457, SRDJ No. 34432, 16 April 1943.

24. Ibid., SRDJ Nos. 34433–34, 19 April 1943. For an account of Ōshima's anti-Soviet work with Abwehr chief Admiral Wilhelm Canaris in the 1930s, see Carl Boyd, *The Extraordinary Envoy: General Hiroshi Ōshima and Diplomacy in the Third Reich, 1934–1939* (Washington, D.C.: University Press of America, 1980), pp. 35, 57–60, 73–74. One reason why Ōshima was found guilty of overall conspiracy and received the sentence of life imprisonment at the International Military Tribunal for the Far East, 1946–1948, was because of his counterespionage activities and collaboration with the Abwehr in anti-Soviet work (see Arnold C. Brackman, *The Other Nuremberg: The Untold Story of the Tokyo War Crimes Trials* [New York: William Morrow, 1987], pp. 207–8.

25. NSA, RG 457, SRDJ No. 34434, 19 April 1943.

26. Ibid., SRDJ No. 37451, 21 May 1943.

27. Ibid., SRDJ No. 37151, 21 May 1943, SRDJ No. 38081, 10 June 1943, and SRDJ No. 39230, 17 June 1943.

28. Ibid., SRDJ No. 34894, 28 April 1943, and SRDJ No. 37151, 21 May 1943. Career diplomat Shigemitsu Mamoru was minister of Greater East Asia when on 20 April 1943 he replaced Tani Masayuki as the Japanese foreign minister. Apparently, Prime Minister Tōjō Hideki selected Shigemitsu for the cabinet post in order to promote more effectively a so-called new China policy (see Mamoru Shigemitsu, *Japan and Her Destiny: My Struggle for Peace*, ed. F. S. G. Piggott, trans. Oswald White [New York: E. P. Dutton, 1958], pp. 286–90).

29. Manchouli (population 6,347 in December 1938), by far the smallest of the sixteen principal cities listed in *The Japan Year Book, 1940–41* (Tokyo: Foreign Affairs Association of Japan, 1940), p. 930, was not listed among the principal cities in *The Japan Year Book, 1943–44* (Tokyo: Foreign Affairs Association of Japan, 1943), p. 958, where population statistics were cited for August 1941. Manchouli was the site of three Soviet-Japanese conferences in the mid-1930s, the purpose of which was to examine various Manchukuo-Mongolia border incidents. The conferences failed, in part, because of the newfound diplomatic strength that Japan gained by concluding the Anti-Comintern Pact with Germany in November 1936. The flagrancy of the initial negotiations leading to the pact centered on then Major General Ōshima, Japanese military attaché in Berlin, and Ribbentrop, Hitler's ambassador at large and, when the pact was signed, the German ambassador to Great Britain.

30. See NSA, RG 457, SRDJ No. 37174, 22 May 1943; Friedrich-Karl von Plehwe, *The End of an Alliance: Rome's Defection from the Axis in 1943*, trans. Eric Mosbacher (London: Oxford University Press, 1971), pp. 39, 42, 100, and Bernd Martin, *Deutschland und Japan im Zweiten Weltkrieg: Vom Angriff auf Pearl Harbor bis zur deutschen Kapitulation* (Göttingen: Musterschmidt-Verlag, 1969), p. 295. It was symptomatic of the weak position Italy occupied in the Axis coalition that there was not always a Japanese ambassador or minister in Rome. Since June 1942, the Japanese government had been represented in Rome by only a chargé d'affaires, Kase Shunichi. Arrangements for the presentation of Ambassador Hidaka's credentials seem to have been difficult to make. Finally, Hidaka was able to schedule a meeting with Mussolini, followed by an audience with King Victor Emmanuel III, the day *after* the Italian dictator was obligated to resign. Thus, Hidaka met, not with Mussolini, but with Pietro Badoglio, the new Italian chief of government, on 26 July 1943. Obviously, Hidaka's tenure was brief. In early August, a month before the king and the government fled Rome and the Germans occupied the capital, Ambassador Hidaka predicted that the Badoglio government would continue the war as a member of the Axis partnership. At the same time, however, Ōshima, the senior and by far most sophisticated Japanese diplomat and army general in Europe, believed that the Italians were already negotiating with the Americans and British. He, therefore, urged the Germans to keep a close watch on the Italian fleet with Luftwaffe dive bombers.

31. NSA, RG 457, SRDJ No. 35401, 30 April 1943. The Japanese referred to "GPU men," in fact, the Soviet authorities were probably NKVD officials (People's Commissariat for Internal Affairs).

32. Ibid., SRDJ No. 35461, 27 April 1943.

33. See John R. Deane, *The Strange Alliance: The Story of Our Efforts at Wartime Cooperation with Russia* (Bloomington: Indiana University Press, 1973), pp. 256–57. General Deane arrived in Moscow in October 1943 to coordinate Soviet and American planning and military efforts in the event of a Japanese attack on the Soviet Union. See also Edward R. Stettinius, Jr., *Lend-Lease: Weapon for Victory* (New York: Macmillan, 1944), and T. H. Vail Motter, *The Persian Corridor and Aid to Russia* (Washington, D.C.: Office of the Chief of Military History, 1952).

34. See NSA, RG 457, SRDJ Nos. 35459–62, 35479–80, 27 April 1943, SRDJ Nos. 34892–98, 35413–16, 28 April 1943, SRDJ Nos. 35387–93, 35405–12, 29 April

1943, and SRDJ Nos. 35394–402, 35449–54, 35481–87, 30 April 1943. See also Martin, *Deutschland und Japan im Zweiten Weltkrieg*, pp. 181, 193, and 204–5. Okamoto did not get to confer privately with Hitler until 29 July, although he visited the eastern front on 8–12 June 1943. Ōshima's reports of Okamoto's observations were translated and reached authorities in Washington much earlier, between 29 April and 11 May 1943.

35. This section on Soviet railroad shipping is based on data included in NSA, RG 457, SRDJ Nos. 35405–16, 29 April 1943.

36. The Soviets have readily acknowledged the value during the war of over 400,000 vehicles supplied by Great Britain and the United States; see, for example, G. Deborin, *Secrets of the Second World War*, trans. Vic Schneierson (Moscow: Progress, 1971), p. 130.

37. Unless otherwise documented, this section on military factors is based on material in NSA, RG 457, Nos. 35387–402, 29 April 1943.

38. Ibid., SRDJ No. 35480, 27 April 1943.

39. Ibid.

40. General Okamoto probably erred in his estimate of the normal displacement of the submarines in the Caspian Sea. These Russian submarines were most likely of the M (*Malyutka*) class and, depending on the particular series, could have had as little as 161 tons surface displacement and as much as 350, but not 1,000 tons. Production of these small boats was concentrated in the Gorki Shipyard on the Volga, and they entered service in 1933. They were transported in sections by rail to the Black Sea, Leningrad, and Vladivostok for assembly and fitting out.

41. Charles F. Romanus and Riley Sunderland, *Stillwell's Mission to China* (Washington, D.C.: Office of the Chief of Military History, 1953), p. 15.

42. For the most part this section is based on NSA, RG 457, SRDJ Nos. 35481–87, 35449–54, 30 April 1943.

43. Ibid., SRDJ No. 35453, 30 April 1943.

44. Ibid., SRDJ Nos. 34896–98, 28 April 1943.

45. The Japanese estimates were reasonably accurate, but not at all inflated; they erred probably on the conservative side (see Deborin, *Secrets of the Second World War*, pp. 129–32, and Alexander Werth, *Russia at War, 1941–1945* [New York: E. P. Dutton, 1964], pp. 621–23).

46. See George C. Herring, Jr., *Aid to Russia, 1941–1945: Strategy, Diplomacy, the Origins of the Cold War* (New York: Columbia University Press, 1973), p. 73, and Motter, *The Persian Corridor and Aid to Russia*, p. 419. Ribbentrop first complained about American matériel reaching Vladivostok in the autumn of 1941. (The first of four U.S. tankers turned over to the Soviet Union for transporting supplies left Los Angeles bound for Vladivostok carrying 95,000 barrels of aviation fuel on 14 August 1941—see *Army History*, no. 19 [Summer 1991]: 21.) Ōshima reported to Tokyo that "Ribbentrop said, 'I have a report that Japan has approved the sailing of American ships straight through [to] Vladivostok. Can this be true?' I [Ōshima] replied, 'Well, I have no report on this from Tokyo, but I certainly do not believe it to be a fact.' Please wire me back what has happened along this line, because I want to know the truth" (NSA, RG 457, SRDJ No. 015385, 2 October 1941). Foreign Minister Tani replied (NSA, RG 457, SRDJ No. 015680, 9 October 1941):

It is not true that Japan has approved the entry of American ships into the harbor of Vladivostok. On the contrary, Japan has taken the stand toward America and Russia that this trade cannot be tolerated from the standpoint, not of international law, but of the whole political situation . . . at the present time. However, America says that trade between America and Russia is a political matter between the two countries and should cause Japan no uneasiness. To Japan's charge that this is an unfriendly act toward Japan and will have to be viewed as such, America invokes the freedom of the seas and says that she can not tolerate interference by a third country in her foreign trade.

However, the number of American ships that have entered Vladivostok from the middle of August [1941] to the present is five tankers and each one is believed to have carried between 60,000 and 95,000 barrels of oil.

The number of Russian ships that have operated between America and the Soviet [Union] during the same period is nine and the cargo was principally oil, (a total of about 300,000 barrels is estimated) and a small number of aeroplane engines and parts, etc.

Clearly, this Soviet-American trade was a matter of considerable concern to the Germans in 1941. Their concern increased with the mounting flow of American lend-lease goods entering Soviet Pacific ports; however, Japanese policy never changed in spite of Washington's fears and Berlin's anguish.

47. NSA, RG 457, SRDJ No. 34893, 28 April 1943.

48. Ibid., SRDJ Nos. 41471–72, 30 July 1943.

49. Ibid., SRDJ Nos. 41747–48, 30 July 1943.

50. Shigemitsu, *Japan and Her Destiny*, p. 301. Shigemitsu was also foreign minister in the three Hatoyama cabinets, 10 December 1954 through 23 December 1956.

Chapter 5. MAGIC *Intelligence during the President's Travels in 1943*

1. GCMRL, George C. Marshall Papers, Box 65, Folder 51: Directives—G-2, 1941.

2. Ibid., Folder 52: Directives—G-2, 1942.

3. Ibid.

4. Willis L. M. Reese (former intelligence officer assigned to the desk concerned with Japan's relations with Russia and certain countries in the Far East) to author, 17 October 1988. See also NSA, RG 457, "Handling of ULTRA within Military Intelligence Service (MIS), 1941–1945," SRH-146.

5. NSA, RG 457, "History of the Special Branch, MIS, War Department, 1942–1944," SRH-035, especially pp. 18, 52, and 55. Wallace Winkler, the NSA declassification officer responsible for making this document available to researchers in July 1979, was a special security officer with the Special Liaison Unit with the Ninth U.S. Army in Europe during the war. He developed an early appreciation of Ōshima's role and the importance of his intercepted messages to the Western Allies in the ETO.

6. Willis L. M. Reese to author, 17 October 1988.

7. Wallace A. Bacon to author, 21 March 1989. B-1-D translated traffic was primarily from three systems (later in the war a fourth system was solved). The first, a simple system, referred to here as "A," sometimes used English language texts and was only used for very routine matters. Traffic was very heavy, and not everything was fully translated, but there was always some notation about the contents of such an intercept made on the message's worksheet. A second system, referred to here as "B," was concerned mainly with economic matters throughout the world, and it was used by Japanese officials at a secondary level, below the ambassador. SSA Japanese translators required a staggering amount of knowledge to translate B messages intelligently because of a very wide range of economic subjects. The highest level traffic, labeled "C" in this study, was PURPLE. Unlike A and B, PURPLE arrived on the desks of American cryptanalysts and translators, not in transliterated code groups, but in a running *rōmaji* text using the Roman alphabet. Thus, missing or garbled parts could not be guessed at by trying other combinations of the letters. Sometimes SSA translators of PURPLE messages had to wait for a second intercept before a full translation was possible. The top translators always handled this traffic, which was separated according to the system and the nature of the message, logged in, and assigned to worksheets. The translation of PURPLE intercepts was usually done by chief Japanese linguists John. B. Hurt, Elmer H. Zaugg, and Wallace A. Bacon.

8. Wallace A. Bacon Papers, Box 2, Folder 1: Japanese Language Course, 1943, Northwestern University Archives, Evanston, Illinois.

9. *The Modern Reader's Japanese-English Character Dictionary* (Rutland, Vt.: Charles E. Tuttle, 1962).

10. Wallace A. Bacon to author, 23 September 1990.

11. Ibid., 21 March 1989.

12. Ibid.

13. Henry F. Graff to author, 28 September 1988.

14. See, for example, the insightful discussion by David Kahn, "Roosevelt, MAGIC and ULTRA," in *Historians and Archivists: Essays in Modern German History and Archival Policy*, ed. George O. Kent (Fairfax, Va.: George Mason University Press, 1991), pp. 115–44.

15. NSA, RG 457, SRH-305, p. 24.

16. See ibid., "War Experience of Alfred McCormack," SRH-185 and "Handling of ULTRA," SRH-146.

17. Ibid., "History of the Signal Security Agency, Volume Two, The General Cryptanalytic Problems," SRH-361, pp. 64, 272–85, and James Rusbridger and Eric Nave, *Betrayal at Pearl Harbor: How Churchill Lured Roosevelt into World War II* (New York: Summit Books, 1991), pp. 110–11, 115.

18. NSA, RG 457, "Marshall Letter to MacArthur on the Use of ULTRA Intelligence, May 23, 1944, and Related Correspondence," SRH-034, p. 2. By 1944, to help establish uniformity in the handling of enemy high-grade cryptographic intelligence in all Anglo-American theaters of operations, joint U.S.-British security regulations stipulated that the term "ULTRA" should be applied to Japanese as well as German signal intelligence. Nevertheless, the U.S. Army continued throughout the war to employ the term "MAGIC" when compiling the Japanese diplomatic summaries (see ibid., SRHs 034, 355, and SRMN-018).

19. See Edward J. Drea, "Ultra and the American War Against Japan: A Note on Sources," *Intelligence and National Security* 3:1 (January 1988): 195–204, and James Walter Zobel, "Signal Intelligence and MacArthur's Use of Military Intelligence (G-2) during the Second World War" (M.A. thesis, Old Dominion University, 1991).

20. NSA, RG 457, "COMINCH File: Weekly Reports on Estimated Locations of Japanese Fleet Units, 1 September 1942-9 August 1945," SRMN-044, p. 9.

21. Memorandum, Knox to Roosevelt, 9 June 1942, President's Secretary's File, Folder: Navy Department, Franklin D. Roosevelt Library, Hyde Park, New York (hereafter cited as FDRL, followed by the appropriate file or folder identification).

22. Ibid., Letter, Ickes to Roosevelt, 17 October 1942, Folder: Navy Department, July-December 1942.

23. In 1943 MIS started to develop the Special Security Officer (SSO) system, patterned after the British Special Liaison Unit (SLU) organization, to provide overseas field commands with COMINT. Each SSO carried a private set of cryptographic equipment and was provided with special pouch service. SSOs were first sent to the theater headquarters in the Pacific in the fall of 1943 and to the ETO early the next year.

24. FDRL, "Plan of Signal Communication," 8 January 1943, Map Room File, Folder: Casablanca Conference.

25. See George Raynor Thompson et al., *The Signal Corps: The Test (December 1941 to July 1943)* (Washington, D.C.: Office of the Chief of Military History, 1957), pp. 431, 454–55.

26. George Raynor Thompson and Dixie R. Harris, *The Signal Corps: The Outcome (Mid-1943 Through 1945)* (Washington, D.C.: Office of the Chief of Military History, 1966), p. 588.

27. FDRL, UTAH 107, 28 January 1943, Map Room File, Folder: Casablanca Conference. Other examples of "Colonel Boone" material are found in UTAH messages 23, 58, and 71.

28. NSA, RG 457, SRS 859, 28 January 1943. Numbered 308, this MAGIC Summary includes an appendix containing the full text of Ōshima's intercepted message, see ibid., SRDJ Nos. 030560–62, 26 January 1943. The message was intercepted on 26 January, deciphered and translated on 27 January, and the next day incorporated in a MAGIC Summary and condensed into a twenty-word UTAH message. The American cryptologic intelligence community was extremely sophisticated by this point in the war.

29. FDRL, UTAH 76, 21 January 1943, Map Room File, Folder: Casablanca Conference; emphasis added. There is little MAGIC material or intelligence with the former ULTRA classification in FDRL because enemy messages were generally only loaned to the White House and had to be retrieved.

30. Cf., Alexander S. Cochran, Jr., "The Influence of 'Magic' Intelligence on Allied Strategy in the Mediterranean," in *New Aspects of Naval History*, ed. Craig L. Symonds et al. (Annapolis: Naval Institute Press, 1981), p. 348n. Since the issue here concerns the protection of MAGIC and the effective communication of MAGIC-based information in disguised form, closer examination of the UTAH message, the MAGIC Summary, and the MAGIC intercept is justified. UTAH 53, 17 January 1943, reads in part: "Tokyo tells Yamaguchi 'ever since outbreak war in Asia Japan has felt

it would be advantageous to take Russia out of anti-Axis camp. To accomplish this we have been constantly on the alert for opportunity to bring about Soviet-Nazi peace. In view recent developments in fighting in Russia fresh studies on this subject now being made. Keep this in your hat until you hear from us but bend every effort to influence Germany toward above end.'"

There is no doubt that MAGIC was the source of this passage quoted in UTAH 53, but the material was not reproduced identically. In part of a message from Foreign Minister Tani Masayuki to Ōshima, the passage is, however, identical in MAGIC Summary, No. 295, SRS 838, 15 January 1943 and SRDJ 030140, 12 January 1943, with one minor exception—"Japan" is substituted for "she" in one instance in the summary. Thus, the intercept and summary read: "Ever since the outbreak of the Greater East Asia war, the Imperial Government has felt that it would be advantageous to Japan, Germany and Italy in their war efforts if Russia could be taken out of the anti-Axis camp. To this end she [or Japan] has watched for an opportunity to effect a German-Russian peace. . . . Now as we look at the results of last year's German-Russian fighting along with the recent resistance on the part of the Russians, we are giving fresh study to the possibilities and terms for peace. . . . Keep this to yourself until further word from us and in the meantime do your very best to influence Germany as her attitude shall permit."

31. See War Cabinet, COS. [Chiefs of Staff Committee] (43) 416 (O), Operation "OVERLORD," Report and Appreciation with Appendices, 30 July 1943; Gordon A. Harrison, *Cross-Channel Attack* (Washington, D.C.: Office of the Chief of Military History, 1951), pp. 46–82; and Maurice Matloff, *Strategic Planning for Coalition Warfare, 1943–1944* (Washington, D.C.: Office of the Chief of Military History, 1959), pp. 126–45.

32. Winston S. Churchill, *The Second World War*, 6 vols. (Boston: Houghton Mifflin, 1948–53), 5:410.

33. Henry F. Graff to author, 11 May 1988.

34. William D. Leahy, *I Was There: The Personal Story of the Chief of Staff to Presidents Roosevelt and Truman Based on His Notes and Diaries Made at the Time* (New York: Whittlesey House, 1950), pp. 198, 215.

35. James Rusbridger, "The Sinking of the 'Automedon,' the Capture of the 'Nankin': New Light on Two Intelligence Disasters in World War II," *Encounter* 64:5 (May 1985): 9.

36. David Kahn, *The Codebreakers: The Story of Secret Writing* (New York: Macmillan, 1967), p. 473. See also Richard A. Stewart, "Rommel's Secret Weapon: Signals Intelligence," *Marine Corps Gazette* 74 (March 1990): 51–55.

37. See Kahn, *The Codebreakers*, pp. 473–77, and Kahn, *Hitler's Spies: German Military Intelligence in World War II* (New York: Macmillan, 1978), pp. 193–94. A less satisfactory account of the Fellers affair is given in Anthony Cave Brown, *"C": The Secret Life of Sir Stewart Graham Menzies, Spymaster to Winston Churchill* (New York: Macmillan, 1987), pp. 358–59. Fellers was granted an interview with President Roosevelt in the White House at the end of July 1942. On this point and other dimensions of the outspoken Colonel Fellers, see the still important study by Maurice Matloff and Edwin M. Snell, *Strategic Planning for Coalition Warfare, 1941–1942* (Washington, D.C.: Office of the Chief of Military History, 1953), especially pp. 246n, 253–54, 297, and 297n.

38. See Arthur Bryant, *The Turn of the Tide: A History of the War Years Based on the Diaries of Field-Marshal Lord Alanbrooke, Chief of the Imperial General Staff* (Garden City, N.Y.: Doubleday, 1957), pp. 348–64.

39. See Edwin T. Layton, *"And I Was There": Pearl Harbor and Midway— Breaking the Secrets* (New York: William Morrow, 1985), pp. 474–76; E. B. Potter, *Nimitz* (Annapolis: Naval Institute Press, 1976), pp. 284–85; Hiroyuki Agawa, *The Reluctant Admiral: Yamamoto and the Imperial Navy*, trans. John Bester (Tokyo: Kodansha International, 1982), pp. 347–67; and Edward Van Der Rhoer, *Deadly Magic: A Personal Account of Communications Intelligence in World War II in the Pacific* (New York: Charles Scribner's Sons, 1978), pp. 134–51.

40. See W. J. Holmes, *Double-Edged Secrets: U.S. Naval Intelligence Operations in the Pacific during World War II* (Annapolis: Naval Institute Press, 1979), pp. 129–36.

41. FDRL, Memorandum, Brown to Director of Naval Communications, 10 November 1943, Map Room File, Folder 1: Sextant Conference.

42. Ibid., "SEXTANT Communications," 11 November 1943.

43. Ibid. and also, from the same folder, "Memorandum Re Radio Traffic for Army-Navy Personnel on Special Project."

44. Ibid., "White House List of Code Words."

45. Ibid., Memorandum, Mathewson to Brown, 14 November 1943, Map Room File, Folder 1: Sextant Conference.

46. Ibid., "F.D.R. Longhand November 12-December 17, 1943, Trip to Cairo and Teheran, Original Diary, 200-3-N," Folder: War Conference, November 11-December 17, 1943.

47. NSA, RG 457, "MAGIC Reports for the Attention of the President, 1943–1944," SRH-111, p. 19.

48. Ibid., p. 18.

49. FDRL, "Log of the President's Trip to Africa and the Middle East, November-December 1943," Logs of F.D.R.'s Trips, September 1942-February 1945 (printed and illustrated).

50. Ibid., Memorandum, "Report of 3 Communications Sent to Tokyo by Japanese Ambassador Ōshima after His Inspection Tour of the German Defenses in France," Folder: Warfare—Germany and German Occupied Countries, 9 September 1943-2 April 1945. The three Ōshima reports were available individually as MAGIC summaries on 12 and 13 November and on 10 December 1943. The original intercepts for these respective summaries and their dates of translation follow: SRDJ Nos. 45444–45; 11 November; SRDJ Nos. 45465–69, 12 November; and SRDJ Nos. 46763–71, 9 December 1943. Complete sets of these intercepts are also incorporated in NSA, RG 457, "Selected Examples of Commendations and Related Correspondence Highlighting the Achievements and Value of U.S. Signals Intelligence during World War II," SRH-059 and in SRH-111.

51. F. H. Hinsley et al., *British Intelligence in the Second World War*, 5 vols. (London: Her Majesty's Stationery Office, 1979–1990), 3, pt. 2, app. 5:771–75.

52. Ibid., 3, pt. 2:33n.

53. NSA, RG 457, SRH-059, p. 2.

54. *Kriegstagebuch des Oberkommandos der Wehrmacht (Wehrmachtführungsstab), 1940–1945*, ed. Percy Ernst Schramm, Andreas Hillgruber, Walter Hubatsch,

and Hans-Adolf Jacobsen, 4 vols. in 7 (Frankfurt am Main: Bernard & Graefe Verlag für Wehrwesen, 1961–1965), 3:1216, 1249.

55. Hensley, *British Intelligence*, 3, pt. 2:32.

56. NSA, RG 457, "Examples of Intelligence Obtained from Cryptanalysis, 1 August 1946," SRH-066, pp. 005–6.

57. FDRL, "Summary of the Second Regular Session of the Teheran Meeting, 4 P.M.—November 29, 1943," Harry L. Hopkins Papers, Sherwood Collection, Folder: Book 8: Teheran (B) Meeting with Stalin.

58. See, for example, Hensley, *British Intelligence*, 3, pt. 2, app. 7, "Decrypts of Signals Reporting the Tour of the Military Defences of Northern France by the Japanese Naval Attaché in Berlin, 4 and 5 May 1944," 787–92.

59. NSA, RG 457, "History of Military Intelligence Service Reports Units," SRH-062, p. 90.

60. See the insightful work of Stephen E. Ambrose, "Eisenhower and the Intelligence Community in World War II," *Journal of Contemporary History* 16 (1981): 153–66, in which ULTRA and signal intelligence generally are discussed, but not MAGIC or Ōshima specifically.

Chapter 6. The MAGIC of OVERLORD and the Surprise of the Ardennes

1. Forrest C. Pogue, *George C. Marshall*, 4 vols. (New York: Viking, 1963–1987), 3:323–24, 374–75; and D. Clayton James, *The Years of MacArthur*, 3 vols. (Boston: Houghton Mifflin, 1970–1985), 2:369–70. Marshall and MacArthur conferred on Goodenough Island and at Port Moresby on 15 and 16 December.

2. Dwight D. Eisenhower, *Crusade in Europe* (Garden City, N.Y.: Doubleday, 1948), p. 216. See also Alfred D. Chandler, Jr., ed., *The Papers of Dwight David Eisenhower: The War Years*, 5 vols. (Baltimore: Johns Hopkins Press, 1970), 3:1632n., 1639–40.

3. Chandler, ed., *Eisenhower Papers*, 3:1639.

4. Stephen E. Ambrose, *Ike's Spies: Eisenhower and the Espionage Establishment* (Garden City, N.Y.: Doubleday, 1981), pp. 3–13.

5. Stephen E. Ambrose (*Eisenhower*, vol. 1 [New York: Simon and Schuster, 1983], pp. 275–76) suggests that Marshall's primary motive for having Eisenhower return to the United States was to give him a rest before taking up his new assignment in England. The U.S. Army official history adds another reason for the trip to Washington: "to discuss with the Joint Chiefs of Staff the allocations of men and matériel for OVERLORD (see Forrest C. Pogue, *The Supreme Command* [Washington, D.C.: Office of the Chief of Military History, 1954], p. 33). Similar explanations are cited in Pogue, *Marshall*, 3:326–27. It is also logical that Churchill and Eisenhower discussed many topics associated with OVERLORD that did not concern Ōshima's reports, for example, control of the bomber command (see David Eisenhower, *Eisenhower at War, 1943–1945* [New York: Random House, 1986], pp. 54–55, 126, 152).

6. Before leaving Washington for London on 13 January, Eisenhower conferred with the president on 3 January, visited his son at West Point the next day, returned to Washington on 5 January to confer with Marshall in the Pentagon and the presi-

dent at the White House, went to White Sulphur Springs, West Virginia, with Mrs. Eisenhower on 6 January, flew to Kansas to visit his mother two days later, returned to White Sulphur Springs on 9 January, went back to Washington on the evening of 11 January, and conferred again with Roosevelt at the White House and with War Department officials in the Pentagon on 12 January. After another day of Pentagon conferences, Eisenhower started the grueling flight to the United Kingdom via Bermuda and the Azores (see Chandler, ed., *Eisenhower Papers*, 3:1651–52n. and 5:140–41).

7. Military Intelligence 14 was the subsection responsible for information on Germany and German-occupied Europe.

8. F. H. Hinsley et al., *British Intelligence in the Second World War*, 5 vols. (London: Her Majesty's Stationery Office, 1979–1990), 3, pt. 2:773.

9. Ibid., 775.

10. See, for example, Eisenhower, *Crusade in Europe*, pp. 229, 244.

11. U.S. Army, Historical Division, *Omaha Beachhead, 6 June–13 June 1944* (Washington, D.C.: Government Printing Office, 1945; facsimile reprint 1984, Center of Military History, CMH Pub 100–11), pp. 23–25.

12. War Cabinet, Operation "OVERLORD," 30 July 1943, B-7. The feint against Pas de Calais was planned and carried out as Operation FORTITUDE; the diversion against the southern coast of France was planned as an actual operation under the code name ANVIL.

13. There is a growing literature on various deception operations. See, for example, Charles Cruickshank, *Deception in World War II* (Oxford: Oxford University Press, 1979); Jock Haswell, *D-Day: Intelligence and Deception* (New York: Time Books, 1979); Juan Pujol, *Operation GARBO* (New York: Random House, 1985); and William B. Breuer, *The Secret War with Germany* (Novato, Calif.: Presidio Press, 1988).

14. NSA, RG 457, SRDJ No. 46835, 8 December 1943.

15. Gordon A. Craig, "The German Foreign Office from Neurath to Ribbentrop," in *The Diplomats, 1919–1939*, ed. Gordon A. Craig and Felix Gilbert (Princeton: Princeton University Press, 1953), p. 420.

16. NSA, RG 457, SRDJ No. 49914, 24 January 1944.

17. Ibid., SRDJ No. 49891, 24 January 1944.

18. Ibid., SRDJ No. 56691, 24 April 1944.

19. Ibid., SRDJ No. 57453, 27 April 1944.

20. Ibid., SRDJ No. 57896, 6 May 1944.

21. Ibid., SRDJ No. 59003, 19 May 1944.

22. Ibid., SRDJ No. 59059, 20 May 1944.

23. See Stephen E. Ambrose, "Eisenhower and the Intelligence Community in World War II," *Journal of Contemporary History* 16 (1981): 154–55; Pogue, *The Supreme Command*, pp. 20, 71; and David Eisenhower, *Eisenhower at War, 1943–1945*, pp. 127, 157–58.

24. War Cabinet, Operation "OVERLORD," 30 July 1943, p. B-59.

25. NSA, RG 457, SRDJ No. 59897, 28 May 1944.

26. Ibid., SRDJ No. 60072, 29 May 1944.

27. Ibid., SRDJ Nos. 59973–74, 28 May 1944.

28. Carl von Clausewitz, *On War*, ed. and trans. Michael Howard and Peter Paret

(Princeton: Princeton University Press, 1976), p. 117. Of course, the U.S. Army report in 1945 used an earlier edition of Clausewitz.

29. GCMRL, Francis Pickens Miller Collection, Box 6, Folder 24: G-2—Information on German Intelligence.

30. Clausewitz, *On War*, p. 118. See also NSA, RG 457, "History of Military Intelligence Service Reports Unit," SRH-062, pp. 90–91, and idem, "The Achievements of the Signal Security Agency in World War II," SRH-349, pp. 20–21.

31. NSA, RG 457, "American Signal Intelligence in Northwest Africa and Western Europe," SRH-391, p. 113. This NSA publication was declassified on 24 March 1988.

32. Ibid., pp. 88–107, 113–33.

33. Ibid., "Problems of the SSO System in World War II," SRH-107, pp. 1–5.

34. Ibid., p. 192.

35. Ibid., SRDJ No. 60973, 7 June 1944.

36. Ibid., SRDJ No. 61183, 8 June 1944.

37. Ibid., SRDJ No. 61272, 9 June 1944.

38. Ibid., SRDJ No. 61321, 11 June 1944.

39. Ibid., SRDJ No. 61788, 15 June 1944.

40. Gordon A. Harrison, *Cross-Channel Attack* (Washington, D.C.: Office of the Chief of Military History, 1951), pp. 386–449.

41. NSA, RG 457, SRDJ Nos. 64107–8, 6 July 1944.

42. See, for example, Cruickshank, *Deception*, pp. 170–89; Pujol, GARBO, pp. 153–77; Ladislas Farago, *Patton: Ordeal and Triumph* (New York: Ivan Obolensky, 1964), pp. 397–438; and Haswell, *D-Day*, pp. 121–33. Patton was given command of the Third Army, then on the Continent, on 28 July.

43. NSA, RG 457, SRDJ No. 65742, 25 July 1944.

44. Ibid., SRH-391, p. 191.

45. Martin Blumenson, *Breakout and Pursuit* (Washington, D.C.: Center of Military History, 1961; reprint, 1984), p. 211.

46. NSA, RG 457, SRDJ No. 65116, 20 July 1944. This message was intercepted, received, translated, and made available to authorities in Washington on the same day, 21 July 1944.

47. Ibid., SRDJ No. 65115, 20 July 1944. Like Ōshima's wire cited immediately above, which was one number later in the SRDJ numbering sequence, this message was also intercepted, received, translated, and made available to authorities in Washington on 21 July 1944.

48. Ibid., SRDJ No. 65771, 22 July 1944.

49. Ibid., SRDJ No. 67741, 24 July 1944.

50. Ibid., SRDJ Nos. 65222–23, 21 July, 1944.

51. Ibid., SRDJ No. 65345, 21 July 1944.

52. Ibid., SRDJ Nos. 65638–39, 25 July 1944.

53. Ibid., MAGIC Diplomatic Summary, SRS-1376, 29 July 1944. Effective 1 July 1944, the title "MAGIC Summary" was changed to "MAGIC Diplomatic Summary," but the numbering of the issues continued in the same series. The attempt on Hitler's life made an enormous impression on Ōshima, who continued to report to Tokyo about the matter in no fewer than eight messages during the remainder of 1944 (see NSA, RG 457, SRDJ Nos. 66941–46, 2 August; SRDJ Nos. 67157–58, 9 August;

SRDJ No. 67624, 11 August; SRDJ Nos. 68479–81, 19 August; SRDJ Nos. 70137–38, 5 September; SRDJ Nos. 72704–5, 26 September; SRDJ Nos. 74438–39, 12 October; and SRDJ Nos. 84506–7, 29 December).

54. Blumenson, *Breakout*, p. 655.

55. NSA, RG 457, SRDJ Nos. 68581–82, 18 August 1944.

56. Ibid., SRDJ Nos. 67849–52, 16 August 1944. The British official history claims that the message of 24 August was "the first of a series of telegrams from the Japanese embassy in Berlin . . . [which] brought to a head Allied speculation about Germany's intentions" (see Hinsley et al., *British Intelligence*, 3, pt. 2:402).

57. NSA, RG 457, SRDJ Nos. 68585–86, 21 August 1944.

58. Hinsley et al., *British Intelligence*, 3, pt. 2:402.

59. See NSA, RG 457, SRDJ Nos. 65955–61, 26 July 1944, and SRDJ No. 67159, 9 August 1944.

60. Ibid., SRDJ Nos. 67376–80, 10 August 1944; SRDJ Nos. 67653–59, 11 August 1944; and SRDJ Nos. 67598–601, 67604–6, 67629–33, 67635–37, 67651–52; and SRDJ No. 67480, 12 August 1944.

61. Ibid., SRDJ No. 68590, 21 August 1944, and SRDJ No. 69210, 29 August 1944.

62. Ibid., SRDJ No. 69900, 5 September 1944.

63. Ibid., SRDJ No. 70139, 5 September 1944. I cite here the revised message, intercepted 6 September, received 7 September, and translated 8 September. The original, which does not differ significantly from the revised message, was intercepted and received on 6 September and translated 7 September. However, the British version claims that Ōshima sent the report on 4 (not 5) September (possibly very late in the evening), but that it was not deciphered until 10 September.

64. Ibid., SRDJ No. 70133, 5 September 1944.

65. Hugh M. Cole, *The Lorraine Campaign* (Washington, D.C.: Historical Division, United States Army, 1950; reprint, 1981), p. 303.

66. Ibid., pp. 168–606, and Cole, *The Ardennes: Battle of the Bulge* (Washington, D.C.: Office of the Chief of Military History, 1965; reprint, 1983), p. 61.

67. Hasso von Manteuffel, "The Battle of the Ardennes 1944–5," in *Decisive Battles of World War II: The German View*, ed. H. A. Jacobsen and J. Rohwer, trans. Edward Fitzgerald (New York: G. P. Putnam's Sons, 1965), p. 391.

68. Ibid., pp. 398–99.

69. Cole, *The Ardennes*, pp. 56–63. Of course, this volume was originally published before ULTRA and MAGIC materials were declassified and released to researchers; no revisions are included in the reprint of 1983.

70. William Casey, *The Secret War against Hitler* (Washington, D.C.: Regnery Gateway, 1988), p. 182.

71. Harold C. Deutsch, "The Influence of ULTRA on World War II," *Parameters* 8:4 (December 1978): 3, and John M. Taylor, *General Maxwell Taylor: The Sword and the Pen* (New York: Doubleday, 1989), p. 120. Cf. Hinsley et al., *British Intelligence*, 3, pt. 2:437–38; Anthony Cave Brown, *"C": The Secret Life of Sir Stewart Graham Menzies, Spymaster to Winston Churchill* (New York: Macmillan, 1987), pp. 644–45, 784–87; Thomas Parrish, *The Ultra Americans: The U.S. Role in Breaking the Nazi Codes* (New York: Stein and Day, 1986), pp. 267–68; and John Patrick

Finnegan, *Military Intelligence* (Arlington, Va.: U.S. Army Intelligence and Security Command, 1984), p. 81.

72. See Hensley et al., *British Intelligence*, 3, pt. 2:402–38. See also Adolph G. Rosengarten, Jr., "With Ultra from Omaha Beach to Weimar, Germany—A Personal View," *Military Affairs* 42:3 (October 1978): 127–32.

73. Hensley et al., *British Intelligence*, 3, pt. 2:418.

74. Ibid., 401–50.

75. Ibid., 414.

76. Ibid., 430.

77. NSA, RG 457, SRDJ No. 83630, 19 December 1944.

78. Ibid., SRDJ Nos. 83702–5, 83734–35, 23 December 1944.

79. Cole, *The Ardennes*, pp. 672–73.

80. NSA, RG 457, SRDJ Nos. 86203–4, 11 January 1945.

81. See, for example, ibid., SRDJ Nos. 88903–4, 13 January 1945; SRDJ Nos. 86545–46, 15 January 1945; SRDJ Nos. 86922–24, 17 January 1945; SRDJ Nos. 87359–61, 87385–86, 19 January 1945; SRDJ Nos. 87700–702, 23 January 1945; SRDJ Nos. 87960–64, 24 January 1945; and SRDJ Nos. 88880–82, 31 January 1945.

Chapter 7. MAGIC and the Question of a German-Soviet Separate Peace

1. The topic of a possible German-Soviet rapprochement has demanded considerable attention in literature on World War II, but in most accounts speculation abounds because of the lack of solid documentation. Nevertheless, it seems likely that some sort of discussions, if only cursory, did occur. Debate was rekindled by one paragraph in Liddell Hart's *History of the Second World War* published posthumously in 1970. Liddell Hart, who had interviewed numerous German officers after the war, claimed that the German and Soviet foreign ministers met behind German lines at Kirovograd in June 1943 to discuss the possibilities of ending the war. The talks were broken off when a report on them was leaked to the western Allies, however, Liddell Hart offered no specific evidence for his account. Following Liddell Hart came Vojtech Mastny ("Stalin and the Prospects of a Separate Peace in World War II," *American Historical Review* 77:5 [December 1972]: 1365–88) who cited no MAGIC material whatsoever because COMINT material was still highly classified at that time. Recently, an essay based largely on a wide variety of Japanese and German published materials has appeared on the topic: Gerhard Krebs, "Japanische Vermittlungsversuche im Deutsch-Sovjetischen Krieg, 1941–1945" in *Deutschland-Japan in der Zwischenkriegszeit*, ed. Josef Kreiner and Regine Mathias (Bonn: Bouvier Verlag, 1990), pp. 239–88. The MAGIC material used in the Krebs essay, however, is restricted to thirteen reels of microfilm of the summaries and to a Pearl Harbor background publication—no original MAGIC messages are cited.

The MAGIC summaries used by Krebs tell only part of the story. They were compiled daily from the massive PURPLE traffic and represent about 2–5 percent of the total volume of original messages. Moreover, many parts of the messages were not immediately available, sometimes taking several weeks or months to be completely deciphered and translated. Thus, not only were the summaries greatly condensed, but they frequently remained incomplete. Nor are the MAGIC-based Special Research Histories (SRHs) used by Krebs. Therefore, MAGIC intelligence forms a small and incomplete part of the Krebs essay.

2. Maurice Matloff, *Strategic Planning for Coalition Warfare, 1943–1944* (Washington, D.C.: Office of the Chief of Military History, 1959), pp. 285–87.

3. There has been very little written about Ōshima's war years in Berlin. In Suzuki Kenji, *Chūdoku Taishi Ōshima Hiroshi* (Tokyo: Fuyō Shobō, 1979), a 290-page biography, there is no mention of MAGIC, and the book covers Ōshima's tour in Berlin in only 18 pages—15 pages for the years 1941–1942, and 3 pages for 1943–1945.

4. NSA, RG 457, SRDJ No. 016845, 21 November 1941.

5. Ibid., "Japan as Mediator in the Russo-German Conflict," (Short Title: PSIS 400–1), Publication of Pacific Strategic Intelligence Section, Commander-in-Chief, United States Fleet, and Chief of Naval Operations (Op-20-3-G50), 29 December 1944, SRH-067, p. 1.

6. Ibid., SRDJ No. 020696, 17 March 1942.

7. Ibid., SRDJ Nos. 021456–61, 6 April 1942.

8. Ibid., MAGIC Summary, SRS–565, 8 April 1942.

9. See, for example, ibid., SRDJ No. 034354, 13 October 1942; SRDJ Nos. 028743–44, 14 November 1942; SRDJ Nos. 028760–61, 28 November 1942; and SRDJ Nos. 028954–56, 12 December 1942.

SRDJ No. 034354 of 13 October 1942 is a message from Japanese officials in Berlin to their government in Tokyo. The date it was intercepted is unknown, but its receipt by U.S. cryptographers is recorded as 16 October 1942. However, this message was not deciphered and translated until 18 April 1943, and the contents are not without significance. Tokyo was told that Germany was completely "uninterested in peace," would push ahead harder than ever, and that Tokyo must not be led astray by rumors in the coming months that Germany would be interested in a rapprochement with the Soviet Union. This precise information did not make its way into the MAGIC Summary, even in April 1943, yet such intelligence needs to be cited for the best possible reconstruction of the historical record.

10. Ibid., SRDJ No. 027500, 26 October 1942.

11. *Stalin's Correspondence with Churchill and Attlee, 1941–1945* (New York: Capricorn Books, 1965), pp. 383–84.

12. NSA, RG 457, MAGIC Summary, SRS–809, 17 December 1942.

13. Ibid., SRDJ Nos. 029010–11, 28 November 1942. Maikop was occupied by the Germans from August 1942 to February 1943, but they never reached Grozny or Tuapse. An explanation of some of the beginning and ending physical characteristics of a typical translated message produced by Arlington Hall Station is included in a letter from Henry F. Graff to the author, 28 September 1988:

> The number 903 is the serial number of message from Tokyo to Berlin. The next message would be 904. Sometimes the files of SIS/SSA translators were more accurate than the Japanese diplomats'. SIS would get a message saying something like "We have not yet received your 903," while Arlington Hall Station had received it, translated it, and put it to use.
>
> The number (92) in parentheses after the date probably indicates the

place of interception. Although many intercepts came from Vint Hill, Virginia, some forty miles away, other intercepts were flown to Washington.

Occasionally SIS/SSA would specifically request speed on an intercept in order to complete an important message that was transmitted in parts, or even request that the intercept stations keep watch for something Arlington Hall wanted.

Each translator had a number or letter identification ["A"], and each translation was checked by a colleague who had a letter identification, lower case "e." Not all intercepts were translated, but everything was examined upon arrival at Arlington Hall; if it was decided not to translate such a message, it was nevertheless filed away carefully. In the diplomatic section at the height of the war there were about 35 translators.

14. Ibid., SRDJ No. 029307, 18 December 1942.

15. Harold E. Zaugg, "The Ultra-American" (Unpublished paper, Lake Forest, Ill.: 1991), p. 145.

16. Toshikazu Kase, *Journey to the* Missouri (New Haven: Yale University Press, 1950), pp. 162–64.

17. Cordell Hull, *The Memoirs of Cordell Hull*, 2 vols. (New York: Macmillan, 1948), 2: 1263–64, 1310, 1462–63.

18. See Bradley F. Smith, "Sharing Ultra in World War II," *International Journal of Intelligence and Counterintelligence* 2:1 (Spring 1988): 59–72.

19. Tōgō Shigenori, *The Case of Japan*, trans. and ed. Tōgō Fumihiko and Ben Bruce Blakeney (New York: Simon and Schuster, 1956), p. 241.

20. NSA, RG 457, SRH-252, p. 169.

21. Ibid., 174.

22. U.S. Department of State, *Foreign Relations of the United States, Diplomatic Papers, 1942*, 7 vols. (Washington, D.C.: Government Printing Office, 1960–1963), 3:415.

23. Valentin Berezhkov, *History in the Making: Memoirs of World War II Diplomacy*, trans. Dudley Hagen and Barry Jones (Moscow: Progress, 1983), p. 166. Negotiations continued in London after Eden returned from Moscow, and finally the Soviet-British Treaty of Alliance was concluded on 26 May 1942.

Originally the Soviets sought Anglo-American agreement to their occupation of eastern Poland as well as their claims on Rumania, but in the eleventh hour Eden proposed to substitute a general and public treaty of alliance for twenty years, omitting all reference to frontiers. The day after the treaty was signed in London, Churchill wrote to Roosevelt: "We have done very good work this and last week with Molotov, and . . . we have completely transformed the treaty proposals. They are now, in my judgment, free from the objections we both entertained, and are entirely compatible with our Atlantic Charter" (Winston S. Churchill, *The Second World War*, 6 vols. [Boston: Houghton Mifflin, 1948–1953], 4:339).

24. Churchill, *The Second World War*, 4:330; see also *Stalin's Correspondence with Churchill and Attlee, 1941–1945* (New York: Capicorn Books, 1965), p. 42.

25. Arthur Bryant, *The Turn of the Tide: A History of the War Years Based on*

the Diaries of Field-Marshal Lord Alanbrooke, Chief of the Imperial General Staff (Garden City, N.Y.: Doubleday, 1957), p. 433.

26. Mamoru Shigemitsu, *Japan and Her Destiny: My Struggle for Peace*, ed. F. S. G. Piggott, trans. Oswald White (New York: E. P. Dutton, 1958), pp. 295–97.

27. Hull, *Memoirs*, 2:1309.

28. NSA, RG 457, SRH-252, pp. 175–76. Curiously, in April 1941 Ōshima feared that Matsuoka did not grasp the magnitude of events about to unfold. Thus, on the night of 6 April, under the pretext of the spirit of the Nazi grand send-off for Matsuoka, Ōshima suddenly decided to accompany his foreign minister as far as the Soviet-German border. In fact, Ōshima sought an opportunity in private to persuade Matsuoka against concluding a Soviet-Japanese neutrality treaty during the scheduled stop in Moscow. However, as Ōshima's Japanese biographer has written: "Matsuoka simply said, 'okay, okay,' and did not deal with Ōshima seriously. When Ōshima got off the train at the border, he grumbled, 'Matsuoka did not understand what Hitler was saying'" (Suzuki, *Chūdoku Taishi Ōshima Hiroshi*, p. 228). Matsuoka, who died 27 June 1946, and Ōshima were both pro-German, although they disagreed on the issue of the Soviet-Japanese Neutrality Pact. In Ōshima's words: "Mr. Matsuoka and I argued a lot. Although there was not much difference in our ideas, I opposed him in April 1941" (Ōshima interviews, 1959 and 1962).

29. NSA, RG 457, SRH-252, p. 176.

30. Ibid., 177.

31. Ibid., SRDJ No. 030140, 12 January 1943.

32. Ibid., SRDJ No. 030560, 26 January 1943.

33. Ibid., SRDJ No. 041095, 27 July 1943; see also SRDJ Nos. 041107–8, 27 July 1943.

34. See, for example, ibid., SRDJ Nos. 046172, 043368, 042815–18, 043038–39, 042854, 042858, 9 September 1943; SRDJ Nos. 042920–22, 10 September 1943; SRDJ Nos. 042935–36, 11 September 1943; SRDJ Nos. 043374–76, 13 September 1943; SRDJ No. 043166, 14 September 1943; SRDJ Nos. 043482–84, 17 September 1943; SRDJ Nos. 043441–43, 24 September 1943; SRDJ Nos. 043455–56, 25 September 1943; SRDJ No. 043597, 28 September 1943; and SRDJ Nos. 043657–58, 28 September 1943.

35. Ibid., SRDJ Nos. 043486–91, 25 September 1943.

36. Ibid., SRDJ Nos. 043854, 043867, 1 October 1943.

37. Ibid., SRDJ Nos. 043820–23, 2 October 1943.

38. Ibid., SRDJ No. 043858, 4 October 1943.

39. Ibid., SRDJ Nos. 043772–73, 4 October 1943.

40. Ibid., SRDJ No. 043969, 4 October 1943.

41. Ibid., SRDJ No. 043986, 4 October 1943. This is an example of how a researcher could be led astray if, for purposes of MAGIC intelligence documentation, only the MAGIC summaries were relied upon. In MAGIC Summary SRS-1110, 7 October 1943, the MIS compiler asserts that the Ōshima-Ribbentrop "conversation [at Hitler's headquarters] is chiefly remarkable for Ribbentrop's confession that the question of peace with Russia was 'a serious one,' and that he was 'going to think about it.'" The next MAGIC Summary that refers to the meetings on the eastern front (SRS-1112, 9 October 1943), probably written by a different compiler, notes that "further reports on Ōshima's trip are now available, and it appears that he also

talked at considerable length with Hitler himself." However, no corrective to the interpretation in the earlier MAGIC Summary is suggested, although in the broader context Ribbentrop's so-called confession does not appear so remarkable after all.

42. Soviet agreement to the unconditional surrender policy had been Secretary Hull's chief agenda item on the eve of the Moscow conference (see, for example, W. Averell Harriman and Elie Abel, *Special Envoy to Churchill and Stalin, 1941–1945* [New York: Random House, 1975], pp. 236–37.

43. NSA, RG 457, SRDJ Nos. 044341–42, 13 October 1943; see also SRDJ Nos. 044335–40, 13 October 1943.

44. Ibid., SRDJ No. 046831, 30 November 1943. Compilers of the MAGIC Summary containing Ribbentrop's statement about not seeking a separate peace with the Soviets (SRS-1147, 13 December 1943) observed in a footnote that "When Ribbentrop last talked to Ōshima—approximately four weeks before publication of the decisions reached at the Moscow Conference [i.e., demanding German unconditional surrender and no separate armistice]—the ambassador asked whether it would not be possible for Germany to make a political settlement with Russia." Ribbentrop replied as indicated in note 41. Thus, the MAGIC summaries continued to perpetuate views that there was still hope that a rapprochement could be reached when a study of all of the daily messages would have dispelled the notion.

45. Ibid., SRDJ Nos. 047070–76, 12 December 1943.

46. Ibid., SRDJ Nos. 046203–4, 23 November 1943.

47. Ibid., SRDJ No. 090337, 26 November 1943. Although this message was intercepted and then received by U.S. cryptographers on 27 November 1943, it was not deciphered and translated until 14 February 1945.

48. Ibid., SRDJ No. 044472BZ, 18 October 1943; SRDJ No. 044721, 23 October 1943; SRDJ No. 044872, 25 October 1943; SRDJ No. 046609, 28 November 1943; SRDJ Nos. 047845–47, 26 December 1943; and SRDJ Nos. 048178–81, 28 December 1943. This Pomeranian house was famous for its immense fortune and beautiful estates. The palace and grounds at Boitzenburg are still beautiful today.

49. Churchill, *The Second World War*, 5:521–22. See, for example, NSA, RG 457, SRDJ No. 046578, 3 December 1943; SRDJ No. 047218, 14 December 1943; SRDJ No. 047272, 18 December 1943; SRDJ No. 048481, 3 January 1944; SRDJ Nos. 049515–18, 18 January 1944; SRDJ No. 049412, 21 January 1944; SRDJ No. 049817, 26 January 1944; SRDJ No. 049574, 28 January 1944; SRDJ Nos. 049672–73, 29 January 1944; SRDJ No. 051274, 12 February 1944; SRDJ No. 051992, 27 February 1944; and SRDJ No. 058757, 18 March 1944.

50. See, for example, Marshall's memorandum to his G-2 of 28 April 1943 in GCMRL, George C. Marshall Papers, Box 65, Folder 53: Directives—G-2, 1943–1945.

51. Edwin O. Reischauer, *My Life between Japan and America* (New York: Harper and Row, 1986), p. 92.

52. NSA, RG 457, SRDJ No. 046756, 4 December 1943.

53. Ibid., SRDJ Nos. 049888 and 049916, 24 January 1944, and SRDJ No. 049705, 30 January 1944.

54. Ibid., SRDJ 060704, 3 June 1944.

55. See, for example, ibid., SRDJ No. 065222, 21 July 1944; SRDJ Nos. 065223–

25, 21 July 1944; SRDJ No. 065345, 21 July 1944; SRDJ Nos. 066941–46, 2 August 1944; and SRDJ No. 067624, 11 August 1944.

56. Ibid., SRDH Nos. 065636–37, 25 July 1944.

57. Ibid., SRDJ No. 068215, 25 July 1944.

58. Ibid., SRDJ No. 068480, 19 August 1944. See also ibid., SRDJ No. 074438, 12 October 1944.

59. Ibid., SRDJ No. 068635, 24 August 1944.

60. Ibid., SRDJ No. 069900, 5 September 1944.

61. Ibid., SRDJ No. 070107, 5 September 1944. The following passages quoted from Ōshima's full message can be found in ibid., SRDJ Nos. 070101–13, 5–6 September 1944.

62. Ibid., SRDJ Nos. 071621–23, 18 September 1944. It should also be noted that the Kremlin was not eager to accept a special envoy from Tokyo. See ibid., SRH-067, p. 8.

63. Ibid., SRDJ No. 080494, 28 November 1944.

64. *Stalin's Correspondence with Roosevelt and Truman, 1941–1945* (New York: Capricorn Books, 1965), p. 168.

65. NSA, RG 457, SRH-067, p. 15.

66. See, for example, ibid., SRDJ No. 085807, 7 January 1945; SRDJ No. 085746, 8 January 1945; SRDJ No. 087703, 20 January 1945; SRDJ No. 088882, 31 January 1945; SRDJ No. 096104, 31 March 1945; and SRDJ Nos. 098241–42, 18 April 1945.

67. Ibid., SRH-067, p. 19.

68. See Herbert Feis, *Japan Subdued: The Atomic Bomb and the End of the War in the Pacific* (Princeton: Princeton University Press, 1961), p. 114. See also V. Larionov et al., *World War II: Decisive Battles of the Soviet Army*, trans. William Biley (Moscow: Progress, 1984), pp. 468–69.

Chapter 8. *MAGIC and the End of the Third Reich*

1. See, for example, Andrew Tully, *Berlin: Story of a Battle* (New York: Simon and Schuster, 1963); Cornelius Ryan, *The Last Battle* (New York: Simon and Schuster, 1966); Earl F. Ziemke, *Battle for Berlin: End of the Third Reich* (New York: Ballantine, 1969); James Lucas, *Last Days of the Third Reich: The Collapse of Nazi Germany, May 1945* (New York: William Morrow, 1986); and Tony Le Tissier, *The Battle of Berlin, 1945* (New York: St. Martin's Press, 1988).

2. For the personal impressions of two diarists see Hans-Georg von Studnitz, *While Berlin Burns: The Diary of Hans-Georg von Studnitz, 1943–1945*, trans. R. H. Stevens (London: Weidenfeld and Nicolson, 1964), and Marie Vassiltchikov, *Berlin Diaries, 1940–1945* (New York: Alfred A. Knopf, 1987). For a scholarly and insightful introduction to the circumstances of political prisons in Berlin near the end of the war, see Peter Paret, "An Aftermath of the Plot against Hitler: the Lehrterstrasse Prison in Berlin, 1944–45," *Bulletin of the Institute of Historical Research* 32:85 (May 1959): 88–102.

3. Between 7 January and 13 April 1945, Ōshima met privately with Ribbentrop

eleven times, sometimes for nearly four hours a session, and he spoke to other high-ranking German military officers and ministers by telephone.

4. The principal source of Ōshima's intercepted five-part message of 8 March 1945 is SRDJ Nos. 92776–81, declassified on 1 June 1980, not the less comprehensive MAGIC Diplomatic Summary, SRS-1607, 15 March 1945, declassified on 1 November 1978. The following extracts closely adhere to the original intercept.

5. NSA, RG 457, SRDJ No. 114447, 22 February 1945.

6. U.K., Foreign Office, *German Zone Handbook No. 1A—Berlin, Part III: Local Directory* (London: His Majesty's Stationery Office, 1945), pp. 29–30.

7. Albert Speer, *Inside the Third Reich*, trans. Richard and Clara Winston (New York: Macmillan, 1970), pp. 548–49.

8. NSA, RG 457, SRDJ Nos. 89328–31, 4 February 1945; see also ibid., SRDJ No. 88436, 27 January 1945 for a similar forecast.

9. Ibid., SRDJ No. 90106, 10 February 1945.

10. Ibid., SRDJ Nos. 89739–40, 5 February 1945, and SRDJ No. 90105, 10 February 1945. See also Susanne Everett, *Lost Berlin* (New York: Gallery, 1979), pp. 8, 11, 15, and 18–19.

11. von Studnitz, *While Berlin Burns* (diary entry 5 February 1945), p. 241.

12. NSA, RG 457, SRDJ No. 114513, 27 February 1945 and SRDJ No. 94099, 19 March 1945.

13. Ibid., SRDJ Nos. 97295–96, 11 April 1945.

14. Ibid., SRDJ No. 91352, 19 February 1945; MAGIC, SRS 1594, 2 March 1945.

15. Ibid., SRDJ No. 91988, 3 March 1945.

16. Desmond Hawkins and Donald Boyd, eds., *War Report: A Record of Dispatches Broadcast by the BBC's War Correspondents with the Allied Expeditionary Force, 5 June 1944–5 May 1945* (London: Oxford University Press, 1946), p. 413.

17. NSA, RG 457, SRDJ No. 90501, 13 February 1945.

18. Ibid., SRDJ No. 97296, 11 April 1945.

19. An American intelligence report of 22 January 1945 concluded that after the failure of the Ardennes offensive, "the Japanese, as a whole, believed that the Germans would hold out at least until the spring or summer of 1945" (see ibid., "Japanese Estimates of Germany's Ability to Continue the Struggle," SRH-068, p. 23).

20. Ibid., MAGIC Diplomatic Summary, SRS 1562, 29 January 1945. See Edward J. Drea, "Missing Intentions: Japanese Intelligence and the Soviet Invasion of Manchuria, 1945," *Military Affairs* 48:2 (April 1984): 66–73, for a good discussion about how the Japanese expected an eventual Russian invasion of Manchukuo, yet were still caught by surprise when the attack came on 9 August 1945.

21. NSA, RG 457, "The Problem of the Prolongation of the Soviet-Japanese Neutrality Pact," SRH-069, p. 34.

22. Ibid., SRDJ No. 89173, 1 February 1945, and SRDJ No. 89539, 6 February 1945; MAGIC, SRS 1570, 6 February 1945; SRDJ No. 91685, 21 February 1945; and SRDJ No. 92547, 5 March 1945.

23. Joseph Goebbels, *Final Entries, 1945: The Diaries of Joseph Goebbels* (29 March 1945), trans. Richard Barry (New York: G. P. Putnam's Sons, 1978), p. 267.

24. NSA, RG 457, SRDJ No. 97542, 13 April 1945; SRDJ No. 95372, 27 March 1945; and SRDJ No. 89542, 6 February 1945.

25. Ibid., SRDJ No. 97633, 14 April 1945.

26. Ibid., MAGIC, SRS 1639, 16 April 1945.

27. Lt. Gen. William W. Quinn, U.S. Army (ret.), interview with author, Washington, D.C., 31 May 1988. See also Charles B. MacDonald, *The Last Offensive* (Washington, D.C.: Center of Military History, 1973; reprint, 1984), chapter 18; "The Battle of the National Redoubt," Reuben E. Jenkins Papers, Archives, U.S. Army Military History Institute, Carlisle Barracks, Pa.; Seventh U.S. Army, *The Seventh United States Army in France and Germany, 1944-1945* (Heidelberg, Ger.: Aloys Gräf, 1946), 3:chaps. 29, 30, and James M. Gavin, *On to Berlin* (1978; reprint, Toronto: Bantam, 1985), pp. 282-83.

28. Frank B. Rowlett to author, 1 July 1987.

29. See, for example, V. Larionov et al., *World War II: Decisive Battles of the Soviet Army*, trans. William Biley (Moscow: Progress, 1984), pp. 422-48; V. I. Chuikov, *The End of the Third Reich* (Moscow: Progress, 1978), pp. 211-40; Gerhard Boldt, *Hitler: The Last Ten Days*, trans. Sandra Bance (New York: Coward, McCann and Geoghegan, 1973), pp. 167-72; G. Deborin, *Secrets of the Second World War*, trans. Vic Schneierson (Moscow: Progress, 1971), pp. 219-29; and Erich Kuby, *The Russians and Berlin, 1945*, trans. Arnold J. Pomerans (New York: Hill and Wang, 1968), pp. 96-161.

30. NSA, RG 457, MAGIC, SRS 1646, 23 April 1945.

31. Hawkins and Boyd, eds., *War Report*, pp. 412-13.

32. NSA, RG 457, SRH-075, p. 12. More often COMINT knew with remarkable accuracy what happened to Japanese nationals in the aftermath of the collapse of Germany. COMINT followed thirteen Japanese nationals led by Vice Admiral Abe when they left Berlin on 20 April; they reached Hamburg, then Flensburg by 24 April, then Copenhagen, and eventually escaped to Sweden by 5 May. In another instance, COMINT knew that by 21 June some 270 Japanese nationals were being repatriated through the good offices of the Soviet Union (ibid., "Russo-Japanese Relations [21-27 July 1945]," SRH-086, p. 16).

33. Frank B. Rowlett to author, 14 February 1989.

34. Thomas Parrish, *The Ultra Americans: The U.S. Role in Breaking the Nazi Codes* (New York: Stein and Day, 1986), pp. 271-84. See also Paul Whitaker and Louis Kruh, "From Bletchley Park to Berchtesgaden," *Cryptologia* 11:3 (July 1987): 129-41.

35. See Ronald Lewin, *Ultra Goes to War* (New York: McGraw-Hill, 1978), pp. 362-63, and F. H. Hinsley et al., *British Intelligence in the Second World War*, 5 vols. (London: Her Majesty's Stationery Office, 1979-1990), 3, pt. 2:587-92, 920-44.

36. Frank B. Rowlett to author, 14 February 1989.

37. NSA SRDJ Nos. 97502-3, 13 April 1945; SRDJ No. 97592, 14 April 1945; SRDJ No. 98549, 21 April 1945; and SRDJ No. 99678, 30 April 1945. Little seems to have survived from the Japanese embassy after the fall of Berlin. In addition to the component of the PURPLE machine, one surviving document found in 1945 names Lieutenant General Banzai, the Japanese military attaché in Berlin, to the honorary rank of Generalkapitän (see photograph on p. 64). The document was signed by Argentinean, Danish, German, Japanese, Rumanian, Swedish, and Spanish naval officers on 21 April 1942 and proclaimed that the bestowal was because of General Banzai's knowledge of submarine warfare in particular and of naval strategy in general; see GCMRL, Francis Pickins Miller Papers, Oversize Items.

In 1991 the Japanisch-Deutsches Zentrum Berlin (JDZB) had two years remaining in the lease of the restored and expanded former embassy building. In the JDZB building is an elaborate fourteen-foot bar with a striking backdrop and mirrors from the old embassy. In 1990 the Japanese embassy building in Bonn underwent extensive reconstruction, yet the Japanese ambassador's official residence will probably be moved to Berlin later in the decade, most likely to more spacious facilities than those available in the present JDZB quarters.

38. Gerald J. Higgins to author, 17 July 1989. See also John M. Taylor, *General Maxwell Taylor: The Sword and the Pen* (New York: Doubleday, 1989), p. 139.

39. See Carl Boyd, *The Extraordinary Envoy: General Hiroshi Ōshima and Diplomacy in the Third Reich, 1934–1939* (Washington, D.C.: University Press of America, 1982), pp. 142–45.

40. Anthony Cave Brown, *Bodyguard of Lies* (Toronto: Fitzhenry and Whiteside, 1975), p. 329; Brown's emphasis. There is some ambiguity in published sources concerning American usage of the terms "MAGIC" and "ULTRA" when applied to Japanese signal intelligence. Brown (p. 69) is a case in point, and also more recent works: Hinsley et al., *British Intelligence*, 2:75n; Ronald Lewin, *The American Magic: Codes, Ciphers and the Defeat of Japan* (New York: Farrar Straus Giroux, 1982), pp. 18–19; Diane T. Putney, ed., *ULTRA and the Army Air Forces in World War II* (Washington, D.C.: Office of Air Force History, 1987), p. 87; and, finally, Brown's newer work titled *"C": The Secret Life of Sir Stewart Graham Menzies, Spymaster to Winston Churchill* (New York: Macmillan, 1987), p. 632, where he writes without much clarification that by 1944 ULTRA and MAGIC were "closely interrelated." The best and most recent explanation of the term ULTRA is Edward J. Drea, *MacArthur's ULTRA Codebreaking and the War against Japan, 1942—1945* (Lawrence: University Press of Kansas, 1992), p. xi.

Unpublished documentary evidence is more precise. On 20 June 1942, Admiral Ernest J. King, commander in chief, U.S. Fleet, and chief of naval operations, ordered that when information obtained from the reading of a Japanese cryptographic system was distributed to lower commanders, "somewhere near the beginning of the message the word 'ULTRA' or the word 'ZEAL'" should be included, but the secret cryptographic nature of the source must never be stated. This was the "other ULTRA" Lewin referred to; it was a caveat applied for security purposes to Japanese naval and military signal traffic. The term "MAGIC," as explained near the beginning of this volume, was an American cover name for Japanese high-grade signal intelligence. By 1944, to help establish uniformity in the handling of enemy high-grade cryptographic intelligence in all Anglo-American theaters of operations, joint U.S.-British security regulations stipulated that the term "ULTRA" should be applied to Japanese as well as German signal intelligence. MAGIC and Japanese ULTRA, unlike German ULTRA, came from a number of widely separated producing centers, and the U.S. Army continued throughout the war to employ the term "MAGIC" when compiling the Japanese Diplomatic Summaries (see NSA, RG 457, SRH's 026, 034, 148, 355, and SRMN-018).

41. David Kahn, *Kahn on Codes: Secrets of the New Cryptology* (New York: Macmillan, 1983), p. 91. Chief of the research and analysis branch of the Office of Strategic Services in Paris and Germany in 1944–1945 and a member of the U.S. State Department's Special Interrogation Mission in 1945, Harold C. Deutsch is a

scholar among intelligence analysts of World War II. Professor emeritus at the University of Minnesota, later Johnson Professor of Military History at the U.S. Army Military History Institute and professor at the U.S. Army War College, Deutsch's investigations continue to open new opportunities for historians of SIGINT.

42. *Hall Herald* (Arlington Hall Station, Virginia), 21 February 1946, p. 1. I am obliged to Frank B. Rowlett for this information. See also Ronald Clark, *The Man Who Broke Purple: The Life of Colonel William F. Friedman, Who Deciphered the Japanese Code in World War II* (Boston: Little, Brown, 1977), p. 200. The Signal Security Agency was renamed the Army Security Agency on 15 September 1945.

43. Frank B. Rowlett to author, 4 February 1989.

44. Ibid. Bradley, Bernard Montgomery's counterpart in the post–June 1944 assault on Berlin, was the Twelfth Army Group commander.

45. Wallace R. Winkler to author, 4 March 1989.

46. NSA, RG 457, "Abrogation of the Soviet-Japanese Neutrality Pact," SRH-071, p. 17.

47. Ibid., "Japanese Reaction to German Defeat, 21 May 1945," SRH-075, p. 15.

48. Ibid., "Russo-Japanese Relations, 18 June 1945," SRH-078, p. 1.

49. Ibid., p. 4.

50. Ibid.

51. Ibid., p. 12.

52. Ibid., "Russo-Japanese Relations (June 1945)," SRH-079, p. 11.

53. Ibid., "Russo-Japanese Relations (13–20 July 1945)," SRH-085, p. 18.

54. Ibid., "MAGIC Diplomatic Extracts, July 1945," SRH-040, pp. 42, 44–45.

55. Frank B. Rowlett to author, 14 February 1989.

56. NAS, RG 457, "Russo-Japanese Relations (28 July–6 August 1945)," SRH-088, p. 11.

Appendix 1. MAGIC Messages Concerning a Visit of the Japanese Ambassador in Berlin to the German Defenses in France

1. NSA, RG 457, SRDJ No. 44762 (23 October 1943). These edited versions of Ōshima's reports to Tokyo take into consideration certain nuances of the Japanese language and differences between British and American translations of the intercepts.

2. Bernd Gottfriedsen, a German Foreign Ministry confidential secretary and liaison, is sometimes referred to in Ōshima's messages as "our usual contact man." He is the man whom Foreign Minster Ribbentrop designated on 24 June 1941 (two days after the German attack on the Soviet Union) to keep Ōshima supplied with information about the war.

3. NSA, RG 467, SRDJ Nos. 45444-45 (9 November 1943).

4. Ibid., SRDJ Nos. 45465-69, 46763-71 (10 November 1943).

5. Ibid., SRDJ Nos. 46763-71 (10 November 1943).

6. Foreign Minister Ribbentrop told Ambassador Ōshima on 11 December 1942 that the Germans

> have an advance line drawn up on the west coast of Europe from northern Norway to the Franco-Spanish border. We also have 50 divisions aligned over that area watching and waiting. Well, if Britain and America want to attack, let them come. The drama will end in a second Dieppe [where in August 1942 a major Anglo-Canadian amphibious raid, including some thirty tanks, ended in complete failure]. We are ready for them. Also on the south coast of France and on the coasts of Italy and Greece we have lately strengthened our lines there for the time being. We Germans feel safe in assuming that Britain and America are planning a landing expedition in Europe, in order to relieve the pressure on Russia and to lengthen our lines of supply. [NSA, RG 457, SRDJ 028952, 12 December 1942]

A secret British report in early 1944 estimated that 7 million tons of concrete fortifications were built along the French coast in 1943.

Appendix 2. Letter from Eisenhower to Major General Sir Stewart Menzies

1. Dwight D. Eisenhower Papers, Pre-Presidential, 1916–1952, Box 77, Melo-Merr (Misc.), Dwight D. Eisenhower Library, Abilene, Kansas. I am obliged to Michael J. Levin, National Security Agency, for this information. This letter was first published in F. W. Winterbotham, *The ULTRA Secret* (New York: Harper and Row, 1974), p. 2.

Appendix 3. Intelligence Agreement between the United States and Great Britain

1. NSA, RG 457, "American Signal Intelligence in Northwest Africa and Western Europe," SRH-391, pp. 171–75. Declassified 24 March 1988.

Appendix 4. Letter from Marshall to Eisenhower

1. NSA, RG 457, "Marshall Letter to Eisenhower on the Use of ULTRA Intelligence, 15 March 1944," SRH-026, pp. 1–4.
2. This is presumably the same agreement dated 17 May 1943 in Appendix 3.

Bibliography

1. Unpublished Documents

Library Sources

Franklin D. Roosevelt Library, Hyde Park, New York.
 Logs of F.D.R.'s Trips, September 1942–February 1945; Map Room File; President's Secretary's File; Papers of Harry L. Hopkins—Sherwood Collection; Toland Papers.
George C. Marshall Research Library, Lexington, Virginia.
 Hanson W. Baldwin Papers; William F. Friedman Cryptologic Collection; George C. Marshall Papers; Francis Pickens Miller Collection.
International Military Tribunal for the Far East (1946-1948). Proceedings, 113 vols.; Exhibits, 131 vols.; Narrative Summary, 14 vols.; Prosecution Summation, 7 vols.; Defense Summation, 17 vols.; Analyses of Documentary Evidence, 29 vols. University of California Library, Berkeley.
Northwestern University Archives, Evanston, Illinois.
 Wallace A. Bacon Papers.
Yale University Library, New Haven, Connecticut.
 Robert F. Wood Papers—Correspondence: Smith, Truman.

Government Sources

Naval Historical Center, Washington, DC. Reports of the U.S. Naval Technical Mission to Japan, 1945–1946. Microfilm JM-200.
U.S. Army Center of Military History, Washington, DC.
 OVERLORD Plans, July 1943; Heinrich Hoffmann Tagesbildberichte, 1941, 1942.
U.S. Army Military History Institute, Carlisle Barracks, PA.
 Richard Collins Papers; Hugh Drum Papers; Chester B. Hansen Papers; Reuben

E. Jenkins Papers; William W. Quinn Papers; William J. Donovan Collection—Office of Strategic Services (OSS) "Boston Series."

U.S. National Archives. Records of German and Japanese Embassies and Consulates, 1890–1945. National Archives. Microfilm Publication No. T-179.

U.S. National Archives and Records Administration, Washington, DC.

Record Group 165, War Department, General and Special Staff. Assistant Chief of Staff, G-2, Intelligence Division, Captured Personnel and Material Branch, Enemy POW Interrogation File (MIS-Y) 1943–45.

Record Group 226, Records of the Office of Strategic Services (OSS).

Record Group 457, Records of the National Security Agency/Central Security Service. Individual Translations, Japanese Diplomatic Messages, SRDJ nos. 1–115,614; Summaries, SRS nos. 1–1838; Special Research Histories, SRH.

SRH-004 The Friedman Lectures on Cryptology. Declassified 22 March 1984.

SRH-005 Use of CX/MSS ULTRA by the United States War Department (1943–1945). Declassified 19 December 1978.

SRH-006 Synthesis of Experiences in the Use of ULTRA Intelligence by U.S. Army Field Commands in the European Theatre of Operations. Declassified 12 December 1978.

SRH-018 Collection of Japanese Diplomatic Messages, 12 July 1938–21 January 1942, Department of the Army Intelligence Files.

SRH-019 Blockade-Running between Europe and the Far East by Submarines, 1942–1944. Declassified 27 July 1979.

SRH-023 Reports by U.S. Army ULTRA Representatives with Army Field Commands in the European Theatre of Operations. Part I, declassified 27 October 1978; Part II, declassified 7 November 1978.

SRH-026 Marshall Letter to Eisenhower on the Use of ULTRA Intelligence, 15 March 1944. Declassified 28 December 1978.

SRH-029 A Brief History of the Signal Intelligence Service by William F. Friedman, 29 June 1942.

SRH-033 History of the Operations of Special Security Officers Attached to Field Commands, 1943–1945. Declassified 22 May 1979.

SRH-034 Marshall Letter to MacArthur on the Use of ULTRA Intelligence, 23 May 1944, and Related Correspondence. Declassified 6 June 1979.

SRH-035 History of the Special Branch, MIS, War Department, 1942–1944. Declassified 9 July 1979.

SRH-037 Reports Received by U.S. War Department on Use of ULTRA European Theater, World War II. Declassified 3 July 1979.

SRH-040 MAGIC Diplomatic Extracts, July 1945: Selected Items Prepared by MIS, War Department, for the attention of General George C. Marshall. Declassified 13 September 1979.

SRH-041 MIS Contribution to the War Effort, MIS, WDGS, December 1945. Declassified 9 October 1979.

SRH-043 Statement for Record of Participation of Brig. Gen. Carter W. Clarke, GSC in the Transmittal of Letters from Gen. George C. Marshall to Gov. Thomas E. Dewey the Latter Part of September 1944. Declassified 30 November 1979.

SRH-044 War Department Regulations Governing the Dissemination and Security of Communications Intelligence, 1943-1945. Declassified 20 April 1982.

SRH-058 The Legendary William F. Friedman by Lambros D. Callimahos. Declassified 16 June 1980.

SRH-059 Selected Examples of Commendations and Related Correspondence Highlighting the Achievements and Value of U.S. Signals Intelligence during World War II.

SRH-061 Allocation of Special Security Officers to Special Branch, Military Intelligence Service, War Department, 1943-1945.

SRH-062 History of Military Intelligence Service Reports Unit. Declassified 23 September 1980.

SRH-066 Examples of Intelligence Obtained from Cryptanalysis, 1 August 1946. Declassified 6 October 1980.

SRH-067 Japan as Mediator in the Russo-German Conflict, 29 December 1944. Declassified 14 October 1980.

SRH-068 Japanese Estimates of Germany's Ability to Continue the Struggle, 22 January 1945. Declassified 14 October 1980.

SRH-069 The Problem of the Prolongation of the Soviet-Japanese Neutrality Pact, 12 February 1945. Declassified 14 October 1945.

SRH-070 Notes on the Crimea (Yalta) Conference, 23 March 1945. Declassified 14 October 1980.

SRH-071 Abrogation of the Soviet-Japanese Neutrality Pact, 23 April 1945. Declassified 14 October 1980.

SRH-075 Japanese Reaction to German Defeat, 21 May 1945. Declassified 14 October 1980.

SRH-078 Russo-Japanese Relations, 18 June 1945. Declassified 14 October 1980.

SRH-079 Russo-Japanese Relations, June 1945. Declassified 14 October 1980.

SRH-084 Russo-Japanese Relations, 1–12 July 1945. Declassified 3 November 1980.

SRH-085 Russo-Japanese Relations, 13–20 July 1945. Declassified 3 November 1980.

SRH-086 Russo-Japanese Relations, 21–27 July 1945. Declassified 3 November 1980.

SRH-088 Russo-Japanese Relations, 28 July–6 August 1945. Declassified 4 November 1980.

SRH-090 Japan's Surrender Maneuvers, 29 August 1945. Declassified 4 November 1980.

SRH-096 Japanese Relations with the Remaining "Listening Posts" in Europe, May–Mid-July 1945. Declassified 19 November 1980.

SRH-102 Identifications, Locations and Command Functions of Significant Japanese Army/Navy Personnel. Declassified 16 December 1980.

SRH-106 Specific Instructions for the Handling and Dissemination of Special Intelligence. Declassified 3 December 1980.

SRH-107 Problems of the SSO System in World War II. Declassified 13 December 1980.

SRH-108 Report on Assignment with Third United States Army, 15 August–18 September 1944. Declassified 17 December 1980.

SRH-110 Operations of the Military Intelligence Service, War Department, London (MIS, WD, London). Declassified 7 January 1981.

SRH-111 MAGIC Reports for the Attention of the President, 1943–1944. Declassified 14 January 1980.

SRH-112 Post Mortem Writings on Indications of Ardennes Offensive, 1945.

SRH-116 Origin, Functions and Problems of the Special Branch, MIS. Declassified 27 February 1981.

SRH-117 History of Special Branch MIS, June 1944–September 1945. Declassified 2 March 1981.

SRH-125 Certain Aspects of MAGIC in the Cryptological Background of the Various Official Investigations into the Pearl Harbor Attack by William F. Friedman. Declassified 22 May 1981.

SRH-131 History of the Intelligence Group, Military Intelligence Service, WDGS, Military Branch. Parts I, II, IV, V, and VI declassified 18 August 1981; Part III declassified 30 July 1981.

SRH-134 Expansion of the Signal Intelligence Service from 1930 to 7 December 1941. Declassified 2 September 1981.

SRH-140 History of the "Language Liaison Group," Military Intelligence Service, War Department, 22 September 1945. Declassified 28 December 1981.

SRH-141 Papers from the Personal Files of Alfred McCormack, Colonel, AUS, Special Branch, G-2, Military Intelligence Division, War Department. Part I, declassified 9 December 1981; Part II, declassified 6 January 1982.

SRH-145 Collection of Memoranda on Operations of SIS Intercept Activities and Dissemination, 1942–1945. Declassified 13 April 1982.

SRH-146 Handling of ULTRA within the Military Intelligence Service (MIS), 1941–1945.

SRH-148 General Information on Local ULTRA Picture as Background for Signal Intelligence Conference, 6 March 1944. Declassified 1 February 1982.

SRH-152 Historical Review of Op-20-G.

SRH-153 MIS, War Department Liaison Activities in the U.K., 1943–1945. Declassified 16 February 1982.

SRH-154 Signal Intelligence Disclosures in the Pearl Harbor Investigation. Declassified 22 February 1982.

SRH-159 Preliminary Historical Report on the Solution of the "B" Machine. Declassified 10 March 1982.

SRH-185 War Experience of Alfred McCormack. Declassified 7 July 1982.

SRH-197 U.S. Navy Communication Intelligence Organization, Liaison and Collaboration, 1941–1945. Declassified 8 August 1982.

SRH-221 SIS Activities of Captain Harrison and Captain Koerner, ETO, 1944–1945. Declassified 30 December 1982.

SRH-232 U.S. Navy COMINCH Radio Intelligence Appreciations Concerning German U-boat Activity in the Far East, January–April 1945. Declassified 2 March 1983.

SRH-252 A Version of the Japanese Problem in the Signal Intelligence Service (Later Signal Security Agency), 1930–1945 by John B. Hurt. Declassified 27 September 1983.

SRH-254 The Japanese Intelligence System MIS/WDGS, 4 September 1945. Declassified 21 November 1983.

SRH-260 Op-20-G File of Memoranda, Reports and Messages on German Blockade Runners, World War II, 1943–1944. Declassified 16 November 1983.

SRH-264 A Lecture on Communications Intelligence by Capt. J. N. Wenger, USA, 14 August 1946. Declassified 6 December 1983.

SRH-266 Japanese Signal Intelligence Service, Third Edition (SSA, 1 November 1944). Declassified 10 January 1984.

SRH-269 U.S. Army COMINT Policy: Pearl Harbor to Summer 1942. Declassified 17 January 1984.

SRH-270 Army-Navy-FBI COMINT Agreements of 1942. Declassified 21 February 1984.

SRH-276 Centralized Control of U.S. Army Signal Intelligence Activities (30 January 1939–16 April 1945). Declassified 1984.

SRH-277 A Lecture on Communications Intelligence by RADM E. E. Stone, DIRFSA, 5 June 1951. Declassified 19 April 1984.

SRH-280 An Exhibit of the Important Types of Intelligence Recovered through Reading Japanese Cryptograms. Declassified 18 May 1984.

SRH-282 Military Cryptanalysis, Part I, Monoalphabetic Substitution Systems by William F. Friedman, 1938. Declassified 10 July 1980.

SRH-283 Military Cryptanalysis, Part II, Simpler Varieties of Polyalphabetic Substitution Systems by William F. Friedman, 1938. Declassified 30 May 1984.

SRH-291 U.S. Naval Communications Station, Guam, Station B. Declassified 3 July 1984.

SRH-305 The Undeclared War "History of R.I.," 15 November 1943 by L. F. Safford, Capt., U.S. Navy. Declassified 19 July 1984.

SRH-306 Op-20-G Exploits and Commendations, World War II. Declassified 18 July 1984.

SRH-349 The Achievements of the Signal Security Agency in World War II. Declassified 15 November 1984.

SRH-355 Naval Security Group History to World War II, Part II. Declassified 1985.

SRH-361 History of the Signal Security Agency, Volume Two—The General Cryptanalytic Problems. Declassified 23 January 1986.

SRH-364 History of the Signal Security Agency, Volume One—Organization, Part I, 1939–1945. Declassified 29 July 1986.

SRH-366 The History of Army Strip Cipher Devices (July 1934–October 1947). Declassified 2 March 1987.

SRH-391 American Signal Intelligence in Northwest Africa and Western Europe. Declassified 24 March 1988.

Discrete Records of Historical Cryptologic Import, U.S. Army, SRMA.

SRMA-003 U.S. Army Converter M-228. Declassified 31 January 1985.

SRMA-014 Intelligence Documents: German Intelligence Activity in the Far East . . . Declassified 27 June 1988.

Discrete Records of Historical Cryptologic Import, U.S. Navy, SRMN.

SRMN-018 U.S. Navy (Op-20-G) West Coast Communications Intelligence Activities Policies and Procedures, 20 June 1942–26 December 1943. Declassified 8 April 1986.

SRMN-044 COMINCH File: Weekly Reports on Estimated Locations of Japanese Fleet Units, 1 September 1942–9 August 1945.

2. Published Sources and Reference Materials

Barker, Wayne G., ed. *The History of Codes and Ciphers in the United States during the Period between the World Wars, Part I, 1919–1929.* Laguna Hills, Calif.: Aegean Park Press, 1979.

———. *The History of Codes and Ciphers in the United States during the Period between the World Wars, Part II, 1930–1939.* Laguna Hills, Calif.: Aegean Park Press, 1989.

Bennett, J. W., et al., eds. *Intelligence and Cryptanalytic Activities of the Japanese during World War I.* Laguna Hills, Calif.: Aegean Park Press, 1986.

Berezhkov, Valentin. *History in the Making: Memoirs of World War II Diplomacy.* Translated by Dudley Hagen and Barry Jones. Moscow: Progress, 1983.

Bezymenski, Lev. *The Death of Adolf Hitler: Unknown Documents from Soviet Archives.* London: Michael Joseph, 1968.

Blewett, Daniel K. "U.S. World War II Naval History: Some Lesser-Known Documents." *Government Publications Review* 17 (1990): 237-49.

Boldt, Gerhard. *The Last Ten Days.* Translated by Sandra Bance. New York: Coward, McCann and Geoghegan, 1973.

"Botschafter Ōshima beim Führer / L'ambasciatore Ōshima ricevulo del Führer." *Berlin-Rom-Tokio* 3:3 (1941): 13.

"Botschafter Ōshimas Ankunft in Berlin." *Ostasiatische Rundschau* 22:2 (1941): 43-44.

Braeckow, Ernst, ed. *Tagesbildberichte—1941, 1942.* Berlin: Verlag Joh. Kasper, n.d.

Burdick, Charles B. *An American Island in Hitler's Reich: The Bad Nauheim Internment.* Menlo Park, Calif.: Markgraf, 1987.

Carl, Leo D. *International Dictionary of Intelligence.* McLean, Va.: International Defense Consultant Services, 1990.

Chamberlin, William Henry. *Modern Japan.* St. Louis: Webster Publishing, 1942.

Chandler, Alfred D., Jr., ed. *The Papers of Dwight David Eisenhower: The War Years.* 5 vols. Baltimore: Johns Hopkins Press, 1970.

Chant, Christopher. *The Encylopedia of Codenames of World War II.* London: Routledge and Kegan Paul, 1986.

Chuikov, V. I. *The End of the Third Reich.* Moscow: Progress, 1978.

Churchill, Winston S. *The Second World War.* 6 vols. Boston: Houghton Mifflin, 1948-1953.

Clausewitz, Carl von. *On War.* Edited and translated by Michael Howard and Peter Paret. Princeton: Princeton University Press, 1976.

Creswell, H. T., et al. *A Dictionary of Military Terms: English-Japanese-Japanese-English.* Chicago: University of Chicago Press, 1942.

Deane, John R. *The Strange Alliance: The Story of Our Efforts at Wartime Cooperation with Russia.* Indiana University Press, 1973.

Doenitz, Karl. *Memoirs: Ten Years and Twenty Days.* Translated by R. H. Stevens. Annapolis, Md.: Naval Institute Press, 1990.

Ehmann, P. *Die Sprichwörter und bildlichen Ausdrücke der japanischen Sprache.* Tokyo: Deutsche Gesellschaft für Natur- und Völkerkunde Ostasiens, 1927.

Eisenhower, Dwight D. *Crusade in Europe.* Garden City, N.Y.: Doubleday, 1948.

Evans, David C., ed. and trans. *The Japanese Navy in World War II: In the Words of Former Japanese Naval Officers.* 2d ed. Annapolis, Md.: Naval Institute Press, 1986.

Farago, Ladislas, comp. and ed. *The Axis Grand Strategy: Blueprints for the Total War.* Harrisburg, Pa.: Telegraph Press, 1942.

Fuehrer Conferences on Naval Affairs, 1939-1945. Annapolis, Md.: Naval Institute Press, 1990.

"Der Führer empfing den kaiserlish-japanischen Botschafter Ōshima." *Berlin-Rom-Tokio* 6:5 (1944): 2.

Galland, Joseph S. *An Historical and Analytical Bibliography of the Literature of Cryptology.* Evanston, Ill.: Northwestern University, 1945.

Gilbert, Felix, ed. *Hitler Directs His War: The Secret Records of His Daily Military Conferences.* New York: Octagon Books, 1982.

Goebbels, Joseph. *Final Entries, 1945: The Diaries of Joseph Goebbels.* Translated by Richard Barry. New York: G. P. Putnam's Sons, 1978.

_____. *The Goebbels Diaries, 1942-1943.* Edited and translated by Louis P. Lochner. Garden City, N.Y.: Doubleday, 1948.

Halder, Franz. *The Halder War Diary, 1939-1942.* Edited by Charles Burdick and Hans-Adolf Jacobsen. Novato, Calif.: Presidio Press, 1988.

Harriman, W. Averell, and Elie Abel. *Special Envoy to Churchill and Stalin, 1941-1945.* New York: Random House, 1975.

Hawkins, Desmond, and Donald Boyd, eds. *War Report: A Record of Dispatches Broadcast by the BBC's War Correspondents with the Allied Expeditionary Force, 5 June 1944-5 May 1945.* London: Oxford University Press, 1946.

Hull, Cordell. *The Memoirs of Cordell Hull.* 2 vols. New York: Macmillan, 1948.

Hunt, David. *A Don at War.* Rev. ed. London: Frank Cass, 1990.

Hunter, Janet, comp. *Concise Dictionary of Modern Japanese History.* Berkeley: University of California Press, 1984.

Ike, Nobutaka, trans. and ed. *Japan's Decision for War: Records of the 1941 Policy Conferences.* Stanford: Stanford University Press, 1967.

Jacobsen, Hans-Adolf, and Arthur L. Smith, Jr., eds. *World War II Policy and Strategy: Selected Documents with Commentary.* Santa Barbara, Calif.: Clio Books, 1979.

The Japan Year Book, 1940-41. Tokyo: Foreign Affairs Association of Japan, 1940.

The Japan Year Book, 1943-44. Tokyo: Foreign Affairs Association of Japan, 1943.

Jones, R. V. *The Wizard War: British Scientific Intelligence, 1939-1945.* New York: Coward, McCann and Geoghegan, 1978.

Kase, Toshikazu. *Journey to the Missouri.* New Haven: Yale University Press, 1950.

Kenkyusha's New Japanese-English Dictionary. Cambridge, Mass.: Harvard University Press, 1942.

Kimball, Warren F., ed. *Churchill and Roosevelt: The Complete Correspondence.* 3 vols. Princeton: Princeton University Press, 1984.

Kriegstagebuch des Oberkommandos der Wehrmacht (Wehrmachtführungsstab) 1940–1945. Edited by Percy Ernst Schramm, Andreas Hillgruber, Walter Hubatsch, and Hans-Adolf Jacobsen. 4 vols. in 7. Frankfurt am Main: Bernard & Graefe Verlag für Wehrwesen, 1961–1965.

Kuby, Erich. *The Russians and Berlin, 1945.* Translated by Arnold J. Pomerans. New York: Hill and Wang, 1968.

Lankford, Nelson Douglas, ed. *OSS against the Reich: The World War II Diaries of Colonel David K. E. Bruce.* Kent, Ohio: Kent State University Press, 1991.

Leahy, William D. *I Was There: The Personal Story of the Chief of Staff to Presidents Roosevelt and Truman Based on His Notes and Diaries Made at the Time.* New York: Whittlesey House, 1950.

Manteuffel, Hasso von. "The Battle of the Ardennes 1944–5." In *Decisive Battles of World War II: The German View*, edited by H. A. Jacobsen and J. Rohwer, translated by Edward Fitzgerald, pp. 391–418. New York: G. P. Putnam's Sons, 1965.

Masterman, J. C. *The Double-Cross System in the War of 1939 to 1945.* New Haven: Yale University Press, 1972.

Morton, H. V. *Atlantic Meeting.* London: Methuen, 1943.

Nelson, Andrew Nathaniel. *The Modern Reader's Japanese-English Character Dictionary.* Rutland, Vt.: Charles E. Tuttle, 1962.

Operational History of Japanese Naval Communications, December 1941–August 1945. Laguna Hills, Calif.: Aegean Press, 1985.

The Orient Year Book, 1942. Tokyo: Asia Statistics, 1942.

Ōshima Hiroshi, "Botschafter Ōshima an *Berlin-Rom-Tokio.*" *Berlin-Rom-Tokio* 3:2 (1941): 11–12.

————. "Doitsu gaikō no rinen" [The idea of German diplomacy]. *Bungei Shunjū* (January 1940). Washington, D.C.: Library of Congress, Reel WT (War Trials) 82, IMT (International Military Tribunal) 623, IPS (International Prosecution Section) Document No. 3268.

————. "Japan, Deutschland und Italien." *Berlin-Rom-Tokio* 4:1 (1942): 9.

————. "Japan und der Dreimächtepakt." *Volk und Reich* 17:5 (1941): 293–94.

————. "Katte kabuto no o wo shimeyo" [After winning, keep the string tight on your helmet]. *Bungei Shunjū* (April 1940): 8.

————. "Neuordnung des Fernen Ostens, Neuordnung Europas." *Die Aktion: Kampfblatt für das Neue Europa* 2 (June 1941): 341–42.

Ōshima Hiroshi and Erich Voss. "Der Neubau der Kaiserlich japanischen Botschaft in Berlin." *Die Kunst im deutschen Reich* 7:1 (1943): 24–40.

Ploetz Geschichte der Weltkriege: Mächte, Ereignisse, Entwicklungen, 1900–1945. Freiburg: Verlag Ploetz, 1981.

Reischauer, Edwin O. *My Life between Japan and America.* New York: Harper and Row, 1986.

Richardson, Stewart, ed. *The Secret History of World War II: The Ultra-Secret Wartime Letters and Cables of Roosevelt, Stalin, and Churchill.* New York: Richardson and Steirman, 1986.

Rohwer, Jürgen. *Axis Submarine Successes, 1939–1945.* Translated by John A. Broadwin. Annapolis, Md.: Naval Institute Press, 1983.

Rosengarten, Adolph G., Jr. "With Ultra from Omaha Beach to Weimar, Germany—A Personal View." *Military Affairs* 42:3 (October 1978): 127–32.

Sevruk, V., comp. *How Wars End: Eye-Witness Accounts of the Fall of Berlin.* Moscow: Progress, 1969.

Shigemitsu, Mamoru. *Japan and Her Destiny: My Struggle for Peace.* Edited by F. S. G. Piggott, translated by Oswald White. New York: E. P. Dutton, 1958.

Sorge, Richard. "Die japanische Expansion." *Zeitschrift für Geopolitik* 16:8/9 (August-September 1939): 617–22.

Spector, Ronald H., ed. *Listening to the Enemy: Key Documents on the Role of Communications Intelligence in the War with Japan.* Wilmington, Del.: Scholarly Resources, 1988.

Speer, Albert. *Inside the Third Reich.* Translated by Richard and Clara Winston. New York: Macmillan, 1970.

Stalin's Correspondence with Churchill and Attlee, 1941-1945. New York: Capricorn Books, 1965.

Stalin's Correspondence with Roosevelt and Truman, 1941-1945. New York: Capricorn Books, 1965.

Stettinius, Edward R., Jr. *Lend-Lease: Weapon for Victory.* New York: Macmillan, 1944.

Stimson, Henry L. *Prelude to Invasion.* Washington, D.C.: Public Affairs Press, 1944.

Studnitz, Hans-Georg von. *While Berlin Burns: The Diary of Hanz-Georg von Studnitz, 1943-1945.* Translated by R. H. Stevens. London: Weidenfeld and Nicolson, 1964.

Tōgō Shigenori. *The Case of Japan.* Translated and edited by Tōgō Fumihiko and Ben Bruce Blakeney. New York: Simon and Schuster, 1956.

Trevor-Roper, H. R., ed. *Blitzkrieg to Defeat: Hitler's War Directives, 1939-1945.* New York: Holt, Rinehart and Winston, 1964.

U.K., Foreign Office. *German Zone Handbook No. 1A—Berlin, Part III: Local Directory.* London: His Majesty's Stationery Office, 1945.

U.S. Air Force. *The Intelligence Revolution: A Historical Perspective.* Special Bibliography Series no. 76. Colorado Springs, Colo.: U.S. Air Force Academy, 1988.

U.S. Department of Defense. *The "Magic" Background of Pearl Harbor.* 5 vols. in 8. Washington, D.C.: Government Printing Office, 1977–1978.

U.S. Department of State. *Foreign Relations of the United States, Diplomatic Papers, 1942.* 7 vols. Washington, D.C.: Government Printing Office, 1960–1963.

U.S. Seventh Army. *The Seventh United States Army in France and Germany, 1944-1945.* Heidelberg, Ger.: Aloys Gräf, 1946.

U.S. Strategic Bombing Survey (Pacific). *Japanese Military and Naval Intelligence.* Washington, D.C.: Government Printing Office, 1946.

Van Der Rhoer, Edward. *Deadly Magic: A Personal Account of Communications Intelligence in World War II in the Pacific.* New York: Charles Scribner's Sons, 1978.

Voigt, Walter. "Begegnung mit Hauptman Ōshima." *Das Deutsche Rote Kreuz* 7 (1943): 32–33.

Wallace, David, comp. *The Magic Documents: Summaries and Transcripts of the*

Top-Secret Diplomatic Communications of Japan, 1938-1945. Frederick, Md.: University Publications of America, 1982.

Warlimont, Walter. *Inside Hitler's Headquarters, 1939-45.* Translated by R. H. Barry. Novato, Calif.: Presidio Press, ca. 1964.

Watson, Bruce W., ed. *United States Intelligence: An Encyclopedia.* New York: Garland, 1990.

Webster's New Geographical Dictionary. Springfield, Mass.: Merriam-Webster, 1988.

Welles, Sumner. *Seven Decisions That Shaped History.* New York: Harper and Brothers, 1951.

Werth, Alexander. *Moscow '41.* London: Hamish Hamilton, 1942.

Winterbotham, F. W. *The Nazi Connection.* New York: Harper and Row, 1978.

_____. *Secret and Personal.* London: William Kimber, 1969.

_____. *The ULTRA Secret.* New York: Harper and Row, 1974.

Yardley, Herbert O. *The American Black Chamber.* Indianapolis, Ind.: Bobbs-Merrill, 1931.

Zacharias, Ellis M. *Secret Missions: The Story of an Intelligence Officer.* New York: G. P. Putnam's Sons, 1946.

3. Secondary Works: Books

Adams, Henry H. *Witness to Power: The Life of Fleet Admiral William D. Leahy.* Annapolis, Md.: Naval Institute Press, 1985.

Agawa, Hiroyuki. *The Reluctant Admiral: Yamamoto and the Imperial Navy.* Translated by John Bester. Tokyo: Kodansha International, 1982.

Albion, Robert Greenhalgh, and Jennie Barnes Pope. *Sea Lanes in Wartime: The American Experience, 1775-1942.* London: George Allen and Unwin, 1943.

Ambrose, Stephen E. *Eisenhower.* Vol. 1. New York: Simon and Schuster, 1983.

_____. *Ike's Spies: Eisenhower and the Espionage Establishment.* Garden City, N.Y.: Doubleday, 1981.

Army Times, ed. *A History of the U.S. Signal Corps.* New York: G. P. Putnam's Sons, 1961.

Baldwin, Hanson W. *The Crucial Years, 1939-1941: The World at War.* New York: Harper and Row, 1976.

Bamford, James. *The Puzzle Palace: A Report on America's Most Secret Agency.* Boston: Houghton Mifflin, 1982.

Beesly, Patrick. *Very Special Intelligence: The Story of the Admiralty's Operational Intelligence Centre, 1939-1945.* Garden City, N.Y.: Doubleday, 1978.

Bennett, Ralph. *Ultra and Mediterranean Strategy.* New York: William Morrow, 1989.

_____. *Ultra in the West: The Normandy Campaign, 1944-45.* New York: Charles Scribner's Sons, 1980.

Blumenson, Martin. *Breakout and Pursuit.* 1961. Reprint. Washington, D.C.: Center of Military History, 1984.

Boog, Horst, et al. *Der globale Krieg: Die Ausweitung zum Weltkrieg und der Wech-*

sel der Initiative 1941–1943. Vol. 6, *Das Deutsche Reich und der Zweite Welt-krieg*. Stuttgart: Deutsche Verlags-Anstalt, 1990.

Boyd, Carl. *The Extraordinary Envoy: General Hiroshi Ōshima and Diplomacy in the Third Reich, 1934–1939*. 1980. Reprint. Washington, D.C.: University Press of America, 1982.

Boyd, Carl, and Akihiko Yoshida, *History of Imperial Japanese Navy Submarine Operations in the Second World War*. Annapolis, Md.: Naval Institute Press. Forthcoming.

Brackman, Arnold C. *The Other Nuremberg: The Untold Story of the Tokyo War Crimes Trials*. New York: William Morrow, 1987.

Bradley, Omar N., and Clay Blair. *A General's Life*. New York: Simon and Schuster, 1983.

Breuer, William B. *The Secret War with Germany*. Novato, Calif.: Presidio Press, 1988.

Brice, Martin. *Axis Blockade Runners of World War II*. Annapolis, Md.: Naval Institute Press, 1981.

Brown, Anthony Cave. *Bodyguard of Lies*. Toronto: Fitzhenry and Whiteside, 1975.

_____. *"C": The Secret Life of Sir Stewart Graham Menzies, Spymaster to Winston Churchill*. New York: Macmillan, 1987.

Bryant, Arthur. *The Turn of the Tide: A History of the War Years Based on the Diaries of Field-Marshal Lord Alanbrooke, Chief of the Imperial General Staff*. Garden City, N.Y.: Doubleday, 1957.

Butler, Ewan. *Mason-Mac: The Life of Lieutenant-General Sir Noel Mason-Mac-farlane*. London: Macmillan, 1972.

Butow, Robert J. C. *Tojo and the Coming of the War*. Stanford: Stanford University Press, 1961.

Calvocoressi, Peter. *Top Secret Ultra*. New York: Pantheon Books, 1980.

Casey, William. *The Secret War against Hitler*. Washington, D.C.: Regnery Gateway, 1988.

Chapman, John W. M. "Japanese Intelligence, 1918–1945: A Suitable Case for Treatment." In *Intelligence and International Relations, 1900–1945*, edited by Christopher Andrew and Jeremy Noakes, pp. 145–90. Exeter, Eng.: University of Exeter, 1987.

Chapman, John W. M., ed. and trans. *The Price of Admiralty: The War Diary of the German Naval Attaché in Japan, 1939–1943*. 3 vols. to date. Ripe, E. Sussex: Saltire Press, 1982–.

Chihiro, Hosoya. "The Tripartite Pact, 1939–1940." In *Deterrent Diplomacy: Japan, Germany, and the USSR, 1935–1940*, edited by James William Morley, pp. 191–257. New York: Columbia University Press, 1976.

Clark, Ronald. *The Man Who Broke Purple: The Life of Colonel William F. Friedman, Who Deciphered the Japanese Code in World War II*. Boston: Little, Brown, 1977.

Cole, Hugh M. *The Ardennes: Battle of the Bulge*. 1965. Reprint. Washington, D.C.: Office of the Chief of Military History, 1983.

_____. *The Lorraine Campaign*. 1950. Reprint. Washington, D.C.: Historical Division, United States Army, 1981.

Craig, Gordon A. "The German Foreign Office from Neurath to Ribbentrop." In

The Diplomats, 1919–1939, edited by Gordon A. Craig and Felix Gilbert, pp. 406–36. Princeton: Princeton University Press, 1953.

Cruickshank, Charles. *Deception in World War II*. Oxford: Oxford University Press, 1979.

Dallek, Robert. *Franklin D. Roosevelt and American Foreign Policy, 1932–1945*. New York: Oxford University Press, 1979.

Danchev, Alex. *Very Special Relation: Field-Marshal Sir John Dill and the Anglo-American Alliance, 1941–44*. London: Brassey's Defence Publishers, 1986.

Deacon, Richard. *A History of the British Secret Service*. Ca. 1969. Reprint. London: Frederick Muller, 1969, 1978.

————. *Kempei Tai: A History of the Japanese Secret Service*. New York: Beaufort Books, 1983.

Deavours, Cipher A., and Louis Kruh. *Machine Cryptography and Modern Cryptanalysis*. Dedham, Mass.: Artech House, 1985.

Deborin, G. *Secrets of the Second World War*. Translated by Vic Schneierson. Moscow: Progress, 1971.

Dewar, Michael. *The Art of Deception in Warfare*. Newton Abbot, U.K.: David and Charles, 1989.

Dippel, John V. H. *Two against Hitler: Stealing the Nazis' Best-Kept Secrets*. New York: Praeger, 1992.

Dorwart, Jeffery M. *Conflict of Duty: The U.S. Navy's Intelligence Dilemma, 1919–1945*. Annapolis, Md.: Naval Institute Press, 1983.

Drea, Edward J. *MacArthur's Ultra Codebreaking and the War against Japan, 1942—1945*. Lawrence: University Press of Kansas, 1992.

Duffy, Christopher. *Red Storm on the Reich: The Soviet March on Germany, 1945*. New York: Atheneum, 1991.

Dull, Paul S. *A Battle History of the Imperial Japanese Navy, 1941–1945*. Annapolis, Md.: Naval Institute Press, 1978.

Eisenhower, David. *Eisenhower at War, 1943–1945*. New York: Random House, 1986.

Erickson, John. *The Road to Stalingrad*. New York: Harper and Row, 1975.

Everett, Susanne. *Lost Berlin*. New York: Gallery, 1979.

Farago, Ladislas. *The Broken Seal: The Story of "Operation Magic" and the Pearl Harbor Disaster*. New York: Random House, 1967.

————. *Patton: Ordeal and Triumph*. New York: Ivan Obolensky, 1964.

Feis, Herbert. *Japan Subdued: The Atomic Bomb and the End of the War in the Pacific*. Princeton: Princeton University Press, 1961.

Finnegan, John Patrick. *Military Intelligence*. Arlington, Va.: U.S. Army Intelligence and Security Command, 1984.

————. *Military Intelligence: An Overview, 1885–1987*. Arlington, Va.: U.S. Army Intelligence and Security Command, 1988. (Unclassified parts).

Fischer, Louis. *The Road to Yalta: Soviet Foreign Relations, 1941–1945*. New York: Harper and Row, 1972.

Friedländer, Saul. *Prelude to Downfall: Hitler and the United States, 1939–1941*. Translated by Aline B. and Alexander Werth. New York: Alfred A. Knopf, 1967.

Fuchida, Mitsuo, and Masatake Okumiya. *Midway: The Battle That Doomed Japan*. Annapolis, Md.: U.S. Naval Institute, 1955.

Garliński, Józef. *The Enigma War*. New York: Charles Scribner's Sons, 1980.

Gavin, James M. *On to Berlin*. 1978. Reprint. Toronto: Bantam, 1985.

Gilbert, Martin. *Road to Victory, 1941–1945*. Vol. 7, *Winston S. Churchill*. Boston: Houghton Mifflin, 1986.

Gondek, Leszek. *Na tropach tajemnic III Rzeszy* [In pursuit of the secrets of the Third Reich]. Warsaw: Wydawnictwo Ministerstwa Obrony Narodowej, 1987.

Grigg, John. *1943: The Victory That Never Was*. New York: Hill and Wang, 1980.

Gudgin, Peter. *Military Intelligence: The British Story*. London: Arms and Armour Press, 1989.

Hamm, Diane L., comp. *Military Intelligence: Its Heroes and Legends*. Arlington, Va.: U.S. Army Intelligence and Security Command, 1987.

Harrison, Gordon A. *Cross-Channel Attack*. Washington, D.C.: Office of the Chief of Military History, 1951.

Hashimoto, Mochitsura. *Sunk: The Story of the Japanese Submarine Fleet, 1941–1945*. Translated by E. H. M. Colegrave. New York: Henry Holt, 1954.

Haswell, Jock. *D-Day: Intelligence and Deception*. New York: Time Books, 1979.

Heinrichs, Waldo. *Threshold of War: Franklin D. Roosevelt and American Entry into World War II*. New York: Oxford University Press, 1988.

Herring, George C., Jr. *Aid to Russia, 1941–1945: Strategy, Diplomacy, the Origins of the Cold War*. New York: Columbia University Press, 1973.

Herzog, James H. *Closing the Open Door: American-Japanese Diplomatic Negotiations, 1936–1941*. Annapolis, Md.: Naval Institute Press, 1973.

Hinsley, F. H., et al. *British Intelligence in the Second World War*. Vols. 1–3, *Its Influence on Strategy and Operations*. Vol. 4, F. H. Hinsley and C. A. G. Simkins, *Security and Counter-Intelligence*. Vol. 5, Michael Howard, *Strategic Deception*. London: Her Majesty's Stationery Office, 1979–1990.

Hodges, Andrew. *Alan Turing: The Enigma*. New York: Simon and Schuster, 1983.

Holmes, W. J. *Double-Edged Secrets: U.S. Naval Intelligence Operations in the Pacific during World War II*. Annapolis, Md.: Naval Institute Press, 1979.

Iklé, Frank William. *German-Japanese Relations, 1936–1940*. New York: Bookman Associates, 1956.

Ingersoll, Ralph. *Top Secret*. New York: Harcourt, Brace, 1946.

James, D. Clayton. *The Years of MacArthur*. 3 vols. Boston: Houghton Mifflin, 1970–1985.

Johnson, Chalmers. *An Instance of Treason: Ozaki Hotsumi and the Sorge Spy Ring*. Expanded ed. Stanford: Stanford University Press, 1990.

Kahn, David. *The Codebreakers: The Story of Secret Writing*. New York: Macmillan, 1967.

———. *Hitler's Spies: German Military Intelligence in World War II*. New York: Macmillan, 1978.

———. *Kahn on Codes: Secrets of the New Cryptology*. New York: Macmillan, 1983.

———. "Roosevelt, MAGIC and ULTRA." In *Historians and Archivists: Essays in Modern German History and Archival Policy*, edited by George O. Kent, pp. 115–44. Fairfax, Va.: George Mason University Press, 1991.

———. "The United States Views Germany and Japan." In *Knowing One's Ene-*

mies, edited by Ernest R. May, pp. 476–501. Princeton: Princeton University Press, 1984.

Katz, Barry M. *Foreign Intelligence: Research and Analysis in the Office of Strategic Services, 1942–1945.* Cambridge, Mass.: Harvard University Press, 1989.

Kimball, Warren F. *The Juggler: Franklin Roosevelt as Wartime Statesman.* Princeton: Princeton University Press, 1991.

Kozaczuk, Wladyslaw. *Enigma.* Edited and translated by Christopher Kasparek. Frederick, Md.: University Publication of America, 1984.

Krebs, Gerhard. "Japanische Vermittlungsversuche im Deutsch-Sovjetischen Krieg, 1941–1945." In *Deutschland-Japan in der Zwischenkriegszeit*, edited by Josef Kreiner and Regine Mathias, pp. 239–88. Bonn: Bouvier Verlag, 1990.

————. *Japans Deutschlandpolitik 1935–1941: Eine Studie zur Vorgeschichte des Pazifischen Krieges.* 2 vols. Hamburg: Gesellschaft für Natur- und Völkerkunde Ostasiens, 1984.

Langhorne, Richard, ed. *Diplomacy and Intelligence during the Second World War: Essays in Honour of F. H. Hinsley.* Cambridge: Cambridge University Press, 1985.

Larionov, V., et al. *World War II: Decisive Battles of the Soviet Army.* Translated by William Biley. Moscow: Progress, 1984.

Lash, Joseph P. *Roosevelt and Churchill, 1939–1941: The Partnership That Saved the West.* New York: W. W. Norton, 1976.

Layton, Edwin T. *"And I Was There": Pearl Harbor and Midway—Breaking the Secrets.* New York: William Morrow, 1985.

Le Tissier, Tony. *The Battle of Berlin, 1945.* New York: St. Martin's Press, 1988.

Lewin, Ronald. *The American Magic: Codes, Ciphers and the Defeat of Japan.* New York: Farrar Straus Giroux, 1982.

————. *The Chief: Field Marshal Lord Wavell, Commander-in-Chief and Viceroy, 1939–1947.* New York: Farrar Straus Giroux, 1980.

————. *Hitler's Mistakes.* New York: William Morrow, 1984.

————. *Ultra Goes to War.* New York: McGraw-Hill, 1978.

Liddell Hart, Basil Henry. *History of the Second World War.* London: Cassell, 1970.

Liddell Hart, Basil Henry, ed. *The Rommel Papers.* New York: Harcourt, Brace, 1953.

Lucas, James. *Last Days of the Third Reich: The Collapse of Nazi Germany, May 1945.* New York: William Morrow, 1986.

Lukacs, John. *The Last European War, September 1939–December 1941.* Garden City, N.Y.: Anchor Press, 1976.

MacDonald, Charles B. *The Last Offensive.* 1973. Reprint. Washington, D.C.: Center of Military History, 1984.

Manning, Paul. *Hirohito: The War Years.* New York: Bantam, 1989.

Martin, Bernd. *Deutschland und Japan im Zweiten Weltkrieg: Vom Angriff auf Pearl Harbor bis zur deutschen Kapitulation.* Göttingen: Musterschmidt-Verlag, 1969.

Matloff, Maurice. *Strategic Planning for Coalition Warfare, 1943–1944.* Washington, D.C.: Office of the Chief of Military History, 1959.

Matloff, Maurice, and Edwin M. Snell. *Strategic Planning for Coalition Warfare, 1941–1942.* Washington, D.C.: Office of the Chief of Military History, 1953.

Mee, Charles L., Jr. *Meeting at Potsdam*. New York: M. Evans, 1975.

Mennel, Rainer. *Die Schlußphase des Zweiten Weltkrieges im Westen (1944/45)*. Osnabrück: Biblio Verlag, 1981.

Meskill, Johanna Menzel. *Hitler and Japan: The Hollow Alliance*. New York: Atherton Press, 1966.

Middlebrook, Martin. *The Berlin Raids: R.A.F. Bomber Command, Winter 1943-44*. London: Penguin, 1988.

Military History Section, Headquarters, Army Forces Far East. *Submarine Operations in Second Phase Operations, April–August 1942*. Pt. 1. *Japanese Monograph No. 110*. Office of the Chief of Military History, 1952.

Montagu, Ewen. *Beyond Top Secret Ultra*. New York: Coward, McCann and Geoghegan, 1978.

Morgan, Ted. *FDR: A Biography*. New York: Simon and Schuster, 1985.

Motter, T. H. Vail. *The Persian Corridor and Aid to Russia*. Washington, D.C.: Office of the Chief of Military History, 1952.

Mueller-Hillebrand, Burkhart. *Germany and Its Allies in World War II: A Record of Axis Collaboration Problems*. Frederick, Md.: University Publications of America, 1980.

Muggenthaler, August Karl. *German Raiders of World War II*. Englewood Cliffs, N.J.: Prentice-Hall, 1977.

Norman, Bruce. *Secret Warfare: The Battle of Codes and Ciphers*. New York: Dorset Press, 1973.

O'Donnell, James P. *The Bunker: The History of the Reich Chancellery Group*. Boston: Houghton Mifflin, 1978.

Paine, Lauran. *German Military Intelligence in World War II: The Abwehr*. New York: Stein and Day, 1984.

Parrish, Thomas. *The Ultra Americans: The U.S. Role in Breaking the Nazi Codes*. New York: Stein and Day, 1986.

Persico, Joseph E. *Piercing the Reich: The Penetration of Nazi Germany by OSS Agents during World War II*. London: Michael Joseph, 1979.

Plehwe, Friedrich-Karl von. *The End of an Alliance: Rome's Defection from the Axis in 1943*. Translated by Eric Mosbacher. London: Oxford University Press, 1971.

Pogue, Forrest C. *George C. Marshall*. 4 vols. New York: Viking, 1963–1987.

_____. *The Supreme Command*. Washington, D.C.: Office of the Chief of Military History, 1954.

Prange, Gordon W. *Target Tokyo: The Story of the Sorge Spy Ring*. New York: McGraw-Hill, 1984.

Pujol, Juan. *Operation GARBO*. New York: Random House, 1985.

Putney, Diane T., ed. *Ultra and the Army Air Forces in World War II*. Washington, D.C.: Office of Air Force History, 1987.

Ransom, Harry Howe. *The Intelligence Establishment*. Cambridge, Mass.: Harvard University Press, 1970.

Read, Anthony, and David Fisher. *The Deadly Embrace: Hitler, Stalin and the Nazi-Soviet Pact, 1939–1941*. New York: W. W. Norton, 1988.

Reese, Mary Ellen. *General Reinhard Gehlen: The CIA Connection*. Fairfax, Va.: George Mason University Press, 1990.

Rocco, Charles C. *The Search for Hitler's Retreat*. Bennington, Vt.: Merriam Press, 1988.

Romanus, Charles F., and Riley Sunderland. *Stillwell's Mission to China*. Washington, D.C.: Office of the Chief of Military History, 1953.

Rusbridger, James, and Eric Nave. *Betrayal at Pearl Harbor: How Churchill Lured Roosevelt into World War II*. New York: Summit Books, 1991.

Ryan, Cornelius. *The Last Battle*. New York: Simon and Schuster, 1966.

Sevostyanov, Pavel. *Before the Nazi Invasion: Soviet Diplomacy in September 1939–June 1941*. Translated by David Skvirsky. 1981. Reprint. Moscow: Progress, 1984.

Sherwood, Robert E. *Roosevelt and Hopkins: An Intimate History*. New York: Harper and Brothers, 1948.

Shirer, William L. *The Rise and Fall of the Third Reich: A History of Nazi Germany*. New York: Simon and Schuster, 1960.

Shulsky, Abram N. *Silent Warfare: Understanding the World of Intelligence*. Washington, D.C.: Brassey's (U.S.), 1991.

Stripp, Alan. *Codebreaker in the Far East*. London: Frank Cass, 1989.

Strong, Kenneth. *Men of Intelligence: A Study of the Roles and Decisions of Chiefs of Intelligence from World War I to the Present Day*. New York: St. Martin's Press, 1971.

Suzuki Kenji. *Chūdoku Taishi Ōshima Hiroshi* [Ambassador to Germany, Ōshima Hiroshi]. Tokyo: Fuyō Shobō, 1979.

Taylor, John M. *General Maxwell Taylor: The Sword and the Pen*. New York: Doubleday, 1989.

Thompson, George Raynor, et al. *The Signal Corps: The Test (December 1941 to July 1943)*. Washington, D.C.: Office of the Chief of Military History, 1957.

Thompson, George Raynor, and Dixie R. Harris. *The Signal Corps: The Outcome (Mid-1943 through 1945)*. Washington, D.C.: Office of the Chief of Military History, 1966.

Trefousse, H. L. *German and American Neutrality, 1939–1941*. New York: Octagon Books, 1969.

Trevor-Roper, H. R. *The Last Days of Hitler*. New York: Macmillan, 1947.

Tully, Andrew. *Berlin: Story of a Battle*. New York: Simon and Schuster, 1963.

U.S. Army, Historical Division. *Omaha Beachhead, 6 June–13 June 1944*. Washington, D.C.: Government Printing Office, 1945. Facsimile reprint, Center of Military History, 1984.

U.S. Army, Intelligence Center and School. *The Evolution of American Military Intelligence*. Fort Huachuca, Ariz.: 1973.

Vassiltchikov, Marie. *Berlin Diaries, 1940–1945*. New York: Alfred A. Knopf, 1987.

Werth, Alexander. *Russia at War, 1941–1945*. New York: E. P. Dutton, 1964.

West, Nigel. *The SIGINT Secrets: The Signals Intelligence War, 1900 to Today*. New York: William Morrow, 1988.

———. *A Thread of Deceit: Espionage Myths of World War II*. New York: Random House, 1985.

Whiting, Charles. *Ardennes: The Secret War*. New York: Dorset Press, 1985.

———. *The End of the War: Europe, April 15–May 23, 1945*. New York: Stein and Day, 1973.

Winks, Robin W. *Clock and Gown: Scholars in the Secret War, 1939–1961.* New York: William Morrow, 1987.

Wojtkiewicz, Stanisław Strumph. *Tiergarten: Powieść z lat 1939–1945* [Tiergarten: A novel from the years 1939–1945]. Warsaw: Kaiążka i Wiedza, 1974.

Ziemke, Earl F. *Battle for Berlin: End of the Third Reich.* New York: Ballantine, 1969.

―――. *Stalingrad to Berlin: The German Defeat in the East.* Washington, D.C.: Office of the Chief of Military History, 1968.

4. Secondary Works: Articles and Papers

Ambrose, Stephen E. "Eisenhower and the Intelligence Community in World War II." *Journal of Contemporary History* 16 (1981): 153–66.

Angevine, Robert G. "Gentlemen Do Read Each Other's Mail: American Intelligence in the Interwar Era." *Intelligence and National Security* 7:2 (April 1992): 1–29.

"Arlington Hall: Monument to Intelligence." *Periscope* (Spring 1987): 4–5.

Army History, no. 19 (Summer 1991): 20–21.

Bennett, Ralph. "Intelligence and Strategy: Some Observations on the War in the Mediterranean, 1941–45." Paper delivered at the Intelligence and Military Operations Conference, U.S. Army War College, Carlisle Barracks, Pa., 23 April 1986.

―――. "Ultra and Some Command Decisions." *Journal of Contemporary History* 16 (1981): 131–51.

Boyd, Carl. "American Naval Intelligence of Japanese Submarine Operations Early in the Pacific War." *Journal of Military History* 53:2 (April 1989): 169–89.

―――. "Anguish under Siege: High-Grade Japanese Signal Intelligence and the Fall of Berlin." *Cryptologia* 13:3 (July 1989): 193–209.

―――. "The Japanese Submarine Force and the Legacy of Strategic and Operational Doctrine Developed between the World Wars." In *Selected Papers from the Citadel Conference on War and Diplomacy, 1978,* edited by Larry H. Addington et al., pp. 27–40. Charleston, SC: Citadel Press, 1979.

―――. "Significance of MAGIC and the Japanese Ambassador to Berlin." *Intelligence and National Security.* "I: The Formative Months before Pearl Harbor," 2:1 (January 1987): 150–69; "II: The Crucial Months after Pearl Harbor," 2:2 (April 1987): 302–19; "III: The Months of Growing Certainty," 3:4 (October 1988): 83–102; "IV: Confirming the Turn of the Tide on the German-Soviet Front," 4:1 (January 1989): 86–107; "V: News of Hitler's Defense Preparations for Allied Invasion of Western Europe," 4:3 (July 1989): 193–209.

Chiles, James R. "Breaking Codes Was This Couple's Lifetime Career." *Smithsonian* 18:3 (June 1987): 128–30, 132, 134, 136, 138, 140–42, 144.

Clarke, William F. "Bletchley Park, 1941–1945." *Cryptologia* 12:2 (April 1988): 90–97.

Cochran, Alexander S., Jr. "The Influence of 'Magic' Intelligence on Allied Strategy in the Mediterranean." In *New Aspects of Naval History,* edited by Craig L. Symonds et al., pp. 340–48. Annapolis, Md.: Naval Institute Press, 1981.

―――. " 'Magic,' 'Ultra,' and the Second World War: Literature, Sources, and Outlook." *Military Affairs* 49:2 (April 1982): 88–92.

————. "Other Front in the Mediterranean, 1943: The Role of Operational Intelligence and Strategic Planning for Coalition Warfare." Paper delivered at the Soviet-American Relations during World War II symposium, Hyde Park, N.Y., 21 October 1987.

Deutsch, Harold C. "The Influence of ULTRA on World War II." *Parameters* 8:4 (December 1978): 2–15.

Drea, Edward J. "Missing Intentions: Japanese Intelligence and the Soviet Invasion of Manchuria, 1945." *Military Affairs* 48:2 (April 1984): 66–73.

————. "Ultra and the American War against Japan: A Note on Sources." *Intelligence and National Security* 3:1 (January 1988): 195–204.

Goren, Dina. "Communication Intelligence and the Freedom of the Press: The *Chicago Tribune's* Battle of Midway Dispatch and the Breaking of the Japanese Naval Code." *Journal of Contemporary History* 16 (1981): 663–90.

Harris, Ruth R. "The 'Magic' Leak of 1941 and Japanese-American Relations." *Pacific Historical Review* 50:1 (February 1981): 77–96.

"Japanese Naval Intelligence." *ONI Review* 1:9 (July 1946): 36–40.

Kahn, David. "The Intelligence Failure of Pearl Harbor." *Foreign Affairs* 70:5 (Winter 1991/92): 138–52.

Kruh, Louis. "British-American Cryptanalytic Cooperation and an Unprecedented Admission by Winston Churchill." *Cryptologia* 13:2 (April 1989): 123–34.

————. "Stimson, the Black Chamber, and the 'Gentlemen's Mail' Quote." *Cryptologia* 12:2 (April 1988): 65–89.

Lewin, Ronald. "A Signal-Intelligence War." *Journal of Contemporary History*. 16 (1981): 501–12.

Mastny, Vojtech. "Stalin and the Prospects of a Separate Peace in World War II." *American Historical Review* 77:5 (December 1972): 1365–88.

Mulligan, Timothy. "The German Navy Evaluates Its Cryptographic Security, October 1941." *Military Affairs* 49:2 (April 1985): 75–79.

Murray, Williamson. "ULTRA: Some Thoughts on Its Impact on the Second World War." *Air University Review* 35:5 (July-August 1984): 52–64.

Paret, Peter. "An Aftermath of the Plot against Hitler: the Lehrterstrasse Prison in Berlin, 1944–45." *Bulletin of the Institute of Historical Research* 32:85 (May 1959): 88–102.

Rusbridger, James. "The Sinking of the 'Automedon,' the Capture of the 'Nankin': New Light on Two Intelligence Disasters in World War II." *Encounter* 64:5 (May 1985): 8–14.

Saville, Allison W. "German Submarines in the Far East." *United States Naval Institute Proceedings* 87:8 (August 1961): 80–92.

Sexton, Donal J. "Phantoms of the North: British Deceptions in Scandinavia, 1941–1944." *Military Affairs* 47:3 (October 1983): 109–14.

Smith, Bradley F. "Sharing Ultra in World War II." *International Journal of Intelligence and Counterintelligence* 2:1 (Spring 1988): 59–72.

Spiller, Roger J. "Assessing ULTRA." *Military Review* 59:8 (August 1979): 13–23.

Stewart, Richard A. "Rommel's Secret Weapon: Signals Intelligence." *Marine Corps Gazette* 74 (March 1990): 51–55.

Stout, Robert Joe. "Cracking the Secret Code." *Retired Officer* (April 1990): 28–34.

Taylor, Blaine. "Ambush in Hostile Skies." *Military History*. 5:1 (August 1988): 42–49.

Whitaker, Paul, and Louis Kruh. "From Bletchley Park to Berchtesgaden." *Cryptologia*. 11:3 (July 1987): 129–41.

Zaugg, Harold E. "The Ultra-American." Lake Forest, Ill., 1991. An unpublished paper on Elmer H. Zaugg, a Japanese linguist at Arlington Hall during the war.

Zobel, James Walter. "Signal Intelligence and MacArthur's Use of Military Intelligence (G-2) during the Second World War." Master's thesis, Old Dominion University, 1991.

Index

Reilly, Michael, 103
Reischauer, Edwin O., 99, 157
Remagen (Germany), 162
Renown (British cruiser), 105
Repin, Alexander, 26
Rhine River, 132, 162
Ribbentrop, Joachim von, 17, 26, 27, 30, 36, 37, 44, 84, 115, 151, 153; and Allied invasion of Europe, 128; on German-Soviet war, 76, 77, 79; illness of, 154; Indian Ocean plan of, 53, 55–56; and separate peace, 68, 69; on Stalin, 160. *See also under* Ōshima Hiroshi
Roehm, Ernst, 131
Rommel, Erwin, 52, 69, 107, 126, 128, 213(n41)
Roosevelt, Franklin D., 23, 28, 32, 37, 38, 66, 100, 160; and all-out war on Japan, 66; code names of, 110; and intelligence reports, 101; and OVERLORD, 104, 117; and possible Japanese attack on Soviet Union, 57, 61, 62, 65; travel and intelligence security of, 102–4, 105, 106, 107, 108–13; and wartime communications, 40–41
Roosevelt Library (Hyde Park), 100, 110
Rosen, Leo, 175
Rostov (Soviet Union), 51
Rotterdam, 132
Rowlett, Edith, 183(photo)
Rowlett, Frank B., 1, 2, 7, 8–9(photos), 38, 42, 66–67, 172, 175, 179, 180(photo), 182, 183(photo)
Royall, Kenneth Claiborne, 179
Rumania, 26, 51, 68, 72
Rundstedt, Gerd von, 114, 128, 186, 189, 190

Safford, Laurence, 100
Saigō Jugō, 25(photo)
St. Malo (France), 127, 132
St. Nazaire (France), 132, 186, 188, 190
Sakhalin, 182
Salmuth, Hans von, 189
Saratoga (U.S. aircraft carrier), 7
Satō Naotake, 146–47, 148–49, 150–51, 159–60, 161, 170, 180; and PURPLE messages, 181–83
Scharnhorst (cruiser), 49, 212(n36)
Scorched-earth policy, 51
Second front, 80, 124–25. *See also* OVERLORD
Secret ink solutions, 16
Separate peace between Germany and Soviet Union, 140. *See also* Germany, and separate peace with Soviet Union; Japan, and German-Soviet peace; *under* Hitler, Adolf; Ōshima Hiroshi
SEXTANT. *See* Cairo Conference
SHAEF, 123

Shigemitsu Mamoru, 84, 92, 93, 94, 95, 150, 152, 154, 155, 157, 158, 160, 161, 163, 164
Shiratori Toshio, 4, 5, 11(photo)
Shirer, William L., 38
Siberia, 58, 61, 63, 93
SIGABA, 115
Signal Intelligence (SIGINT), 126, 135, 136
Signal Intelligence Service (SIS), 1, 7, 10–11, 13–14, 16, 41, 68, 76, 100, 101, 146, 203(n1); and MIS, 149; personnel, 8(photo), 13, 42; security, 42. *See also* MAGIC; Signal Security Agency
Signal Security Agency (SSA), 2, 14, 99, 113, 129, 130, 138, 163, 174, 179, 203(n1)
Sinkov, Abraham, 7, 8(photo)
Sino-Japanese War, 13, 53
SIS. *See* Signal Intelligence Service
Small, Al, 175
Smith, Truman, 59, 215(n7)
Smith, Walter Bedell, 118, 123
Smuts, Jan Christian, 54
Solomon Islands, 58
Sorge, Richard, 58–59, 60
South Africa, 54
Southeast Africa, 55, 61. *See also* Madagascar
Soviet-British Treaty of Alliance (1942), 233(n23)
Soviet-German war. *See* Germany, and Soviet Union
Soviet-Japanese Neutrality Pact (1941), 19, 27, 80, 81, 90, 140, 141, 151, 160; abrogated (1945), 181
Soviet Union, 4, 17; agriculture, 91, 92; air force, 58, 90; army, 58; GPU, 84–85; Japanese ambassador to (*see* Satō Naotake); Japanese observations in, 84–85, 88–93; military strength, 90–91, 92, 93, 182; navy, 90; oil, 85, 88, 91, 92, 145; propaganda, 91–92; U.S. ambassador to, 149; war industry, 81, 91, 92; World War II losses, 92, 208(n31). *See also under* China; Germany; Great Britain; Japan; United States
Spain, 167
Special Branch. *See under* Military Intelligence Service
Special Intelligence, 126, 197, 198
Special research history (SRH), 148
Speer, Albert, 6, 133, 165
Sperrle, Hugo, 189
Spruce (Roosevelt, Franklin D., code name), 110
SRH, 148
SSA. *See* Signal Security Agency
SSO. *See* Military Intelligence Service, Special Security Officer
Stahmer, Heinrich Georg, 25(photo)